MANAGING
THE PUBLIC'S
INTEREST

A Results-Oriented Approach

MANAGING THE PUBLIC'S INTEREST

A Results-Oriented Approach

Douglas M. Fox
The William Paterson College of New Jersey

Holt, Rinehart and Winston
New York   Chicago   San Francisco   Dallas
Montreal   Toronto   London   Sydney

Library of Congress Cataloging in Publication Data

Fox, Douglas M
  Managing the public's interest

  Bibliography: p. 279
  Includes index.
  1. Public administration.   I. Title.
JF1411.F69 1979   350   78-11399
ISBN 0-03-041911-5

Printed in the United States of America

9 0 1 090 9 8 7 6 5 4 3 2 1

For my students at William Paterson College, who have taught me much about public administration—in the hope that there is a Theory Y in their administrative future.

Preface

Most textbooks are written by disgruntled instructors who cannot find a book suitable for courses they teach. *Managing the Public's Interest* is no exception. While many fine treatments of the individual topics covered in separate chapters exist, there has been no book available that pulls results-oriented approaches together so that they can be compared and interrelated. The goal of this book is precisely to perform that task of comparing and inter-relating, so that overall understanding of results-oriented management is increased.

A fault common to many otherwise fine treatments of results-oriented management is neglect of the substantial obstacles, whether technical or political, these approaches often confront. Each chapter in this book dealing with a specific approach discusses these obstacles to implementation and how to minimize them. No miracles are promised, but many commonly made mistakes are can often be easily avoided, and the book advises the reader how to avoid them.

In addition, the text includes actual examples from all levels of government, regions of the country, and types of agencies. Further, a case study of the implementation of each of the methods is to be found in eight of the book's ten chapters. These materials, it is hoped, will make clear that the approaches we discuss are not academic exercises, but managerial methods that have relevance to the real world of government. At the same time, each chapter finishes with a critique of the approach, providing the student with a more balanced view of the subject. If, after scrutinizing the text, the reader decides that some of these methods would not be worth the trouble applying, I will not be disappointed. My goal has been to provide an objective account of the pluses and minuses of each approach. While I advocate results-oriented approaches, I recognize that these approaches may be of limited use in some cases.

The table of contents lists the topics covered. Chapter 1 describes the background to and common elements in results-oriented management. A common framework is used to organize Chapters 2–9, which deal with specific approaches. First, the approach is defined. Second, advice on how to implement it is given. Third, a survey of the record of its use in the United States is made. Fourth, technical and political problems commonly encountered are discussed, and advice on how to minimize them is given. Fifth, a case study illustrates adoption of the approach. Finally, the chapter closes with a critique of the fundamental assumptions and practices of the approach. Chapter 10 is a final summing up of the interrelationships of the various approaches.

Learning objectives for each chapter are stated by the beginning of the chapter as a guide to the reader. An annotated bibliography and list of organizations providing assistance to the reader who wishes to study the topic further, closes the book.

D.M.F.

Acknowledgments

I have been greatly aided by the comments of Ed Bishop, Bob Gilmour, Eli Silverman, and Myron Weiner, who read the entire manuscript. I am also indebted to Ben Dadd, Leo Donohue, Lew Friedman, William Harader, Dick Loverd, Harvey Mansfield, and John Rehfuss, who commented on specific chapters. Denny Fuller was kind enough to make suggestions about style and Jack Burney, Jim Brown, Greg D'Alessio, and Ed Danckwerth furnished valuable case study materials. William Paterson College librarians were unfailingly helpful in aiding my bibliographical search for this project: I am especially indebted to Jane Bambrick, Jess Cooper, Adrienne Korman, Peggy Norris, Eloyse Rinck, and Tim Storch. Holt, Rinehart, and Winston editors Frank Graham, Herman Makler, and Mina Barker made the business of finishing up the job far easier than I would have ever imagined. I could never have begun to write this book without the support of Mildred Weil, dean of the William Paterson College School of Social Science, and I could never have completed it were not working relationships with my colleagues in the political science department so pleasant. The efforts of my extraordinarily efficient and effective research assistant, Sandra Quinn, are also appreciated. A special thank you must be made to Cynthia Mol Ardolino, who produced a flawlessly typed manuscript from the messy morass I gave her. While I would also blame these people for shortcomings if I could get away with it, errors and weaknesses must be attributed to myself alone.

Contents

Chapter

4   Output-Oriented Supervision   80

Chapter

5   Management by Objectives (MBO)   106

Chapter

6   Program Evaluation   141

Chapter

10   *Putting Results-Oriented Approaches Together*   271

1

Introduction

LEARNING OBJECTIVES

TO UNDERSTAND:

Inputs, activities, and results
Efficiency and effectiveness in public programs
The environment of public management
Theory X and Theory Y
Management as a process of planning, organizing, supervising, and controlling

Most government agencies do not know what they are accomplishing. This assertion may seem astonishing, but its accuracy can be easily ascertained. Consider the exasperated outburst of a Flint, Michigan, city councilman, a typical reaction: "Flint looks like hell. The budget is the size of three telephone books; no one can read it, let alone understand it. The city's organization chart looks like a giant spider web; you can't tell who is responsible for what. As a councilman, I do not receive a single report that tells me how our city government is doing."[1]

On what basis can we argue that most government agencies are ignorant of the results of their work? Perhaps the easiest demonstration is to go into a government office and ask the head of the office or his or her subordinates what their work accomplishes. The chances are that the answer will be given in extremely broad terms. For example, a school system will inform the questioner that it is educating children; a police department that it is protecting public safety; a sanitation department that it is protecting public health; and so on. While these answers are not necessarily *false*, they give the questioner no idea of what the agency is actually *achieving*. It is logically possible, and unhappily literally true, that in some cases the work of an agency or one of its programs has little or no positive effect on the conditions it is supposed to improve. That is, if the program were eliminated, no one would miss it, except

1

those who work in it. One example is the tuberculosis sanitoria set up by state governments when the disease was a scourge. But after 1950, when a new drug greatly reduced the incidence of TB, many states continued to operate sanitariums at only a fraction of their capacity, rather than close some down and consolidate their function. Another example which seriously questions a basic agency program is a study of police patrol patterns in Kansas City. After exhaustive experimentation, it was concluded that there was no discernible distinction, as far as the impact on the reported crime rate was concerned, between lots of patrol activity and none at all.[2]

There is no single reason to account for the ignorance of agencies about the effect of their efforts. There are many causes of this situation, a number of which we explore in both this and the other chapters of this book. But before we go further, a few definitions must be given so the reader can understand our argument.

SOME KEY DEFINITIONS

Throughout this book, we will focus on government *programs,* or sets of specific actions designed to implement a plan of providing services to the public. We use the term *outputs* or *results* to indicate what an agency has actually accomplished as the result of its work. If it can be demonstrated that a child has learned to read by attending school, or that the residents of a certain neighborhood are now less likely to be robbed as a result of the work of the police department, we can label these attainments program *outputs* or *results.* This book's purpose is the explanation and critical analysis of several approaches to management which focus on these outputs or results in determining whether agencies are accomplishing what they intend to.

Inputs are the resources an agency uses to produce outputs—for example, personnel, equipment, supplies, and contracted services. No agency can do anything without employees, or materials for those employees to use, whether these be paper clips, garbage trucks, guns, or blackboard chalk. Unfortunately, when asked to specify what they are accomplishing, many agencies will stress their inputs. Officials of a school system may talk to the near exclusion of anything else about its shining new buildings, its well-trained faculty, and the computer it uses for teaching purposes. A fire department may focus on the sophisticated new apparatus it uses to fight fire in multistory dwellings, or a police department may inform the asker that all patrol officers must now have two-year college associate degrees. All of these items may be enviable, but they do not tell anything about what the agency is achieving. They are *inputs,* items necessary to achieve outputs, but they are not to be confused with outputs.[3]

Another key definition is that of agency *activities* or *workload.* These terms denote what the agency does with its inputs to achieve outputs. For example, measures of workload or activity for a schoolteacher would include the number of students taught in a typical day; the number of tests and homework papers graded; the number of hours on duty in the halls, lunchroom, and study halls;

and the number of hours spent in committee or extracurricular work. Typical police workload measures include the number of miles patrolled and the number of tickets, warnings, and summonses given and arrests made. Sanitation workload measures include tons of garbage hauled, while fire department activities encompass the number of alarms responded to.

As the examples illustrate, the workload measures indicate what agency employees are doing on the job. However, they do not in themselves tell us what these activities are accomplishing. If we know that a teacher has taught 400 children in one year, this does not tell us what the children have learned from the teacher's class. If we know that a police officer has arrested 100 people in a month, we do not know whether this activity has increased public safety from criminals. If a sanitation worker hauls 100 tons of trash a day, this workload measure does not tell us what the sanitary conditions are on city streets.

When government agencies are pressed to tell what they are accomplishing, they may stop talking about inputs and begin talking about activity or workload data. One can sympathize with agency officials who stress workload rather than output data in explaining what their agencies have done, because, as we shall see, output is harder to analyze than activities. At the same time, it must be understood that workload data is not a satisfactory substitute for output data. While information on both inputs and activities is absolutely necessary for an agency to determine the factors and costs involved in its job, neither type of information tells us what the agency is accomplishing.

Two related terms which will be defined next are *efficiency* and *effectiveness*. George Berkley has defined efficiency as doing things better, effectiveness as doing the right things better. That is, while a man might be efficient in driving nails into a table, we would question the effectiveness of this activity. Should he be driving nails into a table at all? Peter F. Drucker has argued that some government agencies become obsessed with efficiency and forget effectiveness. An example is the Port Authority of New York and New Jersey, which did a very efficient job at the task it set itself, but failed to handle its part of the area's transportation problem effectively.[4]

While all good managers are concerned with both efficiency and effectiveness, efficiency is closely related to activity or workload, while effectiveness is related to output or results. Activity analysis strives for greater efficiency by asking whether the same task can be performed in a different way so that work of more quantity or higher quality can be done. For example, a workload analysis may discover that a lot of employee time is wasted in filling out poorly designed reports. If the reporting system can be redesigned more efficiently, employees will be able to teach more children, patrol more miles of streets, or visit more welfare recipients at home with this freed-up time. In short, they will be able to get more work done through improved efficiency.

Output analysts will be especially concerned with the effectiveness of these activities. They might ask whether it makes more sense for the teacher to teach children, the patrol officer to cover the streets, or the welfare worker to make home visits. The output analyst will want to determine what the results of these activities are. Suppose the analyst finds, for example, that the pattern of patrolling has no observable impact on the rate of reported crime. Then the effectiveness of patrolling must be seriously questioned, and the practice perhaps eliminated or modified.

In the real world, a concern for efficiency and effectiveness usually go hand in hand. But they are separate concepts and concerns, just as input, activity, and output are, and the distinction should be constantly kept in mind.

THE GROWING CONCERN WITH RESULTS

At no other time in American history has such a large proportion of individuals and groups been concerned with the accomplishments of government programs. The reason for this worry is easily understandable, since the level and cost of government services have risen greatly in the age of the welfare state.[5]

Governments at the federal, state, and local levels do much more than they used to; their functions range from land use controls to student loans to purchase of eyeglasses for the needy. In 1954, government expenditures were 26.5 percent of the gross national product, which is the total of all goods and services produced. By 1976 that figure had risen to 34.2 percent, and all projections were that it would rise still higher in the years ahead.[6] The tax burden of the "average" family rose 92.4 percent from 1953–1975. That is, the 1953 average family had an income of $5,000 and paid 11.8 percent of it in direct taxes. By 1975, 22.7 percent of the average family income of $14,000 went to pay direct taxes.[7]

Given these patterns, it is no surprise to find a growing taxpayer revolt. Several local school systems are temporarily shut down each year because taxpayers refuse to raise funds needed to pay additional costs. In June 1978, California voters passed referendum Proposition 13, which restricted local property taxes to one percent of assessed value. Observers believed that many other states would adopt similar measures.

An imaginative mail-order outfit sells bachelor of divinity degrees, entitling the buyer to be an ordained minister of the Universal Life Church. Since churches are exempt from local property taxes, the buyer declares that his or her house is now a church and claims exemption from the tax. One enterprising New York State "bishop" of the church now holds mass ordinations, raising hundreds of ordinary taxpayers to instant ministerial status. While this ingenious attempt to avoid paying to Caesar what is Caesar's may not stand up to legal scrutiny in the courts, it reflects the anxiety and anger of many taxpayers.

Protests in the capitals of states deliberating tax increases have become commonplace. In 1971, state troopers had to be called in to the Rhode Island capitol building after fistfights broke out during anti-tax demonstrations. Many government officials have been voted out of office because they backed tax increases. For example, in 1972, Illinois Governor Richard Ogilvie was soundly defeated after leading a successful fight for a state income tax. Federal legislators and Congressmen are also faced with growing demands to cut back on taxes.

But perhaps of even more concern than increased taxes is the growing feeling that government is not getting its job done. Opinion surveys show that more and more Americans feel that government is doing an unacceptable job. Surveys also show that most Americans want a high level of services provided by their governments. While they complain about taxes, they do not want their local library or recreation department closed, nor school or police services drastically reduced.

Given these simultaneous demands for a decline in the growth of taxes and a high service level, the only escape from the dilemma is to analyze the outputs of government programs. Then a decision can be made to retain, modify, or eliminate certain services. As we shall see, results-oriented management is not a panacea, but it offers the only alternative to across-the-board cuts, which affect good and bad programs alike, or constantly rising taxes. For this reason, the components of output management merit careful study.

PROBLEMS CONFRONTING OUTPUT MANAGEMENT: THE ENVIRONMENT AND ATMOSPHERE OF GOVERNMENT AGENCIES

Output-oriented managers have to confront a host of hurdles and hindrances. These are of two types. The first is *political,* or disagreement because of values or preferences different from those of the manager. One type of disagreement comes from those not primarily interested in output management. A political leader who wants to staff an agency from the ranks of party campaign workers will have political differences with results-oriented managers, who want to pick the most able employees, regardless of background. Another type of disagreement comes from those who want to manage by results, but who prefer different goals. For example, a city councilperson may want to concentrate on shortening fire response time, rather than increasing fire prevention inspection efforts.

But even where no political problems exist, there are substantial *technical* obstacles, or difficulties inherent in the attempt to set up an output management system. For example, how do we evaluate police output? Number of arrests, summons or warnings given per man-hour on the job may be misleading. The most effective patrol officer might keep order and deter crime while handing out few citations. In each chapter, we will examine political and technical problems peculiar to each output approach and recommend steps to minimize each of them. In the remainder of this section, we will look at some commonly encountered barriers to improved agency management. Note that the focus of the section is on problems, not accomplishments. This emphasis does *not* mean that we are saying that all government agencies are characterized by these conditions.

One all-too-common deficiency of agency administration is weak management. We define *management* as a process which includes planning, organizing, supervising, and controlling personnel and other resources to achieve desired results.[8] This broad definition, which will be elaborated on and related to the topics explored in this book in the last section of this chapter, encompasses all the different subjects we will examine in Chapters 2–9.

Weak management exists in government because top administrators and supervisors are often chosen without regard for their capacity to manage.[9] In 1978, a new head of the Connecticut State Department of Public Works was appointed. His qualifications included selling appliances and friendships with top state politicians. The new head had no background in either management or engineering. Appointment based on personal or political party ties is unlikely to produce good management.

Another problem is that in many departments, administrators are chosen solely because they have a professional background in the field. Educators become school superintendents, doctors head health departments, and engineers run engineering departments—often without training or experience in management. This often results in incompetent management, a phenomenon known as the "Peter Principle." In Professor Peter's words, these managers have been promoted to their level of incompetence.[10] In other words, many managers are not trained in modern management principles, but learn by the seat of their pants.

Another obstacle to output management is inefficient control from the top down. Many agencies insulate their subdivisions from the department head's control. In some, statutes and regulations promulgated by a group with legislative and interest group support grant great independence to the subdivision. A classic example is the separate status of vocational education within departments of education at all levels of American government. This fact means that these agencies can resist attempts to get them to jump on the output management bandwagon, if they desire.

Another problem is caused by excessively detailed regulations and procedures. These often have an admirable goal, to reduce political corruption. If no money can be spent before three administrators "sign off" or approve it, the chances of an employee dipping his hand in the till are substantially reduced. At the same time, the inevitable cost is delay and inefficiency in decision making.

Graft itself is an overpowering obstacle to output management. If employees refuse to deliver services until they are paid off (free meals to the patrol officer) or deliver special illicit services (snowplowing a private driveway for a bottle of whiskey), output management will have a hard row to hoe.

This list could be much longer, but what we have mentioned so far is intended only to illustrate the impressive impediments to output management, impediments which have to be recognized and frankly acknowledged if a *working* output management system is desired. For, as we will argue throughout this book, most of these obstacles can be lessened, but only with hard work.

Perhaps the most fundamental friction between line agency and output management occurs in the clash between what public administration scholar Aaron Wildavsky has labeled the evaluative manager and organization manager. The evaluative manager is the same, to use our term, as the *output-oriented manager:*

> His concern is not that the organization should survive or that any specific objective be enthroned or that any particular clientele be served. Evaluative man cares that interesting problems are selected and that maximum intelligence be applied toward their solution.[11]

The organization manager, on the other hand, is the career bureaucrat who identifies with his agency. The thought that his organization might be dismantled and dismembered causes colossal consternation. To tell the college professor of 20 years' standing that the institution will be closed because it meets no discernible need is to crush that individual. To tell the fire fighter that the fire department is to be totally reorganized and combined with the police and ambulance services as the result of a study is to deliver a blow to the solar plexus. Strong resistance is to be expected in both cases, regardless of the merits of the reports of the evaluative manager. As Wildavsky says, organization and evaluation may well be opposing concepts. The former implies stability and commitment to certain programs and clientele, while the latter implies change, skepticism, and constant analysis of the results of activity.

For these reasons, results-oriented government managers have a large task ahead of them. While details will follow in specific chapters, in this chapter we suggest a general managerial strategy designed to trim away many of these troubles. This strategy is based on a participatory approach to management.

THEORY Y: TAPPING HUMAN POTENTIAL TO GET THE JOB DONE

Douglas McGregor, late professor of industrial management at the Massachusetts Institute of Technology, has argued convincingly that most contemporary organizations operate according to a set of outmoded principles which stifle and stymie achievement on the job. Under these conditions, results-oriented management is much more difficult. McGregor labeled these principles *Theory X,* and describes them as follows:

1. People dislike work and will avoid it if possible.
2. Therefore, they must be threatened, coerced, and controlled if they are to work to fulfill organizational objectives.
3. People have little ambition, wish to be directed and avoid responsibility, and desire security above everything else.[12]

Theory X organizations implement these principles by stressing procedures, outlining the one way to do a job, minimizing the amount of discretion allowed employees, and maximizing control over employees from the top.

These methods are certainly suitable for a manager who believes in Theory X; indeed, they are the only way to follow Theory X principles. Theory X advocates believe that employees use discretion only to goof off. Employees are not naturally results-oriented, so the only way to get results is to carefully control all aspects of their conduct.

McGregor argues that Theory X management produces good results only in very hard times, when loss of a job means severe deprivation (losing one's house, or even starving). But in times of affluence, unemployment insurance, and welfare, such basic subsistence needs are not enough to motivate employees. As McGregor says, "Management cannot provide a man with self-respect, or with the respect of his fellows, or with the satisfaction of needs for self-fulfillment."[13] But he goes on to say that management *can* encourage and enable its employees to seek these conditions for themselves—or thwart them by failing to do so. This can be done if managers subscribe to the principles of Theory Y, which includes beliefs that

1. People do *not* dislike work.
2. They do not have to be threatened to get work done, but can become self-directed.
3. They will be self-directed if, and only if, this satisfies their ego and development needs.[14]

In the right setting, people not only accept but seek responsibility. Although most organizations only partially utilize the potential of their employees because of Theory X, the ability to seek creative solutions to problems is widely distributed in the population. The key to Theory Y is setting up an atmosphere that allows this creative potential to be tapped.

The way to create this atmosphere is to actively encourage employees to participate in organizational problem solving. We are not talking here about a suggestion box, pro forma, or manipulative techniques, but about genuine efforts to encourage and listen to employee ideas. There is no point in even attempting this approach if the manager is not prepared to grant substantial discretion to employees and is not willing to watch them make mistakes as they learn how to use this discretion. Any employee is going to have to go through a learning period in order to cope with a new job situation, but the benefits will far exceed the costs.

One of the underlying assumptions of Theory Y is that no one is perfect. This means that it pays for a manager not only to listen to the ideas of subordinates but also to encourage them to express themselves frankly. If, through experience, it becomes clear to employees that they can say anything, no matter how critical, without fear of personal recriminations from the boss, they can develop their full potential. Unfortunately, many agency employees would never dream of making candid comments, because they are sure that they would suffer for them. Take the example of a department head who just set up a pet project a few months ago and now wants a frank appraisal of its accomplishments. If a Theory Y atmosphere does not prevail, none of the employees will give such an evaluation, because they know it's a pet project and don't want to risk the boss's anger. Silence, noncommittal comments, and vapid praise will be the response. This writer has worked in organizations where employees were told, "Maybe this policy is wrong and foolish, but we don't want any more discussion of it. To do so would be disloyal to the organization." Such an attitude is not explicitly part of Theory X, but is encouraged by it. Results-oriented managers must work to set up a Theory Y atmosphere or suffer the kind of disaster which inevitably results from this kind of lunatic loyalty.

Theory Y management is harder than Theory X management, but achieves superior results. It is difficult for a manager to be open enough to listen to suggestions and criticisms from someone at the lowest level of the organization, because managers are usually as status conscious as anyone else. It is also difficult to decide which of the suggestions make sense and which do not, and to convey this information back without hurting subordinates' feelings or causing them to think that the new Theory Y approach is just another management public relations technique. Implementing Theory Y is not an easy job, but the effort is worth it. Robert Townsend, former president of Avis Rent-a-Car, relates:

> When I became head of Avis I was assured that no one was any good, and that my first job was to start recruiting a whole new team. Three years later Hal Geneen, the President of ITT, . . . after meeting everybody and listening to them in action for a day, said, "I've never seen such depth of management; why I've already spotted three chief executive officers!" You guessed it. Same people."[15]

While some readers would argue that Theory Y can only be applied to business and not to government, we will argue in Chapters 2–9 that it can apply to government.

Other readers may doubt the general applicability of Theory Y, and we are obligated to inform them of several serious critiques of Theory Y:

1. Research on manufacturing shows that, in some situations, workers in a Theory X atmosphere were more motivated and productive than workers in a Theory Y atmosphere.[16]

2. "Contingency" approaches to management argue that managers need to use different strokes for different folks and for different situations. For example, workers who are less psychologically independent will fear participatory management and prefer being told what to do. Likewise, *orders* must be given in many cases, especially in crises and emergency situations which allow no time for debate, like fire fighting or disaster relief.[17]

3. Two important studies note that the large size of many public organiza-

tions, hierarchical relationships, the lack of authority of many public managers, managerial fear of appearing "weak," and the opportunity provided for subordinates to oppose changes make Theory Y difficult to implement in government.[18]

4. The first in-depth analysis of business executives by a psychologist found that the kind of people interested in motivating subordinates to work, develop their skills, and join in a team effort, were manipulators who did not really care about developing subordinate potential. These "gamesmen" are hypocrites, whether conscious ones or not.[19]

5. A brilliant study of federal executive politics argues that the needs for bureaucratic self-protection against political appointees and the divided loyalty of career civil servants who will remain long after any one political appointee is gone complicate consultative management. The study cites numerous examples of the failure of participatory approaches and advocates a course midway between Theories X and Y.[20]

6. Other writers have argued that Theory Y works only where employees "are technically competent, experienced, and mature. An example would be a group of engineers or scientists working with a fair degree of structure on a project where the objective has been established."[21]

Our defense of Theory Y management has several points. First, there are few manufacturing operations in government, so that the research cited may not apply. But we have to admit that there are many highly routinized tasks in government, such as maintenance of buildings or record keeping, and Theory Y may not apply in some of these situations. But this does not mean it should not be tried. No approach is more typical of Theory X than the self-fulfilling prophecy, or giving up without a fight.

Second, as implied earlier, most government agencies are Theory X organizations. Even if Theory Y does not apply to all divisions of the agency, substantial gains may be made if it works in just a few of them. In many of these organizations, it is hard to imagine how a worse job could be done.

After years of teaching management courses to state and local employees, the author is convinced that there are large numbers of capable employees waiting for Theory Y management to release their full job potential. It is well known, for example, that younger police officers make a disproportionate number of arrests and hand out a disproportionate number of traffic violation citations. As they gain experience, their performance record declines, a probable indicator of declining interest in the job. Student after student has described to the author job environments which demand "blind loyalty" above all else and in which employees feel you must "cover your ass" to avoid disaster. Such "covering" means that the employee will go by the book, never taking risks, to avoid being penalized by rigid superiors. Case after case in which potentially valuable suggestions are rejected out of hand and employees are penalized for politely expressing their frank opinions indicate that *Theory Y has yet to be tried in most government jurisdictions.* We advocate giving it a serious try. If it does not work after a truly thorough effort, it can be rejected. In most cases, we suspect a strong positive response to Theory Y would result.

Third, we strongly disagree that employees have to be highly educated professionals for Theory Y to work. Some of the best suggestions for getting the job done better come from clerks, highway brush cutters, and other lower-level employees, as the following chapters will detail.

Let us list two examples here. The first comes from veteran city manager Leroy Harlow, who asked two clerks in one department to come up with some ideas for making their work at a customer reception counter more efficient. "A few days later [they] had some ideas. . . . *They were excited.* [emphasis added] . . . They had thought of two or three other changes. . . . We made the changes, which were really very simple. We got no complaints from the public. I estimate we reduced the energy expenditure of the counter help by 20 percent."[22] Likewise, a researcher reports that the cooperative committees of the Tennessee Valley Authority (TVA), representing both management and unions, regularly put into effect "a large number of suggestions for work improvement."[23]

Fourth, by rejecting Theory Y, the manager usually implicitly accepts Theory X. McGregor notes that management often asks why employees are not more productive, since they have good wages, benefits, and working conditions.[24] The reason is that since their basic needs are satisfied, they have no incentive to perform better unless management can relate to their feelings of self-esteem, competence, and creativity—something only a Theory Y atmosphere can tap.

McGregor sums up the differences between a Theory X and Theory Y atmosphere, as follows:

Theory Y

A working atmosphere without obvious tensions or boredom. People are involved and interested. Much discussion, but always pertinent to the task. The task is well understood and accepted. People listen to each other, and even seemingly outlandish ideas are given a fair hearing. There is disagreement without dominating the dissenter. Decisions are reached by consensus, and are not dominated by the chairman. There is little evidence of a power struggle; the issue is how to get the job done. The group is self-conscious about its operations, looking closely at what interferes with its operation, whether a procedure or an individual. Open discussion ensues until a solution is found.

Theory X

The atmosphere is one of boredom (people whispering or carrying on side conversations) or tension. A few people dominate the discussion, and often their remarks are off the point. The task is unclear, or not commonly agreed on. People do not really listen to each other. Some members do not express their ideas for fear of criticism. Disagreements may be suppressed by the chairman, or a small majority may win a vote over a large, unconvinced minority. Decisions may be unclear—no one is sure who will do what. Criticism becomes personal and destructive. The group avoids discussion about its own operations.[25]

Some readers may think we have created a straw man in Theory X, but we are convinced that many more will recognize Theory X as an accurate picture of the atmosphere in their own government agencies. In such an atmosphere, results-oriented management is impossible. In the chapters which follow, we suggest how to move toward this kind of management via Theory Y.

RESULTS-ORIENTED APPROACHES: AN OUTLINE OF THE BOOK

Since this book is devoted to a discussion of various approaches to results-oriented management, some consideration of how these approaches are *interrelated* is necessary before we deal with each approach specifically. Figure 1–1 outlines four broad management functions—planning, organizing, supervising, and controlling—under which are grouped the chapters relevant to each function. Let us now briefly define each function.

Planning involves setting goals and deciding how best to attain them. If a hospital decides it wants to lower the infant mortality rate in the maternity ward by 10 percent, it has to consider how best to achieve this goal. Should it concentrate on intensive emergency treatment for sickly newborns, a more thoroughgoing prenatal care program, some combination of the two, or another alternative? By setting a goal or deciding on a means to achieve it, the hospital has engaged in *planning*. Chapter 2 and parts of Chapter 7 relate to program planning.

Organizing is the process of grouping activities and responsibilities and establishing relationships that will enable people to work most effectively toward objectives. What relationships between supervisors and subordinates should exist? These are the crucial concerns of organizing, which are explored in Chapter 3.

FIGURE 1–1.   THE INTERRELATIONSHIP OF RESULTS-ORIENTED APPROACHES

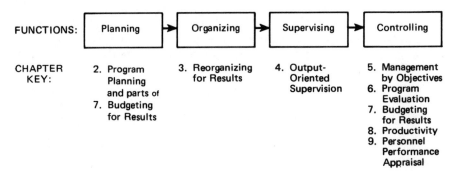

Supervising is leading people to attain the goals set forth in the plan. Effective supervisors need to know how to communicate with, reward, discipline, and train their subordinates. Chapter 4 discusses supervision.

Controlling encompasses all activities meant to ensure that chosen goals will be reached. Chapters 5–9—dealing with management by objectives (MBO), program evaluation, zero-base budgeting (ZBB), productivity, and personnel performance appraisal—are all concerned with controlling.

As the following chapters stress, the four functions of planning—organizing, supervision, and controlling—are parts of a single process, the process of *managing by results.* There is notable overlap both among these four functions and the specific approaches discussed in this book. For example, the reader will be shown that MBO and ZBB have much in common. We know of no public agency which uses all the approaches simultaneously, though it certainly would be possible to do so. One purpose of this book is to enable the manager to understand the basics and the pros and cons of each approach, and thus to try out those which seem useful.

The chapters which follow use the same organizational structure. Each begins with a definition of the subject dealt with in the chapter, and then goes on to discuss how to implement the approach. A look at the actual use of the technique in government is then followed by discussions of the technical and political problems which are usually encountered by those using the method. Finally, there is a case study of the method and a conclusion which raises some provocative questions about the prospects and subtle snares posed by the approach.

NOTES

1. Brian W. Rapp and Frank M. Patitucci, *Managing Local Government for Improved Performance: A Practical Approach* (Boulder, Col.: Westview Press, 1977), p. 347.

2. George E. Berkley, *The Craft of Public Administration* (Boston: Allyn and Bacon, 1975), p. 102, and James Q. Wilson, *Thinking about Crime* (New York: Basic Books, 1975), pp. 88–90.

3. Our definition of inputs differs from that of political scientists, who would stress policy demands and support offered to government by groups.

4. Berkley, op. cit., p. 285; Peter F. Drucker, "Managing the Public Service Institution," *Public Interest* 33 (Fall 1973).

5. Since a searching examination of the causes and consequences of this condition lies beyond the scope of this book, the reader is directed to Seymour Melman, *The Permanent War Economy* (New York: Praeger, 1974), and James O'Connor, *The Fiscal Crisis of the State* (New York: St. Martin's Press, 1974), for two contradictory but provocative analyses of why costs have risen so rapidly.

6. Advisory Commission on Intergovernmental Relations, *Significant Features of Fis-*

cal Federalism, 1976 Edition, I. Trends (Washington, D.C.: Government Printing Office, 1976), pp. 1–3.

7. Peter G. Peterson, "Productivity in Government and the American Economy," *Public Administration Review* 32 (November–December 1972): 745–46, and Advisory Commission on Intergovernmental Relations, op. cit., p. 3.

8. See Donald C. Mosley and Paul H. Pietri, Jr., *Management* (Encino, Calif.: Dickenson, 1975), ch. 1.

9. This section is based on Committee for Economic Development, *Improving Productivity in State and Local Government* (New York: Committee for Economic Development, 1976), pp. 47–48.

10. Laurence J. Peter and Raymond Hull, *The Peter Principle* (New York: Morrow, 1968).

11. Aaron Wildavsky, "The Self-Evaluating Organization," *Public Administration Review* 32 (September–October 1972): 509–20, at 510.

12. Douglas McGregor, *The Human Side of Enterprise* (New York: McGraw-Hill, 1960), pp. 33–34.

13. Ibid., p. 41.

14. Ibid., pp. 47–48.

15. Robert Townsend, *Up the Organization* (Greenwich, Conn.: Fawcett Crest Books, 1970), p. 123.

16. John S. Morse and Jay W. Lorsch, "Beyond Theory Y," *Harvard Business Review*, May–June 1970, pp. 61–68.

17. William F. Dowling, Jr., and Leonard R. Sayles, *How Managers Motivate*, 2nd ed. (New York: McGraw-Hill, 1978), passim; Laurence L. Steinmetz and Charles D. Greenidge, "Realities That Shape Managerial Style," *Business Horizons,* October 1970, pp. 23–32; Michel Crozier, *The Bureaucratic Phenomenon* (Chicago: University of Chicago Press, 1964), pp. 204–5.

18. Donald P. Warwick. *A Theory of Public Bureaucracy* (Cambridge, Mass.: Harvard University Press, 1975), pp. 200–3.

19. Michael Maccoby, *The Gamesman* (New York: Simon & Schuster, 1976), pp. 217–44.

20. Hugh Heclo, *A Government of Strangers* (Washington, D.C.: Brookings Institution, 1977), pp. 191–234.

21. Robert N. McMurry, *The Maverick Executive* (New York: American Management Association, 1974), pp. 44–5.

22. Leroy F. Harlow, *Without Fear or Favor* (Salt Lake City, Utah: Brigham Young University Press, 1977), pp. 88–90.

23. Martin Patchen. "Labor-Management Consultation at TVA," *Administrative Science Quarterly,* September 1965, pp. 149–74.

24. McGregor, op. cit., p. 39.

25. Ibid., pp. 232–38.

2
Program Planning

LEARNING OBJECTIVES

TO UNDERSTAND:

Steps in the planning process

Relating implementation to goals

Technical and political problems in planning and what to do about them

Examining one's assumptions in making plans

Why do the best laid plans of mice and men often go astray? Primarily because planning is a future-oriented activity, and unforeseen events in that future may invalidate the assumptions of the plan. For this reason, it is unlikely that all the aspects of a long-range plan will be achieved exactly as planned. But there are better and worse ways to go about planning, and our purpose in this chapter is to sketch a better way.

DEFINING PLANNING

We define *planning* here as a *process* of interrelated steps, which we have diagrammed in Figure 2–1. The first of these is identification of a problem, such as a high rate of fire loss or low rate of reading achievement, relative to some standard, such as the national average. Once the problem has been pinpointed, broad goals, such as minimizing fire loss or increasing reading ability, can be set. Next, specific objectives can be designed to attain these goals. Over a period of several years, objectives for fire loss might include reducing the losses to 10 percent more than the national average the first year, 5 percent the second year, the same as the national average the third year, and 5 percent less than the national average the fourth year. For reading scores, the first-year goal might be to bring grades 5–8 to within an average reading level of only one grade below actual grade, half a grade the second year, grade level the third year, and half a grade level above grade the fourth year. The fourth step is the

15

FIGURE 2-1.   THE PLANNING PROCESS

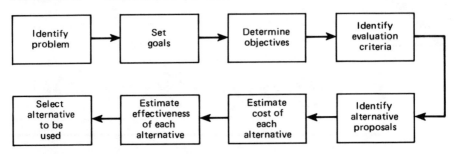

specification of evaluation criteria, such as a standardized reading test in the example just given.

The fifth step is to identify alternative proposals for obtaining these objectives. For example, the fire department might consider a greatly stepped-up fire prevention campaign, purchase of highly sophisticated new apparatus, or new training programs for personnel. It could also come up with a number of alternatives based on different combinations of these three factors. The sixth step would then be to estimate the cost of each alternative, and the seventh step would be to estimate the effectiveness of each alternative. Once this information has been analyzed, the crucial eighth step is to pick one of the alternatives as the action plan for the agency or program, and to get to work on it.

Harry Hatry, a leading authority on results-oriented management, and his colleagues have summed up this planning process as "estimating the impacts—especially the costs and effectiveness—of different ways of accomplishing a public purpose."[1] As defined here, *planning* focuses on the *future*—as opposed to *evaluation*, discussed in Chapter 6, which peruses the *past*. And our focus is on *program* planning. As mentioned in Chapter 1, we define *program* as a proposed set of specific actions intended to implement a plan. A program can be distinguished from a *policy*, which is a broad statement of interrelated goals and the relative importance of each goal. In other words, our concern is more with the planning of specific programs than with the overall process of setting priorities among broad goals.

PLANNING AND SYSTEMS ANALYSIS

It should be noted that many writers, including Hatry, use the word *analysis* to mean the same thing that we mean by planning. They do so because the planning approach described here derives from *systems analysis,* a post–World War II term which incorporates economic and mathematical models and techniques where appropriate. Systems analysis is not a well-defined method with clear-cut procedures, but embraces a number of different approaches,[2] such as operations research (OR), planning-programming-budgeting (PPB),[3] program evaluation and review technique (PERT), and critical path method

(CPM). Let us examine each of these briefly in turn, with the exception of PPB, which is discussed in Chapter 7.

OR is basically a mathematical approach which tries to determine the best procedures to follow in operating a public service. For example, suppose the goal is to maximize traffic flow during rush hour. Existing data can be analyzed with a variety of mathematical techniques to form models which try to predict the likely effect of possible changes, such as urban development, new industry, and different types of private and public transport on traffic patterns so that *optimal* programs can be identified OR techniques have proved very successful in policy areas which lend themselves to quantitative approaches, such as military operations, garbage disposal, and police and fire response patterns.[4] Since these procedures are highly sophisticated, the government official will probably need to bring in a consultant experienced in OR to conduct such studies.

Perhaps the most widely used OR technique is linear programming, a mathematical method for devising optimal solutions. Linear programming can be used to analyze any situation in which people are concerned with maximizing or minimizing economic resources subject to constraints. Linear programming has been used to analyze government warehouse inventory policies, traffic flow patterns, the flow of criminal cases, and a host of other problems.

The following example illustrates the use of linear programming. Imagine that a sewer treatment plant processes both sewage and dry garbage and then puts what is left over in a river. Two tons of garbage must be processed for each three tons of sewage for the plant to operate effectively. Enter a state official who determines that the pollution per ton of sewage is 0.3 damage units and the pollution per ton of garbage is 0.4 damage units. The official notes that state policy forbids the plant to cause more than 8,500 damage units per day. Linear programming can be used to discover the optimal number of tons of sewage and garbage which can be processed each day.[5]

Program evaluation and review technique (PERT) was developed by the United States Navy in the 1950s to help in carrying out the Polaris missile program. PERT charts indicate the interrelationship of steps (called events) necessary to complete the task. (They also typically identify three time estimates for each job—the most optimistic, pessimistic, and probable.) The longest expected time to finish the whole project is labeled the critical path, giving rise to the term *critical path method,* or *CPM.* PERT and CPM techniques have their champions, who claim the approaches have been useful in projects as different as nuclear submarine construction and pothole filling.[6] But, as is true of OR, the typical government office must call in an experienced consultant before proceeding with these techniques.

After this brief introduction to these modes of systems analysis, the reader's reaction may resemble that of a San Francisco city official who said:

> I don't want to know a God Damn thing about the future. I can't take that stuff into the future until I understand where the hell I am . . . that bit about the consequences of your decisions, that the model will tell you policy deci-

sions, is three-quarters bull shit . . . I just want to understand my world and the hell with the model . . . but no, they didn't do that. They had to have a big God Damn model.[7]

While we would argue that systems analysis techniques *can* be useful, the rest of this chapter will focus on more basic approaches to planning which government officials can implement without an army of high-paid consultants.

IMPLEMENTING PLANNING

As the reader might guess from the list of eight steps outlined in the previous section, setting up a planning process is no small job. But, as we shall see in following chapters, it is an integral part of other results-oriented management approaches like management by objectives (MBO) and zero-based budgeting (ZBB). So when an organization becomes oriented to planning, it can incorporate these related approaches relatively easily.

In this section, we examine the recommended steps of the planning process in order. But an analyst working on an actual plan would probably go back and forth among the steps as planning progresses. For example, after some scrutiny, the analyst may redefine the problem or add or modify objectives. Rarely will planning proceed in such a methodically and mechanically meticulous manner as outlined below. But since each step is different and distinct, it makes sense to identify the various phases of the planning process.[8]

Identifying the Problem

To find a problem to study is usually not difficult. The opposite is normally true: there are so many problems that ways have to be found of determining which ones should be studied.

One set of considerations involves the importance of the issue and the study. For example, can the government do much about the problem? In a recession, there is little a city or state government can do in the short run to improve the economy, so studies of this topic would make little sense. (The long run is another matter; the government may want to study ways of improving the business investment climate in the future.)

A second question asks if the problem involves large costs or major consequences for government services. While it may be technically fascinating for the planner to study user patterns for the division of the state or federal Veterans Administration serving World War I veterans, far greater return is likely to result from a study of the divisions dealing with Vietnam veterans. A third question is whether there is a likelihood of improving program performance. If the school system of a city is either doing an excellent job or is doing a miserable job is protected by powerful political allies, it may make more sense to pick a program which spends less but can be improved.

Another consideration is the *practicability*, or feasibility, of the planning study. For example, can the problem be readily measured? Can we study police effectiveness in any definitive quantitative way, or are qualitative factors the only meaningful indicators? Number of arrests made may have nothing to do with real police effectiveness, as already noted in Chapter 1. If the problem area is one in which measurements are difficult, perhaps it should not be studied. At the least, planners should proceed with caution.

Planners should investigate not only the technical but also the *political* feasibility of programs. Erwin C. Hargrove gives the example of a decision about constructing a state medical school in Massachusetts.[9] A professor of management science called in to make a study issued recommendations without any consideration of their political feasibility, thereby earning the enmity and opposition of a coalition of legislators, organized labor, educators, and State Board of Regents members. Alternatives recommended without any appreciation of the politics of the situation may be doomed to failure. With such an appreciation, Hargrove notes, slightly modified options might succeed.

Examples of the statement of a problem include the following:

1. Do we need to build public housing apartment units for the elderly in the city?
2. Private colleges in the state claim that the public colleges are driving them out of business and that public aid to private schools could provide higher education at a fraction of the cost direct public education costs. Is this true, and what should we do about it?
3. Residents in several city neighborhoods complain that the police are neither visible nor responsive. What can be done to improve this situation?

Planners will start with these statements of the problem, but should have their eyes and ears open to determine if the stated problem is the *real* problem. For example, suppose that a study of the first problem stated above concludes that adequate and affordable housing for the elderly already exists, but that other needs which are not being met have led the elderly to demand housing. Further investigation reveals that the elderly feel isolated and ignored because they have no places to gather and no way to get around. A planning study for programs for special transportation and establishment of a senior citizens' center could then be undertaken.

At the same time that he or she considers redefining a problem, the planner must remember that he or she is not able to proceed independently. The same officials—whether mayor, governor, city council, or department head—who put the planner to work will decide whether they want her or him to continue on this new task. The planner must act as a salesperson, convincing these officials to go in the new direction recommended because it will be in their own interest to do so.

One key consideration of a planning study pointed out by Hatry and associates is its *scope*. Should the study be narrow or broad? For example, in the second problem sketched above, what should the definition of higher education be? Should it include any and all post-secondary programs, such as nursing and skilled trade education, or restrict itself to the schools granting bachelors' and graduate degrees? Should it try to measure what students have actually *learned* at the different schools, or roughly equate each school of each type?

Factors determining scope include the interests of the government officials who have called for the study, the amount of information available, the personnel and other resources (equipment, computer time, etc.) allotted, and the time allowed in which to do the study. At the same time, the planner can usually have some say in setting the scope of the study by expressing his or her opinion about what should be studied. Hatry says there is a tendency to define the scope of the study too narrowly, citing a study of an emergency ambulance service which concentrated on response time to the exclusion of the quality of care given after the ambulance arrived. The other extreme is for the scope of the study to be so vast that the questions posed cannot be answered within the

FIGURE 2-2.   "DIAGRAMMING": ONE VIEW OF A HEALTH TREATMENT SYSTEM

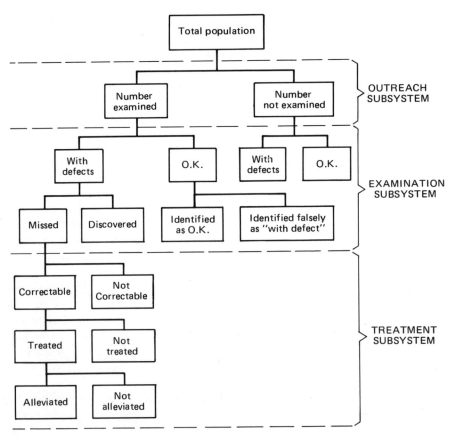

time and with the resources allotted. Our second example, the study of higher education, could easily get out of hand in this way. Hatry suggests a preliminary study by planners to gauge where study efforts would probably be the most effective, but laments that such preliminary workups are rare indeed.

If warranted, the scope of a study can be shifted as the study proceeds. For example, if the study of the third problem listed above began by examining how often police patrolled and how quickly they responded to calls for help, but then discovered that residents felt the police were distant because there was no precinct building in the neighborhood, the study could shift to a consideration of the merits of a police storefront neighborhood presence.

Hatry recommends "diagramming" as a useful aid in learning about the scope of various programs. Figure 2–2 diagrams a health treatment program. Each box represents part of the total population served by different programs. This means that if the *number* of cases in each box could be obtained, we could determine the programs that seem least successful and give them priority in a planning study.

Hatry and his colleagues also recommend several ways of estimating the *need* for a service. Crucial to this task is gauging *demand* for the service, whether it is an explicit one or a latent demand that would be made if the program were better known, more accessible or attractive, or less expensive for users. Information sources which can be used to estimate demand include past incidence of problems, such as the percentage of families below the poverty line. Another source is basic census-type data (age, sex, race, etc.), which can be used to project the likely number of people (e.g., elderly Spanish-speaking women) who may need a particular service. Citizen surveys asking people if they would use a service such as bus transportation can probe latent demand. A fourth technique is to examine conditions, such as the repair of roads, to see if a problem exists. Table 2–1 does not probe all these kinds of information sources, but it illustrates the attempt to project future demand for Colorado colleges.

Identifying Program Goals

The identification of program goals is not as easy as it may sound. Often, agencies carrying out a program have not even specifically identified their broad goals. George L. Morrisey, a management consultant and writer, has suggested the following questions to get agencies thinking about their goals:

Why was our agency established?

Who are our clients?

What are our principal services?

What is different about our services from what they were 5–10 years ago?

What will or should be different about them in 5–10 years?

What special considerations do we have relative to the chief executive and legislature, our clients, our employees, interest groups, and the general public?[10]

TABLE 2–1.   DATA USED TO PROJECT FUTURE DEMAND FOR COLORADO COLLEGES

1. PROJECTED TOTAL ENROLLMENT BY CONSTITUENT UNIT

Institutions	Fall 1972 Actual	Fall 1974 Projected	Fall 1978 Projected
Four-Year Colleges and Universities			
Independent	9,278	10,900	5,250
University of Colorado	20,514	21,450	26,500
State Colleges	32,442	33,400	35,800
Subtotal	63,234	66,750	77,550
Two-Year Colleges			
Independent	1,913	2,000	3,000
Regular Community Colleges	21,477	23,900	29,000
Technical Colleges	5,412	6,300	7,800
Subtotal	28,802	32,200	39,800
TOTAL	92,036	98,950	116,350

2. RATES OF GROWTH SHOWING 1972 AS BASE YEAR (100.0) AMONG POPULATIONS AND ENROLLMENT PROJECTIONS

Year	Colorado 18 year olds	High School Graduates	18–21 year olds	Full-Time Undergraduate Demand 4-year and 2-year	Total Enrollment
1972	100.0	100.0	100.0	100.0	100.0
1973	102.9	104.7	104.0	102.6	
1974	106.5	106.3	107.8	105.8	105.3
1975	108.8	113.2	111.5	108.2	
1976	109.6	114.4	115.0	108.7	
1977	109.5	116.5	117.1	109.9	
1978	111.2	117.8	118.7	111.9	120.0
1979	110.0	119.1	119.7		
1980	107.8	116.8	119.5		

Answers to these questions can hopefully produce a more specific statement of goals. An example Morrisey gives is a hospital center which used to state only that it was in the business of providing health care, which now states that its goals are to

1. Provide superior health care to those who are eligible.
2. Participate in training medical personnel.
3. Expand medical knowledge through research.

Once these broad organizational goals have been clarified, attention can be paid to specific program goals. One goal of the hospital's emergency room program, for instance, could be stated as providing the immediate care necessary to keep critically injured patients alive and ready to begin treatment under long-term programs designed to restore them to health.

Hatry makes the following suggestions for defining and stating goals. First, people-oriented goals should be identified. In other words, how well is a service doing its job for the people who are affected by it? Goals can then be stated in terms of the way the service will affect people ("The goal of this program is to improve citizens' health while treating citizens with courtesy and dignity.") Second, potential unintended results of programs should be considered, especially when these are likely to be negative or to contradict the program's goal. For example, construction of a new hospital in a certain place might create poor traffic conditions and increase the auto accident and injury rate. Third, more than one goal should be stated. Most programs have more than one purpose. A police patrol program, for example, not only enforces the law but also provides information services and keeps public order.

Hatry warns that program goals are rarely neatly packaged for the planner to find. But clues to them can sometimes be found in statements of the legislature, whether ordinances, laws, or resolutions. Another possible source is statements made at public hearings on the program, reported in official minutes or by the press. In addition, government officials and agency employees may have expressed their conception of program goals, and clients receiving the services may have clarified their own concerns about the program.

Identifying Program Objectives

We make a distinction in this book between goals and objectives. Goals are relatively broad statements of purpose of the type listed above. Objectives are much more specific criteria, capable of being measured, which relate to the program goal. Morrisey has argued that the statement of an objective should include an action verb, a measurable result, a date by which the result is to be attained, and the maximum investment of resources to be spent to get the result. An example of a statement of an objective would be "To achieve a minimum of 95% delivery of meals to the shut-in elderly in our community by January 1 at a weekly cost not to exceed $500 and 100 work-hours."[11] Table 2–2 lists an objectives agreement form for results-oriented planning. (While not all writers on the topic would include a cost statement with the objective, they agree that costs are a crucial consideration, as we shall see below.) The planning study for Nashville's program for neglected and dependent children could not use such exact percentages. But it still states very specific objectives, such as "Reduce the number of neglected and dependent petitions filed and the number of children subjected to the system by screening out those cases in which a petition is not justified" and "Keep the child in his or her home or in a family environment when possible until a thorough study can be conducted and the disposition of the case decided. Seek to avoid institutional placements."[12]

TABLE 2–2.   SCHOOL SUPERINTENDENT'S OBJECTIVES AGREEMENT FROM JULY 1 TO DECEMBER 31

KEY RESULTS AREAS Indicators	Objectives

OPERATING RESULTS
  Master plan
  Increase in reading ability,
  grades 3–12
	1. To provide reading instruction as specified in department master operating plan within existing budget.
	2. To increase grades 3–6 reading test scores by 5% before December 31 at no increase in budget.
	3. To increase grades 7–12 reading test scores by a minimum of 3 percent over prior year's level at no increase in budget.

STRATEGIC PLANNING Approved long-range plan	4. To prepare and secure Board of Education approval for a plan for intensive tuition of slow reading learners by September 30 at a cost of 100 work-hours.
PUBLIC RELATIONS Public forums	5. To promote and conduct a minimum of one "how to help your child read" forums each month at specified schools throughout the city at a cost of 150 work-hours and $500.
ANTICIPATION/INNOVATION Brainstorming	6. To personally conduct a monthly meeting of randomly selected teachers; each meeting is to produce a minimum of one new idea for current and future reading programs, at a monthly investment of 40 work-hours.
STAFF DEVELOPMENT Number of qualified replacements	7. To have identified at least two qualified replacement candidates for each key position reporting to me, by August 31 within existing budget.
PROFESSIONAL LEADERSHIP Association participation	8. To serve as a member of the Reading Committee for the State Educational Association at a cost of 60 work-hours and $300 direct expense.
PROGRESS REVIEW SCHEDULE—last working day of each month.	

The following example indicates how to move from general to specific objective statements.

> ORIGINAL: Improve Effectiveness of Highway Safety Patrol's Anti-Speeding Program.
>
> COMMENTS: What is Effectiveness? How will you know when you get there?
>
> REVISED: To lower the number of vehicles traveling at 10 or more miles above the posted speed limit by a minimum of 10 percent, as measured by radar by June 30, at a direct cost not to exceed 100 work hours and $1000.[13]

In short, avoid the general and embrace the specific when stating objectives.

Specifying Evaluation Criteria

In the example given immediately above, an evaluation measure or criterion (improve performance on basic skills tests by 10 percent) is stated. These criteria are crucial; without them it will not be possible to evaluate the success of programs (which is the concern of Chapter 6) later on. In fact, Morrisey argues that evaluation criteria (or "indicators of effectiveness," as he calls them), should be identified *before* objectives are set. He feels this way because of the benefits that will accrue from going through the process of identifying indicators. Often objectives are easy to specify, but just as often an incredible array of indicators might be selected. Wrestling with the choice of indicators, especially in a Theory Y atmosphere where everyone's brainpower is tapped, may result in many practical new ideas for measuring and increasing program effectiveness. Morrisey sets forth the following guidelines for evaluation criteria:

They must be *measurable*.

They may represent "hard numbers" (numbers of clients served), "soft numbers" (absenteeism related to employee morale), or problems to be overcome (intrepreting changes in the law to constituents).

They will usually fall into one of the following time dimensions, in increasing order of usefulness.

Terminal indicators—factors that can be measured only after the project is completed. An example is performance on the basic skills reading test.

Preindicators—factors identified before project completion that will affect the project. Growing unemployment trends will obviously affect a job training project.

Concurrent indicators—factors that can be identified in advance and tracked during performance against objectives. An example is output per hour of work.[14]

Hatry agrees with Morrisey, and declares that programs should use not only multiple objectives but multiple evaluation criteria. For example, a study designed to see whether Fort Worth, Texas, police officers should be assigned to drive a patrol car for private use off duty to deter crime employed these evaluation criteria:

Number and rate of different crimes.

Number of traffic accidents.

Index of citizen feeling of security, based on a survey.

Index of police morale, based on a survey.

Program costs.

Underscoring his point, Hatry warns that too many evaluation criteria are better than too few. It is better to be inclusive rather than exclusive. Less useful or invalid measures can be discarded, but it is hard to introduce new measures in the middle of a study.

Furthermore, evaluation criteria should not be rejected just because they are hard to measure. Police effectiveness is a subject we have already mentioned as being troublesome to determine. Even so, surveys of residents or estimates made by a panel of specialists in the field may provide a means to gauge some aspects of this topic.

Identifying Alternative Choices

Perhaps the most useful task performed by the program planner is the identification of several different strategies for attacking a problem and the pros and cons of each. Spelling out alternative courses of action and their pluses and minuses gives the government official maximum choice in deciding what to do.

Hatry and colleagues suggest several ways to identify alternatives for consideration.[16] Government officials and agency employees should be asked for their ideas, while the proposals of individuals and groups outside government, including the news media and public interest groups such as the League of Women Voters, should also be examined. Approaches of other governments and of research teams often surface at professional meetings like those of the American Society for Public Administration (ASPA), the Ad Hoc Committee on Management Analysis in State and Local Government (MASLG), the National Association of State Budget Officers (NASBO), The International Personnel Management Association (IPMA), The Municipal Finance Officers Association (MFOA), The American Management Association (AMA), The Society for the Advancement of Management (SAM), and the International City Management Association (ICMA).[17]

Hatry also endorses the Theory Y approach of "brainstorming," where several employees meet in a group to throw out ideas to each other. Several experiments have shown that brainstorming generates more ideas than the sum total produced by an equal number of solitary thinkers. Hatry offers a testament to the powers of brainstorming. A fish-processing plant stored fish live in tanks until needed. Management wanted to reduce storage space to cut costs, but found that when the fish were more tightly packed together, they became inactive and less tasty. Many attempts were made to achieve movement of fish in a smaller space, but all failed until a small sand shark was put in the tank. Then, with only slight losses, the fish became very active.[18] While this story may be apocryphal, it shows the utility of both brainstorming and an unorthodox approach. It is hard to imagine this idea emerging in a Theory X atmosphere, where its proponent would probably have been mercilessly ridiculed.

Hatry examines five broad types of alternatives, which we will examine below in order. While these alternatives do not exhaust the range of possibilities, they illustrate a broad range of choices. The first is the extension of the present program at the same level of effort. A plus for this approach is that estimating costs will be relatively easy, since there is a track record to examine; but estimating effectiveness will be far more difficult, unless such a study has already been made. (In the next two subsections, we will examine cost and effectiveness estimates. The reader should also look at the relevant sections in Chapter 7, on budgeting.)

The second alternative is to extend the present program at a different level of support. Estimation of costs becomes more difficult here, especially if it is suggested that the program be expanded. That is, additional personnel costs, relatively easy to estimate, are not the only factors involved, because personnel need facilities and equipment, too.

If the proposal involves a reduction in effort, it will face political opposition from employees and clients. In addition, reduction may impair program effectiveness in ways that are hard to estimate. For example, low employee morale may cause worse job performance than before the cuts.

A third approach, variations in present program procedures, involves a change not just in the level of program support but in the program itself. For example, a sanitation department might switch from backdoor to curbside pickup of garbage. Cost and effectiveness estimates become more difficult here than in the first two approaches and become increasingly more difficult in the two approaches which follow.

The fourth alternative is the initiation of new programs with traditional concepts. An example is a proposal to provide dial-a-bus transportation to the elderly in a city of 150,000. A city that may never have used such a program before can draw on the experience of other cities which have tried it, as well as related programs like meals on wheels to shut-ins. Here the program change has become major enough so that it is not just a variation on the existing program. But this approach is a relatively safe way to introduce change, because there is a record of experience elsewhere from which to draw.

The last type, a new program with a new concept, is the hardest for which to estimate costs and effectiveness. Such a program may be tied to a new technology, in such areas as sewage treatment or educating the blind; and there may be little or no use of similar approaches elsewhere before the new approach is begun. As we shall see below, techniques of estimation are distinctly different for this type of program from those of others.

Estimating Costs

Most modern authorities on planning argue that plans should be formulated on a multi-year basis. This means that both the costs and effects should be projected several years into the future. As can be imagined, this is no simple task. Especially when we get into estimates for the fourth or fifth year, we may be able to get equally good results by reading tea leaves or gazing into a crystal ball. For this reason, Hatry notes that the following are key considerations in getting the most accurate cost estimates possible.

First, it is necessary to describe alternative policies in enough detail to generate cost estimates. For example, for a special education program, the exact number and type of personnel and the type of equipment and supplies must be listed. Suppose one program alternative includes the use of a computer for teaching purposes. Precise information about the type of computer, tie-in arrangements, and number of hours of computer time planned are needed to make cost estimates.

A second consideration is how to determine *which* costs to include. Cost analysis should focus on *major* costs, especially those which vary among alternatives. For instance, in the example above, if computer time is a major cost and is not common to all the alternatives, it should receive a thorough costing scrutiny. If it is common to all the proposals, it need not receive such emphasis.

Another factor to focus on in deciding which costs to include is the distinction among "sunk," "fixed," and "variable" costs. A *sunk cost* is money which has already been spent. For example, buildings already built are sunk costs, and are usually irrelevant considerations. That is, if it is proposed that a program be continued in an inadequate or inappropriate facility because funds have already been sunk in that facility, the planner should reject this line of reasoning. As in the case of the Pruitt-Igoe public housing project in St. Louis, Missouri, which finally had to be dynamited because few people besides criminals would live in it any longer, there is no point in throwing good money after bad.

Fixed costs are those which are unlikely to change, or to change appreciably, from one proposal to another. For example, if all proposals for increased fire protection include much the same apparatus, apparatus costs are largely fixed. But if the personnel and supply considerations vary significantly from one alternative to another, they are *variable costs* and should be closely scrutinized.

It should be remembered that costs are costs, no matter how the accountant enters them in the books. Morrisey gives the example of a manager who stated that his objective would release 1000 square feet of floor space at no cost. But Morrisey pointed out that the manager had already spent 10 hours on the proposal, that operations would be disrupted for a week while equipment was moved around, and that employee morale might suffer from the move. While the move might still be a beneficial one, costs would definitely be involved.[19] Commonly overlooked costs are those for central facilities, such as a town garage which services vehicles for all departments; employee fringe benefits; and future year operating costs of buildings.[20]

Perhaps the greatest cost involved in a program is the opportunity to have used the same amount of money elsewhere, in another program. New recreation costs may mean there is no money left in the budget for expansion of library services. Planners should point out this trade-off to official decision makers.

A number of different sources for estimating costs can be used. One is to apply current data (e.g., employee salary and benefits) to the future. However, this static approach will be less useful the more conditions change and will not take governments very far into the future. Another common approach applicable to equipment is to obtain estimates from sellers. A third cost estimate technique is specialist (in-house or consultant) estimates for new program components, such as operation of a central incinerator. Furthermore, sophisticated statistical analysis or mathematical modeling may be employed by systems analysts to estimate costs. These approaches are likely to be more accurate than the ones mentioned first, but they are also more expensive. Since consideration of these techniques lies beyond the scope of this book, we cite some relevant works in notes 3–6 and at the end of the book in the lists of relevant books and articles.

Estimating Effectiveness

Estimates of effectiveness are even more difficult to make than cost estimates. But hard thinking about realistic expectations for a program is necessary before embarking on the program. Hatry divides approaches for effectiveness estimates into those for alternatives involving minor program change and those involving new alternatives.

The first category involves using past performance data to estimate future effectiveness and estimating likely effects of changes in future conditions on performance. As far as the first of these is concerned, a problem will arise if no evaluation of present programs has ever been run. As mentioned previously, it may be necessary to run one, a process described in Chapter 6, before proceeding further. The second of these two approaches involves extrapolating the effect of changing trends on present performance data. Suppose, for example, that job training programs had succeeded in placing 40 percent of their graduates in skilled jobs over a five-year period. But assume that an increasing number of job trainees are minorities and women, who are harder to place, and suppose further that the local economy is entering a recession. Then there would probably be a decline in the placement rate. If they are to stand any chance of being accurate, estimates must take heed of changing conditions.

Estimates for alternatives new to government will be more difficult. Let us examine some of them here. One approach is to "borrow" information from another government which has already tried the alternative. Unfortunately, if these governments have not done a good job of evaluating program success— which often happens—this information will be inadequate. Even if the data are adequate, they must be carefully analyzed to see if they are relevant to another jurisdiction. Comparing the operation of street-cleaning operations in torrid Texas with those of wintry Wisconsin may be like comparing apples and oranges.

As previously mentioned in regard to cost estimation, information from sellers, in-house or consultant specialist estimation, and statistical or modeling techniques may be employed.[21]

Other approaches include expert judgments of the likelihood of success. For example, specialists in the field of parole and probation could be brought in to give guesstimates of which of several proposed alternatives would probably work best. (Governments employing this approach should be sure to ask the experts to list the reasons they have for their preferences. This will give analysts much more solid ground to work on than simple expressions of preference.)

Another approach is to assign one alternative each to different competing "teams" of planners, who are asked to come up with the strongest possible case for that alternative. Government officials can then scrutinize the reports of the different teams and make their decision. The chief benefit of this approach is that it will probably bring many relevant considerations to the surface which would otherwise have been neglected. This approach, then, could be called competitive brainstorming.

A final approach is the pilot study, or trying out the new approach on a limited trial basis. For example, prisons could try out a weekend furlough experiment, starting first with selected model prisoners. If most of the prisoners return to their cells at the end of the weekend, the program might be tried on a more comprehensive basis. But if the furloughed prisoners decide to ease the burden on the taxpayers by leaving to live elsewhere, it is time for the planners to come up with some other alternatives.

Selecting an Alternative as the Program Policy

The selection of an alternative may not be based on whether it is most likely to achieve the goals set for the program at an acceptable cost. We shall examine some of the political factors affecting program planning later. Suffice it to say that they can often torpedo the best laid plans of mice and mandarins. But for those interested in program results, it makes sense to compare alternatives on the basis of three major factors: likelihood of achieving the program goal, cost, and feasibility.

Morrisey has designed an easel flip chart which provides space to list alternatives next to these three considerations and any others which may arise. He recommends a brainstorming session with this chart as a way of securing the most searching consideration of alternatives.[22] While this session is obviously *not* a substitute for detailed written analysis of the pros and cons of various alternatives, it is a useful final step in summing up all considerations before making the final choice of an alternative.

THE USE OF RESULTS-ORIENTED PLANNING IN AMERICAN GOVERNMENT

Planning has had its greatest use and impact in fields using applied technology. For example, Secretary of Defense Robert McNamara applied systems analysis, in the form of Planning-Programming-Budgeting (PPB) to the Defense Department from 1961–1968. PPB was used to plan many aspects of military strategy and weapons systems research and development. McNamara's approach was characterized as more "bang for a buck," or one of efficiency and effectiveness, by its supporters.[23] However, this vaunted system simply was not used in plans for the Vietnam war, a striking fact which indicates the primacy of politics in many areas of planning, a topic which we examine later in this chapter. The decision to step up our commitment in Vietnam had already been made, and top officials like President Johnson were not interested in planning studies to see what this policy was likely to achieve.

Another technological area where planning has been successfully used is highways. Not only have impressive state highways been built in the postwar period, but a 40,000 mile long interstate system was built from 1956–1976. This enormous achievement required extensive planning. However, this planning was not perfect. In many cases city neighborhoods and the ecology of the countryside were destroyed in the name of Mercury, the god of communication and transportation. And today, the extra energy needed to operate this system is increasingly difficult to come by. In other words, unintended negative effects of this program were ignored or underestimated.

While much planning takes place in applied technology agencies, there are many such agencies, whether public works or sanitation departments, where it is nonexistent. And the lack of adequate and accurate analysis is even more noticeable in human service agencies, whether health, education, police, or welfare. This void looms largest at the local level, becomes smaller at the state level, and is smallest at the federal level, but is still apparent at all three levels of government. While the results of planning the thousands of local, state, and federal governments cannot be reported, we can report findings from some cases where planning has been used and analyze its achievement.

For example, former Illinois Secretary of State Michael J. Howlett describes how he undertook a thorough planning process in his office similar to that described in this chapter. Howlett notes that the results were largely increases in knowledge about how many projects were underway, and at what stage. He concludes that without this knowledge for his department of 4,000 employees, which handles matters as diverse as motor vehicle licensing and the state archives, "far more interdepartmental conflicts would have arisen, to say nothing of delays in completion or decision."[24] While he is surely right on this score, one would like to know more about the total results achieved.

In 1974 the Urban Institute reported on the six studies it had been able to find which examined the usefulness of planning and the factors which determined usefulness.[25] These findings support many of the points we made in the section on implementation. First, issues must be selected far enough in advance to be studied thoroughly before a decision has to be made, if the study is to have an impact. Second, the study will have more impact if the decision cannot be put off indefinitely. Third, planning studies need not use sophisticated methods or techniques to have impact. Fourth, studies of issues on which officials, employees, and affected groups have not already made up their minds are more likely to have impact.

Unfortunately, it is difficult to go beyond these broad generalizations, because we have so few studies of the impact of planning studies. That is, while agencies such as the U.S. General Accounting Office (GAO) have studied planning activity in federal agencies, they have not probed the *results* of this activity. It is surely interesting to know, as the GAO reports, that the Departments of Agriculture and Defense have highly structured planning processes, while the Departments of Commerce and Interior have no planning process.[26] But this does not tell us if Agriculture and Defense get something from their planning work that Commerce and Interior lack. And while energy "czar" James Schlesinger estimated that about one-fifth of the federal planning studies he had seen were implemented, this estimate from experience cannot be generalized.[27]

While it is our position that planning is absolutely essential to results-oriented management, we cannot outline its specific achievements in more detail than this brief summary. The following case study is included to give the reader a sense of the real returns to be had from planning.

CASE STUDY:
IMPROVING SHORT-TERM CARE OF NEGLECTED
AND DEPENDENT CHILDREN IN NASHVILLE

Metropolitan Nashville-Davidson County, Tennessee, had to decide in 1969 how to utilize the county children's home, where neglected and dependent (N-D) children waited before the courts placed them elsewhere. Welfare office employees and mayoral staff felt that this short-term care program was not working well. As a result, a study focusing on the problem was conducted.[28]

Program goals and objectives set were reducing the number of children in the children's home by screening out those who did not need that service, keeping the child at home whenever possible, and achieving the first two objectives at minimum cost.

Evaluation criteria included the number of children named in N-D petitions, the number of children kept in homelike environments instead of institutions, and estimated program costs.

Examination of the current system found that 28 percent of the children who entered it the previous year came in on petitions which were later withdrawn without a court hearing. They and an additional 35 percent were temporarily placed in the county children's home and then returned home. These findings raised doubts about whether the children should have come into the home to begin with.

Alternative programs identified were:

1. Twenty-four-hour intake screening. A welfare worker would always be available to decide where to place a child for whom a petition was filed.
2. Emergency caretakers. A custodian would be available who could enter the child's home to provide care if the parents were away, usually on an overnight basis.
3. Homemaker service. Trained personnel who could stay for a long period could enter the child's home to provide care during the crisis.
4. Emergency foster homes. Certain foster homes could maintain children in family environments prior to the court hearing.
5. County children's home. The existing option.

As the reader can note, these alternatives are not mutually exclusive, and several combinations were considered as alternatives, as Table 2–3 indicates. (Alternative I stressed homemaker service, and II foster homes. Alternatives III and IV provided lower service levels than I and II, but levels higher than those existing. All options included 24-hour screening and emergency caretaker services.)

TABLE 2–3.   INTAKE AND EMERGENCY CARE: ALTERNATIVE PROGRAM COMBINATIONS

	Current program (1969)	ALTERNATIVE (change from current program)			
		I	II	III	IV
24-hour screening	No	Yes	Yes	Yes	Yes
Emergency caretaker	No	Yes	Yes	Yes	Yes
Number of emergency foster homes	2[a]	+5	+13	+5	0
Number of homemakers	13[b]	+30	+15	+4	0
Children placed at Richland Village	469[c]	−325	−325	−167	−37

[a]Used for both N-D children and non-N-D children.
[b]Used only for non-N-D children.
[c]Includes 137 voluntary placements where N-D petitions were not filed; many of these children would be served under Alternatives I, II, and III.

SOURCE: Marvin R. Burt and Louis H. Blair, *Options for Improving the Care of Neglected and Dependent Children* (Washington, D.C.: Urban Institute, March 1971), p. 22.

In *estimating the effectiveness of alternatives,* the analysts assumed that future caseloads would be about the same as that for the last year. Expert judgment by a social worker who reviewed every case led to estimates of how many cases could be screened out by each alternative. *Cost estimation* figured not only the increased cost of additional services but also the reduced costs for the children's home which would result from a drop in caseload. (Table 2−4 presents estimates of costs and effectiveness.) Examination of revenue sources indicated that some foster home financing could come from the federal and state Aid to Families of Dependent Children (AFDC) program, while the children's home was financed by local funds. The exact cost to the local government (roughly proportionate to the *total* costs included in Table 2−4) was calculated, because this cost was of primary importance to the sponsors of the study.

Feasibility of implementation was calculated only for financial costs. Planners did note, however, that workers might not want to work late hours in neighborhoods they considered to be dangerous. No detailed consideration was given to possible reluctance on the part of children's home administrators and employees to seeing the number of employees cut.

The study had maximum impact, since Alternative I (homemaker service) was chosen. It should be noted that favorable conditions not relevant to some other studies obtained here. The study did not threaten any group, government employees found it reasonable, and additional costs involved were small.

The study is not a perfect one. Estimates of the likely number of

TABLE 2-4. EFFECTIVENESS AND COSTS OF SHORT-TERM ALTERNATIVES

Evaluation Criteria	ALTERNATIVE I		ALTERNATIVE II		ALTERNATIVE III		ALTERNATIVE IV	
	First Year[a]	Second Year[b]	First Year[a]	Second Year[b]	First Year[a]	Second Year[b]	First Year[a]	Second Year[b]
1. Children screened out by 24-hour screening	90–200	180–400	Same as Alternative I		Same as Alternative I		90	180
2. Children avoiding institutional care through use of emergency caretaker	12–25	25–50	Same as Alternative I		Same as Alternative I		12–25	25–50
3. Children avoiding institutional care through use of emergency foster homes	36	73	89	179	36	73	0	0
4. Children avoiding institutional care through use of homemaker	126	252	73	146	47	94	0	0
5. Reduction in children placed at Richland Village[c,d]	162	325	162	325	83	167	18	37
Costs ($000)—federal, state, and local	106	179	78	124	19	13	12	16

[a] Based on six-months program development time and only six months operating time.

[b] Also applies to the third and following years.

[c] The 1969 cases examined indicate that most of these children would also need to be served by foster homes or homemakers. Therefore, the total number of reduced placements at Richland Village is conservatively estimated as the sum of criteria 3 and 4, not 2, 3, and 4.

[d] This amounts to reductions per year starting in the second year of more than 12,400 child-days of care (a child-day is one child for one day) for Alternatives I or II, 7,300 for Alternative III, and 300 for Alternative IV.

SOURCE: Marvin R. Burt and Louis H. Blair, *Options for Improving the Care of Neglected and Dependent Children* (Washington. D.C.; Urban Institute, March 1971), p. 24.

children entering the system in future years were rough, while effectiveness criteria did not fully examine the quality of care nor its long-term effects. *Yet this was a useful study, well within the capability of local government.*

Questions

1. Did the Nashville study follow all the steps for a planning study outlined in the section on implementing planning? Would you add any additional steps? If so, describe them and give your reasons for adding them.

2. Do you consider the study deficient in any way? Specifically, are you satisfied with (a) goals, (b) evaluation criteria, (c) cost estimates, (d) effectiveness estimates? If not, explain why not. If so, explain *why* you think each aspect to be satisfactory.

TECHNICAL PROBLEMS AND HOW TO MINIMIZE THEM

The fundamental limitation on planners is their lack of clairvoyance. Since we cannot predict the future, our estimates will hit the target right on the nose only through chance. This is especially true for the period of extremely rapid social and economic change we live in today. Who, for example, forecast that our cities would explode in race riots in the late 1960s—and that race riots would almost disappear in the 1970s? Who forecast the outburst of student activism on college campuses which took place during the Vietnam war? And who said that the Arabs and the oil companies would combine to increase greatly the price of oil in the winter of 1973? To make the best possible estimates, then, we must try to minimize several persistent technical problems.

Several additional persistent problems in planning have already been mentioned in the section on planning implementation, and advice has been offered there about how to deal with them. Here we will discuss some further concerns.

Unclear Goal Statements

One common problem, basic to all results-oriented management, is imprecise statement of the goal. If the program's purpose is unclear, the program is unlikely to accomplish much. An example of this difficulty comes from a 1977 report by the GAO on federal "strike forces" against organized crime. The GAO concluded that not only was organized crime "flourishing" in the six cities with strike forces studied but also that "there is no agreement on what organized crime is, and consequently, on precisely whom or what the government is fighting."[29] This situation is to be expected with unclear goals. If no one can agree on what the target is, it is difficult to shoot bull's-eyes. The job of the planner and the official, then, is to make goals as precise as possible. (Unfortunately, this problem is not only technical but also often has political causes, as we shall see in the following section.)

Cost Estimating

Another problem area in planning is cost estimating. In our inflationary era, prices do not remain constant. Nor do prices for different items—wages, equipment, supplies—vary at the same rate. And in attempts to estimate changing prices in future years, claimants such as contractors or unions may make such forecasts self-fulfilling prophecies by being unwilling to settle for less. There is no easy way out of this dilemma. Hatry and colleagues recommend that perhaps price change projections should be made only when program choice might be significantly affected by price changes.[30] But such advice is not much help. This is an area where planners just have to muddle through, but at the least they should be aware of the problem before they start. They can then avoid unjustifiably precise cost projections which will only embarrass them later on. Indicating that future year costs may range between a minimum and maximum figure may seem sloppy work, but it beats a precise estimate which only holds false hopes.

Projecting into the Future

Another problem arises when we consider the related problem of how far to project program planning into the future. Should we look two, three, four, five, six, or more years hence? While we cannot offer exact guidelines, Hatry et al. have provided some useful advice on the topic.[31] First, we will want to look farther into the future when considering substantial capital spending for such items as a school building or a reservoir. For these very costly expenditures, estimates for 10 or more years hence seem justified. After all, what could be sadder than to spend $10 million on a new school building and find that you don't need it after another six years because of declining birthrates? Many towns have gone through this wasteful process when they could have used temporary buildings to get them through the peak years. But for procedural matters, such as staffing patterns for a hospital emergency room or assignment of welfare workers for family visitations, a shorter planning period of perhaps two or three years can be used. These plans may not involve additional staff or facilities and thus could be modified more easily. Situations where new employees or facilities would be added would fall between these two extremes in length of planning period.

Another consideration is the length of time the program needs to operate before it is likely to start showing results. For a drug treatment program, time must be allotted to hire a staff, obtain a facility (which usually takes a while, since no area wants junkies for neighbors), and recruit and choose patients. Furthermore, the program must run awhile so that analysts can determine whether its graduates are able to stay addiction-free for a long period after they leave. A six-month respite from drugs does not represent a cure if the patient becomes readdicted in his seventh month.

Uncertainty

The basic problem of planning, as we have already mentioned, is uncertainty about what the future will bring. The best way to handle this difficulty is to frankly acknowledge it and incorporate information on uncertainty in the planning study. This can be done by providing rough estimates of the likelihood that various events will occur. The study can then estimate how much these changing events are likely to affect the goals set by the plan. At the least, qualifying statements about potential risks and uncertainties should be included. This is not just to provide an escape hatch for the planner but also to warn those using the planning study that risks are involved all along the line. And if one alternative seems less risky or less changeable than others, this is a major factor to consider when making a choice of program. While information on uncertainty is not the same as a late-model crystal ball, it can make decision makers aware of a crucial dimension that must be considered in results-oriented planning.[32]

In the rest of this section, we will examine two other topics. While these are not problems in themselves, they can become problems if they are not approached or performed in the appropriate manner.

Using Outside Consultants

If an outside consulting firm is brought in to conduct the planning study because government employees are felt to lack the necessary expertise, the following points should be kept in mind. First, those hiring the consultant should be crystal clear about what they want done. As a former New York City budget director has said, "The clearer the notion we had on what we wanted, the better the results we got out of consultants."[33] This may seem an elementary point, but often consultants are hired because the agency has a vague idea that something is wrong and wants advice, but has not done the hard work necessary to pinpoint the nature of the problem. In this situation the consultant ends up telling the agency what the consultant should do—hardly the best way to proceed.

The consultant should also possess skills not readily available within the organization. There is no point in bringing in a civil engineer to look over the civil engineering department unless the consultant also has a specialized background in the kind of planning the organization is interested in.[34]

Management should also specify exactly what employee resources it will provide the consultant, so that the consultant can know if the job can be done adequately and on time. Consultants do not provide their services free of charge. The agency which hires a consultant should take steps to ensure that it gets its money's worth.

Presenting Study Results

As Hatry and colleagues point out, the presentation of study findings is a crucial concern. If the results are not clear, they will be ignored, no matter how brilliant they may be. An incoherent or unintelligible presentation can kill a good study. Hatry suggests the following steps to ensure a positive reception.

First, have the study reviewed by the agency employees who work on the program and by technical staff who did *not* participate in the study. They may well turn up errors or point out important neglected areas. If these employees and staff have strong disagreements with the study team, incorporate them in the study as minority opinions.

To avoid misunderstandings, always report results in writing. Be sure to provide a clear and concise summary for top officials, who may lack the time and interest to read the whole report. Jargon and specialized terms should be avoided, and good visual materials, including photographs, tables, charts, and graphs, should be used to support major points. The study should be tailored to the decision maker who will use it. For this reason, the format preferred by the decision maker (one-page summary, oral briefing, or whatever) should be provided.

Finally, and of great importance, acknowledge the limitations of the study. The official who is left to ferret these out may become suspicious of the merits of the study. One study reported by Hatry et al. noted that the city attorney felt the program proposal violated the state constitution. While the study endorsed the plan, it did not hesitate to point out this potential flaw.

These, then, are some technical considerations of crucial concern to those embarking on a planning study. The next section deals with political obstacles.

POLITICAL PROBLEMS AND HOW TO MINIMIZE THEM

Before we get into the specifics of dealing with political problems, we must note the preconditions necessary if the planning effort is to have a chance of success. First, let us repeat that a Theory Y approach should be employed, drawing on the collective brainpower of everyone in the organization. Only in this way can all unforeseen aspects and obstacles be brought out for close scrutiny. And employees who are involved in planning are going to be far more committed to carrying out the plan than employees who have a plan thrust on them out of the blue. This is the reason we emphasized brainstorming techniques in the implementation section. In sum, agency employees should always be part of the planning team, whether that team includes outside consultants, central planning, budget, or management agency members, or a team of employees from several other agencies.

On the other hand, the agency responsible for delivering services (e.g., education, social welfare, or public transportation) should not have sole responsibility for the planning study. The agency may have a vested interest in certain solutions which it cannot objectively analyze. For example, part of the reason for this country's disastrous experience in Vietnam was that planning was left to the military and their like-minded civilian allies. Only when it became apparent that this planning had been a stupendous failure were planners with other perspectives sought out in 1968 and policy reversed.

Unclear Goal Statements

As mentioned in the previous section, planning goals are often stated imprecisely for political reasons. One cause of imprecision is disagreement within the organization about what its goals are. Indeed, if such is the case, fewer things could be more upsetting to the agency than an explicit and exact goal statement. Take the example of a hypothetical welfare department. Should its goal be providing income to recipients, providing services to them, or trying to get them off welfare? Maybe all three should be goals, but the chances are that identification of any one as *the* goal, or a listing of goals in which one objective will have to appear first will upset employees. Employees in different divisions and programs will emphasize different goals, so that statement of one overall goal will be difficult. Under these circumstances, it is no surprise that many agency or program goal statements are so general as to defy measurement.

And some agency officials may want goals this general because they are apprehensive about measurement of agency output. They may fear, or even know, that the agency will look bad when programs are evaluated. A police department faced with a rising crime rate may feel that it will look bad no matter how good a job it is doing if clear goals are set. While there is no one best way to deal with these political problems, we refer the reader to the last part of this section, "Top Officials in the Planning Process," for some advice about how to proceed.

A closely related problem is agency resistance to consideration of alternative ways to perform a task. If an agency has done its job in a certain way for a long time, its employees may experience great difficulty in considering new ways of work. A teacher who has taught math one way for 30 years is not going to change his or her mind instantly about the best way to do it if he or she is shown a planning study indicating that the "new math" is likely to do the job better. Arnold Meltsner, a program planner for the Defense Department in the early 1960s, reports what happened to him when he tried to explain the importance of contemplating alternatives for military programs to a room full of officers. A Marine colonel who had spent the session doing deep knee bends leaped to his feet and banged his fist on the table, saying, "In the Marines, we have no alternatives."[35] Again, we refer the reader to the following subsection, on top officials; but even these top officials would have their work cut out for them when dealing with this colonel.

Hatry has provided a list and suggestions about how to handle political problems related to agency and clientele resistance to planning.[36] A first concern is the number of agencies that will be involved in program implementation. The more cooks, the more likely the soup will be spoiled. Coordination is a difficult task even under optimal conditions, and if agencies from other levels of government (federal and state) are working with a local agency, there is nothing that even the strongest mayor can do to *make* them cooperate. Thus, alternatives that call for complicated coordination are not going to be as feasible as other alternatives, and planners and officials must not forget this fact.

If an alternative directly affects clientele (school double sessions or admission fee to the municipal park), it is going to be more difficult to implement than a less visible change (dropping the requirement that all teachers have a master's degree or using smaller work crews in the park), other things being equal. Program clientele may bother, badger, and besiege the agency until it agrees to forgo these unpopular alternatives.

If the alternative requires changes in agency behavior which will not be easy to make, it may not be feasible. If police officers, for example, will have to treat suspected criminals very differently from the way they have been doing, they may be unable or unwilling to change.

Finally, if an alternative threatens important officials with a loss of power or prestige, it will certainly be resisted by them. And if these officials are strong enough, it will make more sense to stress another proposal. At the same time, if the officials are results oriented, they may be persuaded to ponder change in their priorities.

Top Officials in the Planning Process

Hatry et al. list several matters which should concern top officials, whether they are chief executives (president, governors, mayors, or managers), legislators, or department heads, who request program planning.[37] While these officials are concerned primarily with broad policy questions rather than the nitty-gritty of carrying out a program, they must be involved with planning in the following ways if it is to get them what they want.

First, they must participate actively in selecting programs and problems to investigate. Only in this way can they be sure that important issues are selected and trivial ones neglected. At the very least, they can go over lists of problems and eliminate less pressing concerns.

The next step is for the top official to do everything possible to facilitate cooperation from agencies concerned with the issue. A personal message from a chief executive will have much more impact than one in a series of memos from the chief executive to a department head. As one New York City department head replied when asked why he was not carrying out a new policy set by the mayor, "Listen, the mayor may be for it, and he may have told you he's for it, and he may have told the press he's for it, but he hasn't told *me* he's for it."[38] And in some cases the mayor may have to do more than send a personal message. He may have to get compliance by reminding the department head to cooperate—or the head's pet project, budget request, or whatever may be in trouble.

A further necessity is provision of a large and competent study group which can focus its efforts on completing the study so that it can be reviewed by top officials before a decision has to be made. Nothing is so frustrating as a study which recommends locks for a house the day after it has been burglarized.

Another step the top official should take is to review the study in its early stages to make sure that its objectives and alternatives are truly important. If a study of fire loss reduction seems to be concentrating on improving police department–fire department relations to the exclusion of other goals, the official should call his study team in and go over the priorities of the program.

A fifth step is the assignment of a member of the official's staff to monitor the study team's work, to make sure the team stays on the mark and will complete the study in time before the day of decision arrives. A detailed schedule fixing dates for the completion of each phase of the study should be constructed by the monitor.

Finally, the officials must carefully review the results of the planning study and make sure that they are used if they seem to hit the mark. Nothing is more wasteful than a good study report which is ignored. The author remembers a police program planner telling how he entered the office of the chief of one police department to begin a study, only to see reports of a similar study by the International Association of Chiefs of Police gathering dust on the shelf. While some top officials may want to run a study as a smoke screen or as a way to get themselves off the hook, the results-oriented manager will want to obtain maximum benefits from the study.

Political obstacles are often even harder to clear than technical hurdles. The suggestions above are not panaceas, but they may be useful to planners and officials who want to see plans implemented instead of gathering dust in the library. And the support of these officials is crucial in avoiding the kind of political compromise (a little from this alternative, some from that, and some from another one) which may make employees and clientele happy but results in an illogical and unworkable "program."

PLANNING PROSPECTS AND PROBLEMS

While we noted earlier that it is difficult to spell out the precise impact of planning under differing conditions, there is no question that planning activity is greatly on the increase. In 1946, few federal agencies had the elaborate planning process which the GAO discovered many of them had in 1976. Likewise, larger state, county, and city governments—and even some medium-sized and smaller units—are more and more concerned with forecasting. Publication of books, articles, and manuals on planning by such organizations as the Urban Institute and the International City Management Association indicate that planning is here to stay and spread throughout many of our 80,000 local governments.[39]

While we heartily endorse this trend and hope to see it strengthened, we have an obligation to point out some hidden snares in planning. These criticisms of the assumptions and approach of planning analysts transcend the technical and political problems confronting the planner. While we do not feel they destroy the efficacy of planning efforts, their impact should be carefully contemplated by the reader.

Political scientist Fred A. Kramer has cautioned that planning contains certain characteristic assumptions which can act as an ideology, blinding the planner to the reality of a situation and thus reducing the value of planning work.[40] Two aspects of this alleged ideology which concern Kramer are its emphases on quantification and social science theory. Kramer warns that stressing the quantitative may drive out qualitative considerations which are all-important to the analysis. That is, a stress on the *numbers* of prisoners paroled under a program may be emphasized more than the *nature* of the guidance and counseling provided by the parole program. These qualitative considerations, which defy quantification, may well be the factors that determine the success or failure of the program.

Kramer's second point is that the social and economic theories behind a plan may be inaccurate and lead to unanticipated and unwanted events. An example given is the social science theory behind the War on Poverty of the Johnson administration. Policymakers were amazed when the poor, instead of being worshipfully grateful, used anti-poverty programs to denounce all levels of government while simultaneously demanding even more program support from them. Likewise, the social science theory that guided advocates of strategic bombing of the civilian population in both World War II and Vietnam was far off the mark. In both cases, enemy war production and morale *increased* as a result of the bombing.

Kramer's advice to the planner whose work is rejected by government officials is to use self-analysis. Perhaps the study was rejected because it did not meet the needs of the official. Maybe the planner did not spell out some implicit assumption of the study, or neglected some aspect with which the official was familiar. Kramer concludes by stating that "More likely, the analysts probably did not spell out the weaknesses in their work because *their perspective—their implicit ideology*—made it impossible for them to see the weaknesses."[41] Kramer's recommendations for avoiding this trap are similar to those made in the preceding section, on political obstacles. But we have repeated Kramer's argument here, because the only way that planners who are off the track are going to get back on it is through serious self-criticism and the willingness to admit that their assumptions are not necessarily eternal verities.

Additional drawbacks have been identified by Kimmel and his colleagues.[42] First, they point out, there is no consensus on what constitutes "good" systems analysis or planning. For example, a survey of Defense Department studies found no agreement on which studies were good, let alone *why* they were good. Public planning, then, is hardly a science comparable to physics or chemistry.

Second, planning may tend to justify ends over means. In their anxiety to achieve results, planners may be expedient about procedural matters, the types of concerns which lawyers, in contrast, tend to stress. And ethics may be of no concern. If it is true that exponents of results-oriented management tend to argue that the end justifies the means, this is a bias they should be aware of. Otherwise they will adopt the same stance as totalitarians determined to triumph regardless of other considerations. Again, planners who are aware of these biases can learn some necessary humility and self-restraint.

Economists Murray Weidenbaum and Linda Rockwood have pointed out that *comprehensive* planning efforts are in for trouble. They argue that it makes more sense to try smaller scale planning in specific agencies, rather than to mount a concerted and coordinated planning effort.[43] They cite the 1965–1971 rise and fall of federal PPB,[44] a topic which will be explored in more detail in Chapter 7. This planning-oriented budgeting system was launched in too grandiose a fashion and collided head-on with existing planning and budgeting efforts. Weidenbaum and Lockwood conclude that even long-range corporate business planning has a poor record, so that hopes of installing such a system in government and seeing it succeed are doomed to disappointment.

These warnings have wisdom. Planning can accomplish much. But its own worst enemies may be the enthusiastic advocates who oversell its merits. Government agencies badly need much more results-oriented planning. But this planning must be flexible and realistic if it is to succeed. Someday comprehensively coordinated planning systems may be feasible, but there is more than enough work ahead in trying to design planning procedures for individual agencies. And these agency planning systems are necessary prerequisites for the eventual establishment of comprehensive planning. A system such as PPB can work only if it is built on a foundation of agency planning capability. The efforts of planning advocates should be made in this direction before we try to erect the imposing but ineffective edifice of a new PPB.

NOTES

1. Harry P. Hatry, Louis Blair, Donald Fisk, and Wayne Kimmel, *Program Analysis for State and Local Governments* (Washington, D.C.: Urban Institute, 1976), p. ix.
2. Wayne A. Kimmel, William R. Dougan, and John R. Hall, *Municipal Management and Budget Methods: An Evaluation of Policy Related Research, Final Report, Volume 1: Summary and Synthesis* (Washington, D.C.: Urban Institute, 1974), pp. 54–55.
3. Perhaps the best introduction to the topic is Charles Schultze, *The Politics and Economics of Public Spending* (Washington, D.C.: Brookings Institution, 1969).
4. See Philip M. Morse, ed., *Operations Research for Public Systems* (Cambridge, Mass.: M.I.T. Press, 1967) and Jack Byrd, Jr., *Operations Research Models for Public Administration* (Lexington, Mass.: D. C. Heath, 1975).
5. This example comes from *Teaching and Research Materials, Public Policy 210 Problem Sets* (Cambridge, Mass.: Kennedy School of Government, 1972).
6. See Federal Electric Corporation, *A Programmed Introduction to PERT* (New York: Wiley, 1963), and John Dearden and F. Warren McFarlan, *Management Information Systems* (Homewood, Ill.: Richard D. Irwin, 1966), ch. 4.
7. Garry D. Brewer, *Evaluation and Innovation on Urban Research* (Santa Monica, Calif.: Rand Corporation, 1970), p. 11.
8. This section is primarily based on Hatry et al., op. cit., chs. 3–5.
9. Erwin C. Hargrove, *The Missing Link* (Washington, D.C.: Urban Institute, 1975), pp. 17–25.
10. George L. Morrisey. *Management by Objectives and Results in the Public Sector* (Reading, Mass.: Addison-Wesley, 1976), pp. 34–37.
11. Ibid., pp. 66–67.

12. Hatry et al., op. cit., p. 41.

13. Morrisey, op. cit., p. 99.

14. Ibid., pp. 55–64.

15. Hatry et al., op. cit., p. 43.

16. Ibid., pp. 47–50.

17. The addresses of these and related organizations are given at the end of this book in the section "Books, Articles, Magazines, and Organizations Relevant to Results-oriented Public Management."

18. Hatry et al., op. cit., p. 48.

19. Morrisey, op. cit., pp. 13–14.

20. Hatry et al., op. cit., pp. 61–64.

21. See Gary Fromm et al., *Federally Supported Mathematical Models* NTIS-PB 241562 (Washington, D.C.: Data Resources, Inc., and ABT Associates, Inc., June 1974); Mathias L. Spiegel and E. S. Savas, *Emergency Ambulance Service for the City of New York* (New York: Office of the Mayor, March 8, 1968); Kenneth L. Kraemer, *A Systems Approach to Decision-Making: Policy Analyses in Local Government* (Washington, D.C.: International City Management Association, 1973); and Environmental Protection Agency, *Evaluation of Techniques for Cost-Benefit Analysis of Water Pollution Control Programs and Policies* (Washington, D.C.: Government Printing Office, 1975).

22. Morrisey, op. cit., pp. 105–12.

23. See Alain C. Enthoven and K. Wayne Smith, *How Much Is Enough? Shaping the Defense Program, 1961–1969* (New York: Harper & Row, 1971).

24. Michael J. Howlett, "Strategic Planning in State Government," *Managerial Planning,* November–December 1975.

25. Kimmel et al., op. cit., pp. 55–58.

26. *Long-Range Analysis Activities in Seven Federal Agencies,* Report to the Congress by the Comptroller General of the United States, December 3, 1976 (Washington, D.C.: Government Printing Office, 1976).

27. See U.S. Congress, Senate Committee on Government Operations, Subcommittee on National Security and International Operations, *Planning, Programing, Budgeting,* 90th Cong., 1st sess., 1970, pp. 127–28.

28. The study is reported in full in Marvin R. Burt and Louis H. Blair, *Options for Improving the Care of Neglected and Dependent Children* (Washington, D.C.: Urban Institute, March 1971).

29. Anthony Marro, "G.A.O. Faults Drive on Organized Crime," *New York Times,* March 19, 1977, p. 1.

30. Hatry et al., op. cit., pp. 69–71.

31. Ibid., pp. 90–92.

32. Ibid., pp. 92–95.

33. Frederick O'R. Hayes, "Things Are Picking Up in the Sanitation Department," *New York Times,* July 9, 1973.

34. George E. Berkley, *The Craft of Public Administration* (Boston: Allyn and Bacon, 1975), pp. 366–67.

35. Arnold J. Meltsner, *Policy Analysts in the Bureaucracy* (Berkeley, Calif.: University of California Press, 1976), pp. 67–68. Meltsner proffers Machiavellian advice to would-be planners on pages 94–102 of this volume.

36. Hatry et al., op. cit., pp. 100–1. Cf. Arnold J. Meltsner, "Political Feasibility and Policy Analysis," *Public Adminstration Review* 32 (November–December 1972): 859–67.

37. Hatry et al., op. cit., pp. 10–11.

38. Edward N. Costikyan, *Behind Closed Doors* (New York: Harcourt, 1966), p. 293.

39. Hatry et al., op. cit., and John K. Parker, "Administrative Planning," in James M. Banovetz, ed., *Managing the Modern City* (Washington, D.C.: International City Management Association, 1971), pp. 238–54.

40. Fred A. Kramer, "Policy Analysis as Ideology," *Public Administration Review* 35 (September–October 1975): 509–17.

41. Ibid., p. 512. Cf. Meltsner, "Political Feasibility . . . ."

42. Kimmel et al., op. cit., pp. 58–59.

43. Murray Weidenbaum and Linda Rockwood, "Corporate Planning versus Government Planning," *Public Interest,* Winter 1977, pp. 59–72.

44. See Allen Schick, "A Death in the Bureaucracy: The Demise of Federal PPB," *Public Administration Review* 33 (March–April 1973): 146–56.

3
Reorganizing for Results

LEARNING OBJECTIVES
TO UNDERSTAND:

Staff, line, and auxiliary agencies and functions

Interdepartmental and intradepartmental reorganization

Span of control, joint accountability, project management, and matrix organization

How to plan and implement reorganization

The record of reorganization

Problems and prospects of reorganization

Reorganization was the rage at the federal and state levels of government in the 1970s. Yet the result of much of this activity is uncertain, as we shall see below. And John Ehrlichman, once an aide to President Nixon, said in 1976 that attempts to reorganize the federal government were "like trying to make water run up hill."[1]

DEFINING REORGANIZATION

Remember that our definition of organizing is the process of grouping responsibilities and activities and establishing formal and informal relationships that will allow people to work together most effectively in setting and attaining the goals of an agency or department.[2] *Reorganization* is the restructuring of these responsibilities, activities, and relationships.

Before proceeding further, we need to define three commonly used terms which distinguish agencies by type. *Line* agencies are those which directly provide services and regulate behavior. Examples include police, fire, school, welfare, transportation, housing, and health departments. *Auxiliary* agencies provide needs common to line departments, such as purchasing, printing, travel, accounting, and computer services. That is, they provide services directly to the line agencies, rather than to a public or clientele, as do the line agencies. (Clientele for the line agencies listed above would include vehicle operators, property owners, students, welfare recipients, bus riders, owners of government-backed mortgages, and people receiving flu shots.) *Staff* agencies are concerned with thinking, planning, and advice; examples include central planning, budgeting, personnel, and management agencies. Such staff operations are usually grouped under the chief executive and share that official's broad, overall perspective on government, rather than the more narrow and limited outlook of a line agency.

Line agencies may contain auxiliary units, such as purchasing, and staff units, such as budgeting, to service the line. These *internal* auxiliary and staff functions are akin to, but not to be equated with, the *external* central auxiliary and staff *agencies* which exist separate from line departments. Looking inside a specific welfare department, we might find a welfare caseworker, who is a *line* employee; an accountant, who is an *auxiliary* employee; and a planner, who is a *staff* employee.

While the distinction among line, staff, and auxiliary is not clear-cut in every case, it is a necessary one to make in this chapter, because there are real differences in function, perspectives, and loyalties among these three types.

INTERDEPARTMENTAL AND INTRADEPARTMENTAL REORGANIZATION

Throughout this chapter we distinguish between *inter*departmental and *intra*departmental reorganization. The former is the rearrangement of functions among departments and is especially concerned with the relationship of the chief executive—whether president, governor, mayor, or manager—to her or his department heads. A recent example of interdepartmental reorganization is the creation of a federal Department of Energy in 1977. This new department was created from components of previously existing departments and agencies, such as the Interior and Defense Departments and the Federal Power Commission.

Intradepartmental reorganization, on the other hand, is concerned with restructuring the lines of authority *within* a department or agency. This type of reorganization focuses on the relationships among top, middle, and first-line management; the degree of decentralization and delegation of authority to be found at lower levels; and the assignments given to different organizational subdivisions. Interdepartmental reorganization is concerned with these matters as well, but on the level of relationships *among* the departments and the chief executive.

Interdepartmental Reorganization

While there are millions of ways to *reorganize,* we use the term to characterize two specific results-oriented packages or organizational changes. The first package, dealing with interdepartmental reorganization, includes the following four principles:

1. Concentration of authority in the chief executive and his or her appointed department heads.
2. Integration of similar functions (for example, solid waste and liquid waste disposal) in the same department.
3. Replacement of multimember boards with single administrators.
4. Coordination of services in central staff (for example, central budget, personnel, and management) agencies.

Administrative reformers have pushed this package and related planks throughout this century. They argue that governments reorganized in this way will be more efficient, effective, and responsive to citizen needs and demands. Reading some of Jimmy Carter's indictment against the federal bureaucracy ("duplications, waste, and inefficiencies")[3] brings to mind the words of the 1937 Brownlow Committee report to President Roosevelt ("waste, overlapping, and duplication, which may be eliminated through coordination, consolidation, and proper managerial control").[4] Both are concerned with trying to apply reorganizational principle 2, integration of similar functions, in the package listed above. Indeed, no President since Roosevelt has not been concerned with these issues. President Nixon offered a massive reorganization plan in 1971 which embodied all four of the principles listed above.[5]

What benefits can be expected from the application of these principles of reorganization? To return to our list, the first principle, concentration of authority, promises increased accountability. If the mayor, governor, or President, and his or her appointees have the legal authority to act, the public can determine whom to blame or praise in given decisions. All too often, executive authority is shared or rests in the hands of semi-autonomous boards (for example, school boards or special district boards) over which the chief executive has little or no authority. In early 1977, Mayor Beame of New York suggested that the city school board be dismantled, to be replaced by a mayorally appointed commissioner of education. The furor this proposal stirred in the educational community indicates how teachers have come to accept organizational autonomy as a given. Mayor Beame's counterclaim was that the educational bureaucracy had no accountability to any elected official. The term *chain of command* is used to describe the hierarchy of officials who report to superiors at different levels. The goal of the administrative reformers is a chain of command from top to bottom unbroken by autonomous agencies. In this way, department heads can manage more effectively to achieve results, or be held accountable for failure to achieve results without passing the buck.

We have already mentioned the second principle, integration of similar functions, which promises greater efficiency. As the report adopted as the basis for reorganizing the Connecticut state government in 1977 stated, "When there are 10 public safety organizational units, 27 health units and 23 education units, questions about accountability, manageability, and efficiency are almost never answered adequately."[6] Central to this efficiency is the concept of *span of control*, which refers to the number of subordinates a supervisor directly oversees. A boss who has 6 employees has a span of control of 6; if someone supervises 28 employees, the span of control is 28. While there is no consensus on the best number of subordinates to have in a span of control, the more agencies that directly report to the chief executive, the more difficult will be the job of management for this top official. For this reason, functional integration should improve management, since it reduces span of control. In some states, the officials directly reporting to the governor number over 200. For example, in Connecticut before reorganization, agencies reporting directly included the American and Francophone Cultural Commission and the Advisory Committee on Mobile Homes. Reducing the span of control from such a swollen number will allow managers to focus more on results.

The third principle recommends the end of government by committee. Multimember bodies—whether school boards, public utility commissions, or the U.S. Federal Reserve Board—are not good at supervision and management. Government by committee is characterized by stalemates, delays, and unworkable compromises, which are the inevitable results of getting all committee members to pull together. Boards and committee can be likened to Dr. Doolittle's Pushmi-Pullyu, an animal with heads at both its front and rear ends. Both beasts often find it difficult to decide where and how to move. They are not cut out for day-to-day supervision and coordination, and the compromises they must often make to function at all lose sight of key goals and objectives.

The fourth principle, coordination of staff services, is designed to give the chief executive the resources needed to manage the complexities of government in the late twentieth century. These staff services include the vital functions of planning, management, evaluation, budgeting, and personnel—all of which are examined in this book. More often than not, they are fragmented from each other and cannot be effectively meshed and coordinated by the chief executive. In 1977, President Carter appointed Alan Campbell as the new chairperson of the U.S. Civil Service Commission, the federal government's personnel agency, to be sure that the personnel function would be carefully considered and coordinated with planned presidential reorganization proposals. One message of this book is that the various management approaches explored here should be carried out in a comprehensive and coordinated manner to achieve maximum results. In addition, auxiliary services such as accounting, purchasing, travel, printing, and computer services are often spread all over the organizational chart outside the chief executive's control. Consolidating them would also increase economy and efficiency.

Intradepartmental Reorganization

The second package, concerned with intradepartmental reorganization, includes the following three principles:

1. *Joint accountability and reward for achieving results.* This approach encourages cooperation by assigning joint responsibility to employees working together on a project. In other words, rather than saying that each person is responsible only for a segment of the project, the work group is evaluated as a group and rewarded on the basis of the overall success of the project.

2. *Decentralization of authority to attain results.* Decentralization has been defined in many different modes and manners. We use it here to mean devolving power to lower levels of an agency, maximizing the number of decisions to be made by first-line and middle managers. Such an approach is consistent with Theory Y, which emphasizes the participation of all members of the organization.

3. *Flexible project management to obtain results.* Project management is an approach borrowed from the highly successful space programs of the National Aeronautics and Space Agency (NASA). Project management is carried out by a temporary unit set up within an organization. The director of the project draws on existing units of the organization for the manpower and material to carry out the project. Project managers, then, cut across jurisdictional lines to perform their assignments.

Bear in mind that the consideration of all these "principles" of reorganization should be guided by a practical and pragmatic concern for the results they are likely to achieve. There is no *science* of organizational principles. Government official and administrative writer Harvey Sherman has sagely discussed what he calls *mutable,* or changeable, principles of organization. Sherman entitled his book on organization *It All Depends*[7] to emphasize that different political, cultural, and agency values determine which administrative arrangement works best in a given context. The reorganizer, then, should apply the advice given in this chapter flexibly, with a constant concern for *results* rather than for stylishly symmetrical organization charts.

IMPLEMENTING REORGANIZATION

Interdepartmental Reorganization

Like most of the other innovative managerial techniques described in this book, reorganization has usually been oversold. Former federal management official and current professor of public administration Harold Seidman makes the following sardonic comment on the reorganization reformers: "Entry into the Nirvana of Economy and Efficiency can be obtained only by strict adherence to sound principles of executive branch organization."[8] Again, anyone who is convinced that reorganization will be a panacea instead of an incremental improvement is destined for disillusionment.

With this point in mind, let us turn to a hypothetical situation in which a green light has been given to make a study of interdepartmental reorganization along the lines of the principles sketched above. (Many, if not all, of the remarks made below will also apply with equal force to intradepartmental reorganizations.)

The Study Phase   A governmental reorganization should be tailor-made. It makes little sense to apply the principles of reorganization in a preconceived and uniform manner. To do so ignores the realities of the "informal" organization. For example, agencies such as the U.S. Army Corps of Engineers or the Veterans Administration may be so powerful that they can not only resist being reorganized but can also torpedo the entire plan. A careful survey should be made to determine the realistic chances of reorganizing. Half a loaf is far better than none. This is what President Nixon's reorganizers concluded in 1971, when they excluded the veterans and engineers from their proposals.

A reorganization study should be as carefully planned as the planning process described earlier. In particular, enough time should be set aside to gather the detailed information about how programs work and how they intersect with each other. A 1972 study of Connecticut human services agencies can be criticized for not allotting enough time and/or staff to this effort. As a result, its report looked like any one of a thousand that had rolled off the consultant's assembly line. The study dealt in generalities, rarely going beneath the surface for a detailed look at the functioning of the system and how it could be improved. This type of superficial study should be avoided. It is almost useless, except as a public relations technique. A more thorough study, of course, will cost more in money and staff time. For this reason, officials who want reorganization should push for an adequate appropriation of funds for the study.

Absolutely essential to the study are staff researchers from outside the line departments who, nevertheless, know these departments well. Only people with this background can bring informed objectivity to the task. A study group made up entirely of line agency employees would be unlikely to examine everything with a dispassionate eye and recommend major changes. A study group made up entirely of consultants from outside government would probably not be able to find out how the agencies really work, and what their personnel think, in the time allotted for the study. A joint team of line agency employees and central staff (management, budget, or personnel departments) employees is recommended, with perhaps an outside consultant thrown in. The central staff employees are the key people in the equation, for they know a lot about the line departments after years of interaction. And they see things through the perspective of their agencies rather than that of the line agency. The Massachusetts reorganization study began in 1969 with outside subject area specialists who did not know the ins and outs of the political labyrinth of the state government. After they fumbled and bumbled for a while, these outsiders were replaced by knowledgeable insiders who shared the bird's-eye view of the governor and his overhead staff agencies rather than the worm's-eye view of the line agencies. (Incidentally, student interns were used by the new study team and were extremely helpful in gathering data. With the growth of college intern programs in public administration and political science, large numbers of interns are available to be tapped by the astute government official. Nearby colleges should be contacted to see if their interns would like to work on reorganization or other governmental matters.)

Theory Y procedures should be followed in the study phase and later. If researchers suddenly show up in the agencies demanding information, the employees' natural reaction will resemble that of clams that have been disturbed. Diplomacy and tact should be used. For example, all interviews with or observation of agency personnel should be cleared in advance with top or middle management. In fact, the agency should be asked if it can appoint an employee to act as a liaison between the agency and the study team. The effort spent on this procedure will yield great dividends in eliminating suspicion and misunderstanding.

At the same time, the goals of interdepartmental reorganization, as embodied in the four principles, should be made clear to employees in the line agencies. Any evasion or fuzziness is going to increase agency mistrust and reluctance to cooperate. Study team members should act as salespeople, pointing out to line agency managers the advantages that might accrue to them with reorganization. While strong agencies who already get what they want are not likely to be quickly seduced by this line, agencies with leaders who are frustrated by not being able to do their job better and weak agencies without strong interest group or legislative support may sign on as ardent supporters of reorganization. Another way of assuaging anxiety is to adopt a policy of not making personnel reductions through layoffs.

It should be noted that former President Nixon did not take this approach to reorganization. As mentioned in the chapter on MBO, he profoundly distrusted bureaucrats and supported reorganization as one way of cracking bureaucratic heads.[9] Had his reorganization proposals been enacted, bureau resistance would no doubt have eviscerated many of them. President Carter's statements on reorganization are in the Theory Y vein. He has talked of the thousands of highly motivated civil servants waiting for an administration that will use their talents and of participation by many groups, including civil servants, in developing reorganization proposals. As the president correctly put it, "Reorganization plans should not . . . spring full-blown from the brow of some presidential counsel or the White House basement. Such approaches have invariably generated tremendous heat, a flash of headlines, and no lasting results."[10] Reorganization studies should tap the collective knowedge and wisdom of all government employees. Unfortunately, as of mid-1978, the president's reorganizers were *not* consulting career employees, thereby nullifying Carter's expressed intentions.

The Legislative Phase   Since interdepartmental organization is usually authorized by statute or ordinance, reorganization must be approved by the legislature, whether federal, state, or local. Federal law and the laws of a dozen states give the chief executive the initiative in reorganization, but allow the legislature to veto proposals if it is displeased with them.

Legislative authority in reorganization means that the astute reorganizer must keep in close touch with key legislators and legislative staff. The legislature must be lobbied from start to finish of the reorganization effort, so that none of the solons slide off the bandwagon. Do not forget that reorganization is but one of many issues to a legislator and is rarely a bread-and-butter issue to his constituents. Legislators will usually be far more concerned with tax issues and the provision of direct benefits to constituents than with a rather abstract matter like reorganization, so that the reorganizers must constantly remind legislators of the issue.

One tactic to *avoid* in selling reorganization is claiming specific dollar savings from it. Reorganization is usually sold in the name of economy as well as efficiency and effectiveness. Roy Ash, director of Nixon's reorganization study, claimed his proposals would save $5 billion a year, if adopted. Yet there is no evidence that reorganization does save money,[11] and claims that it does can cause real problems. Partisan debate may erupt in the legislature over these claims, which cannot be proven. As a consequence, the drive for reorganization may be stalled or sidetracked. Stressing the better management to be expected from application of the principles makes better sense.

The root reason for resistance to reorganization is the fear of bureaucrats and their legislative and interest group allies that an agency will be downgraded and lose its influence. As the 1952 Mississippi Study Committee on Reorganization reported, the almost uniform response received from individual agency heads about reorganization was as follows:

> I think this is one of the very best things that has ever been done in the state of Mississippi, and I have long been of the opinion that this work should have been accomplished in the past. However, my department is of a type, character, and kind that cannot be consolidated with any other agency, as its duties and functions are unique, and a reduction of personnel or transfer of any duties of this department would work a hardship and prevent certain citizens from receiving benefits to which they are entitled.[12]

This knee-jerk response is not necessarily insincere. The most basic reason for it is fear that the administrative and political status quo will be disturbed. We have already proffered some advice on how to deal with agency and ally opposition to change. Suffice it to say here that at least at the state and local level, ample evidence indicates that reorganization can occur. Indeed, reorganization possesses more political appeal in this time of concern for government functioning than it has in the past. Reorganizers should not fear to take on the opposition, because it can be beaten.

Implementing Interdepartmental Reorganization　　　Here we assume that the reorganization proposals have been passed by the legislature. But as the reorganizers break out the champagne, they should recognize that their real work is now ahead. Most reorganizations passed by legislatures do not accomplish even half of what their proponents had hoped for, for reasons we will spell out below.

Reorganizers should get to work at once, as did the North Carolina group which was authorized by a 1970 constitutional amendment. "The committee wisely recognized the need for commencing reorganization when public interest in the issue was highest, i.e., within one year following adoption of the constitutional amendment."[13] Dillydallying will only allow foes of change to entrench themselves more firmly in their bureaucratic bastions.

Crucial to success are the chief executive's strong interest and willingness to expend real effort in pushing to attain the goals of reorganization. If the chief executive's staff and department heads are not equally enthusiastic about monitoring its implementation, the plan has little chance of succeeding. Reorganizers must clearly convey to the chief executive that the battle only begins after the legislature has endorsed the plan. Reorganization is only an opportunity for those who wish to change the functioning of government, not a guarantee that they can do so.

One area to which the department heads must direct their efforts is the breakdown of key boards and commissions which are consolidated with other agencies into new, larger departments. Most reorganizations do not eliminate the power of these boards, which continue to exist as independent entities within a new environment.[14] The department head must use every ounce of willpower and skill to convince board employees that they should pull together with their new neighbors. If this approach fails, tougher methods, including personnel, budget, and management control, may have to be employed. (Unfortunately, these methods may require another trip to the legislature to ask it to clip the wings of the boards, which may retain substantial legal powers.) The mere act of lumping together semi-autonomous agencies in one new large department is unlikely to change anything. As Harold Seidman has noted, "The walls between bureaus within a department may be as impenetrable as those between departments, sometimes more so. . . . Reorganization commissions have concentrated primarily on the organization of the executive branch with only relatively brief reference to internal departmental reorganization. Yet, as a determinant of organizational behavior, the latter is the most important."[15] Seidman notes tht the U.S. Department of Labor has become so rigidly compartmentalized that the only way new programs can be fitted in is to create new bureaus.

For the department heads to transform the sow's ear of autonomous agencies into the silk purse of a well-coordinated department, additional resources are necessary. Reorganization cannot achieve very much unless the kinds of planning, evaluation, and budget approaches described in this book are instituted to increase results-oriented management. Doing so, as already mentioned, requires skilled staff and supporting resources, which do not come free.

Without this staff, change is unlikely. Unfortunately, this is the point at which most reorganizations fail, for rarely are sufficient funds appropriated to mount this kind of effort. But without such an effort, reorganization will remain pretty much a meaningless exercise in moving the boxes on the organization chart.

Why aren't the necessary funds forthcoming? In some cases poor planning efforts may not have foreseen their necessity, but in most cases the request for resources runs into legislative recalcitrance. Paradoxically, requests for funds to increase efficiency and effectiveness are rejected in the name of economy. Take the case of the Massachusetts reorganization, whose success hinged on getting 70 management specialists for the implementation phase, which was due to start in 1971. But 1971 was a recession year, with rising unemployment and a state government deficit. Furthermore, the legislature had just voted down a small raise for itself. While the total funds for the specialists amounted to about one-twentieth of 1 percent of the total budget, the speaker of the house concluded that the votes for the appropriation were not present there and suggested that the governor start out "in a Ford instead of a Cadillac."[16] Robert C. Casselman, the reorganization architect who watched the whole effort fall apart, concluded that failure was due to ignorance on the part of both the governor and legislature. Neither one really understood why the 70 specialists were not a "Cadillac," but an indispensable "vehicle" to achieve the goals of reorganization. Since the governor did not understand the real why and wherefore, he could not convince the legislature. The moral of this story is that reorganizers must work overtime to convince elected officials that reorganization without a real follow-up is a waste of time.

If the necessary follow-up resources are authorized, certain guidelines will maximize their usefulness. First, at least one senior staff specialist within each department should be entrusted solely with the job of implementing the reorganization. If also assigned other day-to-day managerial duties, this person will simply not be able to do the reorganization job. Reorganization is not a part-time task.

Second, reorganizers must work diligently to achieve as much decentralization of management, budget, and personnel matters as possible. That is, they must work to give the new department substantial autonomy in hiring the kind of personnel it needs when it wants, in transferring appropriated funds from one category in which no need exists to another where the need is strong, and in devising new methods to cut red tape. If this kind of decentralization, which is the crux of the Theory Y results-oriented approach to management, cannot be achieved, then efficiency and effectiveness are unlikely to improve. If an agency has to go to a central staff office for approval of minor changes, delay and failure will replace achievement of goals. We will return to this point in our discussion of intradepartmental reorganization. The point of reorganizing into a few broad departments is to delegate authority to these departments to get the job done. Failure to decentralize key management functions means that reorganization will fail to achieve its goals.

Third, a large proportion of staff specialists must be intimately acquainted with the local agency and the political scene. The job of implementation cannot be done by the politically ignorant, who do not know where to tread lightly and where to be tough, where to go to line up allies, or when to give up a hopeless battle and direct efforts elsewhere. The Serenity Prayer is a good guide here: "God grant me the serenity to accept the things I cannot change, courage to change the things I can, and wisdom to know the difference." While managerial experts are indispensable to reorganization, so are political insiders who have acquired, through experience, "wisdom to know the difference."

Finally, reorganization is no more a one-shot or short-term effort than any of the other approaches outlined in this book. It is a lengthy process, with much shakedown time required. This means that the same people should remain in key departmental management positions to see the reorganization through. If there is high job turnover in these posts, the chance for achieving change may vanish. A steady hand is needed on the wheel.

Even when all the advice proffered above is followed, perfection will not be attained. But the outcome is likely to be a lot less imperfect than would be the case if these steps had not been followed.

Intradepartmental Reorganization

Joint Accountability   The principle of joint accountability is likely to outrage and anger many managers, who have been raised for years on a totally opposed concept, that of unique accountability. Unique accountability holds that authority and responsibility for an assignment should be delegated to only one person. It is embodied in the comment, "If you want me to do the job, give me the responsibility for it and the authority commensurate with the responsibility. Then leave me alone to do the job."

Business consultant Edward C. Schleh[17] points out that unique accountability hinders cooperation, forcing managers to devote large amounts of time to coordination—time that could be spent on other work if joint accountability were followed. Unique accountability causes problems because its fundamental premises are false. *In modern management, results do not come from one person.* Rather, more than one person contributes to the result in most cases. To clarify these points, let us examine some sample situations.

Two fire fighters are assigned to conduct a study of departmental policies on fire prevention. One will examine direct departmental efforts and come up with recommendations for improvement, while the other will concentrate on cooperative efforts between the department and other city agencies. The two will combine their findings in a report on fire prevention to be given to the chief. If unique accountability is followed, neither fire fighter will have any incentive to work closely with the other, since each will be held accountable only for his or her part of the report. But if joint accountability is followed and both are evaluated by the total effort, they will have a strong incentive to collaborate and coordinate their efforts. And in this kind of project, as in so many others, such cooperation is a must if effective policies are to result. Without joint accountability, the fire fighters' *manager* is going to have to do the job of coordinating the different parts of the report.

Another reason to institute joint accountability is to give everyone an equal stake in the completion of the project. What incentive do workers have to cooperate if this cooperation will not affect them one way or the other? In Schleh's words, "One should not depend on another to get one's results if the other person does not have the same interest in the outcome."[18]

How do we implement a system of joint accountability? Schleh suggests first that functions that work together be combined, a recommendation similar to the interdepartmental reorganization principle that like functions be put together. If at all possible, this reshuffling should focus on getting one person in charge of a result.

An example is the engineers in one public works department. Engineers representing several specialties were assigned to each division—whether bridge construction and maintenance, roads, or street lighting—because it was felt that all these specialties were needed to get the work done right. But after an analysis was made, it was discovered that one experienced engineer could, in most cases, handle the various specialties competently. It was then possible to cut down time spent in conferring and coordinating by assigning management responsibility in each area to just one engineer.

In a police department, members of the patrol division and the narcotics division might, under joint accountability, share the credit for all drug-related arrests. In this way, the incentive for cooperation to achieve the maximum number of arrests would be provided. Likewise, teaching specialists working with children with learning disabilities should be jointly credited for the overall progress a child makes in the program, not credited by specialties, such as English, math, or art. Joint accountability emphasizes overall results, not narrow specialties. It is not concerned with activities, processes, or titles, but with program results achieved. For this reason, it is an important tool for every results-oriented manager.

Decentralization of Authority   Most public agencies in the United States are overly centralized, which cripples their responsiveness and effectiveness. Most of these controls were originated to prevent various abuses in government, such as graft, corruption, and agency failure to carry out programs assigned by the legislature and chief executive.

Examples of such controls are restrictions to prevent agencies from easily moving budget funds from one category to another as needs change. Thus, a public works department may be hard pressed to shift funds from swimming pool maintenance to snowplowing in a severe winter. Likewise, many agencies are unable to hire employees without going through a central personnel agency, so that badly needed posts go unfilled for months as the applicant goes through lengthy and labyrinthine procedures in the personnel department. The author was once responsible for applying for and administering a grant for student interns in government. The grant, which totaled all of $2,500, had to be approved by the college board of trustees and president before any funds could be disbursed. As a result, the interns were not paid until long after they had completed their work.

Decentralization should be carried out by giving middle and lower level managers maximum authority to hire, fire, and spend funds as they see fit to get a job done, and then holding them accountable for the results achieved. If a mental health clinic can ameliorate emotional problems by instructing patients in Zen Buddhism, why should its manager not be allowed to hire Zen Buddhist teachers in place of traditional personnel if they do a better job of alleviating the problems of depression and neurosis than do practitioners of more conventional modes of treatment? If the Zen Buddhists seem to exacerbate patients' problems, the manager can be sacked and replaced with a new manager who can try a different tack. The emphasis must always be placed on results, not processes and procedures. To advocate such an approach is not to open the doors to embezzlement, misfeasance, and malfeasance. No contradiction exists between decentralized management and careful auditing procedures to make sure that no abuses have occurred in handling funds and equipment used in the agency.

Project Management   Project management is becoming increasingly useful in achieving results. Government and society are increasingly complex, forcing the manager to make special efforts to get jobs done. In addition, public managers usually cannot command in the magisterial manner which some private managers can. The former are, instead, dependent on eliciting cooperation from other managers and agencies in order to get the job done. For these reasons, the results-oriented approach of project management may be most useful.

Project management was first used in the defense and aerospace industries, which had to grapple with the need to construct and coordinate immensely complex projects. The scientists and technicians at work in these projects are accustomed to great discretion, so that centralized authoritarian management would not work in this atmosphere. Furthermore, the need for constant change and redirection of effort demands a flexible approach.

NASA, the National Aeronautics and Space Agency, assigned 100 project managers to the Mercury and Gemini space projects. The overall project manager, George Low, was charged with coordinating the work of the other 99 managers and other organizations over which he had no formal control, including the designer of the spacecraft, the astronauts, and the various technicians and scientists.[19] This approach, far more flexible and less frequently encountered than the usual mode of organization, yielded dramatic program results.

Project management is organized along functional or results-oriented lines, which is often not true of traditional organization structure. This functional form, whether temporary or permanent, is called a *matrix organization*. Table 3–1 illustrates the matrix for a college public administration program, which draws on programs in a number of college departments but does not change the formal structure of these departments. Instead, the director of the program coordinates and consults with the various departments from which program elements are drawn.

How can agencies embark on project management? One way is to create a task force with representatives from the different divisions of the agency. This task force will then inquire whether there are problems for which new programs should be developed. If the answer is yes, the task force will study the issues and then make recommendations.

The next step is to create permanent teams to assist in the implementation of the new program which the task force recommended. The teams are committees made up of representatives from the divisions involved with the new program. The job of the team is to monitor the new program and make adjustments necessary as the program proceeds.

Eventually a project manager must be appointed, to provide a general management perspective and make sure that the various specialists in the terms do not dominate the effort and sidetrack it from its main goal. The project manager, who has the blessing of top management, must then proceed to persuade

TABLE 3–1.   MATRIX ORGANIZATION FOR A SCHOOL OF PUBLIC ADMINISTRATION

Programs / Academic Departments	B.A. or B.S. Degree	M.A.	Ph.D.	Research	Noncredit training
Accounting					
Economics					
Finance					
Management					
Political Science					
Public Administration					
Quantitative Methods					
Sociology					

and coax the permanent divisions of the organization to provide the resources needed to get the job done.

When is project management most appropriate and useful? When the task is unfamiliar, complex, not likely to be a continuing effort, and likely to be too much for any existing division of the agency. Project management is not a useful approach to traditional and routinized agency tasks.[20] But since the pace of program change seems to constantly accelerate, project management may offer increasing returns to results-oriented managers.

THE USE OF REORGANIZATION IN AMERICAN GOVERNMENT

Interdepartmental Reorganization

The Federal Government   Since 1937, when the President's Committee on Administrative Management reported its reorganization recommendations to President Franklin D. Roosevelt, each President has established reorganization study groups. Presidents Truman and Eisenhower had commissions headed by former President Hoover; President Kennedy used informal advisers and a group which studied regulatory agencies; President Johnson established a task force headed by Ben W. Heineman; while President Nixon used the commission chaired by Roy Ash. Even before he got into office, Jimmy Carter had a study group working on reorganization.

While a great deal of federal reorganization has taken place since 1937, most of it was not caused by these study groups. The Departments of Health, Education and Welfare; Housing and Urban Development; and Transportation did not spring from these study groups, any more than did the Environmental Protection Agency or the Energy Research and Development Agency. Each new study group espouses the principles of reorganization and notes that much change is needed to apply these principles.

Public administration scholar Harvey C. Mansfield has noted that there are many motives for reorganization besides the principles discussed in this chapter.[21] They include a desire to change policy; a desire to upgrade or downgrade the status of an agency; or a response to technological innovation, as in the creation of agencies dealing with atomic energy and space exploration. Much, if not most, reorganization activity is not primarily motivated by the wish to improve efficiency or effectiveness. Reorganization acts giving the president the authority to initiate changes, subject to the veto of either house of Congress, have been in effect most of the time since 1939. While these acts "codify the orthodox goals"[22] or principles, this does not mean that the principles are the driving force behind reorganization, because an escape clause ("To promote the better execution of the laws . . . more effective management . . . and expeditious administration") is also included.

While most proposals submitted under reorganization acts (75 of 97, from 1939–1965) have been accepted by Congress, these have not led to earthshaking changes in the executive branch. Congress exempted proposals to create new departments and functions from the act, so that such sweeping changes would be subject to the normal legislative process, where nothing will happen if Congress does not act. And Congress has not acted to endorse broad plans put forth by any President.

Unfortunately, we have no clear idea of what most of the reorganizations have accomplished. Harold Seidman, former Assistant Director for Management and Organization of the Bureau of the Budget, has related his frustration at being unable to get funds to study the effect of organizational change.[23] The few studies that have been made indicate that there is often a discrepancy between the real and stated reasons for reorganization and that the impact of reorganization often lies in a completely unintended direction.[24] While the Nixon administration's proposals were justified in terms of the principles of reorganization, there seems little doubt that the overriding purpose of the proposals was to minimize the power of career civil servants and increase that of presidential appointees. Nixon disliked, distrusted, and feared the career bureaucracy and was determined to minimize its role in federal policy making.[25]

State Government   There has been a great surge of reorganization activity in the states from 1965–1977. Some 20 states, two-fifths of the total, underwent extensive reorganization along the lines enunciated by the reorganization principles. Several factors contributed to this change, including the rapid growth and resultant red tape in state government; soaring expenditures and taxes; the growth of "good government" groups concerned with revitalizing such moribund institutions as state legislatures; and the availability of federal money to help finance planning studies.

While a definitive analysis of the impact of state reorganizations would be both costly and premature, a study of organization and spending patterns in the states was published by political scientist Thomas Dye in 1969. Dye concluded that there is "very little evidence to support the notion that executive fragmentation itself affects the content of public policy in the state,"[26] since he found no difference in spending patterns, when controlling for other factors, between more fragmented and less fragmented agencies. Of course, Dye's measure cannot tell us whether the agencies became more efficient or effective. It simply tells us that fragmented agencies do not receive higher or lower levels of appropriations than agencies organized according to the four principles of interdepartmental organization. Again, we are struck by the failure of scholars to examine the effect of reorganization, because major studies of the impact of this surge of activity in the states simply do not exist.

A closer look at one state may tell us a little more about what we can realistically expect from reorganization.[27] Since the state is Georgia, reorganized under Jimmy Carter, it is of particular interest to observers of the federal as well as the state scene.

Because Georgia is one of the few states in which a governor cannot succeed himself, Carter had to move fast. Right after taking office, he got the legislature to pass a reorganization act giving him the authority to make changes subject to a veto by either house. Then he drafted his plan, with the assistance of a 100-person study group. The reorganizaton consolidated 300 agencies into 22 departments. For instance, the state Parks Department, Department of Mines, and the Game and Fish Commission were consolidated along with 30 other agencies into the Department of Natural Resources.

To determine what the reorganization accomplished is more difficult. It did not stop or curtail the growth of government, since the budget rose by 58.5 percent in four years and 8,000 more employees joined the payroll. Claims that more would have been added without reorganization cannot be tested. While the rate of growth of Georgia state employees slowed down compared to previous years, this drop was a trend across the nation and cannot be attributed solely to reorganization.

The largest department created was Human Resources, which combined health and welfare agencies with a total of 22,000 employees. The department has remained a storm center, strongly criticized by opponents of reorganization. Professionals in different agencies, jealous of their own prerogatives and status, live in uneasy coexistence. Rivalry among such groups as social caseworkers, court service workers, and mental health associates was exacerbated by different pay levels and lack of funds to bring everyone up to the same level. This and other restrictions have hampered harmony; as the department's commissioner said, "Building an after-the-fact consensus on the mission of a unified department is a difficult task at best."[28]

The governor's rush to complete the job before his term was up did not allow the careful planning process we have argued is a prerequisite for success. As one participant stated, "you accept the fact that you are unable to have full discussion of issues, explain completely, ease anxieties, bring people along at their own pace, and minimize resistance."[29]

Perhaps the most serious blow to Human Resources was the decision to reduce administrative staff in budgeting, management, and personnel by 100 positions the first year. While the Governor of Massachusetts had been unable to add necessary staff here, Carter *cut* the staff with a meat ax. The commissioner reports that this decision, made on the basis that the reorganized department would run more efficiently and thus need fewer employees, has lead to a great increase in delays and errors of all kinds.

The Georgia reorganization, then, has been at best a mixed bag. If the approach used in the Georgia Human Resources Department serves as a model for the President's recommendations for the federal government, the Carter reorganization effort will be counterproductive. Certainly, the decline of managerial expertise within the Office of Management and Budget under Carter is not an encouraging sign.

Local Government   Since there are 80,000 local governments, we would expect to find a wide range of differences in reorganization activity among them. One type of change is in the form of government itself. Municipalities, townships, and counties have become increasingly enamored of the manager form of government, in which an appointed professional serves as chief executive at the pleasure of the legislature. Over 10 percent of our 3,000 counties now have managers, as do 57 percent of cities with populations between 10,000 and 500,000.[30] (In 1900, there were *no* professional manager governments.) Since manager government is characterized by adherence to the principles of reorganization, it would be safe to assume that a quantum jump had been made in administrative coherence since 1900—had not other factors been at work. These include the enormous growth in government functions and the spread of single-purpose special district governments. In no city or county does the manager have full authority over the biggest governmental activity, education, which is governed by a lay board and the superintendent it appoints. There are 16,000 boards of education and 25,000 special districts providing everything from cemetery operation to mosquito control for multitown areas, though these districts rarely offer more than one service. These special districts are outside the legal control of local chief executives.

Even though professionalism in local government has increased greatly, administrative chaos will remain unless there is substantial consolidation of the 80,000 local governments. But such consolidation, in the form of "metro" government embracing a broad geographical area, has taken place in only a handful of cases. And even in these cases—which include Miami, Florida; Indianapolis, Indiana; Nashville, Tennessee; Minneapolis–St. Paul, Minnesota; and Jacksonville, Florida—hundreds of other governments continue a semi-autonomous existence. The need for government reorganization according to the four principles is far greater at the local level than at the national or state level.

Intradepartmental Reorganization

We must admit that few, if any, governmental jurisdictions in the United States practice joint accountability, an approach found in the private sector. And even there most firms do not use it.

Further, definitive conclusions on the effects of decentralization in public organization are not possible. While such decentralization has yielded dramatic results in the private sector, lifting a near-bankrupt General Motors to a position far above other auto manufacturers,[31] we have no such stellar examples of success in government. Indeed, we do not even have studies from which to draw conclusions about the effects of decentralization.

The reader, then, may accuse us of unfounded optimism in advocating these approaches. We would reply that they are fully consistent with a results-oriented Theory Y approach and should thus be very likely to work if other such approaches are being implemented and working successfully.

One area in which we do have numerous examples is project management. And here we have an example of a public organization achieving results as spectacularly successful as General Motors. NASA put men in orbit around the earth and sent them to the moon while running under project management. Numerous examples of the successful use of task forces, matrix approaches, and the like can be found in organizations as diverse as the federal Social Security Administration; the California State Insurance Compensation Fund; and the city governments of Dayton, Ohio; Brea, California; and Syracuse, New York.[32] The use of project management seems likely to increase in the future, as government and society became increasingly complex and the need to pull together organizational resources rapidly to address changing conditions increases.

TECHNICAL PROBLEMS IN INTERDEPARTMENTAL REORGANIZATION AND HOW TO MINIMIZE THEM

One perennial problem of reorganization is *layering,* or the creation of another organizational level. Lumping existing agencies together into new larger departments means that a new top level is needed. For instance, before reorganization, the Georgia Health and Welfare departments were separate entities, each with its own head. Now that they have been combined in the Human Resources Department, they each have their own head, but there is also a new Commissioner of Human Resources at the top level.

Connecticut State Auditor Leo V. Donohue has pointed out that in states where 200 or more agencies report directly to the governor, "The horror of the span of control is greatly exaggerated."[33] Donohue observes that many of these agencies require little, if any, attention from the governor; and many licensing boards are already assigned to major departments for budgetary and auxiliary service purposes, so that consolidation of like functions may achieve little or nothing in some jurisdictions. Donohue also cites with approval Wayne L. Tyson's remarks in a study of the reorganization of state government: "Management is not the primary function of government . . . the first and foremost function of government is the reconciliation of interests in a pluralistic society, and the most important characteristic is not how well the function is managed, but accountability."[34] We have argued that accountability is increased by concentrating authority in the chief executive and the subordinate department heads. But Tyson feels that the introduction of additional bureaucratic layers between the chief executive and lower levels of administration instituted to reduce the span of control works against accountability. Tyson states that the chief executive cannot check closely on agencies with these intervening administrative layers.

The most undesirable result of layering is delay and red tape, caused by the creation of another level in the hierarchy through which all communications must go. (Layering also costs more money for new staff and facilities.)[35] Other things being equal, an agency which replaces four levels of supervision with five is going to see a slowdown in decision-making response time and communication flow.[36] Critics of Mayor John V. Lindsay's 1966 reorganization of New York City's government into "super departments" claimed that exactly these kinds of delays happened.[37]

The antidote to the troubles caused by layering is the departmental decentralization we spoke of earlier. If decision-making authority is moved in large part to lower levels of the organization, there will be no need for extensive communication flow from top to bottom. Communications can be restricted primarily to those involving new policy or crises for the organization. Such decentralization, of course, can take place only in a Theory Y atmosphere, which indicates that Theory Y yields many dividends, including this red tape reduction fringe benefit.

Herbert Simon, one of the leading figures in the development of modern organization theory, pointed out over 30 years ago that some "principles" of public administration were conflicting and contradictory.[38] We will look here at the conflict between two of these principles which relate to reorganization. The first is that the span of control should be small. In other words, it is better for a chief executive to have 20 departments reporting directly than to have 300 doing so. The second principle is the one we have just examined, that levels within the organization should be kept to a minimum, preventing layering and its attendant difficulties.

Note, unfortunately, that there is no way to implement both these principles at once. The smaller the span of control, the larger the number of hierarchical levels that have to be established. The relationship is a simple matter of arithmetic. The only way for the chief executive to reduce the span of control from 300 to 20 is to create new hierarchical levels. In other words, there is no way to stop increasing the number of hierarchical levels if one wants to reduce the span of control, and no way to stop increasing the span of control if one wants to reduce the number of hierarchical levels. Again, we recommend decentralization as the best way to deal with the problem of layering; but we have examined this built-in difficulty to make reorganizers aware of the very definite and discernible limits to increases in efficiency made possible by reorganization.

Another one of the principles of reorganization which is easier to state than to implement is the integration of similar functions. In today's integrated and interdependent society and economy, it is hard to find governmental activities which are not related to each other. For example, attempts by energy and natural resource agencies to conserve energy will obviously impact directly on environmental protection agencies. The less the need to develop new energy sources, the less the environment will be despoiled. In 1971, while sparring over Nixon administration reorganization proposals, Congressman Chet Holifield told Office of Management and Budget (OMB) Director George Schultz that "A critic would say that everything the government does affects the economy, and on that theory all the mission affairs would be placed in one giant department"; Schultz had to admit that "to a certain extent it is true that everything is related to everything else."[39] Note that no two of the 20 states reorganizing between 1965–1977 reorganized in exactly the same way. In some, health and welfare agencies were consolidated; in others, they were kept separate. Some states reorganized into 13 agencies, while others reorganized into as many as 25. While politics and the size of the states and their governmental activities had something to do with these differences, they do not explain all the variations. Attempts to apply the principle of functional integration turn out to be difficult in practice. Reasonable people can easily disagree on just how the principle should be applied. No perfect solutions are to be found here.

One well-known cost of reorganization is the turmoil it creates. Any family which has moved knows that moving is physically, financially, and often emotionally disruptive. The change from familiar surroundings and procedures can be equally disturbing for an administrative agency; and this is why we have made several recommendations in the section on implementation designed to reduce disruption. Another warning should be sounded here: Agencies should not be reorganized frequently (once in a decade seems to be the outside limit) if the reorganizer wants to avoid administrative chaos. Case studies of frequently reorganized agencies have found that they use most of their energy in reorganizing and cannot get their assigned tasks done as well as they used to.[40] An agency which has been reorganized five times in ten years may feel as confused and worn out as a family which has moved that often. In other words, unless one cannot imagine a recently reorganized agency doing a *worse* job than it is doing, another reorganization may be the last thing it needs to be straightened out.

In conclusion, the words of the late scholar of public administration Wallace Sayre make good sense. Sayre spoke of "the triumph of technique over purpose" in public administration. Reorganizers must keep in mind that reorganization is a means to the end of greater effectiveness and efficiency, and not an end in itself. It makes no sense to reorganize in situations where very little or no change for the good seems likely. As OMB Director James T. Lynn said in 1976, "It doesn't do any good to take garbage out of an old can and put it in a new can. It'll stink just as much."[41]

POLITICAL PROBLEMS IN INTERDEPARTMENTAL REORGANIZATION AND HOW TO MINIMIZE THEM

The crux of reorganization lies in implementation. And unless the legislature is reorganized, in some sense, along with the executive, reorganization is unlikely to get very far. We have already seen how the Massachusetts legislature—because it refused to provide the follow-up staff needed—made it impossible for reorganization in that state to achieve much. Reorganization of the executive failed because the legislature was unable to reorganize its own values so that a premium would be placed on such a change. Until state legislatures become more professional, with competent staffs of their own and a desire to listen to those staffs, reorganizations will not change much. We are *not* saying that the legislatures must become less political for reorganization to work. Rather, reorganization must join the other political demands made on the legislature. Only then will the legislature become responsive to the rationale of reorganization.

Unfortunately, the growth of a full-time, professionally staffed legislature is not sufficient to bring about a large-scale reorganization, or the federal government would have reorganized itself on this basis some time ago. And as Harold Seidman has pointed out, even if Congress were to buy a broad-scale reorganization scheme like Jimmy Carter's whole bag, the reorganization would not work unless Congress reorganized its own committee jurisdictions. If jurisdictions were left unchanged, several different committees would have jurisdiction over each department, with obvious problems in coordination and control. No one committee would have the same perspective as the department head, but would identify with specific agencies inside the new department. Thus, as far as the legislature would be concerned, the dynamics of government would not have changed in any important way. The reason behind the principles of reorganization would be lost in the shuffle if Congress did not reorganize itself. [42]

Another political difficulty which should be avoided at all costs is the temptation for the department head to run the new organization in a strict Theory X manner. This is a temptation because the principles stress increased managerial control. This strategy would be counterproductive not only for reasons previously discussed in this book but also because of a reason noted by political scientist Erwin C. Hargrove. Hargrove points out that if departments were run as strict hierarchies with unified missions, department heads would become the prisoners of civil servants. Why? Because there would be a relative lack of competition between different groups within the department, causing all information and recommendations to be biased in the long-term interests of the civil service, which will outlast almost any chief executive. Hargrove advocates spurring competition among different groups as the best way for the department head to get differing information and perspectives. [43] It is another good reason to stick to Theory Y.

PROBLEMS IN INTRADEPARTMENTAL REORGANIZATION AND HOW TO MINIMIZE THEM

Joint Accountability

Joint accountability will not be easy to sell in government, because advocates of increased efficiency have long argued that unique accountability is needed. These advocates have deplored organizational tangles in which an employee reports to several superiors and is thus never sure to whom he or she is most directly accountable. Unique accountability and stress on the principle of unity of command—that each employee have just one boss—was pushed as the remedy to such a confusing state of affairs. Unity of command is still advocated as a desirable principle of organization in many textbooks, which argue that authority must be commensurate with responsibility.

Persons trained in this tradition are likely to be appalled at the prospect of joint accountability, which flies in the face of many notions associated with unity of command. For this reason, full consultation must be made with employees in deciding how to implement joint accountability. Ample time must be allotted to understand the concept and to discuss problems and prospects likely to arise in different situations. Once employees understand that the purpose of joint accountability is to attain better *results,* rather than to penalize hard workers or control those who have not worked so hard, they are likely to respond to the concept more favorably. But we would be kidding ourselves and the reader were we to claim that making the concept clear, selling it, and implementing it will be easy.

Decentralization

One of the critical roadblocks to governmental decentralization is lack of centralization. What is meant by this paradoxical statement? The explanation lies in the failure of most governments to develop adequate central staff agency capability in such areas as personnel, budgeting, and management information systems. That is, while these staff agencies impose a host of controls to prevent line agencies from decentralizing, the former usually do not have the capacity to discover what line agencies are doing or achieving. Most state personnel departments, for example, have difficulty finding out how many employees are at work in state government on a given day and how many jobs are vacant. And information about what these employees are actually *doing* is far harder to come by. Because of this lack of basic information, the central staff agencies are not in a position to release additional funds or personnel to the agencies which need them the most or are likely to do the most with them. Because of central staff agency inability to gather these data in one central place, line agencies cannot effectively decentralize and be rewarded for the results they achieve.

To allow line agencies to decentralize, then, overhead agencies need both to evaluate and eliminate cumbersome controls and to gather meaningful information in a central location. Without these steps, decentralization is simply impossible.

While decentralization should lead to faster and better decisions, development of employees, more original ideas, and improved morale, it is not a one-way street. Typical problems of decentralization include increased difficulty of coordination, inconsistent policies; and increased costs due to addition of staff.[44] No more than any other results-oriented approach discussed in this book is decentralization a panacea. It is, rather, an opportunity to manage more effectively, especially if carried out in a participatory fashion. Full involvement by personnel, with a stress on goals, will reduce problems of coordination and inconsistency to their minimum possible levels.

Project Mangement

The manner in which the project manager must extend influence is at once a restriction and an opportunity. The project manager can rely only on persuasion, not command, and must reason with division managers to obtain project wants and needs. This means that project managers will inevitably feel some frustration. But they also enjoy a freedom that other managers do not have, because they have a mandate to draw on the resources of the entire organization to complete their project. And since such a project is typically a priority for the agency's head, who would not have gone to the trouble to create it otherwise, the manager is in a good position to bargain. He or she may only need to give reminders to division managers that their help is expected and that they will be accountable if the project fails because they did not help it. More positively, they can be reminded that they will share in the glory and rewards if it does succeed.

CASE STUDY:
WATCHING THE SUN SET IN COLORADO

"Sunset" laws are the latest attempt to control government agency growth. Such laws amount to a special kind of reorganization, for the legislature mandates that a program or an agency will be terminated after a certain number of years if a required legislative review concludes that it has not done a good enough job to continue. Hence the title—the sun will set on the agency or program if it does not pass legislative muster.

While legislatures are legally free to abolish agencies or programs at any time, sunset laws have become popular because legislators feel that they have not been giving programs a careful enough examination. A 1975 Harris poll indicated that 72 percent of the public "no longer feel they get good value from their tax dollars."[45] As Senator Edmund Muskie, leading congressional backer of a federal sunset law, said in March 1977, "Sunset can help us take a closer look at the components of the budget . . . and sunset can have the added benefit of reining in so-called uncontrollable spending . . . which . . . takes up 75 percent of the budget."[46]

Certainly sunset has struck a sympathetic nerve. While there were no state sunset laws in January 1976, there were 11 by May 1977.[47] And in June 1977, the House of Representatives voted to create a Cabinet-level Department of Energy subject to a five-year sunset review. In the rest of this section we will examine the passage and operation of sunset in the state of Colorado, the first government to enact a sunset law.

In 1976, the Colorado legislature required that the 38 commissions, boards, and divisions of the state Department of Regulatory Agencies be subject to sunset review. This modest beginning makes sense, for, as we have stressed over and over again, across-the-board reviews are usually more trouble than they are worth. In addition, since there were only 300 employees in this department, the state employees' organization was persuaded not to oppose sunset. Another reason for picking regulatory agencies is that many of them restrict competition and drive up prices.[48] Several of the other states adopting sunset have followed Colorado's lead and focused on their own regulatory agencies.

How does the Colorado legislature conduct its sunset reviews? Guidelines set up consider whether the number of licenses issued is unduly low; whether women and minorities have been licensed; whether the agency works for the public interest or for the benefit of its licensees; the extent to which the agency is willing to listen to and act on criticism aimed at improvements; and how the agency handles public complaints concerning its licensees. In addition, a performance audit is required three months before the sunset expiration date, so that legislators can use the data in making their decisions.

Colorado sunset requires that each regulatory agency be reviewed every six years. This means that in each of its two-year sessions, the legislature will review the performance of one-third of the regulatory agencies. The legislature has several options besides merely renewing the agency or program for six more years or destroying it. These include not renewing the program, which wipes out future—but not past—licensing. The legislature then has the option to retain or discard consumer protection statutes relative to the agency or program or not to do so. Another option is to transfer program or agency functions to another agency.[49]

While a comprehensive review of the impact of Colorado sunset will not be possible until the six-year period is up in early 1983, a progress report is possible now. The law had an immediate impact on some aspects of agency performance. For one thing, it became easier to get a license. Despite a shortage of court stenographers, for example, only 2 percent of the applicants were passing the shorthand test. But after sunset the passing figure rose to 48 percent.[50] The Department of Regulatory Agencies has recommended that four boards, including morticians and sanitarians, be abolished; that three more boards be transferred; and four more, including the public utilities and insurance commissions, be substantially reformed to make them more responsive to citizen complaints. Department Secretary Paul Rodriquez states that the boards are cleaning up sloppy administrative procedures and becoming more responsive to certain complaints. Indeed, several agencies scheduled for future review have asked the legislature to reform their operations so that they can do a better job.

During the first year of sunset review, 3 of the 13 agencies examined were eliminated: the State Athletic Commission; the Board of Registration for Sanitarians; and the Board of Shorthand Reporters. The annual budgets of these agencies totaled $6,810. At the same time, 3 other agencies were combined with other agencies, 2 were allowed to continue to exist as they had before the review, and 5 were still being studied as of April 1978. The cost of the review to that date was $212,000. Rosalie Schiff, director of Colorado Common Cause, commented that "legislators have lacked the courage to stand up to lobbying efforts to retain or perpetuate these agencies. But I think for the most part the sunset law has been successful here, perhaps more in requiring the legislature to do the oversight not done in the past, and in requiring accountability from state agencies. Maybe that's more important than getting rid of them"[51]

Some critics warn prospective buyers of sunset that they should look over the merchandise carefully. Alan Rosenthal, a political scientist who has specialized in helping state legislatures improve their analytical capabilities, argues that "Sunset is just another mechanistic solution for complicated and subtle problems," which ignores advances in program evaluation by state legislatures and substitutes a "black or white, live or die, justify your damned existence approach."[52] Former OMB Director Roy Ash argues that a comprehensive review of federal programs, as proposed by Senator Muskie, would be "like attempting to jump aboard a 747 in full flight."[53] In addition, some programs—such as the decennial census, cancer research, and space exploration—are perhaps not appropriately reviewed after five or six years. Finally, some critics feel that legislative committees conducting a sunset review may end up as program *advocates* rather than objective critics, "since their ability to obtain reenactment may depend on how convincing a case for reenactment they can make through those studies."[54]

The controversy over this novel attempt to reorganize government so that it is more responsive, effective, and efficient should continue for quite a while.

Questions

1. How useful an approach do you think sunset is for improving each of the following: (a) agency responsiveness, (b) agency effectiveness, (c) agency efficiency? Explain your reasons.

2. Would you suggest any changes in Colorado sunset review procedures to improve legislative review of agencies and programs? If so, detail the changes and explain why you feel they would be improvements. If not, explain why you feel the process could not be improved.

3. What do you see as the cost and benefits of sunset? List these various costs and benefits. Do you think benefits outweigh costs? Explain your reasons.

4. How valid do you think the objections to sunset listed at the end of this section are? Examine each one, indicate your reaction to it, and explain the reasons you feel as you do.

PROBLEMS AND PROSPECTS FOR REORGANIZATION

Reorganization will exist as long as organizations do, and reorganization according to the principles examined in this chapter should continue for some time. But exactly what the principles of reorganization accomplish when applied is not a topic that has been seriously studied by scholars of public administration. And some writers are caustically critical of the inadequacy of these principles for late twentieth-century organizations. Indeed, skepticism about reorganization has existed since organizations have.

As Gaius Petronius Arbiter, setter of social protocol for the court of ancient Rome, remarked in A.D. 66: "I was to learn later in life that we tend to meet any new situation by reorganizing, and a wonderful method it can be for creating the illusion of progress while producing confusion, inefficiency, and demoralization." Modern-day writers have been no less unsparing in their judgments.

Harold Seidman has written the most trenchant and incisive critique of the principles of reorganization.[55] In his treatise on federal organization, Seidman argues that whatever relevance to federal organization the principles once had is now gone; in fact, the principles do a disservice, since they help to perpetuate the "myth . . . that we can solve deep seated and intractable issues of substance by reorganization."[56] In Seidman's opinion, the principles neglect the political realities of public organization. If we do not live in a nice, neat, orderly society, how realistic is it to expect a nice, neat, orderly governmental structure? Seidman argues that the most important characteristics of bureaucracy in a democracy are representativeness and responsiveness. In other words, agencies should reflect the interests of competing groups in our society. If there is no administrative diversity and pluralism, have-not groups will suffer. When President Nixon proposed reorganization, it is noteworthy that agencies such as the Office of Economic Opportunity (OEO), which was the premiere anti-poverty agency, were designated for destruction. This is nothing new. The 1949 Hoover Commission recommended that the Farmer's Home Administration (FHA) be divided up between two other Department of Agriculture agencies because its functions overlapped theirs. However, the FHA was established to help small farmers with little influence, while the record of the rest of the Department of Agriculture showed that it marched in step with the bigger, more conservative members of the American Farm Bureau Federation. Lumping FHA functions with those of other bureaus would have brought FHA functions to an end in this new and unfavorable environment. Seidman also notes that even "have" groups like bankers and scientists prefer particular organizational arrangements which do not follow the principles of reorganization.

The point here is that there is a lot more to organizational reality than is to be found in the principles. The creation of a neat and orderly bureaucracy will help some groups and agencies, while hurting others.

In a similar vein, former federal official and current public administration professor Rufus Miles states that "Wide span of control satisfies many con-

stituencies; narrow span of control satisfies few. If the [chief executive] wishes
to fend off . . . special pleaders, he is likely to prefer a small number of officials
directly answerable to him; if he can take the time and wants to hear what
people have to say, he will enlarge the range of important membership in his
official family."[57]

Reorganization does much more than aid efficiency and effectiveness; it
affects the power of agencies and may have completely unintended consequences. Applying the principles in a vacuum is the height of naivete, as we have
warned the reader in the section on implementation.

Other writers have joined Seidman in criticizing the obsolescence of the
principles. Public Administration Professor Edwin O. Stene has lamented the
failure of newer writings on organization to provide operational guidelines for
reorganizers.[58] Harvey C. Mansfield notes that the Brownlow Committee report "no longer furnishes an agenda for action."[59] Seidman states that it is far
easier to criticize the principles than to develop acceptable alternatives.

Seidman concludes that the amount and nature of federal reorganization
occurring since 1937 have largely overcome the problems the principles address. Whether this is so at the federal level, it is certainly not true in many
state and most local governments, where the organizational restraints on executives are often enough to make strong managers weak. Furthermore, the fourth
interdepartmental principle—coordination of central staff agency operations—does not now apply at any level of government. The federal government
has a long way to go to improve defects in its central budgeting, personnel, and
management activities. And deficiencies in these areas mean that there will be
corresponding deficiencies and inability to decentralize line agency management. As we have already argued, this decentralized management is crucial to
reorganization. If it is not achieved, reorganization has not accomplished very
much.

We endorse the principles of reorganization, while disclaiming any beliefs
about their completeness and perfectibility. At the same time, reorganizers
should constantly keep aware of the points raised by Seidman, who has provided a list of questions to ponder:

> 1. What is the nature of the interest group constituency created or ac-
> quired as a result of the reorganization? To what extent will it influence
> policies and administration? Is it broadly based or is it narrow and opposed to
> some of the goals of the program?
> 2. What is the internal environment of the agency being given program
> responsibilities? Will it help, hinder, or ignore the program? Does a particu-
> lar type of professional outlook which may regard certain programs unfavor-
> ably dominate?
> 3. Are safeguards assuring that no group or class of people is excluded
> from the program provided? Are there any built-in obstacles to joint adminis-
> tration with related government programs?[60]

These are some of the questions that must be asked if we are to prevent the principles from becoming a straitjacket which will make the goals of effectiveness, efficiency, and responsiveness more difficult to reach. The principles of reorganization are neither all encompassing nor perfect, but they are not useless. They can change many governments for the better if used with the focus Seidman recommends.

─────────

NOTES

1. "Ehrlichman Says Carter Can't Reorganize," *News-Times* (Danbury, Conn.), July 20, 1976, p. 2.
2. Harvey Sherman, *It All Depends: A Pragmatic Approach to Organization* (University, Ala.: University of Alabama Press, 1966), p. 22.
3. Jimmy Carter, "The Management of the American Governmental System," *ASPA News and Views*, October 1976, p. 3.
4. President's Committee on Administrative Management, *Report with Special Studies* (Washington, D.C.: Government Printing Office, 1937), p. 32.
5. *The President's Proposals for Executive Reorganization* (Washington, D.C.: Government Printing Office, 1971).
6. *Better Organization for Better Government* (Hartford, Conn.: Committee on the Structure of State Government, 1976), p. 5.
7. Sherman, op. cit.
8. Harold Seidman, *Politics, Position, and Power: The Dynamics of Federal Organization* (New York: Oxford University Press, 1975), p. 4. This book is indispensable for the serious student of federal reorganization.
9. Douglas M. Fox, "The President's Proposals for Executive Reorganization: A Critique," *Public Administration Review* 33 (September–October 1973): 401–6.
10. Jimmy Carter, "Making Government Work Better: People, Programs, and Process," *National Journal*, October 19, 1976, pp. 1448–49.
11. Seidman, op. cit., p. 12.
12. Karl A. Bosworth, "The Politics of Management Improvement in the States," *American Political Science Review* 47 (March 1953): 84–99, at 90.
13. Alva W. Stewart, "Executive Reorganization: The North Carolina Process," *State Government*, Summer 1972, pp. 207–21, at 210.
14. See George A. Bell, "States Make Progress with Reorganization Plans," *National Civic Review*, March 1972, pp. 115–27, and George A. Bell, *Reorganization in the States* (Lexington, Ky.: Council of State Governments, 1972).
15. Seidman, op. cit., pp. 308–9.
16. Robert C. Casselman, "Massachusetts Revisited: Chronology of a Failure," *Public Administration Review* 33 (March–April 1973): 129–35, at 132.

17. Edward C. Schleh, *The Management Technician* (New York: McGraw-Hill, 1974), pp. 54–68.

18. Ibid., p. 58.

19. Howard E. McCurdy, *Public Administration* (Menlo Park, Calif.: Cummings, 1977), pp. 255–57.

20. Grover Starling, *Managing the Public Sector* (Homewood, Ill.: Dorsey Press, 1977), pp. 192–93.

21. Harvey C. Mansfield, "Federal Executive Reorganization: Thirty Years of Experience," *Public Administration Review* 29 (July–August 1969): 332–45.

22. Ibid., p. 334.

23. Douglas M. Fox, ed., "President Nixon's Proposals for Executive Reorganization," *Public Administration Review* 34 (September–October 1974): 487–95, at 489.

24. Loc. cit.

25. Fox, "The President's Proposals . . . ," pp. 404–5.

26. Thomas Dye, "executive Power and Public Policy in the States," *Western Political Quarterly* 22 (December 1969): 932.

27. James Parham, "Constraints in Implementing Services Integration Goals: The Georgia Experience," *Human Services Integration* (Washington, D.C.: American Society for Public Administration, 1974), pp. 15–18; and David E. Rosenbaum, "4½ Years Later, Carter's Reorganization of Georgia Government Is Controversial," *New York Times,* October 19, 1976, p. 30.

28. Parham, op. cit., p. 16.

29. Ibid., p. 17.

30. *Municipal Yearbook* (Washington, D.C.: International City Management Association, 1976), p. 22. See also George F. Berkley and Douglas M. Fox, *80,000 Governments* (Boston: Allyn and Bacon, 1978), chs. 10–11.

31. Ernest Dale, *The Great Organizers* (New York: McGraw-Hill, 1960), pp. 71–112.

32. George E. Berkley, *The Craft of Public Administration*, 2nd ed. (Boston: Allyn and Bacon, 1978), 521–26.

33. Personal communication from Leo V. Donohue, July 28, 1977. See also Leo V. Donohue and Henry J. Becker, Jr., "The Fears behind Reorganization," *New York Times,* October 2, 1977, Connecticut sect., p. 11.

34. Wayne L. Tyson, "A Dissenting Point of View," mimeograph, no date.

35. G. Ross Stephens, "Monetary Savings from State Reorganization in Missouri, or You'll Wonder Where the Money Went," *Midwest Review of Public Administration,* January 1973, pp. 32–35.

36. See Herbert Kaufman, *The Limits of Organizational Change* (University, Ala.: University of Alabama Press, 1971), pp. 76–78.

37. U.S. Congress, House Committee on Government Operations, *Executive Reorganization: A Summary Analysis,* 92nd Cong., 2nd sess., 1972, p. 28.

38. Herbert A. Simon, "The Proverbs of Administration," *Public Administration Review* 6 (Winter 1946): 53–67.

39. Fox, "The President's Proposals . . . ," op. cit., p. 403.

40. See John F. Wall and Leonard B. Dworsky, *Problems of Executive Reorganization:*

The Federal Environmental Protection Agency, Cornell University Water Resources and Marine Science Center Publication No. 34, September 1971.

41. Mercer Cross, "Revamping Government: Usually Tough," *Congressional Quarterly,* October 16, 1976, pp. 3009–13, at 3011.

42. Seidman, op. cit., ch. 2.

43. Erwin C. Hargrove, *The Power of the Modern Presidency* (Philadelphia: Temple University Press, 1974), p. 241.

44. Sherman, op. cit., p. 80.

45. Neal R. Pierce, "Climbing on the Sunset Bandwagon," *Bergen Evening Record* (Bergen County, N.J.), October 3, 1977, p. 8.

46. Richard E. Cohen, "Management Report: Sunset Legislation," *National Journal,* April 2, 1977, pp. 514, 518–20, at 518.

47. Neal A. Peirce, "Sunset Laws Need Twilight Zone," *News-Times* (Danbury, Conn.), May 15, 1977, p. 9.

48. Gerald H. Kopel, "Sunset in the West," *State Government,* Summer 1976, pp. 135–38, at 136.

49. Ibid., p. 137.

50. Bob Cunningham, " 'Sunset Law'—More Red Tape?" *Bergen Evening Record,* August 2, 1976, p. 1.

51. Peirce, "Sunset Laws . . . ," op. cit., and Associated Press, "With New Law, Colorado Spends $212,000 to Abolish 3 Agencies," *New York Times,* April 23, 1978, p. 37.

52. Peirce, "Sunset Laws . . . ," op. cit.

53. Peirce, "Climbing on the Sunset Bandwagon," op. cit.

54. Judy Gardner, "Doubts over Sunset Bill Fail to Deter Backers of Concept," *Congressional Quarterly,* November 27, 1976, pp. 3255–58, at 3257–58.

55. Seidman, op. cit.

56. Ibid., p. 4.

57. Rufus E. Miles, Jr., "Considerations for a President Bent on Reorganization," *Public Administration Review* 37 (March–April 1977): 155–62, at 158.

58. Edwin O. Stene, "Reorganizing Kansas State Governments: The Persistence of Classical Theory," *Midwest Review of Public Administration,* January 1973, pp. 26–28, at 27.

59. Mansfield, op. cit., p. 341.

60. Seidman, op. cit., pp. 315–16.

4

Output-Oriented Supervision

LEARNING OBJECTIVES

TO UNDERSTAND:

The rule of depersonalization

Different ways to tell employees what to do

Ways to communicate more effectively

Why reward is more effective than punishment

Problems confronting participatory supervision and what to do about them

T-groups, transactional analysis, and double-loop learning

Supervision is the process by which government programs are carried out on a day-by-day basis. No work can be done without supervision, and inadequate supervision will cripple attempts to produce effective and efficient programs.

DEFINING SUPERVISION

As we noted in the first chapter, *supervision* is the leadership of employees in the attempt to reach goals stated in a plan. Supervision is a process of *motivating* workers to work. The best supervisors are able to get their subordinates to work at close to their full potential, while less effective supervisors are unable to get their subordinates to perform so well. This book recommends a supervisory style consistent with Theory Y and with the outlook expressed by former President Dwight D. Eisenhower:

Leadership is a word and concept that has been more argued than almost any other I know. I am not one of the desk-pounding types that likes to stick out his jaw and look as if he is bossing the show. I would far rather get behind and, recognizing the frailties and the requirements of human nature, I would rather try to persuade a man to go along—because once I have persuaded him, he will stick. If I scare him, he will stay just as long as he is scared, and then he is gone.[1]

IMPLEMENTING THEORY Y-STYLE SUPERVISION

In this section, we examine the various aspects of supervision, including relationships with employees, directing the work, communicating, rewarding and punishing, and leadership by consensus.

Probably the most important rule to follow in supervising is to focus on the work done by subordinates rather than on the subordinates themselves. This principle of "depersonalization" is one we shall return to at various points in the chapter. A manager following this rule will not praise or denigrate the personal worth of a subordinate, but will focus on the subordinate's results. "That was a fine job you did straightening out the books" and "Are you having any problems in interviewing applicants for aid?" are examples of a focus on *work* rather than *workers*, points we shall return to below.[2]

THE NEW MANAGER'S FIRST DAYS[3]

Few managers start work in newly created organizations with a newly assembled staff. Most are promoted to a managerial position in an office which has existed for a number of years and which has employees with substantial service in the office. These conditions mean that the new manager should proceed cautiously in surveying the lay of the land.

First impressions may be the most persistent and powerful perceptions we have of other people. For this reason, the new manager should be doubly sure to go slow initially. A sure recipe for disaster is to announce that the way the previous manager did things was inappropriate and that some big changes are going to be made. The prospect of change usually causes anxiety and insecurity, because to change is to venture into unknown territory. Employees will wonder if the way they have learned to do their jobs will be considered inadequate and, ultimately, whether they themselves will be declared unfit for further service. As a result, they will react negatively—directly or indirectly, consciously or unconsciously—decreasing their performance to a point where the new manager is going to be in hot water. As Howard E. Ball, a veteran federal career employee has written, "Never knowingly let your boss repeat a mistake already made by his predecessor [although] I have broken this rule . . . where the arrogance level of my supervisor was so high that I felt he had to go through the disaster and fully and directly experience the put down."[4] An insistence that the new broom will sweep the office clean will be interpreted as arrogance, since this approach rejects previous practices and procedures without carefully investigating them and consulting with the staff to see whether they make any sense. More mature managers will assuage the anxieties of their employees by ensuring them that no changes will be made immediately. The wise manager begins by studying how the office works, *in consultation with subordinates,* and works to gradually introduce needed changes.

A temptation beckoning new managers is to make promises to keep their new employees happy. Assurances that "Sure, you can keep on working on that shift" or "Don't worry about following that new procedure set by the accounting department" may return to haunt the manager, who may find out later that the only way to keep such promises is to anger other employees, damage relations with other offices, or decrease the efficiency or effectiveness of the office's operations. And reneging on a hastily made promise will surely create bad blood between superior and subordinate. The same point can be made about careless remarks of any kind. Subordinates will interpret them as management policy, so the manager must avoid such offhand comments. Note above all that these careless promises are inconsistent with a Theory Y approach, in which the manager would consult all the employees together, as a *group.*

Blaming your subordinates for your mistakes is a sure way to lose the respect and loyalty of your workers. Yet how many times have we asked supervisors why they had not yet done something that was supposed to have been done yesterday, only to be told that their failure was due to a subordinate? This writer once called two editors to ask why they had not made a decision on a proposal he had made. One editor frankly acknowledged that he had goofed, and made no excuses, while the other blamed his secretary. The poor impression made by the latter editor would surely have been aggravated even further had his secretary been present to hear this remark. Managers should never pass the buck, because admissions that they are to blame are unlikely to hurt them unless they fail constantly. And buck-passing managers will soon have a completely disloyal and disrespectful staff.

Another constant concern should be to avoid even the appearance of treating employees of equal status unequally. If subordinates come to believe that some of their number are favorites of the manager or are on an enemies list, morale will quickly decline and performance will follow. For example, if one worker always gets desired assignments and equally qualified peers do not, trouble is bound to result. While it is not possible to treat equally qualified workers equally in every instance, a good manager will strive to do so, or trouble will surely occur.[5]

A final crucial point to be made in this section is that the new manager should strive to be respected, rather than liked. The manager should strive for maximum participation by subordinates in getting the work done, and be fair and humane. Great care should be taken to avoid social or emotional entanglements with subordinates off the job. A supervisor who drinks or socializes with subordinates will be tempted to look the other way when they perform below par. How are you going to deal with your *friends* for tardiness and absenteeism or poor work? To avoid this bind, the manager should not accept favors from subordinates, make decisions that are popular but unwise, or look the other way when a worker should be disciplined. To do so, the supervisor need not be rude or crude, but can politely refuse favors and say why, refuse to do the popular thing and explain why, and discipline subordinates in the manner discussed later in this chapter. A night shift supervisor whose wife was in the last month of a difficult pregnancy asked a subordinate to cover for him for one or two hours every night so that he could go home and comfort her. Later, the subordinate demanded pay raises, promotions, and unexcused absences, reminding the manager of the favors he had done. Interestingly enough, when the manager decided to confess his faults to his own boss, the boss did not fire him. Instead, the boss told him that he had now learned the valuable lesson that you cannot accept favors from subordinates, and would be a much better manager as a result.[6]

DIRECTING THE WORK

As we mentioned earlier, managers should strive to follow the rule of depersonalization, focusing on the work rather than on the worker. Theory Y-oriented management styles avoid unnecessary supervision, seeking instead to give the employee maximum discretion in deciding how to get the job done. Results-oriented managers include the chef who samples every dish as it leaves the kitchen and the trash route foreman who checks the route to see if garbage has been neatly carted away. A chef who keeps telling the cooks to mix sauces with a certain motion regardless of the way they taste and a foreman who insists that workers lift garbage cans with a particular motion have failed to follow the rule of depersonalization. They have lost interest in results and become obsessed with matters of style. Predictably, their subordinates will chafe under this unreasonably close supervision and become less productive.[7]

Telling Employees What to Do

Even managers with a participatory approach must often tell subordinates what to do.[8] There are several ways to do this, and one is the *command.* "Do this" should be used if there is some *danger*, such as an accident, fire, or disobedience of safety rules. Or a command may have to be used as a last resort with employees who have not responded to the other approaches used below.

The *request* is the most useful way to direct everyday work. "Could you give me that report this week?" beats "Get the report to me by Friday!" by a long shot. Most employees today do not like to be ordered around in a heavy-handed way. A request implies that a worker is a respected member of a team, whose cooperation is needed by the manager. If some employees view the request as one that they can ignore, the manager will have to sit down and talk over their relationship and his or her managerial style. Again, the manager should be considerate and careful not to strongly criticize the employee. But if the employee does not respond to this kind of approach, the command may have to be substituted for the request.

The *suggestion* can be used effectively with experienced employees. "Do you think you could do it this way?" may be a very effective manner of management. It indicates that the manager views the subordinate as an equal whose judgment can be relied on in the task at hand, and who does not have to be told what to do. The suggestion is very much a part of participatory, team-oriented management. However, it will probably not work very well with inexperienced employees, who may not be able to take the suggestion and analyze it. And since a suggestion is usually not unambiguous, nothing may result.

Subordinates naturally prefer directions which indicate that the manager trusts their judgment and discretion. They want to feel that their supervisor considers them valuable members of the team, who have positive contributions of their own to make. Thus, "Would you please have the council room cleaned and presentable for tonight's meeting?" beats "Empty the ashtrays, sweep, dust tables, empty wastebaskets, and get the council room ready for tonight!" by a wide margin. The employee is likely to resent a supervisor who shows so little confidence in subordinates.

By the same token, most employees today do not like to be called by their last names. Such a practice smacks of the command approach; indeed, it will remind military veterans of the way they were treated by their sergeants. Far better to use the first name, calling someone "Bob" or "Doris" instead of "Reilley" or "Brown." If there are a lot of "Bobs" in one office, some confusion may result. But it is better to use the first name, perhaps together with the last one, in this case, then to use the last name alone. In our culture, use of the last name alone denotes that the employee is little more than an object or piece of equipment.

Likewise, the manager often has a lot to gain by asking subordinates to address her or him by first name. If superior and immediate subordinates are on a first-name basis, a team spirit will be fostered. Being called Mr., Ms., Dr., or whatever while you call employees by their first names is unlikely to promote a cooperative environment. Instead, employees are likely to feel that so-and-so is the boss and I'm the worker who is merely ordered around. This situation creates maximum resentment when the manager is a lot younger than some of the employees.

At the same time, the manager who used these approaches in an obviously manipulative way would quickly be seen by his subordinates as a phony. Even Dale Carnegie has stressed that his approach to winning friends and influencing people will not work if the user is insincere. More important than using first names and making requests is results-oriented fair-and-equal treatment of subordinates. John R. Coleman, President of Haverford College, labored incognito for two months as a blue-color worker in 1973. One of his supervisors, in charge of a pipelaying job, did not exemplify the management approach we have spelled out. For example, he once said, "The trouble with you guys is that you're all ironheads. You don't think. You use your muscles and your feet when you should use your heads"; yet Coleman concluded that although this managerial style "wouldn't look too good in the personnel books I've read . . . his directness works on this job. And there is so much fairness and competence in him that he earns respect. . . . So far as he is concerned, my life is my own affair. He will judge me by how I act on the job."[9] While this management style is not an optimal one—indeed, it would fail miserably in most white-collar jobs—it is superior to fake public relations approaches.

What Should Employees Be Told to Do?

The manager should be sure the need for a request or order exists before he gives it. A manager does not need to issue orders constantly to be effective. In fact, the opposite may be true. In a participatory working environment, subordinates will exercise substantial discretion and will not need close supervision.

Managers should be sure to issue the correct order. Management consultant James Van Fleet tells of a case where employees were ordered not to go to the company cafeteria via an outside walk that they had used previously. The employees resented this restriction tremendously, because the heat inside the plant was extreme, and the walk outside provided welcome relief. When Van Fleet asked management why it had restricted use of the walk, he was told employees had littered along the way. Van Fleet replied that the wrong order had been given: Trash containers should have been put out, with a request that employees please use them. When this was done, the resentment the original order incurred began to subside.[10] We would add that consultation with employees at the outset probably would have avoided this problem.

An order which cannot be enforced should not be given. Suppose you tell a highly skilled employee to do something not in his or her job description. The worker refuses to do it on the basis that it is unskilled work, and tells you that if you press the matter he or she will file a grievance with the union or civil service. All you have done in this case is to antagonize the employee and illustrate your own impotence. This problem might have been avoided if you approached it by saying, "I know this isn't part of your job, but I'm in a bind and would really appreciate it if you could help me out." Of course, such a request is much more likely to succeed in a Theory Y than in a Theory X environment.

Delegation

One mark of a good manager is the ability to delegate tasks. The temptation to try to do the job oneself can be overwhelming. In fact, management authority Louis A. Allen has enunciated the principle of operating priority, which states that "when called upon to perform both management work and operating work during the same period, a manager will tend to give first priority to operating work."[11] But this is a mistake, since the manager's job is *to supervise others to get work done.* A manager wastes time by doing work subordinates should do, and indirectly conveys a lack of confidence in subordinates' ability to do the job—a surefire way to destroy morale. After such practices, attempts to introduce a participatory working style will be met by employee incredulity.

A manager who feels that subordinates cannot do the job adequately must do everything possible to have these employees trained so that they can improve their performance. At the same time, the manager should indicate to employees that however the office was run in the past, more authority will now be delegated. Indeed, Theory Y management is dependent upon delegated discretion. Without it, Theory X becomes the assumption on which the office operates.

Delegating authority will develop the initiative and resourcefulness of subordinates and increase their respect for their boss. At the same time, the manager will be less likely to be surrounded by "yes men."[12] A domineering boss attracts subordinates who agree with everything he or she says, while driving away those with independence and creativity. Once the organization encounters a crisis, yes-men are worse than useless, because they stop the boss from seeing how serious the situation is. What the manager needs in an emergency is a subordinate who will clearly sketch the dismal picture and help formulate a solution, no matter how drastic or unpopular.

Some managers detest delegation because they fear their subordinates will outshine them. For the same reason, they resolutely refuse to groom someone to take their place while they are away from the job. In this way they hope to be seen as indispensable. What they fail to realize is that the most valuable managerial skill is developing talent, especially talent that may come to outshine them.[13] And in results-oriented organizations, managers' achievements in developing talent will be richly rewarded. By the same token, an organization may be reluctant to promote someone who has not trained a successor. After all, who can do that supervisor's work if she or he is promoted? Finally, the manager will have more time to get managerial work done with help from an assistant. Many, or most, managers complain that there is not time enough in the day to do everything. An assistant can make it possible to lengthen the day by sharing the burden.[14]

COMMUNICATION

Effective communication is much harder to achieve than one might think. Indeed, the problem is pressing enough for large numbers of consultants to be able to make a living advising organizations how to improve their communications. Managers may save themselves much grief by practicing the procedures listed below.

Emotions and Facts[15]

Emotions are more readily communicated than facts. The manager who remembers this can profit from it. We communicate not only through words but also through actions, facial expressions, bodily gestures, and the like. A subordinate who receives permission to do something from a boss who has a contemptuous facial expression is not going to appreciate the boss's approval. Instead, the employee will remember the antagonistic look on the boss's face and respond with similar antagonism at a later date.

The manager should strive not only to keep negative emotions out of communications but also to replace them with positive ones. A factual message will be communicated more effectively if the supervisor can relate it to employees' personal interests ("The productivity plan will yield individual bonuses if successful").

Negatively phrased communications (*"Don't* delay in getting the job done, *don't* use that machine, and *don't* let anything fall out.") are guaranteed to evoke negative emotions. There are few ways to get employees more resentful than accentuating the negative. They will assume that the boss thinks they are untrustworthy boobs of the first order. Negative communications should be negated.[16]

Precision[17]

Communications should be precise, containing the answers to the questions Who? What? When? and Where? In communicating, the manager should keep in mind the *why,* or purpose, of the communication. This will help to make the who, what, when, and where clearer. Communications should be put in concrete terms, using examples where appropriate. Plain, everyday English rather than esoteric jargon or bureaucratese should be used.

Since correct communication is a difficult art, the manager should check to see if subordinates understand the communication. "Do you understand?" is inadequate. Employees may think they understand when they do not, or they may be embarrassed to say that they do not. The manager should *check* to see that employees understand what has been said or written. One way of doing so is to ask employees to repeat what was said in their own words, or to demonstrate what they thought the superior meant. In this way, the manager can see whether any flaws in communications exist and should be corrected.

Unfortunately, many managers neglect this necessary step and then blame their subordinates when things go haywire. Business administration professors William F. Dowling, Jr., and Leonard Sayles give the example of a busy manager who gave several communications in a brief time to his secretary. One of these instructions was to call another manager and remind him how important it was that his current assignment be finished by a specific date. But then the manager said no, the secretary had better not say this because it might get the other manager's back up. On returning from a week's trip out of the office, the manager found that his colleague had not finished the assignment, and took his frustration out on the secretary. He asked in a caustic tone why she had not called the other manager to tell him to get the job done, only to be told that she had called and said that her boss was concerned and would appreciate whatever could be done. With those words, her boss collapsed with a groan, but he had only himself to blame.[18] His instructions to his secretary were ambiguous, to put it mildly, and he never asked her to confirm that she knew what he wanted her to do.

Two-way Communication

A one-way communication process—where managers tell subordinates what to do, but are not interested in suggestions of subordinates—is typical of Theory X–oriented organizations. But by definition, Theory Y participative management requires managers who will not only listen to their subordinates but also actively solicit their advice. Managers should not feel magnanimous in so doing. Rather, they are drawing on the collective experience of their workers to enable themselves to make better managerial decisions. At the same time, they are indicating to employees that they are indeed members of a team, whose advice is appreciated and respected by the team leader.

Listening is *not* easy—it takes practice.[19] Remember to ask Who? What? Where? When? How? and Why? For example, "Did you go to the meeting?" is not as useful a question as "What happened at the meeting?" And be ready to listen when the subordinate initiates the conversation. Some managers do not want to "waste the time" involved in listening, but they should view this time as a worthwhile investment in improving communications, morale, and performance.

A good listener will often spot underlying causes of problems which may not be apparent at first. Suppose that a dependable employee suddenly begins to fall down on the job. The manager should not bawl him or her out and order improvement, but ask what the matter is and listen carefully. This may take time, because the employee may be reluctant to divulge the problem, whether or not it is work related. The manager should not only listen to the employee but also talk to others and observe and think about what might be causing the problem. This is the best way to identify the difficulty, whether it be some unpleasantness at work or off the job, and then try to do something about it. A draftsman in a public works department began to fall down on the job and to manifest obviously hostile feelings toward the manager. The manager looked patiently into the matter, listened carefully, and found out that the draftsman was angry because his desk had been moved and he felt cramped in his new location. This problem was speedily solved by moving the draftsman's desk back to its former location. A reprimand to this employee would have doubtlessly caused more hostility and even less achievement, where careful listening solved the problem.[20] Note, again, that advance consultation with the draftsman would probably have kept the problem from arising.

A *responsive* listener is one who has time for employee comments even when they may not seem directly related to the task at hand. Dowling and Sayles give the example of an employee who tells the boss that nothing seems to be going right today. The responsive boss notes that everybody has such days, and asks what's gone wrong. The subordinate proceeds to explain. The *unresponsive* boss responds that the employee has been falling down on some aspect of the job and should master it right away, or says that there is no time to listen to the employee.[21] This is a great mistake, for the recognition or attention the employee wanted can contribute greatly to morale. Simply restating what the worker has said makes him or her feel that the manager understands and thereby sympathizes with the problem—which is certainly true, if the manager is taking time out to listen.[22]

There is no better way to destroy team spirit and end two-way communication in the organization than to refuse to listen. This can only hurt the organization's performance in the long run.

Communicating Bad News

Managers must often deliver sad tidings to employees. In so doing, they should be expeditious. There is a great temptation to delay conveying bad news, which is painful for both superior and subordinate. Yet delay only aggravates the situation, increasing employee suspicion or allowing an unsatisfactory situation to continue.

Depersonalization is essential in conveying bad news. Suppose a worker with many years of dependable service shows up drunk after lunch one day and is obviously unfit for work. The manager should take the employee aside and calmly stress the facts. "We both know you can't get the job done today, so why don't you go home now and report back in the morning?" is a far better approach than "You're drunk! Go home and sober up!" At the same time, of course, the manager should try to find out what has caused this behavior.

Business administration professor Lewis R. Benton gives another example, that of an employee who asks to be let off work early on a busy workday to receive delivery of some furniture. A manager who practices depersonalization tells the employee she or he would be glad to do so if it were not so busy, and suggests that the furniture store be told to delay shipment two days, when the big push will be over and the employee can be let off. The wrong way to refuse the request is to say "Absolutely not! We're too busy, and this office does not revolve around your desires!"[23] In the first case, the subordinate is not going to be happy at the news, but can understand why the boss acted this way, and will appreciate that the request is being deferred, not denied completely. In the second case, the employee is going to feel rejected, frustrated, and angry.

Benton has a number of suggestions to follow in giving out bad news.[24] All requests should be listened to in full, even if the manager realizes early that the request will have to be rejected. Cutting the employee short indicates that the manager does not care about the employee's wants and needs. And sometimes the request may be based on a misunderstanding, which the manager can correct after listening.

In responding to the request, the manager should make clear that he or she takes the request seriously and realizes that the subordinate feels it is an important matter. And even if the reasons for rejection are manifestly clear to the boss, they should be spelled out to the subordinate, who may not be aware of some of them (e.g., "This would favor you over other employees with equal performance records"). Possible alternatives to the request should then be discussed, and the subordinate should be told what to do in the future to increase the chances of having the request granted.

One thing to avoid at all costs is to treat the employee whose request has been rejected in a special or apologetic way afterwards. This will only convey that the manager feels guilty because there was something wrong in turning down the request, which will redouble resentment. The manager should continue to treat the subordinate the same as always. The rule of depersonalization should always be followed.

Communication as the Road to Cooperation[25]

Cooperation in doing a job can only be gained through consultative communication. Managers must strive to get the advice of employees in their own and other offices. Furthermore, they must keep others informed of actions which affect them. *Cooperation cannot be ordered.* It can only occur in a Theory Y–oriented communications process. The manager who does not follow the steps outlined above is unlikely to preside over an office where employees cooperate well with each other.

REWARD AND PUNISHMENT

Managers give out rewards and punishment every working day. A word of praise, a sarcastic remark, permission to leave early, denial of a request for a raise, and listening to a distraught employee's problems are all rewards or punishments. While punishment is sometimes necessary, reward is a far more effective means of motivating workers.

Problems with Punishment and Returns from Reward

We live in a punishment-oriented society, which endorses penalties as the best way to make sure crimes and undesired actions will not recur. But punishment is a problematical procedure to use in motivating employees and should be employed only as a last resort. For one thing, punishable behavior is likely to happen again when the punisher is absent. Second, the punisher is perceived as the bad guy: the whole relationship between subordinate and supervisor may be jeopardized. Third, punishment has many undesirable consequences. The subordinate can get even with the punishing superior in a thousand different ways, whether slowing down work or slandering the manager in front of other employees.[26] Fourth, it is impossible to enforce penalties in a fair and evenhanded way. Just as some speeders are never caught, while others receive a ticket, some workers who should be punished are never caught. A feeling of being treated unfairly will rankle in a subordinate and may eventually cripple performance.[27]

With all these problems, it makes sense to stress reward over punishment. Reward focuses on what the employee is doing right and contributes to a positive relationship with the manager. Praise ("Thanks for doing that," "That was an excellent job,") can be a highly effective reward, even better in some cases than monetary (pay raise), status (new title), or power (more authority) rewards. Since most people like rewards, they may modify their behavior so that they will continue to be rewarded.

Managers will do well to follow certain principles in giving rewards. One is to discover which rewards mean the most to which employees. Some will prefer money raises, others challenging assignments, others recognition. Each person is different, and the manager should analyze what makes each subordinate tick.[28] Another principle to follow is rapid reward, so that the employee realizes just what is being rewarded. Do not defer rewards, or the subordinate will not be so highly motivated to repeat desirable behavior. Third, rewards should be given only when they are deserved. If employees find they are rewarded without having done anything to be rewarded for, they lose all incentive to improve. Fourth, getting employees to keep records of their own behavior can pay large dividends. This step at once rewards subordinates by indicating the manager trusts them, and allows employees to see that rewards are given on an objective, results-oriented basis. For example, employees could keep records to see how many units of work at what level of quality were finished.[29]

Readers may balk at the advice that undesirable behavior should be ignored unless it jeopardizes the safety and health of other employees or clients. But we would urge them to try this approach for a while and to focus on reward to see if subordinate behavior can be modified. This writer once surprised two blue-collar subordinates taking an unauthorized break. Instead of saying a word, he ignored the infraction, and these two dependable and productive workers continued their excellent work in the future. If unacceptable behavior persists, punishment can always be used as a last resort.

Principles and Procedures of Punishment

Remember that punishment is like surgery, a remedy to be tried only after other approaches have failed. And when punishing or disciplining employees, never forget to follow the principle of depersonalization.

Perhaps the most necessary reason for punishment is to show other employees that the person who does not obey the rules that they do is not going to get away with it. Remember that few things can infuriate so much as the feeling that a person is being treated unfairly or invidiously. If someone else can disobey the rules, why not you? Indeed, the record shows that tolerating one goof-off's absences, tardiness, or other infractions is likely to lead other employees to emulate the goof-off.[30]

A manager who contemplates taking a disciplinary action should ask whether the subordinate understood that a rule had been broken. If there has been a communication error or inadequate training, punishing the worker would have disastrous consequences. Supervisors should be especially careful when the violator is a new employee, who may be confused on beginning work in a new environment. Only when the manager can be sure that the employee definitely knew that a rule was being broken should disciplinary measures be taken.

In meting out discipline, the manager should seek to remove the *cause* of the violation wherever possible. For example, if smoking is forbidden in certain areas for safety considerations, it should be allowed in other well-publicized areas.

Before applying discipline, the manager must investigate the circumstances. Is this the subordinate's first infraction or the latest in a long line of similar occurrences? Was it done by accident or on purpose?[31] The manager should sing along with Gilbert and Sullivan,

> My object all sublime,
> I shall achieve in time,
> To let the punishment fit the crime,
> The punishment fit the crime.

Again, the rule of depersonalization is critical. Stress the facts, instead of rushing up to an employee and shouting "How did you do this, you jackass?" One approach is to show an employee an error or point out a rule infraction, and simply ask in a friendly tone what happened. The employee may be completely innocent of any blame for the error. But if not, the supervisor should not greet obviously lame excuses with derision. A remark to "Cut the baloney and own up!" is only going to cause the employee to hate the manager. Instead, by patiently listening to the explanation and failing to express any irritation, the manager is much more likely to get improvement. The manager can then say, "Let's review the procedure to make sure you understand it." In this way, the subordinate has been able to save face and avoid humiliation. At the same time, the appropriate behavior has been made crystal clear.[32]

As mentioned in the section on communication, managers who have to resort to stronger disciplinary measures such as fines or suspensions should not act apologetic to the disciplined worker afterwards. Likewise, saying to the worker that "I've really gone out on a limb for you—how could you do this to me!" is a mistake of the first magnitude. It diverts attention from the work to the worker, focusing on allegedly undesirable personal qualities.[33] Indeed, the remark above translates as "How can you be such a rotten person?" The proper procedure is the factual one outlined earlier to be used when giving bad news to employees.

As we have acknowledged earlier, there will be situations where Theory Y may not work. Just as managers should tailor rewards to individual employees, so should they tailor disciplinary measures. Take two employees who left the office to "visit" other offices. One employee did so because she was too intelligent for her job, which frequently bored her, but was a reasonable person. Her supervisor checked on her absences, made a facsimile time sheet spelling out what her pay would be if the "visits" were deducted, and showed it to the employee. The visits stopped, and the supervisor then began to discuss with the employee the possibility of trying for a more challenging assignment. The other "visitor" was a social butterfly who was not as bright as the first subordinate. The butterfly's manager simply tracked the employee down several times and ordered a return to work at once, which cured the employee of the visiting habit. Both managers applied individually tailored discipline based on their knowledge of the personality of their subordinates.[34]

LEADERSHIP THROUGH CONSENSUS[35]

Theory Y management is participatory management. The manager strives to involve all subordinates in making and implementing decisions. In this sense, decisions are made by mutual agreement. Of course, there will be times when decisions will have to be made immediately, but a leader in a participatory milieu will have some sense of the group's preferences even then. Consensus leadership pays several dividends, which we shall examine below.

Why Consensus?

Rensis Likert, a management scholar and consultant, whose "System 4" style greatly resembles Theory Y, has pointed out that most group deliberations are "win-lose" situations.[36] That is, proponents of one viewpoint usually prevail over advocates of other approaches. While the winner may feel elated, the loser is likely to remain hostile. Likert points out that the only way to get maximum cooperation from all concerned is for all sides to believe they have won at least enough so that a satisfactory solution has been found. "Win-win" must be substituted for win-lose.

The astute manager, then, will search for integrative solutions to problems which will leave all or most of the decision-making team satisfied. An example is the approach taken by New York City Tax Collector Lawson Purdy in leading the way to zoning and building regulations in 1916. Purdy went into a meeting room full of real estate operatives vehemently opposed to any kind of governmental regulation of land and just waiting for the chance to denounce zoning. So Purdy's first words were, "Let's all agree to propose no regulations that do not enhance the values of the properties affected." Opposition suddenly faded and consensus building began.[37]

Win-win decision making may be a long and difficult struggle in organizations with a history of acrimonious conflict. One tactic is to try to get the group to agree to a trial run of a proposal, even though everyone is not keen on it. The group then agrees to meet again at a specified time to see how the trial run has gone. If this approach is to work, the manager must take pains to make sure that special attention is paid to the needs of group members who went along with the trial run even if they did not want such a policy. Note that the agreement to try something on a pilot basis is a real step forward for a deadlocked group, and can be the foundation for eventual harmony.

When the trial run is not acceptable, the manager can ask the group to start all over again. This time, the group has to be sure that it is considering the real problem and stating it clearly. At the same time, an energetic search for more and better integrative goals, similar to Lawson Purdy's work in New York City zoning, is necessary. It may be necessary to start over more than once. Chances for success will be improved if all involved realize that their interests will suffer if no solution is reached.

If the situation remains stalemated, some action will have to be taken so that the organization can keep functioning. The manager should make such a decision only if she or he cannot convince the group to endorse a temporary measure favored by those who will have the major responsibility for implementing it. Other factions may well go along with this approach, but if they don't, the manager will have to act, while continuing to work with the group towards a long-run solution.

Consensus does not mean that a discouraging word is never heard. The group should strive for a full airing of differences and dirty linen. Otherwise, it will fail to get below the surface and no real progress in resolving conflict will be made.

Some critics feel that group decisions are mediocre ones because they reduce to the lowest common denominator, but research has proven again and again that not everyone in a group has equal influence. If the manager guides the group deliberations properly, those who are best informed and most experienced will be listened to most carefully, and their advice will be heeded.

Likewise, leadership is present in a group setting, even though Theory X–type orders are absent. The Theory Y leader guides the discussion, keeps the group on target, and summarizes the feelings of the group. These are the resources of leadership and can be used by a sensitive manager to wield great influence.

Tactics for the Leader to Follow to Reach Consensus

Groups not used to participating in decisions may find the going rough at first. The leader must not yield to temptation and try to solve the problem, but should make clear that the group is expected to do it. In particular, the temptation to lead the group to a prearranged solution through manipulation should be resisted. The group will quickly see through this tactic and realize that the new participatory style is a fraud. And even if they do not, the manager will gain nothing from such deception.

Managers should not be reluctant to air their true feelings, calmly and coolly, if they feel that the group is not making adequate progress. At the same time, group members have to feel they can also speak frankly. Nor should managers feel they have to be perfect. Such a fear will impede frank discussion and stop the session in its tracks.

While managers must make sure the group sticks to the topic, they should not be overly obsessed with this. It may be useful for the group to dissipate tension by beginning with small talk, for example. And when the discussion has clearly wandered, the question "How does that relate to the topic?" is the remark to make, *not* "Stick to the point!"[38]

Managers must relate all comments made to the main point, especially if the remarks are unclear. Nor should managers move ahead to further discussion until the group thinks this is appropriate and that its members are ready to proceed.[39]

It also helps for the manager to be generous in giving credit to others, to accept more blame than is actually due for failure, and to encourage the group to examine his or her proposals more critically than those made by other group members. These steps will encourage candid comments and go far to make group members feel that this really *is* a team.

Depersonalization in Consensus Building

Depersonlization is just as essential in rendering participatory decisions as it is in any other aspect of management. For example, proposals should not be labeled as "Doug's" or "Linda's," but stated as "One of *our* proposals is X; another is Y." In this way, individual egos are kept out of the picture as much as possible.

Letting the facts speak for themselves is a standard way of depersonalizing. T. W. Gamble, who ran bond drives in World War II, first tried to persuade state directors to use his approach by personal appeals. When this failed, he assembled all the facts and figures, which disclosed that his procedure attracted more contributors than any other one. In making his presentation, he did not urge state chairpersons to use his approach. After the presentation, however, most chairpersons adopted his technique. The facts, not Gamble's personal appeals, proved to have been the clincher.[40]

It is often useful to tackle broader general problems before specific ones. Group members are likely to be more attached to their viewpoints on specific problems (e.g., Should paramedics double for nurses in the physical therapy department?) than on general ones (should we strive to get maximum, flexible use of manpower in the hospital?). It is easier to depersonalize in the general than the specific case, and once progress has been made in the general area, solutions can be more easily reached in specific cases.

Sometimes a consultant can be of enormous help in assisting a group to move toward depersonalization. When a new department was created by consolidating several smaller ones, the head of one of the divisions was bitter at not having been promoted to head the new department, and went out of his way to undermine the authority of the new head. One strategy the division head followed was to bring problems for solution to the top managerial team which he should have settled himself and to state them so they involved win-lose decisions. He would also ask for decisions on controversial proposals involving his division, which again created win-lose situations. The department head, flustered by his failure to build a cohesive team, called in a consultant. Meetings of the management group were then observed, tape recordings were made, and analyses indicated that the division head was at the bottom of the problem.

With this new awareness, the department head asked the group to look more deeply into the reasons for conflict. In so doing, they found that a disproportionate amount of friction was generated by the division head's proposals. They then decided to look into the underlying causes of problems rather than the specific proposals. They also concluded that many of the problems they dealt with should have been solved at lower levels. With these new insights and procedures, it was no longer possible for the division head to disrupt the management team, which moved towards win-win decision making.[41]

If leadership through consensus sounds too good to be true, keep in mind Likert's counsel that the road is not easy and must be traveled slowly. The following sections discuss some typical problems involved in introducing Theory Y supervision and advise the reader about how to deal with them.[42]

PROBLEMS OF PARTICIPATORY SUPERVISION AND HOW TO MINIMIZE THEM

The principal problems confronted by those trying to introduce Theory Y–style supervision are political, since they are caused by differing values and emotions of employees. As was emphasized in the previous section, implementing participatory supervision is not going to be an easy task in organizations that have a previous history of Theory X management. Employees may not feel comfortable with Theory Y approaches or may doubt that managers are sincere in saying they will adopt Theory Y. What can be done to bring about change under these conditions?

Organizational Development (OD)[43]

Organizational development (OD) is a process of planned change designed to modify the behavior of agency employees. OD resembles the results-oriented management model we have sketched in this book. There is a problem recognition phase, program planning, implementation, and evaluation. Crucial to our concern here is the *training* phase of OD, typically called *T-groups* (T for "training"), or sensitivity training.

Developed by National Training Laboratories, T-groups usually include 10–16 people, one of whom is a trainer, who is usually an outside consultant. The goal of the training is for the participants to gain a better understanding of their *job-related* feelings and the feelings of their co-workers. T-groups are *not* group therapy sessions, but work-related training groups. While the trainer guides the group, there is no structure, agenda, or set procedure. Trainees are encouraged to express their true feelings and ask others how *they* feel. The trainer's job is to focus on the way the group is working, individual relationships to the group, and issues facing the group.

Well-run T-groups can help foster Theory Y management, for the T-group approach is participatory. If, with the trainer's help, trainees express themselves frankly without being punished, they may well be ready to participate more fully when Theory Y management goes into effect on the job. Researchers have found that T-group participants become more skilled in communication, leadership, group effectiveness, and acceptance of change than do matched groups which do not undergo sensitivity training.[44]

Lest the reader conclude that T-groups are a panacea, let us hasten to point out several common problems. First, the typical T-group lasts only a week. This is only long enough for some kind of change to begin. T-groups should continue for a much longer period of time.[45]

Second, T-groups must involve all levels of the organization if they are to work. If middle managers undergo training but top managers do not, much less is likely to change than would if all managers underwent training.

Third, according to Dr. Harry Levinson, an industrial psychologist, T-groups focus too much on confrontation, hoping thereby to draw out the negative feelings of participants. Levinson urges greater use of other techniques as well, because he feels that confrontation alone quickly becomes a gimmick.[46]

The related technique of *transactional analysis* (TA) can also be used in OD. This approach is based on the writing of psychoanalyst Eric Berne, author of *Games People Play*.[47] Berne argued that everyone behaves in three different ways: as parent, child, and adult. Parent behavior is paternalistic and authoritarian; child behavior is impulsive and dependent; and adult behavior is factual and results oriented. Every human relationship is a transaction between these different states. For example, a manager may say to a subordinate, "Give me that report by 5 o'clock," and the subordinate will reply "Yes." This is a *complementary* transaction between boss (parent) and subordinate (child), for it goes off without a hitch. But if the subordinate were to think or to reply "Go to hell!", this would be a *crossed* transaction, with negative rather than positive results.

TA training attempts to get trainees to recognize whether they are acting as parent, child, or adult at various times. This training can be extremely useful in developing a Theory Y atmosphere, where employees will learn to behave in the adult role and to practice depersonalization. Organizations can become far more effective by avoiding games that utilize parent and child roles, such as "Kick me" (criticize me for failure); "Now I've got you, you son of a bitch!" (entrapment of someone else, forcing an admission of failure); and "Yes, but" (nothing you say can influence me). When players of these negative games learn that a game cannot be continued if one of the players acts the adult role, great progress has been made. Since Theory Y aims for a working group of adults, TA may be very useful in helping some organizations to move toward participatory management.

Problems Common to All Training Techniques

Whether T-groups, TA, or other training approaches designed to change behavior are used, certain limitations on their effects will exist. These must be pointed out so that the real benefits to be gained from training are not dissipated after disappointment.

First, substantial change takes quite a while. Behavior learned over many years cannot be modified overnight. Management Professor James A. Lee recommends that top management "double a behavioral scientist's estimate of the time required for change and triple its own."[48]

Second, middle management needs guidance and support from top management in introducing change. A T-group alone is unlikely to change a manager who will not delegate authority. The manager's superiors will have to do things like asking the manager what subordinates think about the problem, and stress that the better one's subordinates, the higher top management's opinion of one as a manager. In short, training must be integrally related to management philosophy, or no benefits will result. Training without follow-up will not be taken seriously by managers.

CASE STUDY:
MANAGEMENT PROBLEMS IN A
HIGH SCHOOL DEPARTMENT

Community A, Louisiana, is a town of 20,000. In 1977, a rancorous conflict raged around the town's high school guidance department. The public became aware of the problem when several parents discovered that the records of evaluations written for their children's application to college and other postsecondary endeavors had been changed. The parents were surprised to find that the original evaluations, written by guidance counselor Stephen Knil, had been expunged and replaced by new recommendations. The parents and their children were upset, because the new recommendations did not seem to be as favorable as the original ones.

Why and how had these changes been made? High school principal Tito Gobbi had ordered guidance department chairperson James March to direct Knil to correct fifteen "misleading" recommendations to make them "more realistic and more in keeping with what the records actually showed." Knil refused to do so, stating that this was both his professional judgment and a matter of integrity. Knil reviewed the recommendations he had made, but felt he could not change them. Both March and Knil had been guidance counselors for ten years and had never before been asked to change a recommendation except to correct an error of fact.

After his refusal, Knil was asked directly by the principal to make changes, which he again refused to do. Gobbi then told March to make such changes. March asked the school board's lawyer whether he was required to do so, and was told yes, although the instructions for writing regulations stated that "Counselees you are not familiar with should have their comments and recommendations done by another counselor who may have better knowledge of them." Since each of the three counselors had several hundred students to advise, March did not know Knil's counselees personally. In light of this legal advice, March did make the changes requested by the principal.

Knil's personnel evaluations for the previous two years had been written by department head March, and were quite positive. The next one, written by principal Gobbi, was not a good one. Knil was then transferred from the high school guidance department to the middle school teaching staff, effective the next academic year. He did not fight the transfer, since he felt that he could no longer be effective as a counselor in the high school

Superintendent Albert Dulles, who approved the transfer, had refused the request of a parent whose child's recommendation was changed to meet jointly with her, Knil, and Gobbi. According to the parent, Dulles stated that he "would not be in the same room with this man [Knil]. I can't get along with him."

Knil's transfer was not the only one involving the guidance department. Chairperson March was transferred to the middle school as a guidance counselor for the next academic year, losing the position of chair and $2,400 in salary. March claimed that principal Gobbi told him he was being demoted and transferred because of pressure from the superintendent and some members of the Board of Education because March had discussed the Knil affair with the press. Gobbi denied that March's statements to the press had influenced his decision, though they might have influenced other people. Beyond that, Gobbi said he could not discuss this personnel matter. Parents supporting March pointed out that his annual personnel evaluation, made by the principal and dated February 1, 1977, recommended that he be reappointed chairperson, and that a May 6, 1977 evaluation was also very positive. But by June 30, 1977, he had lost the position of chair.

March's parting words were angry ones. "I'm glad to get out of that narrow-minded place [the high school]. I've had enough of their pettiness for 11 years."

The transfers left the middle school with four guidance counselors, and the high school with one. While new counselors would presumably be found for the high school, they would not have the personal knowledge of students that Knil and March had. Parents and the high school parent-teachers organization expressed great concern about the personnel changes, since they felt the high school guidance department had been understaffed even before the transfers.

While school board members stated that March's transfer had nothing to do with the case of the changed records, on July 12, 1977, the board directed Dulles to conduct a professional evaluation of the high school guidance department by October 1. The study would consider record-making and record-keeping procedures, assignment of personnel, and the overall quality of the services provided.

QUESTIONS

This case study outlines the development of a serious conflict in an administrative agency. The questions that follow ask you to relate the material in the rest of this chapter to the case study. Ask yourself whether any of the procedures described earlier in the chapter might have been able to lessen the conflict and its negative consequences.

1. Suppose you were the principal and found that one of your guid-

ance counselors was writing recommendations you could not support. Would you have followed a course different from that of principal Gobbi in trying to resolve this difference. If so, what would you have done? Explain the reasons for your stand, whether affirmative or negative, in detail.

2. How good a job do you think the superintendent did in helping to mediate this conflict? Explain your reasons in detail.

3. If you were department chairperson March, would you have acted any differently in this matter? Explain.

4. If you were guidance counselor Knil, would you have acted differently? Explain.

5. What effect do you think the handling of this case had on guidance personnel morale? On the morale of teachers and other professional staff within the school system?

6. Would you characterize the end result of this conflict as a win-win, win-lose, or lose-lose situation? Explain.

7. Do you think the superintendent's evaluation of the guidance department would be likely to improve matters? Explain.

PROBLEMS AND PROSPECTS FOR PARTICIPATORY SUPERVISION[49]

Management scholar and consultant Chris Argyris has pointed out some perennial training problems which he feels can only be solved by what he calls "double-loop learning." *Single-loop learning* occurs when agency employees detect
and attempt to correct an error in carrying out a task (our definition of *efficiency*). *Double-loop learning* confronts the question of whether they should be
carrying out the task to begin with (our definition of *effectiveness*). Argyris says
that his research indicates that training designed to help double-loop learning
confronts the obstacle of trainees' inability to understand that they wear blind-
ers which restrict them to single-loop learning. He gives the example of one
executive who told his training session of five other executives and a trainer that
his vice president was too submissive to succeed him. Eventually, after careful
questioning, the rest of the group convinced the executive that *he* was the cause
of his subordinate's dependence. The executive eventually accepted this
analysis, and invented a new "solution," which was to "lay off the vice president
and give him breathing space." But now his peers in the training session
pointed out that the vice president might wonder if his boss had suddenly given
up on him. The executive then tried another solution that he devised with the
group's help, testing it out on group members playing the role of the vice president. *Every time he tried this approach on a group member, what he carried out
was not the solution he and his peers had devised.* In other words, in spite of intelligence and effort, the executive was unable to immediately master double-
loop learning.

Argyris attributes this dilemma to the set of assumptions he finds govern
most managerial behavior:

1. Define in your terms the purpose of the situation you find yourself in.
2. Win.
3. Suppress your own and others' feelings.
4. Emphasize intellectual and deemphasize emotional aspects of problems.

Argyris's collection of 3,000 cases of executive behavior leads him to believe that double-loop learning can take place only under a different set of assumptions:

1. Gather valid information.
2. Make informed and free choices.
3. Be internally committed to the choice and constantly monitor evaluation.

Argyris found that shifting from the first set of assumptions (Model I) to the
second (Model II) is difficult because employees withhold information to protect themselves. Like the messengers of ancient times, they fear that they will
be punished if they bring bad news. Argyris believes that T-groups and similar
sessions will have only limited benefits, because they do not deal directly with

the organizational learning systems that caused the problems in the first place. The only way to change is to instruct *top* executives in double-loop learning and then have them return to their organizations and implement double-loop learning there themselves.

Argyris, like Likert and McGregor, is a convinced exponent of Theory Y. He is not saying that we should give up, but that plenty of effort is required to shift to effective participatory management. We would only urge the reader here not to despair if his or her department head will not make a full-time commitment to Theory Y. This would be optimal, but Theory Y can achieve results in units of an organization, even if it is not applied throughout the agency.

NOTES

1. Press conference, November 14, 1956.
2. Mary Parker Follett was the writer who pointed out the crucial importance of depersonalization. See Henry C. Metcalf and Lyndall Urwick, eds., *Dynamic Administration: The Collected Papers of Mary Follett* (New York: Harper & Row, 1942).
3. This section is based primarily on Robert E. Bouton, "The Supervisor Looks at His Job," *Effective Supervisory Practices, Bulletin No. 1* (Washington, D.C.: International City Management Association, 1965).
4. Howard E. Ball, "The Art of Disobedience," *The Bureaucrat* 2 (Fall 1973): 248–55.
5. Theodore Caplow, *How to Run Any Organization* (Hinsdale, Ill.: Dryden Press, 1976), pp. 161–62.
6. James K. Van Fleet, *The 22 Biggest Mistakes Managers Make and How to Correct Them* (West Nyack, N.Y.: Parker Publishing, 1973), pp. 121–34.
7. Caplow, op. cit., pp. 93–94.
8. Robert E. Bouton, "Directing the Work," *Effective Supervisory Practices, Bulletin No. 5* (Washington, D.C.: International City Management Association, 1965).
9. John R. Coleman, *Blue-Collar Journal: A College President's Sabbatical* (Philadelphia: Lippincott, 1974), pp. 38, 44.
10. Van Fleet, op. cit., pp. 67–68.
11. Louis A. Allen, *The Management Profession* (New York: McGraw-Hill, 1964), p. 77.
12. Van Fleet, op. cit., p. 74.
13. Allen, op. cit., p. 204.
14. Van Fleet, op. cit., pp. 209–11.
15. This section is based primarily on Allen, op. cit., p. 278.
16. Bouton, "Directing the Work," op. cit., p. 6.
17. Loc. cit.
18. William F. Dowling, Jr., and Leonard R. Sayles, *How Managers Motivate: The Imperatives of Supervision* (New York: McGraw-Hill, 1971), pp. 199–200.

19. F. J. Roethlisberger, *Man-in-Organization* (Cambridge, Mass.: Harvard University Press, 1968), pp. 31–32, 155.
20. Vincent W. Kafka and John W. Schaefer, *Open Management* (New York: Peter H. Wyden, 1975), is full of illustrative examples and incisive analysis supporting this point.
21. Dowling and Sayles, op. cit., pp. 239–40.
22. This is usually called the "nondirective" approach and originated with the psychologist Carl R. Rogers. See his *Counseling and Psychotherapy* (Boston: Houghton Mifflin, 1942).
23. Lewis R. Benton, *Supervision and Management* (New York: McGraw-Hill, 1972).
24. Ibid., p. 214.
25. This section is based on Robert E. Bouton, "Co-operation within the City Service," *Effective Supervisory Practices, Bulletin No. 14* (Washington, D.C.: International City Management Association, 1965).
26. Clemm C. Kessler, III, "Influencing Employee Behavior," in *Developing the Municipal Organization* (Washington, D.C.: International City Management Association, 1974), pp. 85–101, at 100.
27. Dowling and Sayles, op. cit., p. 133.
28. Kafka and Schaefer, op. cit., explore this topic in depth.
29. Kessler, op. cit., pp. 100–1.
30. Dowling and Sayles, op. cit., p. 134.
31. Benton, op. cit., p. 225.
32. Ibid., p. 227.
33. Dowling and Sayles, op. cit., p. 134.
34. Ibid., pp. 140–41.
35. This section is based primarily on Rensis Likert and Jane Gibson Likert, *New Ways of Managing Conflict* (New York: McGraw-Hill, 1976).
36. Ibid., pp. 142–55.
37. Ibid., pp. 142–43.
38. Benton, op. cit., p. 337.
39. Wallace G. Lonergan, "Groups and Meeting," in *Developing the Municipal Organization* (Washington, D.C.: International City Management Association, 1974), pp. 113–24.
40. Likert and Likert, op. cit., pp. 163–64.
41. Ibid., pp. 171–73.
42. This chapter has no secton on the use of Theory Y supervision, since a number of examples have already been discussed in Chapter 1.
43. This section is based on W. B. Eddy, "Beyond Behavioralism: Organization Development in Public Management," *Public Personnel Review,* July 1970; and Charles Seashore, "What Is Sensitivity Training?" *Management Forum,* June 1968.
44. See E. G. Miller, "The Impact of T-Groups on Managerial Behavior," *Public Administration Review* 30 (May–June 1970): 296–97.

45. Chris Argyris, "The CEO's Behavior: Key to Organizational Development," *Harvard Business Review*, March–April 1973.

46. Harry Levinson, *The Great Jackass Fallacy* (Cambridge, Mass.: Harvard University Press, 1973), pp. 160–62.

47. Eric Berne, *Games People Play* (New York: Grove Press, 1964), and Eric Berne, *Transactional Analysis in Psychotherapy* (New York: Ballantine Books, 1973).

48. James A. Lee, "Behavioral Theory vs. Reality," *Harvard Business Review*, March–April 1971, pp. 20–28, 157–59, at 157.

49. This section is based primarily on Chris Argyris, "Double Loop Learning in Organizations," *Harvard Business Review*, September–October 1977, pp. 115–25, and Chris Argyris, *Increasing Leadership Effectiveness* (New York: Wiley, 1976).

5

Management by Objectives (MBO)

LEARNING OBJECTIVES

TO UNDERSTAND:

The relationship of planning, implementation, and review in MBO

Types of corrective action

How to reduce technical and political problems

Avoiding potential traps in MBO

DEFINING MBO

Management by objectives (MBO) is an approach to output-oriented management which encompasses all the steps outlined in Chapter 2, on planning, and all the steps in this chapter. The reader may wonder why we have chopped up MBO and present only part of it in this chapter. The principal reason for this procedure is to emphasize the common ground shared by results-oriented management approaches. Since the planning process we have outlined in Chapter 2 is identical with the planning process used in MBO, there is no reason to repeat the material presented in that chapter.

MBO is a comprehensive approach which includes planning, implementation, and review, as Figure 5–1 indicates. In this chapter, we will focus on the implementation and review phases of MBO. This is more than enough for one chapter, as the reader will see. She or he should not forget, we repeat, that MBO includes the subject matter in Chapter 2 as well.

There is no single commonly accepted definition of MBO. Indeed, it seems that every month brings forth a new article declaring an additional twist to MBO and distinguishing the new approach from the old.[1] Kimmel, Dougan,

FIGURE 5-1.   PRINCIPAL COMPONENTS OF MBO

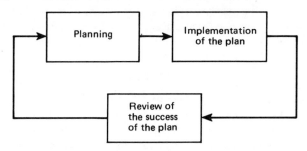

and Hall define MBO as "an approach to the internal management of an organization in which individual managers set performance goals in terms of output or achievement rather than input or activity. . . . Beyond this activity, an MBO program may be as unique as the organization that uses it."[2]

Indeed, MBO is used for different reasons or combinations of reasons in different organizations. It can be used as an *evaluative technique* for employee or program performance; as an *incentive technique* to motivate employees; as a *system to enhance job satisfaction;* or as a means to attain *mutual understanding* among different levels of the organization.[3] A well-designed and implemented MBO system can perform all these functions. MBO is nothing if not flexible, since it is a system which decentralizes management by granting a larger decision-making role to subordinates.

IMPLEMENTING MBO

Alternative Approaches

MBO is a very flexible management approach, which can be introduced at any level of an organization and implemented in a variety of ways. There is no one best way to introduce MBO. For example, Morrisey lists a half-dozen alternatives, which range from across-the-board implementation to an individual manager's practicing MBO alone to set an example.[4] While there is no one best way, *commitment* to MBO is a crucial concern. Managers who want to implement MBO must examine their own level of commitment and ask whether it will suffice to make the plan workable. At the same time, managers must gauge the support likely to be given by colleagues, whether peers, subordinates, or superiors. If they are unlikely to support MBO to the same extent as the manager, its chances for success will be adversely affected. There would be little point to going ahead with MBO if the manager was committed to the concept but had little desire to put more than a couple of hours a week into it and colleagues were opposed to or uninterested in it. Certain failure and disillusionment with MBO would be the result.

While MBO can be introduced at a number of different points, one survey of several hundred managers found that it was most likely to be accepted by them if introduced by top management. Such sponsorship indicates to managers that MBO is to be taken seriously, because it is more than the passing fancy of just one part of the organization, such as the personnel department, which can be ignored without penalty.[5]

Preconditions

A substantial training effort is necessary if MBO is to succeed. We are not talking about a weekend seminar, but a prolonged and protracted period of several months. Special training sessions are a must, but most of the learning will come on the job, as managers seek to apply the principles of MBO and are instructed further in their efforts by the project director or trainers.

As a result of training, managers must know the general principles of MBO and how it fits into their agency before they can get into the nitty-gritty of fashioning and implementing specific objectives. A substantial amount of time during the training period should be allotted to both the costs and benefits of MBO. Since MBO is a Theory Y approach intended to maximize participation of individual managers in agency decision making, the training process should stress individual self-assessment of skills and judgments about the utility of MBO.[6] MBO is a complicated system; plunging into it without extensive training is a guarantee of failure. A common experience in agencies that fail to train managers in this way is for managers to wait passively for their superiors to set objectives for them instead of fixing objectives themselves.

Plans which are not carried out resemble those New Year's resolutions we can never deliver on. Both are worthless. At this point the best laid plans of mice and men most often go astray. The attempt to implement, then, deserves thorough scrutiny. Several different steps are involved in this implementation process, as Figure 5–2 indicates.[7]

FIGURE 5-2.   IMPLEMENTING MBO

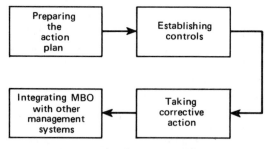

Preparing the Action Plan

Once an alternative has been choosen, an action plan must be drawn up to implement it. The statement of the plan should be brief, but should be broken down into different phases as well. One example of an action plan follows.

The city of Podunk welfare department finds that a large number of welfare checks are going out to ineligible clients. It forms the following action plan to correct this problem. A new information system designed to end these errors is to be installed in six months, at a cost of $100,000 and 2,500 work-hours of effort. The first step in the plan is to gain agreement and support for it within the agency. One week and 50 work-hours of *specifically designated personnel* are allocated to this phase. Next, the design and installation of the new computer-based information system is allotted $50,000, 75 days, and 850 work-hours. Third, training staff to use the new system will take 50 days, $35,000, and 1,000 work-hours. Implementation of the new system is allotted $15,000, 35 days, and 500 work-hours. The final step is review and evaluation, for which 13 days and 100 work-hours are allocated.

Figure 5–3 outlines an action plan followed by the U.S. Civil Service Commission to attain the objective of improving the accuracy of estimates of new employees hired by federal agencies. While the cost element is not included, steps, timetable, and individual responsibility are detailed in the figure. Figure 5–4 is an action plan for the Wisconsin Division of Family Services. Note that both costs and assignment of individual responsibility have been left out of this otherwise exemplary plan.

In the examples just given, we have sketched a five-step implementation plan which involves several tasks. These tasks include *programming*, or determining the steps to be followed to gain objectives; *scheduling*, or determining the amount of time necessary to accomplish each step; *budgeting*, or allotting resources—whether money, men, or merchandise—necessary to attain each objective; and *accountability*, or assigning the responsibility for getting each

FIGURE 5-3.   U.S. CIVIL SERVICE COMMISSION ACTION PLAN

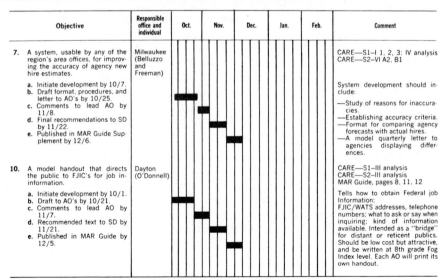

SOURCE: *Civil Service Journal,* July/September 1975, p. 15.

FIGURE 5-4. EXAMPLE OF AN OBJECTIVE STATEMENT AND PROGRESS REPORT

OBJECTIVE

To reduce inadequacies and errors in payment levels and eligibility determinations in income maintenance programs.

BACKGROUND

The quality control program is a federally mandated program to all states, which involves the selection of a specified monthly sample of cases on AFDC, adult categories and Medical Assistance and a review of active cases and those terminated or denied by the county. The case record is read and the recipient(s) is interviewed on all active sample cases and also on terminated and denied cases if an error exists. The factual material gathered is recorded on HEW-APA 341 worksheets and after all collateral checks have been completed, the data is entered on the case review schedule for submission to central office. There it is tabulated and updated periodically as the review schedules are received in central office. Individual cases are reviewed in the regional offices for case remedial action, i.e. the county will be asked to correct the error and regions may take a financial exception on the case. The corrective action taken is based upon significant statistical findings of errors in three programs which require basic change in policy, procedure or administration of program.

Currently, federal standards for program tolerance are set at 3% for ineligible cases and 5% for payment errors. Based on our most recent figures, compiled on February 1, 1973, the state has a 2.91% ineligibility rate for AFDC with an estimated monthly cost of $$310,000 $\pm$ $140,000 involving 1275 cases; 12.10% overpayments with an estimated monthly cost of $170,000 $\pm$ $35,000 involving an estimated projected 5,100 cases and 13.32% underpayment with $120,000 $\pm$ $23,000 involving an estimated 5,600 cases. In the adult categories there is 3.8% ineligibility rate involving 1140 cases and 7.2% overpayment rate involving 2,100 cases and an underpayment rate of 7.6%.

The broad area of corrective action needs immediate attention, particularly in Milwaukee County. This County generates 47% of the total state AFDC population and accounts for an 18% error rate in this category alone based on overpayments and ineligibles. It is essential that immediate steps be taken to correct the error levels in Milwaukee County and we believe that this should be underway by

110

FIGURE 5–4 (cont.)

July 1973. We would assume that if immediate action is initiated in the Milwaukee Region a significant error reduction would result by the third quarter of September 1973.

We are uncertain as to the formula the federal government will apply when the state is out of tolerance. On overpayments, the dollar sanction might be based upon the average amount of overpayment determined by the sample estimated to the entire population.

It now appears that the output compliance issue will be met in Health, Education and Welfare samples. This does not cover the Food Stamp quality control program administered by United States Department of Agriculture. Barriers to achieving tolerance compliance in the assistance payments programs are focused primarily around mis-interpreted manual material and failure to apply policies where needed. Efforts are underway to clarify manual material and train the case aides within each county to apply policy material in accordance with state and federal law.

Adult categories are to be administered by the Social Security Administration by January 1, 1974. The Social Security Administration is developing a quality assurance program similar to the HEW quality control programs to monitor these cases.

Also, it would appear that a flat grant system would reduce the overpayment/underpayment errors to within tolerance limits to a significant degree as it would eliminate the source of most agency errors in the determination of the case budget.

RESPONSIBILITY FOR ACHIEVEMENT

Deputy Division Administrator—Operations.

PERFORMANCE INDICATORS

The primary performance indicators in the quality control program are the error rates determined for the various categories of assistance. In the AFDC and adult (old age, blind, and disabled aid) categories three error rates are determined: what percentage of the cases are receiving grants in excess of what they are entitled (overpayment), what percentage of the cases are receiving grants that are less than they are entitled to (underpayment) and what percentage received a grant to which they were not entitled (ineligible). In addition, the proportion of negative action cases (cases which are distontinued and applications for assistance which are denied) for which the agencies reason is invalid is calculated. In the Medical

FIGURE 5–4 (cont.)

Assistance program, only the proportion of those inappropriately receiving Medical Assistance benefits and the proportion invalidly denied or discontinued medical benefits are determined.

The federal government has established error tolerance limits of 3% for measures of ineligibility and 5% for the measures of payment errors. The criterion for success for the QC program is to <u>reduce</u> any error rates which exceed the tolerance limits to within those limits. In addition, it is the responsibility to maintain error rates within these acceptable limits. All fiscal disallowances will be directly related to the Division's capability of reducing error rates and maintaining them within acceptable error levels.

Error Rates as Performance Indicators

AFDC	Wisconsin's Current Rates	Federally Tolerated Error Rates
overpayments	12.10%	5%
underpayments	13.32%	5%
ineligibles	2.91%	3%
invalid negative actions	19.29%	3%
Adult		
overpayments	7.21%	5%
underpayments	7.69%	5%
ineligibles	3.84%	3%
invalid negative actions	14.00%	3%
Medical Assistance		
ineligibles	5.26%	3%
invalid negative actions	6.25%	3%

IMPLEMENTATION TIMETABLE

First quarter—completion of July–December 1972 HEW sample.
Second quarter—corrective action on Milwaukee County problems
        and Training of QC reviewers on new manual material.
Third quarter—completion of January–June 1973 sample.
Fourth quarter—operational remedial and corrective action system.

FIGURE 5–4 (cont.)

PROGRESS REPORT

Objective: Quality Control

DIVISION: Division of Family Services   REPORT PERIOD:
September-December 1973

OBJECTIVE STATEMENT: Reduction of Errors in AFDC Program

OVERALL STATUS:

Current Reporting Period	Preceding Reporting Period
☐ Ahead of Plan	☐ Ahead of Plan
☐ Satisfactory	☐ Satisfactory
☒ Minor Problem	☐ Minor Problem
☐ Major Problem	☒ Major Problem

SUMMARY OF PROGRESS AND PROBLEMS:

1. The April–October sample was completed. The following data becomes the base for the next two QC sample reviews:
   Ineligibles 4.7%   Overpayments 14.5%   Underpayments 16.5%
   In spite of actual increase in ineligibles (4% April to 4.7% November) Wisconsin has a good record compared to national average of 10.2%.
2. Corrective Action Plan was submitted to NEW, a DFS Corrective Action Panel has been formed and a Regional Task Force has been organized.
   Problem: The Corrective Action Plan to be successful depends in part on CRN which will have no impact during the current sample period.
3. AFDC-U statewide review is now taking place. Milwaukee AFDC-U review has reached $2.5 million to be recovered.

   We are drawing and reviewing cases in the January-June sample.

   Note: Minor problem is indicated at this time. Hopefully the use of the first grant will reduce some of the previous errors. In spite of AFDC-U reviews, etc., there is no guarantee that QC sample will show the one-third reduction in errors which is expected by HEW.

step of the job done to each person. While we will not discuss the details of the last three tasks here, since such detailed consideration is not necessary for each and every action plan,[8] the key task of programming is examined next.

Programming   Morrisey warns that the concerns to consider in programming seem so commonsensible that we may overlook them and fall flat on our faces. For example, gaining agreement and support is a deceptively simple step. It should be done before the plan is put in final form. Input from subordinates, superiors, peers, and groups outside the agency may point out ways in which the plan is inappropriate or mistaken. It may be noted, for example, that a plan to relocate the town dump to neighborhood A is not going to be acceptable to residents there, who have shown impressive ability in the past to reverse similar decisions. Or it may be pointed out that the dump cannot be located in the swampy area of neighborhood B because of new state environmental laws banning such use of swamps. Secondly, this kind of Theory Y consultation is much more likely to enlist support for any plan than would simply ordering staff to carry it out. Managers who are in a hurry to get on with the job should not try to save time by neglecting this step. If they do, their fate may resemble that of a person with a bad cold who was ordered to rest in bed for a few days by the doctor. Ignoring the physician's advice, the patient returned to work the next day, only to collapse with pneumonia and spend a *month* in bed. Such shortcuts are penny-wise and pound-foolish.

The most complicated step is usually outlining the sequence of events to be followed to gain the objective. Morrisey suggests that three concerns are crucial to the determination of the number and nature of the steps involved. First, *major* steps involving broad areas of accomplishment under the plan must be specified. In the Podunk welfare example, major steps include the design and use of the new computer-based information system.

A second concern is determining priorities. Which steps must precede others? In the Podunk example, the information system had to be designed before staff could be trained to use it.

Third, major steps must be broken down into smaller ones, following a logical sequence. The procedure to be followed in each of these steps (for example, training staff in use of the new information system) should be left up to the manager or subordinate in charge, with the sole concern of the superior being the results achieved, unless legal or ethical problems are involved. For example, if training is enhanced by using Hatha Yoga techniques, fine; but if the subordinate suggests using hypnotism, problems of prying into personal privacy may arise.

Next, Morrisey suggests a test or review of the action plan. Such a step could range all the way from a pilot run of the program (trying out the new Podunk welfare information system on a trial basis) to a brief brainstorming session with program officials to guesstimate what is likely to happen when the action plan goes into effect.

The moment has now arrived to implement the action plan. Its success can then be gauged by evaluating the results achieved after the program has run for a while, the subject of the next chapter.

Establishing Controls

Control is defined here as the process by which we make sure that MBO is actually implemented. It should not be conceived of as a set of dictatorial devices to manage employees, but as an approach which helps those responsible for implementation of the plan to stay on the right track. Highway traffic lights are a means of control, and some drivers might not like them for this reason. But if we did away with traffic lights, we would have chaos, terrible accidents, and traffic backed up for miles. Likewise, implementing an action plan without adequate controls will result in failure. But controls should follow the guideline set forth by George S. Odiorne, a leading authority on MBO: "Leave me alone as much as possible to do my job."[9]

Morrisey notes control is intended to warn us when we are going to get in trouble so that we have enough time to change direction to avoid disaster. For this reason, too much control should be avoided, for it is a waste of organizational resources. If managers are constantly looking over their subordinates' shoulders and telling them what to do, MBO does not have a chance to be established. Subordinates will never learn to do the work on their own, and managers will waste valuable time that could be put to productive effort elsewhere.

Controlling should focus on the most important concerns the organization deals with, whether these are input costs or outputs. For example, a health department should be more concerned with establishing controls for the cost and quality of its public innoculation programs than with working out elaborate controls to reduce the number of pencils and paper clips used each year.

Standards   *Standards,* also discussed in Chapter 8, on productivity, are accepted levels of performance, or yardsticks by which to measure achievement. They can cover almost any aspect of organizational input, activity, or output. Examples might include the amount of sewerage purified per workhour, the employee absentee rate, and the number of welfare client complaints per week. Some standards, such as those relating to employee morale, may be very difficult to qualify or measure, but Morrisey recommends that the attempt be made regardless. Otherwise, we would have no criteria to gauge objectives-oriented performance, and thus no way to tell early enough (when it is preventable) which is likely to go wrong. For example, if Dutch water engineers know that a certain amount of dike leakage is inevitable and easy to deal with, they know that it is not a critical problem. But if leakage exceeds a certain amount, they know a crisis is coming and must immediately be dealt with. Without such standards, they could not adequately respond to leaks and would either ignore the crumbling of the dike or treat each leak as if it forecast a flood.

In either case, the consequences for agency efficiency and effectiveness should be obvious; and the need for standards applies equally strongly—though usually not so dramatically—to every organization.

It must be emphasized once more that if they are to be appropriate and accepted, these standards should emerge from a Theory Y atmosphere of cooperative consultation among superiors and subordinates. Managers who expect their subordinates to meet standards which the latter neither understand nor accept are asking for trouble. Odiorne notes that controls should not be carried out merely through the exchange of memos, but on the basis of personal, face-to-face contact. As he puts it, memos "used in the absence of such face-to-face dialog . . . can be poisonous. The MBO system becomes bogged down in a morass of forms, memoranda, and unintelligible evasions. The logic of MBO alone won't carry it off if the system is depersonalized and mechanistic."[10] Personal contact carries with it a conviction and commitment that meaningless myriad memos can not muster. As business executive Arthur H. Kuriloff has put it,

> By "saying it" instead of writing it we have opened up numerous channels of communication instead of confining ourselves to the medium in which many people have limited capability anyway. When people talk face-to-face, their understanding is almost invariably improved—tone, inflection, facial expression, and all such nuances reinforce the message that is being transmitted. Above all, there is a fair guarantee that the message has actually been received.[11]

We are not talking here about a public relations technique, but a clue to commitment. If managers are taking the trouble to personally convey their convictions, this usually indicates that they care about MBO. But if they are carrying out a charade, they are not going to fool anyone. The sincere spoken word signals conviction; insincerity is even more counterproductive than a multitude of memoranda.

Factors Fouling Up the Forecast   Morrisey identifies four factors that necessitate conscious and careful adjustment of the action plan if it is to succeed.[12] These include *uncertainties,* such as the volume of clientele demands, employee illness, or a legislative investigation of the agency. There is no way to prevent all uncertainty, but standards are needed so that we will know when uncertainties have begun to undermine the action plan and threaten accomplishment of objectives. If employee absenteeism was estimated at 3 percent per day on the average and a severe winter raises this to 10 percent, implementation of the plan may be in jeopardy. Standards relating to uncertainty or to the other factors listed below can help us identify *what* went wrong so we can take corrective action. Otherwise, we will only know that *something* went wrong, and now know where to begin to remedy the situation. *Unexpected events,* such as the death of a powerful political ally or an agency scandal uncovered by the media; *failures*, such as computer breakdown, which are beyond the control of employees; and *human error*, whether due to incompetence or to an inappropriate workload, can also necessitate readjustment of the plan.

In selecting control measures, we have to ask which factors are likely to be identified by the measures. A standard of employee performance based on skill is likely to identify human error, for instance, but another type of control measure will have to be employed if we are to deal with the consequences of uncertainties or failures.

Another critical concern is how much lead time is needed to correct the situation. Radar systems give the military early notice of enemy intentions, increasing the amount of time available to deal with the situation. All organizations benefit if they can design warning systems that make information available at the earliest moment possible.

Another key concern is the amount of time and effort required by the control measure. Morrisey recounts a top executive's request for a report which required so much work and overtime that the executive might well have settled for a more modest effort had he known the cost involved.

Finally, controls should be carried out in a Theory Y atmosphere. If employees feel that an "efficiency expert" is dogging their steps, or that other employees are spying on them, the control measure will be counterproductive. A problem common to all organizations is the proliferation of paperwork forms, because they are used as instruments of control from above. Few things are as wasteful of effort as to have skilled personnel spend endless hours filling out such forms instead of doing productive work. Peter F. Drucker, the famous management consultant, reports how he once recommended that a company abolish all its reports except those demanded by managers living without them. The company was able to cut back forms by 75 percent.[13] To repeat Odiorne's injunction: "Leave me alone as much as possible to do my job."

Taking Corrective Action   We have now arrived at the crucial juncture of MBO. The whole point of establishing controls is to be able to change course. One type of action is *self*-correcting. Competent and motivated individuals can adjust their own behavior when it is inadequate to achieve objectives *if* they are aware of the objectives and how they are doing in relation to them. Such self-correcting behavior, of course, can take place only in a Theory Y environment.

A second type is *operating* action. If problems develop, managers may step in and do the work themselves; or they may direct another employee to take over. But while this may sometimes be necessary, managers should not do so if it is not. Otherwise, subordinates will never learn how to deal with a crisis, and will thus never develop their full potential. The author remembers well how his father, a motel manager, turned over the office to a new employee on his first day, walking out and leaving him alone on his shift after five minutes' instruction. This manager was willing to risk some mistakes so that the employee could learn how to handle any situation which might arise by himself. Perhaps the most important benefit of this action was its impression on the employee, who interpreted the manager's action as a vote of confidence in his ability to do the job.

A third type is *management* action. Here the manager must review the *process* which has caused the discrepancy between the action plan and actual events. Was the discrepancy due to a fault in the planning process for the action plan; or did it arise from uncertainty, unexpected events, failure, or human error? This difficult determination is the measure of a manager, for the plan can only be implemented if the supervisor is able to determine why it went wrong and take steps to correct it.

John W. Humble, a British specialist in MBO, has suggested the following checklist to be used in the implementation of MBO:

> Do managers have control information on all the key results they must achieve?
>
> Is it simple? relevant? timely? acceptable? a good basis for self-control?
>
> When did you last make a critical study of the information and control systems and paperwork?
>
> Is there too *much* information?·
>
> Is it costing too much?[14]

Integrating MBO with Other Systems

Another crucial question remains. Is MBO integrated with other organizational procedures, or is it set up as a system which functions independently of personnel, budgeting, and other key areas of organizational decision making? As business administration scholars Stephen J. Carroll, Jr., and Henry L. Tosi have put it, "Unless the MBO program is integrated with other organizational procedures and systems, it will be viewed as something outside normal operating procedure and will receive inadequate attention. In addition, it will create a source of conflict, as it is likely that action required by the MBO program will contradict other procedures and requirements."[15] Carroll and Tosi note that unless other organizational subsystems, such as data processing, forecasting, and budgeting are tied into MBO, MBO will lack the data it needs to operate. Conversely, they observe that "The more that the MBO system is made interdependent with other subsystems of the organization, the more the use of MBO will be reinforced and will become a natural aspect of management."[16]

Of course, this is much easier said than done. There is no substitute for hard work and careful thought when it comes time to try to integrate something like the budget with MBO. For example, the budget for the coming fiscal year has to be prepared before the current fiscal year is over. This means that an MBO implementation scheme for the next year must be devised before all the returns for the current year are in.

While there is no way to eliminate this time lag, employees preparing MBO action plans can compensate by setting up a system of review that will focus on the kinds of data relating to uncertainties, unexpected events, failure, and human error which we looked at previously. For example, if budget data for the last quarter of the current fiscal year indicate that human error has sharply increased costs in one action plan area, the action plan for the next fiscal year will have to be adjusted. This kind of problem is to be expected and can be dealt with *if* the budget information system is closely integrated with MBO. But if the two systems do not share a common language of category titles and operating assumptions, and if the employees in charge of each subsystem do not have a close working relationship, such adjustments cannot be made. And then MBO becomes an academic enterprise without real significance for the agency. "Unintegrated" MBO cannot work.

An illustration of this point is the case of a manager who restructured the work system in his office so that 39 employees were able to accomplish what had previously been done by 44. For this reason, he did not ask for replacements when 5 employees quit or retired. But when the manager was told that he would be paid less because he now supervised less than 40 employees, he immediately asked for 5 more employees and gave them busy work. Thus, failure to integrate MBO with personnel department procedures wiped out all the gains made possible by MBO.[17]

GOVERNMENTAL USE OF MBO

Before beginning this section, the reader should not forget that MBO is a management approach which includes planning, implementation, and review. Although the preceding material in this chapter deals only with the implementation phase of MBO, MBO consists of more than an implementation phase. Thus, we do not concentrate solely on MBO *implementation* in the material in this section.

The Federal Government[18]

On April 18, 1973, President Nixon ordered 21 agencies which were spending 95 percent of the federal budget to institute MBO. The President's reasons for backing MBO were twofold. He stated, "I am confident that this conscious emphasis on setting goals and then achieving results will substantially enhance Federal program performance"; and perhaps even more important, Nixon wanted to exert greater control over a federal bureaucracy he did not trust and suspected of sabotaging his programs.[19] The President believed that career civil servants did not share his values and resisted the attempts of his managers to implement new programs.[20] MBO was part of a larger scheme to increase presidential control which included proposals for reorganizing agency structure, changing the civil service system, withholding funds budgeted by Congress, training federal executives in technocratic loyalty, and using the illegal methods of surveillance that came to light in the Watergate affair.[21] As the reader might suspect, an approach born out of such mixed motives is going to achieve mixed results. We will focus in this section on what MBO has achieved as a program-oriented management tool, rather than as a device for political control.

A number of federal agencies such as the Department of Health, Education and Welfare (HEW) and the National Aeronautics and Space Administration (NASA) had already been using MBO-type systems, while other agencies such as the Justice and State departments were far away from having anything remotely similar to MBO. Not surprisingly, then, MBO got a mixed reception from the agencies. Some resisted and suspected MBO, while others were receptive.

Officials of the President's Office of Management and Budget (OMB), charged with implementing MBO, made sure that their initial meetings with the line agencies to discuss MBO were held in line agency offices. OMB took this approach to emphasize, in the words of Director Roy Ash, that "We are not imposing goals and objectives on any agency. All of these agencies are already aware from various Presidential policy statements of the general direction of Presidential policy. It's their job to translate their concept of Presidential direction to their own goals and objectives."

At the beginning of the program, meetings between OMB and line agency staff were held every two or three months to monitor agency performance in implementing action plans. As the line agencies learned MBO procedures, these meetings became less frequent. OBM set a fall 1973 deadline for the agencies to define their objectives, which 19 of the 21 agencies met. (Defense was late and State never filed a list of objectives.)

In the first year of MBO, OMB let the agencies select their own objectives and their own mechanisms for monitoring program accomplishment. By April 1974, 18 of the 21 agencies had established such mechanisms.

After President Nixon resigned in August 1974, President Gerald Ford endorsed the 172 objectives formulated by the agencies for the second year of MBO. However, Roy Ash and some key assistants left shortly after Nixon did, and federal MBO began to change emphasis. The new Deputy Director of OMB, Paul O'Neill, wanted to be more selective in applying MBO, rather than tracking hundreds of objectives throughout the entire federal bureaucracy. Political reporter Joel Havemann wrote in May 1976 that MBO was in "suspended animation . . . Federal . . . agencies have not been required to identify their most important objectives since fiscal year 1975, and they have not been meeting with OMB to report progress toward objectives."[22] Since President Carter introduced zero-base budgeting (ZBB) in the federal goverment in 1977, MBO has been supplanted by ZBB.

What conclusions can we draw about the impact of federal MBO? Joel Havemann wrote in 1974 that MBO had had little effect on middle managers and their subordinates.[23] Since the essence of MBO is decentralized discretion, lack of middle management involvement indicated a critical problem for federal MBO. In addition, OMB itself, or, more properly, its budget examiners, often continued to work as if MBO did not exist. At this critical central staff level, then, MBO was not integrated with other ongoing management systems.

Ralph C. Bledsoe of the Federal Executive Institute, a training center for federal employees, stated in 1975 that MBO had caused improvements in federal programs, but only slight ones. Among the problems he saw MBO encountering were agency resistance based on antagonism toward attempts to exert control from above, the latest management "fad," the goals of the Nixon and Ford administrations, increased visibility of line agency programs caused by MBO, and the changes necessitated by MBO.[24]

British political scientist Richard Rose identified five factors influencing the extent to which federal agencies implemented MBO.[25] These included previous experience with similar systems, support from the department head, agency size, whether agency objectives were easily quantifiable, and whether departments thought MBO would benefit them rather than OMB. Rose concluded that the prospects for strengthening MBO were dim, because of the technical and political obstacles discussed in later sections of this chapter. Yet he concluded that the cost of MBO was relatively low ($6 million annually), that friction between OMB and line agencies was also low, and that MBO was not an unrealistic attempt to improve federal management. While Rose's assessment is the best overall picture we have of federal MBO efforts, there is unfortunately no comprehensive factual study of MBO impact in the federal government. This fact says volumes about the motives of some MBO proponents, who ask the onlooker to accept MBO as an article of faith. While a few isolated studies of specific MBO impact indicate that MBO has indeed had positive results,[26] we cannot accurately assess its total impact. In any case, as the reader should note, the federal example is not a model to follow, given the mixed motives of Nixon's MBO managers. Certainly federal MBO was not guided solely by Theory Y precepts. Such a future effort might achieve superior results.

State Government MBO

At the state level, individual departments or agencies are more likely to have used MBO than has the state government as a whole. For example, the Wisconsin Department of Health and Social Services instituted an MBO system in 1970. Writing in 1974, Bruce Faulkner, the budgeting chief of the department's Bureau of Planning and Analysis, argued that MBO does not have to be applied across the board to be useful. Not only was MBO not used in all Wisconsin State agencies, it was not used in all divisions of the Health and Social Services Department. We agree with Faulkner's contention, because decentralization is the logic of MBO. Individual managers can use MBO to improve their divisions' operation, regardless of whether anyone else in the organization does the same.[27]

Dennis E. Butler, Personnel Director of the Pennsylvania State Department of Environmental Resources, became interested in MBO right after the department was established in January 1971. Among the achievements he credits to MBO are doubling the number of students taught per staff member in the training division and organizing a new personnel development team without adding any employees. Butler says that while installing MBO is not without its trouble and turmoil, "it's the 'only way to run a railroad.' At least it's far ahead of what's in second place."[28]

These two examples do not make a case for MBO, because we have to accept at face value the authors' claims that MBO works the way the textbooks say it's supposed to. Unfortunately, unearthing systematic information about use and impact of MBO at the state government level is even more difficult than investigating federal MBO.[29]

Local Government MBO

Multitudes of municipalities have adopted MBO. New Orleans, Louisiana, installed it in 1973; and Little Rock, Arkansas; Overland Park, Kansas; Fort Worth, Texas; Virginia Beach, Virginia; Pasadena, California; St. Petersburg, Florida, and Seattle, Washington are among the local governments employing MBO. Cities ranging in size from New York City to Gobbler's Nob have taken a crack at MBO. While we examine the experience of one county government department in more detail in the case study later in this chapter, we survey here an illustrative local experience with MBO.

Fort Worth, Texas, set up MBO in 1972, and tied it directly to the budgetary process. Budget examiners now review budget requests in light of the statements of objectives provided with the requests. The examiners make recommendations based on their opinion of whether objectives are realistic and whether the departments have the resources to reach their objectives. A slow and careful approach has been taken in implementing MBO, rather than trying to establish it across the board in one year as a crash program, according to Budget Director William B. Gordon.[30]

In Fort Worth, department heads meet quarterly with the city manager, who is the city's chief executive. Director Gordon claims this process has enabled all involved to see problem areas better. Communications between department heads and the manager have improved as well. MBO has enabled city officials to identify duplication of effort and program results. Drawbacks include the tendency of some departments to get lost in a paperwork shuffle because they focus on MBO process rather than purpose. And, not surprisingly, Gordon notes that "it is extremely difficult to make MBO type decisions in a political environment." Gordon claims that department heads are "generally enthusiastic about MBO" because it was implemented gradually rather than being imposed by overnight edict from above. Figure 5–5 is a Fort Worth MBO plan.

This example is intended more as an illustration of local government use

FIGURE 5-5. ACTIVITY SUMMARY, CITY OF FORT WORTH, TEXAS

411

ACTIVITY TITLE	ACCOUNT NUMBER	DEPARTMENT
CUSTOMER ACCOUNTS & COLLECTIONS	016-60300	WATER AND SEWER

RESOURCES	ACTUAL 1974-75	ADOPTED BUDGET 1975-76	PROPOSED BUDGET 1976-77	ADOPTED BUDGET 1976-77
Allocations	-	-	$548,527	
Authorized Positions	-	-	25.25	

ACTIVITY DESCRIPTION:

The Customer Accounts and Collections Activity is responsible for administering office procedures related to the billing of and collecting from water customers. Functions of this activity include processing bills, checking accounts, providing customer service and information, and transmitting information to the Meter Shop concerning installing, removing, and exchanging water meters.

The 48.5 employees and related expenses previously reflected in the combined Water and Sewer Customer Accounts and Collection Activity are re-allocated into two accounts on a 50 percent Water, 50 percent Sewer basis.

Additional appropriations for this activity are partially due to the addition of two account clerks to handle the additional billing steps required with the separation of the water and sewer funds. Also, increased appropriations for anticipated postal rate increases and increased data processing charges account for some of the additional appropriations.

ACTIVITY GOALS:

To promote an effective public relations program by providing immediate response to customer requests for service and by processing customer bills and collections in an accurate and efficient manner, additionally, to insure equal employment opportunities for women and minorities within the Water and Sewer Department.

1976-77 OBJECTIVES:

To continue to improve customer relations by maintaining present average time required to process customer requested service through the use of on-line computer teleprocessing system.

To insure that each customer receives an accurate water bill through continued improvement in our computer analysis procedures on number of rechecks required.

To continue working toward meeting standards of employment as set forth by the Affirmative Action Program.

To maintain level of staff training sessions to insure that each employee understands policies and procedures.

To maintain present level of lost time and vehicular accidents through continued emphasis on safety program.

To maintain equitable distribution of water costs to each customer by reducing unauthorized water usage through investigation of all inactive accounts showing consumption.

To increase the accurate systematic monthly processing, billing, collecting and accounting of all water customers.

MEASURES OF EFFICIENCY AND/OR EFFECTIVENESS:	Actual 1974-75	Estimate 1975-76	Target 1976-77
Average time required to process all customer requests	5 minutes	4-5 minutes	4-5 minutes
Number of rechecks required	65,359	62,000	60,000
Minorities employed (percent)	25.0%	23.0%	29.0%
Females employed (percent)	85.0%	84.0%	76.0%
Staff training sessions held	54	50	50
Lost-time and vehicular accidents	0	0	0
Percent of inactive accounts showing consumption investigated	70%	100%	100%
Number of water meters billed, collected and balanced	1,380,300	1,391,650	1,406,940

123

of MBO than a conclusive summary of its impact at the local level. Again, we lack such studies, which will hopefully be forthcoming.

TECHNICAL PROBLEMS AND HOW TO MINIMIZE THEM

A basic problem in implementing MBO is verifying whether or not objectives have been attained. Since 1976 the New York City Highway Department has installed MBO on an experimental basis.[31] One of the objectives of its MBO action plan is to fill a certain number of potholes per month, but department managers have no way to run an independent check to see if the number of holes reported filled have indeed been filled. Even more difficult to ascertain is the quality of the job done. Will the repair last a year or just a month? Short of doubling the number of department employees by creating a huge force of inspectors, there is no completely satisfactory way for managers to verify reports.

The history of administration is replete with false reports of program effectiveness. Haroun El-Raschid, a Turkish sultan of the twelfth century, used to disguise himself and walk around the capital to check on the status of public works, and to find out what ordinary citizens thought about his administration. As the German army was pushed back by the Russians at the end of World War II, some field commanders gave Hitler misleadingly optimistic reports in the hope that they would avoid angering him with bad news. South Vietnamese officials soon became aware that the U.S. Department of Defense thrived on statistical reports of the war during the 1960s, and the South Vietnamese manufactured data which would make the Americans happy.

These examples can be multiplied a millionfold, for they illustrate a classic stumbling block in administration which has no easy solution. But the best general strategy to minimize the problem is to establish a Theory Y ambience. If employees participate in setting goals and believe that these goals are appropriate, they will be less likely to file misleading reports. But if the goals are merely dictated from above, workers will use their ingenuity to beat the system and protect themselves. The New York City MBO experiment attempts to decentralize power, thus giving managers at all levels more authority to carry out their duties. While it is too early to judge the success of this effort, such decentralization is an integral part of the Theory Y approach. It represents a vote of confidence in the ability of managers to get the job done. The only alternative to such an approach is close Theory X inspection, which breeds resentment and stifles positive commitment to the task.

Most authorities on MBO agree that it takes several *years* for MBO to become fully operational.[32] This comprehensive results-oriented approach, which encompasses planning, implementation, and evaluation, is too complex and multifaceted to be installed and run smoothly overnight. When first operated, even machines such as computers confront problems and must go through a "debugging" period. Naturally, management systems involving human beings with different attitudes, values, and abilities must go through an even longer debugging period. Further, MBO is a learning experience, and learning something both new and important takes time. Preconceived ideas interfere with our ability to implement a new system. Some habitual practices must be unlearned in a trial-and-error process which takes time. In addition, MBO must be coordinated with other organizational subsystems, a multiyear task in almost all organizations. Thus, MBO will inevitably take a good while to operate. But managers can minimize the amount of additional *unnecessary* time required for implementation by making clear that the organization is committed to MBO, and by sincerely striving to create a Theory Y atmosphere. In these ways the organization will be able to harness maximum energy to the MBO effort.

MBO is not free, unfortunately. A substantial number of resources, particularly employee work-hours, must be invested in it. To ensure that unnecessary expenditure is minimized, the procedures recommended for estimating the period of time necessary to acquire a fully functioning MBO system should be followed. For time is money. The extra cost of MBO should be viewed as an investment that will more than pay for itself in increased effectiveness, but there is no point in covering up the fact that the investment costs resources. In Bruce Faulkner's words, "it won't work if there is no staff to run it. . . . [MBO] has functioned well where there has been a heavy dose of planning staff time injected to coordinate, promote, and move it along and has not functioned well when and where staff attention to these functions has been minimal."[33]

Flexibility is essential to MBO. If MBO procedures become overly structured and rigid, the system will break down. For example, the Wisconsin Department of Health and Social Services originally designated MBO as an *annual* process, congruent with the budgetary process. But after it was realized that many objectives were likely to be achieved in less than a year, while some would take more than a year, MBO was redesignated as an *operational* process.[34] MBO action plans were given whatever timetable seemed appropriate, regardless of the annual budget cycle.

Morrisey warns that there will be a "disenchantment period" after MBO efforts are begun.[35] This period usually occurs after about six months, when the novelty of MBO has disappeared. Some objectives now look like they will not be achieved, and managers realize that MBO is a long-term approach, not a panacea that yields quick results.

Disenchantment can be minimized by several approaches which should be part of any MBO implementation plan. MBO is a dynamic process in which action plans should constantly be adjusted on the basis of the latest data available. Means and methods of making such adjustments include group progress reviews scheduled as an integral part of MBO; a no-holds-barred frank dialogue with top executives; and problem-solving "clinics" conducted by managers. While these regular reappraisals will not make everyone happy, they should reduce disappointment with MBO.

In the previous chapter, we mentioned that some organizations may bring in an outside consultant to help in formulating a plan of action. As George

126   Management by Objectives (MBO)

Berkley, a former government official and current public administration scholar, has noted, "Too often the consultant is hired for a certain study, does it, and then is sent on his way. The agency should, instead, make sure that he plays a role in putting the proposal into effect."[36] Indeed, the consultant may be able to play a key part in reducing disenchantment by articulating the experience other organizations have had with MBO and their eventual success.

Another frequent frustration encountered by MBO is the problem of jurisdiction. Two or more agencies or their subdivisions may both be operating in the same area at the same time, producing duplication or a standoff. Morrisey asks "What's the point in planning your work if some other organization is going to undo everything you have done already?"[37] Morrisey answers his own question by first recommending a clear statement of goals and responsibilities to lay all the issues on the table. In this way, both the "competing" agency and the chief executive, if necessary, can be made aware of the way an agency defines its role. Second, before action is taken, statements of objectives should be shared with other agencies that might be affected by them. Third, action plans should include steps to coordinate operations with other agencies operating in the same area. While one would have to be extraordinarily naive to believe that these actions would change interagency conflict into harmonious serenity, they should minimize the conflict as much as possible.

An additional problem encountered by MBO is faulty communications, found especially in larger organizations. Oftentimes managers will hear from an outside source such as a reporter or legislator about a problem in the organization, or find out on Tuesday that there is a problem which should have been solved by Monday at the latest. What can be done to implement action plans under such conditions?

Morrisey stresses that regularly scheduled progress reviews between superior and subordinate will help to dispel much of the communication distortion.[38] This periodic review is essential to MBO if the plan is to be successfully implemented, because only through such reviews can each party gather the information needed to stay on top of implementation.

Carroll and Tosi emphasize that many managers do not provide enough feedback to their subordinates. These managers hold group staff meetings and consider them adequate progress reviews, but their subordinates rarely do. Superiors must tell each subordinate on a one-to-one basis how they feel about the individual's work; otherwise, subordinates will not get all the information they need. This evaluation cannot be done in a group session, because it might seem critical or could embarrass the subordinate, since co-workers are looking on. Progress review must be personalized if it is to be truly effective two-way communication.[39] In this way, MBO sets up its own communication channels to avoid being trapped by the faulty communication system in the organization. Note that if this system were to follow MBO principles, communication would improve markedly.

A classic problem which can plague MBO and the other results-oriented approaches covered in this book is what Odiorne calls the quantitative fallacy. This pathology, already noted in Chapter 2, compels the victim to ignore phenomena that cannot be quantified. One firm which introduced MBO gave out awards for achievement at year's end, recognizing only those with precisely measurable outcomes. Ignored were a great improvement in company-community relations and a general drop in employee hostility to management. Furthermore, the manager who got the most MBO awards had broken faith with union leaders, who now vowed revenge for next year; fired two promising subordinates whose competence threatened him; and neglected equipment maintenance to show "savings." The quantitative fallacy caused top management to reward a manager who was crippling the organization.[40]

A final problem to be aware of in implementing MBO is the necessity to limit the number of objectives to a critical few. Public administration professor David S. Brown has advocated, tongue in cheek, SLO—System of Limited Objectives.[41] Only high-priority items should be included—or management, lost in a sea of paper, will equate objectives involving use of paper clips with objectives involving the prevention of polio. Such was the case in the Wisconsin Department of Health and Social Services. When the number of objectives being monitored declined because some had been achieved, a search was begun to find new ones. "As a result, objectives have occasionally been established which are only of secondary importance."[42] Quantity must never be confused with quality.

POLITICAL PROBLEMS AND HOW TO MINIMIZE THEM

Managerial Resistance to MBO

It would be extraordinarily unusual to install a new management system without a hitch. If managers are told that they will have to manage in a new manner, they are going to resist some or all of these changes, consciously or unconsciously. In fact, the better the job of management they have done or think they have done, the more likely they will be to resist a new system like MBO. After all, if they feel they are doing a good job, why should they want to change?[43] Managerial resistance to MBO should be anticipated so that it can be dealt with. Otherwise, the implementation of MBO is going to be all blood, sweat, toil, and tears. Some commonly encountered reasons for managerial resistance to MBO are catalogued below.[44]

A full-fledged formally structured MBO system requires training for those who will use it, as we have previously mentioned. Managers cannot simply implement the system overnight. And veteran managers may resent having to be trained to work in the new system. Carroll and Tosi found that managerial complaints such as "I've always managed this way. Why do I have to spend time in training? . . . My people know what is expected" were commonplace.[45] The best way to deal with these complaints is to explain to the managers, in the training sessions themselves, what the benefits of MBO are likely to be for both them and the organization. At the same time, the flexibility of MBO should be stressed: If an action plan is not working, managerial advice can lead to changes in the plan. If managers understand that MBO will give them much more discretion and freedom in managing, they will be much more likely to take this particular problem in stride.

Another frequent cause of managerial resistance involves the manager's relationships with subordinates. For example, a manager may argue that subordinates are not competent enough to implement MBO. But if the underlying causes of managerial resistance can be analyzed, it may be found that the real reason for resistance is fear of losing control. Managers may feel that they are no longer real managers if their subordinates exercise greatly increased discretion under MBO. This kind of problem is not easily solved. Perhaps the best way to try to sell MBO to managers is to ask them to see the results achieved by MBO after the system has run for a while. Managers should be reminded that they will get much of the credit if the effectiveness and efficiency of their employees improve as a result of MBO. Unfortunately, some long-term veteran managers will probably not be able to make the shift from Theory X to Theory Y. After all, a whole life's habits are not easily discarded in late middle age. But many managers will be able to make the change, even if it takes time.

Another cause of managerial resistance indicates again how crucial it is to create a Theory Y ambience. One study of several hundred managers found that they felt forced to endorse what they considered unrealistic or inappropriate objectives.[46] The managers felt that if they expressed their true feelings, top management would think they could not, or did not want to, handle the job and would downgrade them accordingly. Managers also felt handicapped in determining objectives and action plans, compared to MBO planners. It is easy to see how this situation occurred. Change usually causes anxiety, because the stable structure of the past is taken away. If this anxiety—which need be only short-lived when installing MBO—is compounded by faulty communication, MBO is in trouble. In the case just cited, management either did not try or tried unsuccessfully to create a Theory Y atmosphere which would allow for frank talk among managers and MBO planners. A manager who feels that an action plan will not work should be encouraged to explain the reasons for her or his opinion. If the manager is afraid to state these reasons, Theory X still reigns supreme, and MBO will not be able to yield the dividends it is designed to give. Establishing a Theory Y atmosphere is easier said than done, but one crucial step is making clear—by actions as well as words—that candor will be rewarded and not punished.

Morrisey has noted several frequent frustrations encountered by government agencies attempting to implement MBO, and has offered advice about how to deal with these obstacles.[47]

One general rule of government is that agencies are headed by people who have short tenure in office. This means that a champion of MBO may be replaced by someone who does not care about it at all. While admitting that this is a frustration, Morrisey argues that the key to MBO is its decentralized nature. That is, it can be used by individual managers to run their own divisions regardless of whether any other part of the organization is using it. While MBO would achieve maximum results if an entire department of transportation used it, the manager of the ferry boat division could use it on his own to strive most effectively to meet the objectives set in his division. Furthermore, the new commissioner of transportation would be more likely to look with favor on the ferryboat manager than upon other managers who were not achieving the same kinds of results.

Another closely related problem occurs when there is a lack of external support (usually meaning support from the chief executive's office or the legislature) for MBO.[48] The chances for innovative results-oriented management systems are maximized when they are supported not only by the top management of the department but also by the legislature and chief executive. Such support is crucial because the legislature and chief executive can usually reward or punish an agency when appropriating funds or authorizing new programs for it. Unfortunately, there is not much that MBO proponents can do beyond trying to sell MBO to the chief executive and legislature by stressing the results it can achieve in government. Whether these officials will buy MBO on this basis is another question.

Another problem posed by legislators is that such solons may not be interested in MBO, especially in election years. They may want a project to show their constituents, rather than a carefully planned program. For example, a representative who can point to a park that he or she has set up in the district is more likely to interest constituents than one who stresses overall work on a city, state, or nationwide park system. And this park may be one that park planners feel is inappropriate or should not be included in an MBO system for parks. While there is no way to eliminate this problem entirely, Morrisey argues that agencies using MBO have some positive bargaining points with the legislature. After all, they can point to a clear statement of goals, an action plan, and understandable criteria for measurement. Morrisey suggests that a well thought out action plan will include steps to gain legislative approval. While no agency is going to win every legislative battle, this approach should increase its chances for victories.

The current period is one of increasingly tight budgets. This poses problems for MBO, for what if someone's thorough job of MBO planning is upset by a chief executive and legislature who are cutting funds to the bone? Morrisey argues that this predicament can be made more bearable if managers do not set up action plans which use 100 percent of anticipated funds. He is not advocating budget "padding," but taking into account that all action plans will undergo some adjustment as they are implemented. Some funds have to be allocated for contingencies, whether or not they are so designated formally in the budget submitted to the chief executive and legislature. In fact, this kind of MBO planning will minimize the problems caused by tight budgets. The MBO plan will identify priorities among objectives, so that less urgent action plans can be shelved until more funds become available later on. MBO minimizes the pain inherent in such trade-offs.

Another set of obstacles to output-oriented management is the barrier erected by civil service systems, lockstep wage increases, and employee unions. Firing an incompetent employee in a civil service system may rank as one of the labors of Hercules, and rewarding extraordinary performance through promotion and salary increase may be just as difficult. While lengthier analysis will be devoted to this topic in following chapters, suffice it to say here that our general approach to employee motivation is Theory Y. If employees are given the authority to do the job and they know they have the full support of their supervisor to do it, then—and only then—is their full potential likely to be unleashed.

CASE STUDY:
THE PASSAIC COUNTY, N.J., PROSECUTOR'S OFFICE[49]

This sketch of how one division of an agency has used MBO over a one-year period is intended to illustrate some of the practical payoffs and pitfalls of MBO. It demonstrates how MBO will not obtain pristine perfection, but is nonetheless very valuable.

Passaic County, New Jersey, is located about 15 miles due west of New York City. Principally urban, the county has 500,000 residents and a very high rate of all incidences of crime. Before it was reorganized in June 1975, the county prosecutor's office had been written about in newspapers and national magazines as representing law enforcement at its worst. Lacking equipment, adequate and appropriate office space, adequate employee salaries, and professional management, the agency was ineffective. "The office was a haven for political appointees who had little or no law enforcement experience and background. . . . Permeating all was the stench of political corruption."[50]

Burrell Ives Humphreys, the new prosecutor, carried out a series of wide-ranging reforms to change this negative environment. Of interest to us are attempts to use MBO in this office. The goals of the prosecutor's office are set by state statutes. In addition, the New Jersey State Department of Law and Public Safety, which supervises the country prosecutors, has endorsed the goals of the National Advisory Commission on Standards and Goals for Police, Courts, and Corrections. Specific objectives within the office are set by Prosecutor Humphreys himself, who is reported to encourage a Theory Y atmosphere of free and frank discussion with his staff before he sets an objective. While the prosecutor is not a proponent of MBO, one division of the office uses MBO, and MBO concepts are used in applying to the federal Law Enforcement Assistance Administration (LEAA) and the State Law Enforcement Planning Agency (SLEPA) for funds. Indeed, these agencies require such a format—as Figure 5-6, detailing the SLEPA grant application instructions, and Figure 5-7, the SLEPA narrative report, indicate. Sample objectives formulated by the prosecutor's office to use in grant-assisted programs include:

1. The period between arrest and grand jury hearing for persons jailed after arrest shall not exceed 30 days. (The national standard is 60 days.)
2. Increase individual staff prosecutor caseloads by 5 percent.
3. Increase the rate of successful prosecution (defendant found guilty) by 2 percent.

FIGURE 5-6. STATE LAW ENFORCEMENT PLANNING AGENCY GRANT APPLICATION INSTRUCTIONS

Each of the following attachments must be included as part of the application: (Note: If this is not an initial application for this project, refer to the continuation application information at the bottom of this page before proceeding).

ATTACHMENT ONE: Description of Project

Each of the following sections must be included as part of this attachment:

A. The Problem
B. Goals
C. Objectives
D. Project Activities
E. Project Management
F. Personnel

G. Brief Personnel Biographies or Job Specifications
H. Participating Agencies
I. Project Evaluation
J. Alternative Methods
K. Assumption of Costs
L. Civil Rights Compliance

ATTACHMENT TWO: Budget Detail/Budget Explanation

ATTACHMENT THREE: Non-Supplanting Certification

ATTACHMENT FOUR: Negative Environmental Impact Statement

REFER TO THE CURRENT APPLICANTS GUIDE FOR DETAILED INSTRUCTIONS OUTLINING THE COMPLETION OF ATTACHMENTS ONE AND TWO ABOVE. INSTRUCTIONS FOR ATTACHMENTS THREE AND FOUR ARE CONTAINED WITHIN THIS APPLICATION AND CAN BE FOUND ON EACH RESPECTIVE ATTACHMENT.

CONTINUATION APPLICATION. In the case of a continuation application, the applicant must present an overview of the activities funded with the previous year's grant, and an assessment of project results supported by data. This overview should be developed in line with the stated goals and objectives of the previous project, and should be presented in addition to each of the Attachments referred to above. Continuation applications should be submitted approximately three months prior to expiration of the preceding project.

SLEPA 101.2

A federal grant was obtained to hire an office manager/business administrator to deal with such matters as the budget, procurement, record keeping and security, and selection and supervision of non-legal personnel. The office manager, Edward T. Danckwerth, who was hired in March 1976, has to a large degree begun implementing MBO in his sphere of activity. Interviewed after a year in the job, he noted that installing MBO was not an easy task, but that the measurable and definable results were well worth the efforts.

The office manager currently sets the objectives of his staff, but allows them to formulate their own action plans. One current example occurred with the recent hiring of a chief of security, a position the office had previously lacked. The office manager gave this new employee and the police legal advisor the broad objectives of formulating narrative instructions for local police departments and internal personnel handling evidence. He also gave them a deadline, but let them decide how to proceed. Their work would be subject to review and possible change at regular intervals, but no one would be looking over their shoulders. Some other programs are a central supply program, case file control, paper flow, word-processing manual, statistical reports, and the creation of an office policy and procedure manual.

The office manager noted that "selected" MBO implementation in the office had just finished its first year, and that it was a long-range program. He expressed the hope that in the future employees could begin to set their own objectives, but felt that the full maturation process would take place only after a constant bombardment of successfully implemented programs. The shift to MBO which has taken place to date was quite an adjustment for some staff persons who had never before used anything like it.

The office manager monitors progress toward objectives by keeping progress records and then going over them with employees. He has to be a salesperson and a humanist, rather than a despot, to get employees to accept his suggestions. One example is a new word-processing system designed to make more efficient use of secretaries. Under the system, assistant prosecutors dictate memos, letters, reports, and correspondence into recording equipment rather than directly to stenographers. After arranging for instruction in the techniques of machine dictation and further explaining the objectives of the new system, the office manager had the satisfaction of seeing the use of this new system triple in a two-month period. Specifically designed performance reports indicated the level of use by prosecutors. A detailed plan to implement the system was set out. All participants were trained. Employees were assured that no jobs would be lost because of the modern technology.

FIGURE 5-7. STATE LAW ENFORCEMENT PLANNING AGENCY QUARTERLY NARRATIVE REPORT

<table>
<tr>
<td>
STATE OF NEW JERSEY

STATE LAW ENFORCEMENT PLANNING AGENCY

QUARTERLY NARRATIVE REPORT
(Submit in Duplicate)
</td>
<td>
For SLEPA Use Only

Date Rec'd. _____

Analyst _____

Chief _____

Refer to _____

Comments Attached:
</td>
</tr>
</table>

Passaic County Prosecutor's Office   A-163-75
IMPLEMENTING AGENCY   SLEPA NO.

77 Hamilton Street   (201)525-5000
STREET ADDRESS   PHONE NO.

Paterson, New Jersey   07505
CITY   ZIP NO.

For Quarter:

Project Duration (if SLEPA approved extension, use latest date)

[X] January 1 to March 31   From February 1, 1976
[X] April 1 to June 30
[ ] July 1 to September 30   To   January 31, 1977
[ ] October 1 to December 31
[ ] Other/Final Report From February 1, to June 30, 1976

1. GOALS (List the goals from the body of the grant application). a) To establish policy guidelines and implement a system of prosecutorial case screening so that the public interest and justice is better served by early use of the prosecutor's discretionary authority. b) To improve the work flow in the prosecutor's office by refining case evaluation earlier in the criminal justice process. c) To reduce the detention time of persons accused of criminal activity by enabling the prosecutor to make speedier decisions regarding cases. d) To provide to each municipality in the County the presence of an assistant county prosecutor for the purposes of: case screening; representing the State at all arraignment or indictable complaints and preliminary hearings, including bail and sentence recommendations; advising whether a complaint should charge an indictable crime, or a disorderly persons offense; eliminating from the criminal process those complaints that do not merit such actions; and initiating supplementary investigations relating to the crime charged in the complaint.

2. OBJECTIVES (List the objectives from the body of the grant application). a) To work with the police legal advisor to inform the sheriff and police departments of the views of the Prosecutor on various crimes. Such efforts would instill cooperation between the police and prosecutor in the enforcement of the law. b) To select candidates for conditional discharge under the Controlled Dangerous Substance Act and other pre-trial intervention programs. c) To increase the effectiveness of the prosecutor's office by recommending personnel assignments based on case priority and difficulty. d) To have a system under the direct supervision of the Prosecutor, which would screen 100% of the complaints charging indictable crimes in Passaic County over the next twelve (12) months. To reduce the number of Grand Jury remands to 5% over the next twelve (12) months. To reduce the number of No Bill action by the Grand Jury to 10% over the next twelve (12) months.

SLEPA 106

134

FIGURE 5–7 (cont.)

3. ACTIVITIES (Specific activities related to achievement of goals and objectives) **The Case Screener and Evaluator Unit will be under the supervision of the Prosecutor. Two assistant prosecutors will be assigned to the Case Screener and Evaluator Unit. Each assistant county prosecutor so assigned will be responsible for the following functions: a. The Case Screener and Evaluator shall receive and review complaints or requests for prosecution from police or the** public and make decisions as to further action needed, including the issuance of warrants where required. The Case Screener will establish guidelines as to what factors are considered when deciding whether to prosecute. These guidelines will be circulated to other members of the Prosecutor's Office, the County Sheriff, and other police units located within the County. An example of such guidelines might be those proposed by the American Bar Association in its Standards on prosecution and defense. These include:

a. the prosecutor's reasonable doubt that the accused is in fact guilty;
b. the extent of the harm caused by the offense;
c. the disproportion of the authorized punishment in relation to the particular offense of the offender;
d. possible improper motives of a complainant;
e. prolonged non-enforcement of a statute, with community acquiescence;
f. reluctance of the victim to testify;
g. cooperation of the accused in the apprehension or conviction of others;
h. availability and likelihood of prosecution by another jurisdiction.

(Activities cont'd on last two pages)

4. SUMMARY OF PROJECT PROGRESS (Relate to goals, objectives and activities, highlighting significant accomplishments and problems. Quantify where possible).

From February to June 1 arrangements were made for the implementation of the project. Starting in June Assistant Prosecutors Rocco and Abdy screened every case coming into the Courts of Paterson, Clifton, Passaic, Wayne and other smaller municipal courts in the County. In screening these cases we made determinations as to whether a particular complaint should be sent to the Grand Jury or whether it should be downgraded to a disorderly persons offense. When downgrading a complaint a recommendation was made as to the sentence to be imposed. When making such a recommendation the defendant's age, past record and the chances for successful rehabilitation were considered.

SLEPA 106.2

135

The office manager noted several frustrations in implementing MBO. Since the entire office is not on MBO, top officials can ignore his MBO-based requests and suggestions, if they desire. While the prosecutor has given him carte blanche to use MBO within his own sphere, this does not mean that he necessarily gets managers in other divisions to use it. The problems of implementing MBO seem to go beyond the immediate office of the prosecutor. The county legislature does not vibrate to the MBO wavelength, and probably has not had the opportunity to understand the concept itself. The time frame of the legislature does not extend beyond the next election, and the usual political trade-offs sometimes conflict with an MBO approach. In spite of these troubles, the office manager feels that the results produced by MBO are worth the work involved. One of the office manager's goals is to apply an MBO approach to as many administrative programs as possible which are not in the daily limelight, over the course of a two-year period. Top administrators in and out of the office will then recognize the importance of a programmed approach and apply the MBO techniques to other areas.

Questions

1. Do you believe that this application of MBO is an example of a model MBO system? Explain your reasons.

2. Do you believe that this application of MBO is worth the effort involved? Explain your reasons.

3. Does the fact that only one division of this office uses MBO weaken or invalidate MBO's utility for this office, in your opinion? Explain your reasons.

4. Do you think full-scale implementation of MBO could be speeded up? Explain your reasons.

PROBLEMS AND PROSPECTS FOR MBO

MBO is being used increasingly by American state and local governments, even though it is not being pushed as strenuously at the federal level as it was in the 1973–1975 period. The chief advantage of MBO is its flexibility. It can be used in one division of an agency or throughout an entire government. Not all of its component parts need to be implemented at once to begin an MBO program that will yield benefits. We feel that MBO is a management approach which can yield great dividends.

Nevertheless, there has been some trenchant criticism of MBO, which we must consider here. Harry Levinson, a specialist in industrial psychology, has argued that MBO is usually counterproductive.[51] He sees MBO as a potential trap for managers. A manager who sets his own objectives and then is evaluated on how well he achieves them is like a rat in a maze who is given only two alternatives, according to Levinson. The rat, it is assumed, will choose the alternative he is given a food reward for selecting; but just to make sure of this, the experimenter starves the rat. Levinson says that MBO differs only in that it allows the manager himself "to determine his own bait from a limited range of choices. Having done so, the MBO process assumes that he will (a) work hard to get it, (b) be pushed internally by reason of his commitment, and (c) make himself responsible to the organization for doing so."[52] Managers thus feel increasing resentment, guilt for neglecting job duties not in their objectives, and resistance to pressure to meet new more difficult goals.

Levinson believes that MBO as generally practiced misses "the whole human point." Objectives can tap human potential only if they relate to the innermost personal needs and wants of employees. Levinson cites examples of successful employees who have resigned because they felt that their organizations were only using them to meet goals, and considered them otherwise expendable.

Happily, Levinson does not believe that the situation is hopeless. In fact, his remedy is the same as ours: large doses of Theory Y. But he argues that most MBO is self-defeating because it is *not* based on Theory Y. If MBO is not a process that develops from the bottom up, with real instead of pro forma participation, it is not going to work.

In addition, we should emphasize that it is easy to bungle the implementing of MBO or any of the other results-oriented approaches described in this book. It is a lot easier to talk about Theory Y than it is to create a Theory Y atmosphere. The job will be bungled if a careful survey of the terrain of the agency is not made. Agency managers and MBO implementers must be sure that they understand the attitude of employees to their work. Otherwise, MBO will appear confusing, frightening, or frustrating to them. MBO implementers, in other words, must be sensitive to nuances of human behavior. One government official has related to the author the story of how he had an outside consultant come in to study his purchasing department to make some MBO-type recommendations. But the consultant was so inept at communicating with human beings that he offended and antagonized people in that department. Since future MBO would now be associated in employees' minds with this unsympathetic figure, the agency was worse off than before it had brought the consultant in. Time and effort would have to be used to repair the damage wrought.

The same official stressed that MBO cannot be unduly hurried, especially if employees are not highly skilled or professional. They need an extensive period of training and orientation before they can pick up the MBO ball and run with it. And training should be a permanent, periodically used part of any MBO program.[53] But if this task is performed well, employees may respond so effectively that their managers will be amazed.

What this all boils down to is the frustrating fact that Theory Y is easier to talk about than to establish. Every agency has a hidden agenda, or a subculture of values which are not performance oriented. MBO implementers have to be superb at communication and personal relationships so that they can gradually wean employees away from this hidden set of values and interest them in output-oriented management. Even without other obstacles, such a task will take a long time and will often involve exquisite anguish. But there is no other road to travel to a functioning MBO system. And such a system—while it will greatly aid management—is not a panacea for all that ails an organization and should never be sold as one. The only result will be disillusionment and less effectiveness.

NOTES

1. For instance, see Steven D. Norton, "Management by Results in the Public Sector," *Public Productivity Review* 2 (Fall 1976): 20–31.

2. Wayne A. Kimmel, William R. Dougan, and John R. Hall, *Municipal Management and Budget Methods: An Evaluation of Policy Related Research, Final Report, Vol. 1: Summary and Synthesis* (Washington, D.C.: Urban Institute, 1974).

3. Ibid., pp. 29–30.

4. George L. Morrisey, *Management by Objectives and Results in the Public Sector* (Reading, Mass.: Addison-Wesley, 1976), pp. 203–7.

5. J. M. Ivanevich, J. H. Donnelly, and L. Lyon, "A Study of the Impact of MBO on Perceived Need Satisfaction," *Personnel Psychology* 23 (1970): 139–51.

6. Stephen J. Carroll, Jr., and Henry L. Tosi, Jr., *Management by Objectives* (New York: Macmillan, 1973), pp. 52–54.

7. The rest of this section is based primarily on Morrisey, op. cit., pp. 105–69.

8. Morrisey, op. cit., pp. 122–48, discusses these three steps in detail.

9. George S. Odiorne, "MBO in State Government," *Public Administration Review* 36 (January–February 1976): 28–33, at 31.

10. Loc. cit.

11. Arthur H. Kuriloff, "An Experiment in Management: Putting Theory Y to the Test," *Personnel* 40 (November–December 1963): 8–17, at 12.

12. Morrisey, op. cit., p. 157.

13. Peter F. Drucker, *The Practice of Management* (New York: Harper & Row, 1954), pp. 133–35. Drucker is generally acknowledged as the originator of the MBO concept.

14. John W. Humble, *MBO in Action* (Maidenhead, Berkshire, Eng.: McGraw-Hill, 1970), p. 283.

15. Carroll and Tosi, op. cit., p. 107.

16. Ibid., p. 108.

17. George S. Odiorne, *Management Decisions by Objectives* (Englewood Cliffs, N.J.: Prentice-Hall, 1969), p. 140.

18. This section is based primarily on C. David Billings, "MBO in the Federal Government," in Robert T. Golembiewski et al., eds., *Public Administration*, 3rd ed. (Skokie, Ill.: Rand McNally 1976), pp. 71–92, and three articles by Joel Havemann: "OMB Begins Major Program to Identify and Attain Presidential Goals," *National Journal*, June 2, 1973, pp. 783–93; "OMB's MBO Produces Goals of Uneven Quality," *National Journal*, August 18, 1973, pp. 1201–10; and "Ford Endorses 172 Goals of MBO," *National Journal*, October 26, 1974, 1597–1605.

19. Nixon had reasons to believe this. See Joel D. Aberbach and Bert A. Rockman, "Clashing Beliefs within the Executive Branch: The Nixon Administration Bureaucracy," *American Political Science Review* 70 (June 1976): 456–68.

20. Frank P. Sherwood and William J. Page, Jr., "MBO and Public Management," *Public Administration Review* 36 (January–February 1976): 5–12, at 7.

21. For background, see ibid., and Frederick C. Mosher et al., *Watergate: Implications for Responsible Government* (New York: Basic Books, 1974); and Richard P. Nathan, *The Plot That Failed: Nixon and the Administrative Presidency* (New York: Wiley, 1975).

22. Joel Havemann, "Congress Tries to Break Ground Zero in Evaluating Federal Programs," *National Journal*, May 22, 1976, p. 706.

23. Joel Havemann, "OMB's MBO," *National Journal*, April 27, 1974, pp. 609–18.

24. Ralph C. Bledsoe, "Is MBO Working in the Public Sector?" *The Bureaucrat*, Occasional Papers Service, 1975, pp. 15–16.

25. Richard Rose, "Implementation and Evaporation: The Record of MBO," *Public Administration Review* 37 (January–February 1977): 64–71; and Richard Rose, *Managing Presidential Objectives* (New York: Free Press, 1976).

26. See Joseph E. DeSio and John E. Higgins, Jr., "The Management and Control of Case Handling, Office of the General Counsel, NLRB," *The Bureaucrat* 2 (Winter 1974): 385–94. Note, however, that this article reports on the use of MBO-type procedures in this agency before 1973.

27. Bruce Faulkner, "Policy Execution Using MBO: Lessons from a State Human Services Agency," paper presented at the National Conference of the American Society for Public Adminstration, 1974.

28. Dennis E. Butler, "The Evolution of MBO in a State Governmental Agency," in Morrisey, op. cit., pp. 249–60.

29. Claims like those of Fred Luthans that "the literature does contain a fair number of success stories of MBO in the public sector" (in his "How to Apply MBO," *Public Personnel Management*, March–April 1976, pp. 83–87, at 85) turn out to be based largely on superficial or hortatory studies.

30. Letter from William B. Gordon to the author, October 26, 1976.

31. Steven R. Weisman, "New Management System Tightens Beame's Control," *New York Times*, September 27, 1976, p. 1.

32. Morrisey, op. cit., 196; William L. Ginnido, "A View of MBO . . . From the Middle," *Civil Service Journal*, July–September 1975, pp. 13–17, at 17.

33. Faulkner, op. cit., p. 33.

34. Ibid., p. 12.

35. Morrisey, op. cit., p. 197.

36. George E. Berkley, *The Craft of Public Administration* (Boston: Allyn and Bacon, 1975), p. 367.

37. Morrisey treats this in both his book, op. cit., pp. 213–25, and his article, "MBO Questions and Answers," *Public Personnel Management*, March–April 1976, pp. 96–102.

38. Ibid.

39. Carroll and Tosi, op. cit., p. 58.

40. George S. Odiorne, *Management and the Activity Trap* (New York: Harper & Row, 1974), pp. 122–27.

41. David S. Brown, "MBO: Promise and Problems," *The Bureaucrat* 2 (Winter 1974): 413–20.

42. Faulkner, op. cit., p. 31.

43. Ibid., p. 28.

44. Carroll and Tosi, op. cit., pp. 49–52, is the source for these common troubles.

45. Ibid., p. 49.

46. Ibid., p. 68, footnote 6.

47. See note 37 above.

48. Cf. Faulkner, op. cit., p. 28.

49. This section is based primarily on John M. Burney, "MBO in the Prosecutor's Office," unpublished paper, December 1976.

50. *Annual Report of the Passaic County Prosecutor's Office*, June 23, 1975–June 23, 1976, pp. 4–5.

51. Harry Levinson, "Management by Whose Objectives?," *Harvard Business Review*, July–August 1970, pp. 125–34. See also Sherwood and Page, op. cit., pp. 9–11.

52. Levinson, op. cit., p. 128.

53. See Faulkner, op. cit., pp. 32–33.

6
Program
Evaluation

LEARNING OBJECTIVES

TO UNDERSTAND:

The difference between review and evaluation
Different types of results-oriented evaluation
How to reduce technical and political problems
Ethical concerns evaluators should consider

Evaluation is the moment of truth for output-oriented managers, because it is the way they discover how well their programs are doing. But this search for the truth can become as arduous as the quest for the Holy Grail, as we shall see below.

DEFINING EVALUATION

There is a large body of literature on evaluation concepts and procedures, and many definitions of the term. But most definitions of *evaluation* involve probing the impact of a program using predetermined criteria of success.[1] (These criteria are part of the planning process discussed in Chapter 2.) Federal program evaluator Joseph S. Wholey and colleagues have given a comprehensive definition of the purposes of evaluation which we will use in this chapter:

> Evaluation (1) assesses the effectiveness of an ongoing program in achieving its objectives, (2) relies on the principles of research design to distinguish a program's effects from those of other forces working on a situation, and (3) aims at program improvement through a modification of current operations.[2]

The reader should not blanch at this long definition, because we will go over each of its component parts in some detail in the next section.

141

What is the difference between the review process in management by objectives (MBO), discussed in the last chapter, and evaluation? The MBO review process is a form of *monitoring* intended to document whether goals and objectives are being attained. Evaluation goes beyond monitoring to try to determine if a program has caused the results observed, or to identify the program aspects which have caused success or failure.[3] Monitoring would indicate that the Grand Teton Dam had burst and flooded the countryside, where evaluation would try to explain *why* it had burst. Program evaluation is a more elaborate process than the usual MBO review. Because this evaluation is more careful, costly, and cumbersome, it is not likely to be part of a monthly review, though it may well utilize the same information as the review. Furthermore, MBO reviews often focus on the work of individual managers who set their own objectives. Program evaluation focuses on the total program.

Evaluation is logically integrated with MBO. At the same time, evaluation can be used independently of MBO or a planning process. While we recommend that evaluation be linked to planning or MBO, it is better to have evaluation alone than no evaluation at all.

IMPLEMENTING EVALUATION

Deciding the type of evaluation procedure to use is a bit like shopping for a new car. A bewildering array of alternatives, with different price tags and features, confronts the shopper. (Harry P. Hatry has even referred to one approach as the "Cadillac.")[4] In this section, we will examine several of these alternative approaches to evaluation.

The Controlled Experiment[5]

The experimental approach to evaluation is likely to give the most accurate picture of program accomplishment. Not surprisingly, it is also the most expensive and most difficult method of evaluation to implement.

The distinctive approach of the controlled experiment is the division of program clientele into two or more groups. Typically, the first, or *controlled*, group will have a service (e.g., garbage pickup or education) performed just as it has been in the past. The second, or *experimental*, group will be served in a new and different manner. At the end of a specified period, an investigation of the results of the two approaches will be made. It can then be determined which procedure picked up more garbage, or which group of students learned more. In this way, a judgment can be made about the quality of the alternatives.

For the experimental approach to work, the control and experimental groups have to be roughly equivalent. That is, it makes no sense to have a control group of very bright students contrasted with an experimental group of average or below-average students. The bright students will almost certainly do better than the other group, regardless of the type of teaching method used.

Likewise, if different approaches to garbage collection are applied in neighbor-hoods with greatly differing topography (flat ground and straight streets versus twisting and tortuous terrain), the results will be meaningless.

In implementing this approach, steps should be taken in the following order. First, the control and experimental groups should be selected in a scientifically random manner. This will assure that they are indeed comparable. (Random selection involves choosing a group in a manner which gives each person considered an equally good chance to be selected for the group. The simplest method is drawing names out of a hat, and there are several other more sophisticated and less clumsy methods.)[6] Next, the pre-experiment per-formance of each group should be measured according to the evaluation criteria (e.g., reading skill level or cleanliness of streets) established for the program. Third, the experimental program (e.g., teaching children with color TV as well as traditional methods) is applied to the experimental, but not the control group. Fourth, the experiment must be carefully monitored to detect anything that might bias the results. For example, program personnel working on the experiment might be very pro- or anti-experiment, compared to control group personnel. This kind of behavior must be changed through conferences with the personnel. But if sufficient change is impossible or comes too late, the problem must be acknowledged in the evaluation so that the two groups are not judged to have been equally insulated from extraneous events. Next, the per-formance of each group should be measured according to the evaluation criteria, after the experiment has run its course. This is the crucial and critical phase of the experiment: If better results are attained by the experimental rather than the control group, a promising new program approach may be in the works. If the opposite is true, it is time to go back to the old drawing board.

But before one can come to such definitive conclusions, two further checks are in order. First, the pre-experimental performance of each group should be compared to the postexperimental performance. This is the reason the pre-ex-perimental data were gathered in the first place. After all, even if the different groups are very similar, they will not be identical, so that a record of their exact performance is needed to make precise comparisons. For example, the conclu-sion that the experimental program produced a 5 percent decrease in fire department response time would be false if the squad in the experimental program already had a 6 percent faster response time than the squad in the control program.

The final check to be made is a search for causes of different performance between the experimental and control groups which lie outside the program. For example, if the traffic accident rate declines in an experimental area where a major road has been closed for repairs, the closed road, and not a new traffic enforcement program, may be responsible for the decline.

The experimental approach is a complex task. It is not for amateurs un-trained in procedures of experimental design, including statistical measure-ment and random selection. Likewise, higher cost and many problems investigated in later sections are associated with the controlled experiment. But it is the best of the evaluation procedures, because it is the only one which allows precise estimation of program impact.

The Quasi-Experiment

Quasi-experimental design is the next best thing to the controlled experiment. The quasi-experiment can be used when meaningful control or random selection are not possible. For example, parents or teachers may object to students being reshuffled into control and experimental groups, just as government employees may not want to be reshuffled.

Carol Weiss, an authority on evaluation, has argued that quasi-experimental designs are more than poorly executed experimental designs.[7] Instead, they have a definite logic, admitting what they do and do not control for. Thus, evaluators who proceed carefully can draw conclusions. One type of quasi-experiment is the nonequivalent control design,[8] which does not require random selection of subjects. Rather, it may utilize volunteers or self-selection. A drug treatment program, for instance, may ask for volunteers to try a new method of treatment. The volunteers would then be compared with a selected group, chosen from those in the program who did not volunteer. To get around the lack of random selection of each group, the groups would be matched as closely as possible on various performance measures, whether written tests or staff appraisals. The volunteer and nonvolunteer groups (which are called "comparison groups") would then be compared much as a control and experimental group would be.

As indicated, there are a number of shortcomings in the quasi-experiment, but a good quasi-experiment is inferior only to experimental procedure. For as we shall see below, several other methods of evaluation do not involve anything like this type of direct comparison.

Nonexperimental Approaches to Evaluation[9]

While all of the nonexperimental approaches examined here are based on comparisons of the results of new programs, they do not involve anything similar to a comparison of control and experimental groups. While inferior to the controlled experiment, they are much less difficult and costly to run and far better than no evaluation at all.

One approach is *before-and-after program comparison.* It compares program results before a new program was implemented and immediately afterwards. Changes in program results should be carefully scrutinized to see if conditions other than the new program caused them. After this step, an estimation of actual program impact can be made. Such as evaluation procedure was applied to Pennsylvania state prison vocational education programs in 1970. It was discovered after comparing pre- and postprison jobs and earnings that prison education had little or no effect.[10] The program was not achieving any positive results.

TABLE 6–1.   SUMMARY OF INDIANAPOLIS POLICE FLEET PLAN EFFECTS AND COSTS

A. Reported Crime, Clearance Rates and Traffic Accident Records,1969–1970.[a] Compared with Projections Based on Previous Trends

	Projected Result without Fleet Plan[b]	Actual Result with Fleet Plan	Percent Difference
Reported Crime (in numbers)			
Total Crime	21,978	22,451	+ 3
Larceny	9,458	10,996	+16[c]
Burglary	6,281	6,308	0
Robbery	1,294	1,207	− 7
Outdoor Crime Index	7,467	6,431	−14[c]
Purse Snatching	306	241	−21[c]
Street Robbery	820	762	− 7
Theft from Auto	2,420	2,378	− 2
Auto Theft	3,921	3,050	−22[c]
Clearance Rates (in percent)			
Total Crime	21	22	+ 5
Larceny	17	20	+18
Burglary	20	17	−15
Robbery	27	27	0
Auto Theft	23	26	+13
Vehicle Accidents (in numbers)			
Total Accidents	10,846	9,356	−14[c]
Killed	60	40	−33[c]
Injured	4,197	4,000	− 5

B. Cost of Fleet Plan Operation[d]

Initial Investment	$650,000
Subsequent Annual Cost	
Equipment Replacement	$200,000
Operating Expense	250,000
Total	$450,000

a. Based on the "Fleet-Plan year" comprising September, October, and November of 1969, and January, February, March, April, and May of 1970.
   b. Projection based on trends from 1963 through 1969, using months of "Fleet-Plan year."
   c. Indicates that change is significant according to standard statistical test.
   d. Full year cost; not Fleet-Plan year.

Source: Donald M. Fisk, *The Indianapolis Police Fleet Plan* (Washington, D.C.: Urban Institute, 1970), p. 2.

A second method is *time-trend projection of preprogram data versus actual postprogram data.* Unless some unanticipated events have intervened, the difference between actual program results and what was likely to have happened under the old program is assumed to be due to the new program. Table 6–1 illustrates the use of this approach in the Indianapolis Police Department. The program under examination involved having police officers drive patrol cars at all times, whether on or off duty, to see if crime would be deterred.

A third nonexperimental method is *comparisons with other jurisdictions not served by the program.* If a city health department initiates a new method of innoculation of the public against polio, it can compare its program results with those of other jurisdictions not using the program. If the city is found to be innoculating fewer people per cost-dollar than other cities, it may be time to redesign the program. Such an evaluation was made for the State of Connecticut after it implemented a strict traffic enforcement project in the 1950s. When traffic fatalities declined, evaluators measured the record in other states to make sure that something other than the new program had not caused the decline. The results, depicted in Figure 6–1, show that the program did have a positive impact.

FIGURE   6–1.   CONNECTICUT   AND   CONTROL   STATE   TRAFFIC FATALITIES (PER 100,000 POPULATION), 1952–1959

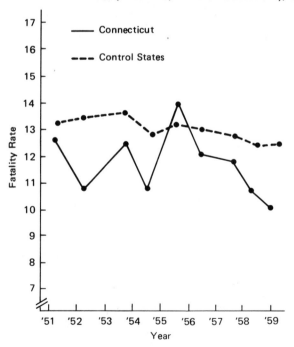

Note: Speeding crackdown program was introduced in
       FY 1955-56

Data Collection

Hatry calls data collection the "dirty job" of evaluation,[11] but notes that it is a crucial task which cannot be done haphazardly if the evaluation is to be a success. There are many possible sources of data, some of which we examine here.

Existing Records   The evaluator can draw on much data already in existence (pupil reading scores, police arrest records, etc.). Usually, however, it is necessary to dig further, putting together different information sources to come up with details on program cost, residence of clientele by neighborhood, and so on.

Unfortunately for the evaluator, procedures or definitions used in gathering data often change, so that reports from different years may not be directly comparable. The federal Census Bureau, for example, delights in changing the boundaries of its "census tracts" (neighborhoods within cities) from census to census, making it very difficult for analysts to measure the changes which have taken place in these neighborhoods.

Interviews   Existing records will usually provide only a fraction of the data needed for evaluation. More often than not, the evaluator will have to arrange to systematically interview certain categories of people.

One category is *persons who have left a government program,* whether it be health, education, or welfare. This is the only way to find out the long-term effect of the program on these individuals, since agencies usually do not keep records on their "alumni."

Another category is *those who use (or do not use) government services.* First, factual information can be gathered ("Do you use service X? How frequently? When?"). Second, and perhaps even more important, are questions framed to measure citizens' perception of the adequacy of certain services ("Does the sanitation department do a good job of garbage collection in your neighborhood? Explain").

In both cases, scientifically selected random samples of residents or clientele must be made, or the survey is likely to be inaccurate. This is no job for the dilettante. Better that the survey not be done than that it produce a false picture. (It is possible to conduct such surveys by telephone, which is much easier and less expensive for the agency.)[12] Figure 6–2 is part of such a survey dealing with urban transportation. It was designed to be administered face to face, since mail questionnaires are unlikely to be as accurate. They are never answered by 100 percent of the sample, which causes results to be biased. In most cases, no more than 100 people need to be interviewed to produce accurate findings.[13]

Professional Ratings   The technique of professional ratings is similar to one mentioned earlier in Chapter 2, on planning. Outside specialists can be

FIGURE 6–2.   EXCERPT FROM A CITY SERVICES QUESTIONNAIRE

Transportation[1]

Q14. How would you rate your overall satisfaction with the transportation in this city/county:

Excellent ____   Fair ____

Good   ____   Poor ____

Q15. How often have you used public transit in the last month? _____

[ONLY ASK Q16 IF USED PUBLIC TRANSIT]

Q16. As a rider, how would you rate the transit vehicles in this city/county on the following (comfort) factors:

a) Temperature/humidity: usually comfortable ____, occasionally uncomfortable ____, often uncomfortable ____, usually uncomfortable ____?

b) Crowdedness (peak hours): almost always get a seat ____, occasionally have to stand at least part of the way ____, usually have to stand at least part of the trip ____, usually have to stand all the way ____?

c) Noisiness: quiet ____, mostly quiet ____, fairly noisy ____, very noisy ____?

d) Cleanliness: clean ____, mostly clean ____, fairly dirty ____, very dirty ____?

e) Courteous of drivers: usually very courteous ____, fairly courteous ____, unpleasant ____?

f) Odors: no problem ____, occasional bothersome fumes or odors ____, usually unpleasant ____?

Q14, Q15, Q16, & Q17 indicate: satisfaction with the overall local transportation system (Q14), ridership (Q15), perceptions of selected quality aspects of public transit (Q16) and reasons for non-use of public transit (Q17).

1. A more extensive list of illustrative questions is contained in Appendix D.

148

FIGURE 6–2 (cont.)

IF NO TO Q15, ASK

Q17. How would you rate the following factors as reasons why you have not used public transit for travel within this city/county in the last month?

	Major Reason	Minor Reason	Not a Reason
a) Takes too long			
b) Transit stop not close enough			
c) Transit runs too in-frequently			
d) Routes do not go to desired destination			
e) Prefer convenience of automobile			
f) Transit vehicles too uncomfortable and unpleasant			
g) Don't like crowds			
h) Too dangerous			
i) Too expensive			
j) Other (Specify)			

Recreation [2]

Q18. Recreation is sometimes thought of as the pleasant activities that are available during your free time after school or work and on weekends. What do you think of the recreation available in your neighborhood?

Very Good ____   Fair ____

Good ____   Poor ____

The data on the questions on recreation will provide estimates of the quality of recreation (Q18), the percentage of households using nearby recreation facilities (Q19),

2. A more extensive list of questions is contained in Appendix C.

149

FIGURE 6–2 (cont.)

and reasons for liking or disliking them (Q20).

No Opinion ____   Don't Know ____

IF FAIR OR POOR, ASK

Would you tell me why you say that? _____

_____

Q19. Did anyone in the household use any Public Recreation facilities in the city during the past month?

Yes ____   No ____   No Reply ____

What is the name and address of each?

a. _____

_____

b. _____

_____

c. _____

_____

IF YES TO Q19, ASK Q20 FOR EACH FACILITY GIVEN

called in to rate an agency's performance. Agencies hiring such professionals should be sure to make them detail their reasons for feeling as they do. Vague statements that the agency is doing a good, mediocre, or bad job are useless. Statements that, for example, fire response time compares in a certain way to the national average are far more valuable. In fact, a rating system should ideally be established before the raters come in. They could then use this system to indicate for example, whether police behavior toward all ethnic groups is the same.

Supporting Evaluation and Deciding When to Use It

Hatry and his colleagues note that an effective evaluation will have to have the same kind of support from the department head or higher government officials which a successful planning effort needs.[14] In Chapter 2, we discussed how planning studies must be assigned to units that can carry them out objectively, be relevant to the needs of officials, be adequately staffed and supported, be carefully monitored while in progress, and be thoroughly reviewed and actually used, when reported. All of these conditions must also apply if an evaluation is to be useful.

Evaluations of programs are most useful if the following criteria are met. First, when decision makers have to determine whether a program should continue, be modified, or end, an evaluation is highly desirable. Of course, the decision makers have to be serious about the decision. We are not talking about a pro forma review, such as the periodic federal tax "reforms" which always end up sheltering the income of the very wealthy through numerous loopholes. Second, it must be determined whether the evaluation can be done, and done in time for the decision makers to use it in making up their minds. If adequate data and sufficient resources for the evaluation are lacking, the evaluation cannot be undertaken. Third, evaluations should focus on certain types of programs. These include large expensive programs, programs which appear to be operating in a substandard manner, new programs, and programs touted for expansion. Evaluation is likely to have more impact on such programs than on older medium-sized ones which seem to be running well. Since evaluation is costly, it should concentrate on programs in which savings and enhancement of effectiveness are likely to be greatest. As Kimmel and his colleagues have put it, "Local managers should remember that program evaluation, like anything else, is not infinitely valuable. . . . Not all government programs can or should be evaluated."[15]

THE USE OF OUTPUT-ORIENTED EVALUATION IN AMERICAN GOVERNMENT

The Federal Government

Evaluative studies of federal programs have increased greatly since 1969, when the Nixon administration began. After the great expansion of programs which took place under the Johnson administration, program expansion slowed and Congress, President, and the agencies took a look at what some of these programs were accomplishing. Congress, for example, required that agencies evaluate programs authorized by such acts as the Energy Reorganization Act of 1974, the School Lunch and Child Nutrition Act Amendments of 1973, and the Rangeland and Renewable Resources Planning Act of 1973. Legislation in 1970 and 1974 called for extensive program evaluation to be performed by the General Accounting Office (GAO), which is the audit arm of Congress. (Such evaluations by a legislative audit office are usually called *performance audits*.) In fiscal year 1977, for example, GAO spent $68 million on such evaluations and estimated that the agencies themselves had spent $116 million on evaluations in 1976.[16] (Lest these seem like vast sums, bear in mind that the total federal budget was close to $400 *billion*, so that evaluation costs were less than 0.0005 percent of the budget total).

Federal evaluations have encompassed productivity in the Postal Service (discussed in Chapter 8), federal crime strike forces, and alternative approaches to welfare. Elaborate and careful evaluative approaches such as the one illustrated in Table 6–2 were used by the Office of Economic Opportunity (OEO) in 1969. Several extensive and expensive controlled experiments of welfare have been conducted.[17]

But while much has been learned about the likely impact of variations in welfare programs, our floundering welfare system remains intact. As Joseph S. Wholey wrote in 1972, "after investment of significant resources and effort, *not one* federal agency has an overall evaluation system and few programs are able to make any use of the evaluations produced."[18] Interviewed in 1976, Wholey saw little reason to change his earlier opinion.[19] He felt that the technical and especially the political problems we examine in later sections of this chapter had prevented *use* of evaluation. Evaluations were being run, but few agencies were using evaluation reports to modify their programs.

While federal use of evaluations to date may be dismally deficient, as the case study in this chapter demonstrates, interest in evaluation is growing. (We have noted in Chapter 3 the growing interest in sunset laws, which mandate the end of a program after so many years unless it is reauthorized by the legislature after an evaluation has been conducted.) Similarly, President Carter implemented zero-base budgeting, which incorporates program evaluation in the budgetary process, and which we discuss in Chapter 7. But while the future impact of program evaluation may increase, at present many an evaluation is born to blush unseen and waste its fragrance on the desert air.

State Government

State government use of evaluation has also increased greatly since 1969. We have already examined the record of sunset laws and will look at that of zero-base budgeting in promoting evaluation in chapter 7 of this book. In

TABLE 6-2 PARADIGM FOR OEO PROGRAM IMPACT EVALUATION[a]

ANTI-POVERTY PROGRAM[b]

EVALUATION DATA	COMMUNITY ACTION PROGRAMS									Delegated Programs	Non-OEO Project
	Job Corps	VISTA	Organization Coordination Functions	Legal Services	SERVICE PROGRAMS						
					Head Start	Follow Through	Upward Bound	Health Services	Others		
A. Universe of need											
B. Program reach											
C. Program coverage (A/E)											
D. Program cost											
E. Cost per person reached (D/E)											
F. Cost of total coverage (E) × (A)[c]											
G. Measures of program effectiveness											
1. Immediate objectives											
2. Poverty reduction											
H. Benefit-cost ratio (G/D)											

[a]John Evans explained the use of the matrix as follows: "Going down the Evaluation Data column from A through H will indicate how the competeled paradigm would be useful in overall agency planning and programming. With extensive and dependable data for each program or universe of need (A) and program reach (B), we can calculate and compare programs on the extent to which they are reaching their target populations (C). A solid figure on program coverage (C) would be very useful in planning and budgeting within a given program and across the total array of OEO programs. Bringing together for all programs the information on their total costs (D) (on which we have good data) and information on the number of people they reach (B) (on which we don't) would allow us to compute, and compare programs on, the cost per person reached (E). With information on program costs (D), the total universe of need (A), and the present program reach (B), we could determine for each what the cost of total coverage would be and how much of an increment over present budget outlays they would require (F)."

[b]A number of the programs listed have since been delegated to the Departments of Labor and of Health, Education, and Welfare.

[c]A correct computation would not be this simple but would take into account the marginal cost required to expand programs at different levels.

153

this section, we examine the activities of state legislative auditors, whose performance audits are the most noticeable program evaluation activity at the state level. The auditors have assumed this role in the past few years. In 1970, not a single state legislature had a full-time program evaluation staff. By 1974, more than a dozen had such a component.[20]

The New Jersey Office of Fiscal Affairs, for example, has published scores of evaluations, ranging from the operation of the state Civil Service Commission through urban renewal to protection of migrant farm workers. Figure 6–3 illustrates some findings of the migrant worker study. The overall impact of these evaluations is difficult to gauge without an evaluation of the evaluators. Certainly, there is no question that many of the audit recommendations have not been followed up by the governor, legislature, or state agencies.

But a report by New York State auditors claims that the legislative audit has had substantial impact. They cite a large decrease in manpower training

FIGURE 6-3.   SUMMARY RATING OF MIGRANT LABOR CAMP CONDITIONS

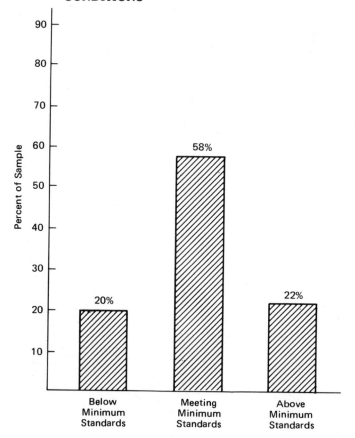

funds and abolition of a program to attempt marital reconciliation in divorce cases, after performance audits showed that these programs were achieving very little. Following a state university dormitory construction audit, room rents were increased, a subsidized phone system was terminated, and the governing body of the construction agency was modified.[21]

On the other hand, some states have not yet, or have just, begun to get into performance auditing. Connecticut, for example, issued its first performance audit in February 1977. The report was a blockbuster which probed the operation of the State Department of Education and gave it very low grades for enforcing state standards in local schools. Since the report was unpopular among educators, the question remains whether it will have any impact.

State evaluation activity is on the upswing, and some states claim it has substantial impact. Overall, we can be sure that its effect has been marginal, though it seems certain to increase in the future. For line agencies themselves, as well as legislative auditors, are beginning to use evaluation more frequently.

Local Government

Many attempts at evaluation have been used in our 80,000 local governments. In a 1976 article, Wholey lists a number of effective evaluations, including one which stopped an attempt to end the Cincinnati police paraprofessional program and another which led to better performance by the Washington, D.C., sanitation department.[22] Savannah, Georgia, has implemented an extensive evaluation of city services to determine if all neighborhoods get an equal break.[23] Rockford, Illinois; St. Petersburg, Florida; and Nashville, Tennessee, have used a common recreation program evaluation approach, while Palo Alto, California, has used evaluation for its police department.[24]

One area in which local government is taking an increasing interest is measuring and evaluating educational programs. In the winter of 1977, the parents of a recent high school graduate from Copiague, New York, sued the school district for $1 million because their son could not read. New York City schools announced in April 1977 that they were going to require that higher reading, writing, and arithmetic standards be met before a high school diploma would be awarded. Student performance relative to these standards would be measured by a written test.[25]

While interest in, and use of, evaluation is increasing at the local level, Kimmel and his colleagues noted in 1974 that there was "a very limited body of evidence *from research and formal study* on the utility, impact and effectiveness of conducting program evaluation."[26] As Wholey said in December 1976, "For many years evaluators have been meeting in conferences. . . . I'd like to see an evaluation conference in which all the papers have the same title: "How Evaluation Was Used in Improving the Programs in Our Agency.""[27] Such a desire, of course, indicates that evaluations are not yet heavily used.

TECHNICAL PROBLEMS AND HOW TO MINIMIZE THEM

Experimental Designs

The controlled experiment is technically more demanding than any other output-oriented management technique examined in this book. The study must be run by people versed in the intricacies of such subjects as random selection of a sample, statistical analysis, and reliability and validity.

Reliability[28]   One basic problem in evaluation is *reliability*, or the extent to which results found by the same type of evaluation approach will be consistent from one study to another. Suppose, for example, that two randomly selected equivalent samples of students are selected, subjected to a similar program, and then graded according to a set of evaluation criteria. The evaluation finds a large difference in what students have learned. Group A has surpassed group B. Curious about why this might be so, the evaluation is repeated. This time the results are reversed, and group B has surpassed group A.

These findings question the reliability of the evaluation criteria. Since the results obtained are widely different with each use, the criteria have low reliability. What can be done about this problem?

First, the evaluator must recognize that all measurement is likely to contain some error. Rarely is the data gathering and measurement process carried out with perfection. Since typical samples feature 5 percent–10 percent margins of error and correlation techniques performed on sample data also involve 5 percent–10 percent error margins, between 10 percent–20 percent of correlated findings from sample data will simply be wrong. The key question then becomes whether the degree of error is critical. Unfortunately, there is no precise criterion to distinguish a reliable from an unreliable measure. The best way to ensure reliability is to pay careful attention to factors that permit large chance errors to enter into the evaluation measurement. For example, sloppy or careless handling of data could cause unreliability. Or failure to make sure that control and experimental groups were treated in consistently different ways could also result in errors.

Validity[29]   *Validity*, or the extent to which evaluation criteria succeed in measuring what they claim to measure, is "by far the most important single methodological criterion for evaluating any measuring instrument."[30] If an evaluation is valid, its reliability can usually be taken for granted.

A valid evaluation of student reading skills would be one which accurately reflected student ability. If, for example, freshmen who received low scores on reading evaluations could read Melville's *Moby Dick* with speed and full understanding, we would be correct in suspecting that the evaluation was not valid. Likewise, if students pass a twelfth-grade level reading test, but have trouble getting through *Dick Tracy*, the test would be invalid.

Edward A. Suchman, a medical sociologist and a leading authority on evaluation, details seven different sources of invalidity.[31] These lie beyond the scope of this section, but we have defined the concepts of reliability and validity here to indicate that there is no place for the rank amateur in the experimental type of evaluation.

Lack of Logic in the Design   Pamela Horst and her colleagues at the Urban Institute found that federal agency managers did not feel that most of the evaluations conducted for their programs were useful.[32] Typical complaints were that the evaluations were not geared to user needs; different evaluations of the same program were not comparable; and evaluation results were inconclusive.

After digging deeper, Horst concluded that these complaints were symptoms, not causes. Often, the very design of a program indicated a lack of clear logic, since there was no adequate statement of the assumptions behind a program. An example is that of drug treatment programs. Evaluators found that what was a "therapeutic community" in one town did not resemble an operation called by the same name in another. In other words, what seem on the surface to be identical programs may turn out not to be the same.

Under these circumstances, the evaluator cannot determine which program works best. Even if one program has results dramatically superior to others, the difference may be due to external factors such as the type of clientele or community. The only way to determine which approach is best is to institute several approaches simultaneously in several different kinds of locale, and then evaluate the results of each therapeutic community program. Without such an arrangement, all the evaluator can do is report what is going on in a program and how the program's success cannot be evaluated because one cannot compare apples with oranges. The evaluator can argue for the planned variation approach sketched above as a future means of evaluation, but this is not likely to satisfy the program administrator who will complain that the evaluator has failed to describe how well the program is doing.

This perennial problem indicates why evaluators should be called in during the *planning stages* of a new program, so that they can indicate whether alternative proposals can be adequately evaluated. Otherwise, the program results, whether experimental or nonexperimental in nature, are likely to remain unknown.

The Hawthorne Effect   A study made during the 1920s at the Hawthorne plant of the General Electric Company discovered a problem that plagues the evaluation of any controlled experiment.[33] The study was designed to see what kind of working environment (lighting, work breaks, types of supervision, etc.) would result in maximum productivity. The researchers were puzzled when productivity rose no matter what they did. They concluded that the workers were performing better because they knew they were part of an experiment. Interestingly enough, the principle of interdeterminacy in modern physics is similar: The experimenter's observations effect the outcome of the experiment. Perhaps the best way to compensate for the Hawthorne effect is to tell control group members that they are also part of an experiment.[34] In this way, both groups may respond in the same way to the experiment, canceling out the bias caused by the Hawthorne effect.

Experimental and Nonexperimental Designs

All of the problems and examples discussed in this section apply equally strongly to experimental as well as to nonexperimental designs, but the emphasis is on nonexperimental approaches.

Goal Statement   One problem with the statement of goals, already alluded to in Chapter 1, is lack of clarity. Horst et al. have identified as "vaporous wishes" goals such as "adequate quality of life" and "improved mental health," which were never followed up with much more specific criteria. (Such criteria for the mental health goal might include ability to hold a job outside of a mental health institution, improved family relationships, etc.). In addition, Horst commonly encountered terms like *outreach capability* and *upgraded job skills*, but rarely were adequate definitions and measures provided for them. The evaluator cannot evaluate when there are no stated criteria of evaluation.[35]

To avoid this problem, evaluators should be in on the design of a program from the beginning. (As we mentioned in Chapter 2, political problems are also involved in stating goals; we will discuss these problems in the next section.) A number of other problems relative to goal statement exist. Rarely, for instance, do agencies or programs have only one goal. As Figure 6–4 indicates, multiple goals are the rule, not the exception. This raises the question of how the evaluator separates these goals from each other and determines priorities. Perhaps the best way to assign a priority rating to a goal is to research the legislative history of the program and to ask government officials what their priorities are. But if a consensus is lacking, this will not be easy. How to separate closely related goals (reduction of odor emanating from sewage treatment plants and reduction of germs from the same plants) is a task for which, unfortunately, there is no substitute for hard work and ingenuity.

The way goals change over time also causes complications. The submarine service of the U.S. Navy is now largely a nuclear missile system, whereas up until the 1950s its function in war was to sink enemy ships. Comparisons between the submarine service of 1976 and 1956 will be extremely misleading if these changes in goals and functions are not carefully considered.

Evaluation Criteria   The search for quantitative measures can produce inappropriate measures of evaluation.

What are the most satisfactory indexes of output for a given agency? How do we measure how many crimes have been deterred by a police force or how much a child has learned in school as distinct from the other environments of

FIGURE 6–4   RECREATION OBJECTIVES AND ASSOCIATED EVALUATION CRITERIA

Objectives

To provide all citizens, to the extent practicable, with a variety of leisure opportunities which are accessible, safe, physically attractice, and enjoyable. They should contribute to the mental and physical health of the community, to its economic and social wellbeing and permit outlets that will help decrease incidents of antisocial behavior such as crime and delinquency.

Evaluation Criteria

1. *Overall Citizen Rating:*   (Overall Enjoyableness)
   a. Percent of households which feel that recreation opportunities are very good.
   b. Percent of households which feel that recreation opportunities are poor.

2. *Overall User Rating:*   (Enjoyableness)
   a. Percent of user households which feel that recreation opportunities are very good.
   b. Percent of user households which feel that recreation opportunities are poor.

3. *Crowdedness:*   (Enjoyableness)
   a. Percent of user households which feel that the amount of facility space is poor.

4. *Facility Upkeep:*   (Physical Attractiveness)
   a. Percent of user households which feel that facility cleanliness is poor.
   b. Percent of user households which feel that maintenance of equipment is poor.

5. *Helpfulness — Attitude of Staff:*   (Enjoyableness)
   a. Percent of user households which feel that helpfulness — attitude of staff is poor.

6. *Hours of Operation:*   (Accessibility)
   a. Percent of user households which feel that hours of operation are poor.

7. *Safety:*
   a. Percent of user households which feel that safety is poor.
   b. Number of serious accidents per 100,000 hours of use.
   c. Number of deaths per 1,000,000 hours of use.

8. *Participation:*   (Enjoyableness)
   a. Percent of citizens who have used a government facility or program one or more times during a given time period.
   b. Percent of citizens who have not used a government facility or program one or more times during a given time period, categorized by reason for nonuse.

9. *Attendance:*   (Enjoyableness)
   a. Total attendance at government facilities or programs.

10. *Hours of Attendance:*   (Enjoyableness)
    a. Total citizen attendance hours at government facilities or program.

11. *Physical Accessibility:*   (Accessibility)
    Percent of citizens who live within "X" miles of a government recreation facility.

12. *Variety:*
    a. Average number of different programs per facility.

NOTE: The phrase in parenthesis is the objective to which the specific evaluation criterion most directly applies.

family, peers, and media? Unfortunately, for many programs, we either have no way or only very costly ways which require an analysis over several years to measure results. There is no way to minimize this difficulty. Perhaps the best that can be hoped for is to make government officials aware of this technical problem and thus avoid inappropriate or inimical approaches to evaluation. An example of such counterproductive steps is the practice some cities follow in awarding bonuses to patrol officers on the basis of the number of arrests made. Such a system could easily result in scores of false arrests or arrests for minor offenses, rather than in measures which would serve to deter or cut down serious crime.[36] There are no shortcuts or substitutes for careful analysis and confrontation of the difficulties inherent in defining output measures.

POLITICAL PROBLEMS AND HOW TO MINIMIZE THEM

Experimental Designs

A controlled experiment means that two or more groups are treated differently. When agency clientele discover this differential treatment, they are unlikely to be ecstatic.[37] Take the case of a reading experiment in school. The principal is likely to hear from parents who are upset about the experiment soon after it begins. Some parents will want to know why junior is not in the new program. After all, they are paying taxes, too, aren't they? Others will want to know why their child is in this new program when she or he was perfectly happy in Ms. Smith's class. Carrying out a controlled experiment, in short, is going to upset the status quo and raise the question of whether some clients are being unfairly favored over others.

While not a panacea, the best way to proceed here is with candor and honesty. Before an agency begins a controlled experiment, it should publicize its intentions and hold a public hearing to explain them. It could send out a mailing to explain the program to those who will be affected. Through such pre-experimental openness, misunderstanding of program interest can be minimized. In addition, the feeling that the agency has tried to pull a fast one should be minimized. Often opponents of the experiment will be up in arms not because of the experiment itself, but because it was suddenly dropped on them out of the blue. If possible, program administrators should be ready to make minor adjustments in the experiment when clients are highly incensed about one part of it. For example, people in one neighborhood who violently object to being part of the police or fire department experimental group can perhaps be shifted to the control group, and a similar neighborhood shifted to the experimental group to take their place. While such a shift may not always be possible, it makes sense to try to build some flexibility into the experimental plan. For what is the point of running a valid experiment which is so unpopular that there is no chance of implementing its findings as a new program plan?

Experimental and Nonexperimental Designs

Agency Resistance   Perhaps the most important political obstacle to evaluation comes from the agency itself. As mentioned in Chapter 1, Aaron Wildavsky has argued that the very concept of evaluation, denoting change, may be incompatible with organizations, which denote stability. It is certainly not difficult to find example after example of agency resistance to evaluation which is difficult to explain on any other ground.

For instance, a study of federal funding of local police departments in the New England states found that police officials believed that the concept of evaluation was unimportant or nonsensical.[38] The police believed that only those with extensive experience in police work could make rational decisions, based on their intuitive knowledge. Former Secretary of Defense McNamara ran into a similar problem during the 1962 blockade of Cuba, when he asked the head of the Navy how he was going to conduct the blockade. Admiral Anderson replied by holding up a copy of navy procedures to be followed in such a case. McNamara replied, "I don't give a damn what John Paul Jones would have done! What are *you* going to do?" Here we have in a nutshell the difference between agency adherence to traditions and intuition and the approach of the output-oriented evaluator. The same point can be illustrated in more detail by the following example, a 1975 confrontation between a Pennsylvania State Police major and the chairman of the House Appropriations Committee in that state:

> *Chairman Wojdak:* I had asked several questions about the means of collecting data, hard data, to establish and determine the effectiveness of certain programs. One was . . . traffic supervision. . . . I would like you to furnish me as soon as possible with how you are determining the effectiveness of these programs and if you have no means at present of determining the effectiveness, how you plan to determine the effectiveness of it. . . .

> *Major Buchinsky:* Yes, I did want to offer something, Mr. Chairman, if I may. I don't know who put some of these statements in and that is concerning the low number of accidents and the fact that patrols do not have a major impact on accident rate. I would like to find where the reference is. In other words, what documentation there is to support that general statement for this particular reason. . . .

> *Chairman Wojdak:* Major, everything you say may very well be true. My question was to determine on the basis of what some recent studies have shown and we will furnish those to you if you want them.

> *Major Buchinsky:* I would appreciate that.

> *Chairman Wojdak:* Okay. That patrolling really was not a significant factor in reducing the occurrence of accidents. Now, you may disagree with that. We will furnish you with those studies.

My questions to you before were what considerations you were using in determining how many numbers of officers you would use in traffic control . . . in light of these studies.

Major Buchinsky: May I cite one particular instance where the presence of other patrols would have gone ahead and prevented a fatality?

Chairman Wojdak: There is no doubt in my mind that in individual cases, and I am not certain how many cases that would be or what percentage it would be, I am certain there are instances where patrol does prevent accidents.

Major Buchinsky: And this is one that we could document very definitely, sir. . . .

Chairman Wojdak: I think everyone's ultimate goal is running things most efficiently and if, in fact, studies show that . . . traffic patrols don't have a major impact on accidents, all I am really trying to determine is what alternative plans, or how that affects your thinking in allocating officers because ultimately, if you disagree with the plan, your requests will be for additional officers.

All I am trying to determine is what your thinking is and it is the same thing with the determination of the effectiveness of the municipal police training program and with the crime prevention program.[39]

Suchman has noted how many agencies prefer "pseudo-evaluations" which make them look good to probing output-oriented evaluations.[40] Variations on this theme include the *eyewash*, which selects for evaluation only the aspects of a program which look good on the surface. Another approach is the *whitewash*, or cover-up of the real nature of a program. The Nazis tried in 1945 to impress world public opinion by inviting three observers to visit a concentration camp especially spruced up for the occasion. Large numbers of inmates were hidden from view, and inmates who would repeat what the Nazis wanted them to say were selected as guides for the observers. This whole farcical "inspection" tour viewed nothing that was representative of the reality of the camps, and won high grades from the naive observers.[41]

The *submarine* is an attempt to destroy or torpedo a program unpopular in the agency, regardless of the program's accomplishments. It is a hatchet job which overlooks the positive achievements and focuses on the shortcomings of a program.

Another variation is *posturing*, which points to the use of evaluation as a "gesture" of objectivity. Most evaluations used in government today fall into this category, because they are not output oriented. "We have evaluated our program and found that it meets professional standards" is a comment which usually begs the question. The real question should be, "So what if we meet professional standards? Are these standards meaningful, and if so, how do they affect program results?"

A final ploy is *postponement*. Needed action is delayed through the pretense of seeking the "facts." The author once went through a year of frustration while the administrative officials at the college where he worked decided to fill a position they had previously authorized only after they had made an evaluation of the entire department's programs. This move was clearly designed to punish the department rather than to accomplish any useful purpose.

Having detailed a host of obstacles posed by agency resistance to evaluation, we must now discuss what can be done to combat such hindrances to results-oriented management. The overall strategy to follow is to try to convince agency personnel that evaluation will work for them, because the better the job they do, the more recognition and budget resources they are likely to get.

While such salesmanship makes sense, it will not always work. Low performance agencies will see nothing to gain by it. And other agencies may not be willing to sell their bureaucratic souls for a mess of increased appropriations. The U.S. military's leadership greatly preferred Defense Secretary Melvin Laird (1969–1973) to Secretary McNamara (1961–1968). They felt as they did even though budget pickings were much leaner under Laird than McNamara. While they prospered under McNamara, they had to prosper on his terms. He demanded evaluation and justification before he would endorse proposals by the professional military. Under Laird's tenure, however, the services were allowed to cut up their smaller budget pie pretty much the way they wanted to.

Public administration professor Bruce Rocheleau studied the impact of evaluation in 14 mental health agencies in Florida.[42] His findings were paradoxical, since he discovered both substantial support for and opposition to evaluation within the agencies. While agency personnel agreed with many of the evaluators' recommendations, they felt that it would be political suicide to try to carry out some of them. Rocheleau found that the key factor in effective evaluation is authority, or the ability to evoke compliance in others. In this case, authority was based on good personal relationships between the evaluator and program directors. This goodwill was built up by the evaluator's assuming service jobs such as data gathering and replying to information requests from local, state, and national funding agencies. On the other hand, evaluators had to be careful while performing these tasks not to be sidetracked from their job of evaluation.

Attitude of Top Officials   Equally critical if evaluation is to work is a commitment by top management. Rather than repeat the recommendations made in Chapter 2 on planning we refer the reader back to them. Department heads must make clear their commitment to evaluation, must assign adequate resources to the task, must monitor efforts, and must act on evaluation recommendations.[43]

Unfortunately, none of these suggestions is a cure-all. Different opinions and beliefs will always combine to kill certain recommendations of evaluators. The Nixon administration, for example, ignored the recommendations of advisory commissions set up to investigate marijuana and pornography, just as the

Johnson administration ignored the findings of both the Advisory Commission on Civil Disorders and the Douglas Commission on Urban Problems. In none of these cases did the recommendations of the commissions jibe with the political preferences of high officials and their perception of how the adoption of such recommendations would affect their political party at the polls. Sometimes the results of evaluations are ignored in the attempt to see a proposed bill become law. For example, President Nixon's proposal for welfare reform included a work requirement provision which he privately admitted would accomplish no useful purpose, since all studies showed that the vast majority of welfare recipients (including mothers of small children) could not work. Yet Nixon kept this questionable provision in his bill to ensure conservative support for it in Congress. While the bill did not become law, its chances would probably have been even dimmer without this counterproductive or useless requirement.[44] But while there are no panaceas in getting officials to accept evaluation reports, the steps we recommend will minimize such problems insofar as they can be minimized.

The Evaluator's Own Attitude   A final problem appropriately considered in this section is the intrusion of the evaluator's own values into the report. We have defined politics as the realm of differing values, and there is no question that two equally competent evaluators might be led by their values to different recommendations. As evaluation specialist Carol Weiss has noted,

> Different people looking at the same data can come up with different conclusions in the tradition of the "fully-only" school of analysis. "Fully 25 per cent of the students . . ." boasts the promoter; "only 25 per cent of the students . . ." sighs the detractor.[45]

Some researchers have been so influenced by their own values that they have wilfully distorted their research findings. For example, a world-famous authority on intelligence tests who argued that intelligence was principally determined by hereditary factors was found after his death to have fabricated data pointing to that conclusion. While few evaluators are likely to go this far, they should squarely confront their own preferences and ask themselves if these biases are unduly influencing them.

CASE STUDY:
EVALUATING MODEL CITIES[46]

The Model Cities program was enacted by Congress in 1966, at the request of President Lyndon Johnson. Model Cities was designed to coordinate different federal programs within a city so that local problems could be met in a more flexible and effective manner. Model Cities distributed a large amount of resources to a limited number of cities and was designed, as its name indicates, to generate programs that could be used in a much larger number of cities.

Given these purposes, it is surprising that evaluation was not given priority in the task force study report which recommended the program to President Johnson. The act itself mandated local evaluation and called for determination of overall program "magnitude" and "impact" by the federal department of Housing and Urban Development (HUD).

By the spring of 1967, a program development and evaluation office for Model Cities had been established. An initial draft of an evaluation study suggested that changes in attitudes and behavior of neighborhood representatives; in physical, social, and economic characteristics of model neighborhoods; and in public and private institutions serving the neighborhoods be examined. The draft did not explore the technical difficulties confronting evaluation attempts, nor did it mention potential political problems.

After extensive interoffice disputes, contracts with consultants to study the program were signed in the summer of 1968. At the same time, local governments were asking what HUD wanted from them for evaluation. Directions from the program development and evaluation office were looked on with some misgivings by HUD's office of research and technology and the deputy undersecretary of the department. The latter were apparently concerned that evaluation not be so wide in scope that unfavorable analyses of the performance of local officials or HUD could complicate matters for the Model Cities program.

These technical and political obstacles resulted in confusion at the local level and stalemate at the federal level. The situation remained stymied even after the advent of the Nixon administration, in January 1969. No further evalution studies were authorized by HUD, demoralizing the Model Cities evaluation staff.

Assistant Secretary Floyd Hyde, in charge of Model Cities, now demanded some kind of evaluative study, even if it were not methodologically elegant or completely reliable or valid. At the very least, he needed *some* kind of study to protect himself from outside critics of the program. The evaluation team, however, balked at providing such potentially misleading reports. After 1970, Hyde changed the entire emphasis of Model Cities evaluation efforts to short-term "quick and dirty" examinations of policy areas rather than to the overall, long-term perspective originally advocated by the evaluation office.

At the same time, local evaluation efforts never really got off the ground. In spite of HUD threats to withhold funds unless local evaluations were run, most cities were able to placate HUD by filing paper plans for evaluation.

Friedman and Kaplan conclude that "HUD was not able to mount a nationally relevant, coordinated, and sustained evaluation effort."[47] These authors feel that there were several reasons for this failure. One was a lack of consensus on the goals of Model Cities, which caused the interoffice disagreement and lack of coordination mentioned earlier. Second, there was no consensus on the scope and methods to be used, causing disagreement between Assistant Secretary Hyde and the Model Cities evaluation staff. Third, the need to produce immediate visible results to placate congressional and interest group critics pulled HUD away from a comprehensive evaluation. Fourth, as mentioned above, some local and federal officials feared that evaluation might make the program look bad.

The Model Cities evaluation effort ran into several of the difficulties described in the two previous sections, which combined to destroy its effectiveness. The only useful effect of this evaluation is the guidance it can give to evaluators who wish to avoid some of the pitfalls which destroyed this attempt at evaluation.

Questions

1. Do you think that political or technical causes were most important in destroying this effort at evaluation? Explain the reason for your opinion.

2. If you were in charge of the Model Cities office of program development and evaluation, how would you have handled (a) departmental wariness about your evaluation efforts, (b) lack of response by local governments to the evaluation effort, (c) Assistant Secretary Hyde's demand for short-term evaluations?

3. Do you think your answers to the previous question might have made possible a more extensive and valuable evaluation of Model Cities? Explain the reasons for your opinion.

EVALUATION: PROBLEMS AND PROSPECTS

There seems little doubt that results-oriented evaluation will continue to grow in popularity at all levels of government in the United States. Such growth is not an unqualified good thing, as we will argue in this section. So far in this book we have not had much to say about ethical questions. Questions of values cannot be resolved through factual research, as we have mentioned. Certainly not all readers will share the values espoused below. But the author feels these matters are of utmost importance and must be seriously considered by all results-oriented managers before they implement evaluation systems.

Ethics and Evaluation

Central to most systems of ethics which have evolved over the last several thousand years is the belief that human beings should not be treated as objects. The golden rule—do unto others as you would have them do unto you—can be found in different forms in a wide variety of religious and ethical creeds. The idea that human beings possess an inherent dignity which should not be violated by other human beings, organizations, or government is an ideal espoused by almost all governments today.

Of course, this ideal has often not been observed by the very governments which loudly proclaim it. It is all too easy to find government persecution, whether it be of business people and farmers in Communist China, dissidents in the Soviet Union, or leftists in the United States. While we fully endorse government evaluation, we feel it must be hedged in by measures designed to protect the rights and dignity of individuals.

How can evaluation interfere with human freedom and dignity? A clue is provided by a chapter in a leading book on social science research techniques, entitled "Contrived Observation: Hidden Hardware and Control."[48] In this chapter, the authors, who include Donald T. Campbell, one of the leading experts on output evaluation in the United States coolly discuss the use of manipulative techniques, hidden recording equipment, and means of "entrapment." In other words, any individual right to privacy or "right to know" is waived in the interest of social science research or evaluation. Indeed, the individual, or "subject" (a very revealing word), may never find out what was done to him or her by the evaluator.

Even Campbell feels uncomfortable about this chapter, written in 1966. In 1975, he admitted that "we published the book with little self-consciousness about the invasion-of-privacy issues . . . . I believed I was being more scientific if the people I studied did not know what I was up to. . . . After 20 years of research, I feel that this . . . stance . . . exploits others."[49]

At the same time, this dean of evaluators went on to justify not getting informed consent from subjects and stressing how the privacy issue often becomes a way to avoid evaluation. Old habits die hard.

The reader may wonder whether this is a problem confined to laboratory controlled experiments in psychology. We feel strongly that it is not. It is easy, on the contrary, to find examples of ethically egregious evaluations. A study of victims of syphilis conducted by the federal Department of Health, Education and Welfare (HEW) from the 1940s through the 1960s continued even after a cure for many types of this dread degenerative disease had been found. Rather than administer the drug to all the victims, HEW-funded researchers continued to study their decline and fall. And while the practice is decreasing, prisoners have historically been used for experiments of new drugs. One of the authors's acquaintances once met an ex-convict who had had a chance to have his sentence shortened by "volunteering" to take a drug which he later claimed damaged his brain. In this kind of situation, what could be more coercive of the aptly named "subject"? His "freedom" to make a choice was strictly of an academic nature. A final example of evaluative abuse is the federally funded study run by the New York State Health Department on the effects of abortion on 48,000 women. This study, it was revealed in 1977, was carried on without the consent of the women and contained no safeguards for their privacy. State Senator Karen Burstein noted that a progress report on the study contained the names of 28 women who had had abortions and were subsequently married. The senator said, "I should not have this information . . . [which] is not just being kept, but is being disseminated casually, almost randomly"; neither Senator Burstein nor Assemblyman Mark A. Siegel objected to the study itself, but, as the Assemblyman said, to "the idea that it is being done without consent."[50]

These examples all come from the field of public health. But, as Alice Rivlin, Director of the Congressional Budget Office and an authority on evaluative techniques, has put it, "In the social action area, where experiments rarely involve death or physical damage, the problem seems less serious, but is perhaps only less obvious."[51] She notes, for instance, that new kinds of experimental teaching methods or child care techniques might inflict psychological damage.

A related problem, already mentioned in its political context, is how to separate people into control and experimental groups. How can such a decision be made without discriminating against the rights of individuals? As one author asks,

> Is it right, for example, to deny service to a man who lives on the wrong side of the street merely because his inclusion might obscure the statistical base for evaluation of the project? And what are we to say of the use of control groups, chosen to be as similar to the aided groups as possible, but denied benefits in order to serve as a base for comparison?[52]

Another related problem involves the experimental group. If temporarily provided a new service, clients may feel betrayed after this service is terminated at the end of the experiment. They may have grown used to it, only to have it taken away.[53]

Conclusion

Many other legal and ethical problems are involved in the use of controlled experiments.[54] The review above is intended to make the reader aware of some of these concerns. While controlled experiments seem to pose the greatest threat to human dignity, the steady accumulation of information about individuals by government—whether from evaluations, census data, tax returns, school records, or whatever—must also be hedged in with careful controls. The abuses of individual rights made by the Federal Bureau of Investigation (FBI) and Central Intelligence Agency (CIA) in the 1960s and 1970s indicate that some agencies will stop at nothing in gathering information about individuals. Witness the FBI break-ins and the plundering of the office of the psychiatrist of Vietnam war opponent Daniel Ellsberg by White House "plumbers." Information gathered by any type of evaluation procedure must not be abused.

Recent federal legislation has moved to protect this information, but, as the New York State abortion study indicates, enforcement is another matter. Officials should carefully protect their confidential data. Otherwise, in the fervor to conduct badly needed evaluation studies, our society may come increasingly to resemble totalitarian nations like the Soviet Union.

NOTES

1. Wayne A. Kimmel et al., *Municipal Management and Budget Methods: An Evaluation of Policy Related Research, Final Report, Volume 1: Summary and Synthesis* (Washington, D.C.: Urban Institute, 1974), p. 39.

2. Joseph S. Wholey et al., *Federal Evaluation Policy* (Washington, D.C.: Urban Institute, 1970), p. 23.

3. John D. Waller et al., *Monitoring for Government Agencies* (Washington, D.C.: Urban Institute, 1976), pp. 7–8.

4. Harry P. Hatry et al., *Practical Program Evaluation for State and Local Government Officials* (Washington, D.C.: Urban Institute, 1973), p. 56.

5. This subsection is based primarily on ibid., pp. 56–62, and "Program Evaluation," chapter 15 in Barry Bozeman's *Public Administration and Policy Analysis* (New York: St. Martin's Press, 1979). See also Carol A. Weiss, *Evaluation Research* (Englewood Cliffs, N.J.: Prentice-Hall, 1972), and Peter H. Rossi and Walter Williams, *Evaluating Social Programs* (New York: Seminar Press, 1972).

6. See John Madge, *The Tools of Social Science* (Garden City, N.Y.: Doubleday Anchor Books, 1965), pp. 232–35.

7. Weiss, op. cit., p. 68.

8. Ibid., pp. 69–72, and Bozeman, op. cit.

9. This subsection is based primarily on Hatry et al., op. cit., pp. 39–56, 62–70.

10. Hatry et al., op. cit., p. 44.

11. Ibid., p. 71.

12. Joseph S. Wholey, "The Role of the Evaluation and the Evaluator in Improving Public Programs," *Public Administration Review* 36 (November–December 1976): 679–83, at 681.

13. U.S. Bureau of the Budget, Executive Office of the President, *Household Survey 1969*. (Washington, D.C.: Government Printing Office, 1969).

14. Hatry et al., op. cit., pp. 107–26.

15. Kimmel et al., op. cit., p. 47.

16. Joel Havemann, "Congress Tries to Break Ground Zero in Evaluating Federal Programs," *National Journal*, May 22, 1976, pp. 706–13, at 708.

17. See Joseph A. Pechman and P. Michael Timpane, eds., *Work Incentives and Income Guarantees: The New Jersey Negative Income Tax Experiment* (Washington, D.C.: Brookings Institution, 1975).

18. Joseph S. Wholey, "What Can We Actually Get from Program Evaluation?" *Policy Sciences* 3 (1972): 361–69.

19. Havemann, op. cit., p. 710.

20. Neal R. Peirce, " 'Productivity' is Slogan For Taming Spiraling Expenses," *National Journal*, April 12, 1975, p. 536.

21. Richard Brown and Ray D. Pethtel, "A Matter of Facts: State Legislative Performance Auditing," *Public Administration Review* 34 (July–August 1974): 318–27, at 325.

22. Wholey, "The Role of the Evaluation . . . ," op. cit., p. 681.

23. Frank Wise, Jr., "Toward Equity of Results Achieved: One Approach," *Public Management*, August 1976, pp. 9–12. Mr. Wise was Assistant City Manager of Savannah at the time.

24. "Measuring Basic City Services," *Search*, May–August 1974, pp. 8–10. (*Search* is a periodical newsletter of the Urban Institute.)

25. Leonard Buder, "High School Graduation Standards to Be Stiffened by New York City," *New York Times*, April 25, 1977, p. 1.

26. Kimmel et al., op. cit., p. 38.

27. Wholey, "The Role of the Evaluation . . . ," op. cit., p. 682.

28. This subsection is based primarily on Edward A. Suchman, *Evaluative Research* (New York: Russell Sage Foundation, 1967), pp. 116–20.

29. This subsection is also based primarily on ibid.

30. Ibid., p. 120.

31. Ibid., p. 122.

32. Pamela Horst et al., "Program Evaluation and the Federal Evaluator," *Public Administration Review* 34 (July–August 1974): 300–8.

33. Elton Mayo, *The Human Problems of an Industrial Civilization* (New York: Macmillan, 1933).

34. Hatry et al., op. cit., p. 60.

35. Horst et al., op. cit.

36. An excellent treatment of this problem is V. F. Ridgway, "Dysfunctional Consequences of Performance Measurements," *Administrative Science Quarterly* 1 (September 1956): 240–47.

37. See Alice M. Rivlin, *Systematic Thinking for Social Action* (Washington, D.C.: Brookings Institution, 1971), pp. 110–11.

38. Laurence W. O'Connell and Susan O. White, "Politics and Evaluation in LEAA: New England States," paper presented at the annual meeting of the American Political Science Association, New Orleans, 1973.

39. Pennsylvania House Appropriations Committee hearings, April 2, 1975.

40. Edward A. Suchman, "Action for What?" in Weiss, op. cit., pp. 52–84.

41. Richard Petrow, *The Bitter Years* (New York: Morrow, 1974), 300–13.

42. Bruce Rocheleau, "Evaluation, Accountability, and Responsiveness in Administration," *Midwest Review of Public Administration*, October 1975, pp. 163–72.

43. Cf. Hatry et al., op. cit., pp. 107–23.

44. Daniel P. Moynihan, *The Politics of a Guaranteed Income* (New York: Random House, 1973).

45. Weiss, *Evaluation Research*, op. cit., p. 32.

46. This section is based on Bernard J. Frieden and Marshall Kaplan, *The Politics of Neglect* (Cambridge, Mass.: M.I.T. Press, 1975), 169–86.

47. Ibid., p. 183.

48. See Eugene J. Webb et al., *Unobtrusive Measures* (Skokie, Ill.: Rand McNally, 1966), pp. 142–70.

49. Carol Tavris, "The Experimenting Society: To Find Programs That Work, Government Must Measure Its Failures," *Psychology Today*, September 1975, pp. 47–56, at 47.

50. Richard J. Meislin, "Legislators Say Abortion Study Invades Privacy," *New York Times*, May 12, 1977, p. 1.

51. Rivlin, op. cit., p. 109. See also Alice M. Rivlin and P. Michael Timpane, *Ethical and Legal Issues of Social Experimentation* (Washington, D.C.: Brookings Institution, 1975).

52. Alanson R. Wilcox, "Public Services under a Government of Laws," in U.S. Department of Health, Education and Welfare, "What's Going On In HEW?" *HEW Forum Papers*, 1967–1968, p. 106.

53. Hatry et al., op. cit., p. 61.

54. See Rivlin and Timpane, op. cit.

7

Budgeting for Results

LEARNING OBJECTIVES

TO UNDERSTAND:

Input, performance and results-oriented budgeting
Planning-programming-budgeting systems (PPBS)
Zero-base budgeting (ZBB)
Political and technical obstacles to budgeting for results
Differences in the perspectives of planners and budgeters

---

*T*he beginning student of budgeting is often bothered, baffled, and bewildered by the host of budgeting systems he or she encounters. Besides the standard line-item budget, there are things called performance budgets, program budgets, planning-programming-budgeting systems (PPB, or PPBS), and zero-base budgeting (ZBB). We define these below, and explain the nature of achievement-oriented budgeting approaches.

DEFINING BUDGETING AND VARIOUS BUDGET APPROACHES

The word *budget* derives from the Middle English word for *pouch* or *purse*. As economist Jesse Burkhead has noted, "In Britain the term was used to describe the leather bag in which the Chancellor of the Exchequer carried to Parliament the statement of the Government's needs and resources."[1] Eventually budget came to mean the statement inside the pouch, rather than the pouch.

Such a statement presents information on the finances of an organization, including its income, spending, and activities. A *budget* is future oriented, estimating what the organization is likely to receive in revenue, to spend, and to accomplish over a future period.[2] As the reader can see, this is a very broad definition. It *has* to be broad to encompass the different budgeting systems existing in the United States today.

While there are almost as many variations on budgeting as there are governments in this country, we can classify budget systems into one or a combination of three general approaches.[3] The first is the *input*-oriented approach, generally referred to as the line-item or financial-legal budget. Under this approach, items purchased, rented, or hired (which are called objects of expenditure) are listed as in Table 7–1. They indicate what the budgetary inputs are—whether these be wages, equipment, or supplies—but do not provide any information about the activities or outputs which the inputs will accomplish.

An *activity* approach to budgeting indicates what kind of workload the inputs will result in. Such an approach is usually called a performance budget and is characterized by the layout depicted in Figure 7–1.
Note that Figure 7–1 indicates the activities to be performed with appropriated funds.

An *output* approach to budgeting sets goals and attempts to evaluate success in achieving these goals. This approach to budgeting should be familiar to the reader who has gotten through the preceding chapters, since it is the general approach advocated throughout this book. Figure 7–2 illustrates output budget categories. Output-oriented budget approaches include program budgets, PPBS (which also attempts to evaluate alternatives over a multiyear period), and ZBB, the principal emphasis of this chapter.

THE PLANNING-PROGRAMMING-BUDGETING SYSTEM (PPBS)

PPBS is the most ambitious of the results-oriented approaches we examine in this book, for it is a budgetary system which combines long-range planning (up to five years into the future) with results-oriented programs and evaluation.

TABLE 7–1   PROPOSED STREET MAINTENANCE INPUT BUDGET, CITY OF PHOENIX DEPARTMENT OF TRANSPORTATION, 1977

Street Maintenance	$10,950,662
Salaries and Wages	6,230,162
Equipment	
7 Trucks	300,000
3 Steamrollers	150,000
Other	850,000
Maintenance of Equipment	910,000
Supplies	
Asphalt	1,570,000
Other	520,000
Miscellaneous	420,500

FIGURE 7-1. PROPOSED STREET MAINTENANCE ACTIVITY BUDGET, CITY OF PHOENIX TRANSPORTATION DEPARTMENT, 1977

Program Goals

Assist in providing for the safe and expeditious use of public streets and alleys through a regular street maintenance program, minimize danger to life and property through the control of irrigation and storm water, and assist in maintaining acceptable aesthetic standards for public streets and alleys.

TOTAL BUDGET $10,950,662

1976-77 Program and Objectives Highlights

Service levels relating to significant departmental objectives which will be achieved wit wtith 1976-77 recommended budget allowances:

- Fog seal 340 miles of Class A streets out of a desired level of 500 miles per year.
- Repair all chuckholes on major and collector streets within 72 hours of notification compared to a desired level of response within 24 hours.
- Continue to grade 85 out of a desired 121 miles of unpaved Class D streets monthly.
- Continue to achieve objective of grading all 700 miles of unpaved alleys every two years and gravel as needed.
- Mow weeds from the 162 miles of unimproved shoulders of major and collector streets four times a year to achieve desired objective.
- Sweep all 50 curb miles of downtown streets daily.
- Sweep 425 curb miles of heavily traveled major and collector streets weekly out of a desired level of 550 miles weekly.
- Sweep 3,824 curb miles of local and low-use major and collector streets every 5½ weeks compared to a desired level of every four weeks.
- Clean 800 out of a total 1,000 inlets and catch basins once a month to achieve 80% of the desired service level.
- Clean 95 miles of drainage ditches once every 7 months to achieve 85% of desired objective of cleaning every 6 months.
- Sealcoat 40 miles of major, 20 miles of collector and 200 miles of Class A local streets to avert further street detioration — $1,500,000.
- Provide required sealcoating for State highways in Phoenix as requested by the State Highway Department (reimbursed by State of Arizona) — $50,000.
- Continue the dust control program for south Phoenix streets implemented in 1974–75 — $50,000.

Governmental PPBS had its origins in the Defense Department in the early 1960s, where President Johnson was so impressed by its work that in 1965 he directed PPBS be used in all federal agencies. At the same time, a number of states and localities adopted PPBS.

PPBS budgeters follow the same kind of planning process outlined in Chapter 2. The programs which result from this process should then be evaluated by the approaches discussed in Chapter 6. Such evaluation, as noted

FIGURE 7–2   PROPOSED STREET MAINTENANCE OUTPUT BUDGET CITY OF PHOENIX DEPARTMENT OF TRANSPORTATION, 1977

Program Goals

Assist in providing for the safe and expeditious use of public streets and alleys through a regular street maintenance program, minimize danger to life and property through the control of irrigation and storm water, and assist in maintaining acceptable aesthetic standards for public streets and alleys.

Program Objectives Highlights

1. Reduce street flooding 10 percent from last year's levels (criterion: number of square feet flooded to a depth of six or more inches × minutes flooded) $457,832.00

2. Reduce dwelling flooding 10 percent from last year's levels (criterion: amount of estimated property damage) $119,830.00

3. Reduce automobile damage from potholes by 10 percent from last year's levels $384,296.00

4. Increase traffic flow on class A streets 5 percent from last year's levels through prompt repair . . . $872,419.00

5. Increase aesthetic standards by 10 percent (criterion: citizen questionnaire) $82,117.00

---

in that chapter, is often referred to as a *performance audit*. The term is confusing, since performance budgeting is activities-workload oriented, while performance auditing is results oriented.

While a number of governmental jurisdictions still use PPBS, interest in it has declined while enthusiasm for ZBB is increasing. For this reason, we will not describe the workings of PPBS in detail, but will sketch its achievements before going on to a more intensive examination of ZBB.

The Record of PPBS

The Federal Government   Federal PPBS was instituted across the board with a bang in 1965, but died with a whimper in 1971. Expert observer Allen Schick concludes that its demise was due to multiple wounds: lack of preparation, inadequate support and resources, lack of skilled manpower, and a clash of perspectives between PPBS implementers and traditional budgeters. But PPBS did not die, in his opinion, because of subversion by the line agencies, most of which gave it a serious try. Schick concludes that PPBS was doomed by the failure of the federal Bureau of the Budget, the central staff budget agency, to adequately support the new system.[4]

While the overall effort floundered, there were successes in various federal agencies. Thomas Lynch's study of PPBS in the Department of Transportation concluded that the Coast Guard "took quite seriously the presidential order to develop a PPB system,"[5] using it as a decision-making tool in planning for aids to navigation. According to Lynch, some federal agencies, including the Coast Guard, continue to use PPBS today even after its systemwide demise.

State Government   PPBS was taken up by a number of states, including New York, Pennsylvania, California, Wisconsin, Florida, and Hawaii. (In 1971, Harry Hatry reported that 20 states had undertaken some PPBS activities.)[6] In some states, such as New York, PPBS was dropped shortly after it was introduced. New York State budgeter Stephen M. Fletcher concluded that PPBS was too ambitious in scope and depth to be applied in New York; and Fletcher also felt that the same reasons listed by Schick for the death of federal PPBS applied in New York. New York did not completely abandon results-oriented budgeting, but switched to a narrower approach which selected specific priority areas for analysis.[7]

Other states have stuck with PPBS. One of these is Pennsylvania, which Schick designated in 1971 as the state that had taken PPBS the furthest.[8] Yet a 1974 study concluded that only about half the study budget is governed by PPB criteria. Stated objectives are not specific enough to be measured, so that evaluation of results is impossible. A case study of the Department of Education concluded that most budgetary decisions are made in the same manner they were before PPBS was introduced.[9]

A more optimistic conclusion is found in a 1977 study which concludes that results-oriented approaches are employed in Pennsylvania, if not so comprehensively or ambitiously as originally hoped. In many cases, analysts in the governor's budget office reported using output data as the primary basis on which at least part of their recommendations were made. The study concludes that progress toward a results orientation has been made, even if optimal goals have not been reached.[10]

While state PPBS has not achieved revolutionary change, PPBS is still used in a number of states.

Local Government   A 1972 survey of 214 cities and 120 counties found that 22 percent of the former and 17 percent of the latter reported using at least some elements of PPBS.[11] It has also been used in a large number of school systems, since federal and state aid program officials pressed for its use. A 1971 guesstimate by Harry Hatry concluded that "perhaps between 50 and 100 of the approximately 1,000 city and county governments of over 50,000 population have made some significant use of PPBS."[12] No doubt this is true, as a budget official of Orange County, California, insisted to the author in 1974. Regrettably, we cannot go beyond this level of generality because of the lack of follow-up studies.

ZERO-BASE BUDGETING (ZBB): ASSUMPTIONS AND CHARACTERISTICS

As mentioned above, input-oriented line-item budgeting is the predominant budgeting approach found in the United States today. While line-item budgeting may sometimes be combined with activity data, only rarely will output data be used.

The practice of line-item budgeting is often incompatible with an output-oriented approach. That is, there is usually no evaluation of how well programs work, and no subsequent curtailment or modification of programs which do not seem to be accomplishing very much. Frequently, the budget appropriation which an agency or program received the year before is regarded as its "base" for the next year's budget. That is, the base is treated as something to be left intact, with an increment added. In hard budget times, there may be some minor reduction in the base, but rarely will there be major (over 10 percent) cuts. In typical incremental budgeting, agency "success" is determined not by results achieved by programs, but by the amount of funds appropriated to the agency by the legislature.

In zero-base budgeting, the base is not to be regarded as a given which should not be analyzed. President Jimmy Carter, an advocate of ZBB who has implemented it in the federal government, has defined ZBB as follows: "Under this novel concept, every dollar requested for expenditure during the next budget period must be justified, including current expenditures that are to continue. It also provides for examining the effectiveness of each activity at various funding levels."[13] Such an approach obviously dovetails with the other approaches advocated in this book, and just as obviously involves a good deal of work. The next section deals with setting up ZBB.

After Jimmy Carter was elected governor of Georgia in 1970, he happened to read an article on ZBB by business consultant Peter A. Pyhrr. Intrigued by Pyhrr's arguments, Carter called him down to Georgia to set up ZBB for the Georgia state government. After setting up the system, Pyhrr published a book on ZBB which forms the basis for this section.[14] Pyhrr divides ZBB into two basic steps, developing and ranking "decision packages."

Developing Decision Packages

A *decision package* describes an activity or function in terms of its goals, its activities, its performance measures, its costs and benefits, the consequences of not performing it, and alternatives to it. Figure 7–3 is an actual decision package for the Georgia State Highway Patrol's field operations. Note that there are specific statements for each of the items listed above.

Like MBO, ZBB is a decentralizing approach which delegates to managers the task of putting decision packages together. Decision packages can deal with people, projects, programs, services, costs, and expenditures as long as they focus on *what is being achieved* by these personnel and items . For example, a people-centered decision package might focus on the principals for two neighboring elementary schools. It would focus on what they accomplish and could raise for consideration alternatives such as eliminating one principal and turning over both schools to the remaining principal.

Figure 7–3 illustrates a program-centered decision package. *Services* such as ambulance costs paid for by a welfare department, *cost overruns* beyond the amount projected, and *line-item expenditures* such as travel or consultant fees

FIGURE 7-3 GEORGIA STATE HIGHWAY PATROL DECISION PACKAGE

(1) Package Name
Georgia State Highway Patrol–Field Operation (1 of 5)
(6) Statement of Purpose
To patrol the rural and public roads and highways throughout the State, to prevent, detect and investigate criminal acts, and to arrest and apprehend those charged with committing criminal offenses appertaining thereto, and to safeguard the lives and property of the public.
(7) Description of Actions (Operations)
Patrol the rural roads of the State and respond to civil unrest. Operate 45 patrol posts 365 days per year; utilizing a staff of 64 radio-operators, 45 clerk dispatchers, 45 sergeants, 45 corporals and 382 troopers for a total staff of 581.
· Replace 47 trooper positions with clerk dispatchers or radio operators to perform office duty, at a savings of $180 thousand.
· Reduce obligated and other service hours (for example: putting mail boxes at each station, rather than having 45 troopers spend one hour each day picking up the mail from the post office, saves 16 thousand man hours per year)—implement in FY 1972 rather than waiting until FY 1973.
· Increase preventative patrol 14% over the FY 1971 level.

FIGURE 7–3 (cont.)

(8) Achievements from Actions

Troopers already patrolling the roads can react faster to accidents and emergencies than if they were performing their other duties. The increased free patrol time will improve trooper service, plus reduce the time required by troopers to answer emergency calls—thus increasing even more the free patrol time available.

(9) Consequences of not Approving Package

The State would not have a patrol force to patrol the rural areas nor would local law enforcement agencies have access to a statewide law enforcement communication network.

(10) Quantitative Package Measures	FY 1971	FY 1972	FY 1973
Operate Station Hours	280	286	286
Obligated Service Hours	191	163	163
Other Service Hours	175	113	113
Preventive Patrol Hours	526	703	600
Total Hours Available	1172	1265	1162
(Hours in thousands)			

(11) Resources Required ($ in Thousands)	FY 1971	FY 1972	FY 1973	% FY 73/72
Operational	7005	7846	7131	91
Grants				
Capital Outlay	110			
Lease Rentals				
Total	7115	7846	7131	91
People (Positions)	586	631	581	92

FIGURE 7–3 (cont.)

(12) Alternatives (Different Levels of Effort) and Cost

(2 of 5) Reassign 34 troopers from license pickup duties to the State Patrol. By changing the license pickup method, only 20,610 hours of obligated service will be transferred with these 34 troopers, providing a net gain of 49,464 hours for preventive patrol (cost $417K)

(3 of 5) Fifty State Troopers for 103 thousand hours of preventive patrol (cost $501K)

(4 of 5) Pay Troopers for overtime rather than giving compensatory time-off—equivalent to 20 troopers, provides 41,229 hours of additional preventive patrol (cost $173K)

(5 of 5) Upgrade 45 Trooper positions to corporal positions (cost $25K)

(Note: Approval of all packages would increase free patrol time 42% at a 5% increase in cost over FY 1972, and increase free patrol time 90% at a 16% increase in cost over FY 1971).

(13) Alternatives (Different Ways of Performing the Same Function, Activity, or Operation)

Abolish the Georgia State Patrol and let local jurisdictions-provide traffic law enforcement in the rural areas. Not feasible because: (1) Local jurisdictions would be deprived of the statewide communication system. (2) The mobility of todays population, made possible by the motor vehicle, makes it impossible for local jurisdictions to deal with traffic law enforcement problems effectively. (3) In cases of civil disorder or natural disaster, there would not be trained force available to augment local effort other than the National Guard.

could all become the subjects of decision packages. ZBB, then, is a flexible tool for managers, adaptable to a wide variety of uses.

Description of Purpose or Goals   The goal statement of a decision package should always be specific to the function performed. That is, the purpose of a state police laboratory is to identify the victims or criminals in various crimes, not to prevent crime and apprehend criminals. This broader goal is the goal of the entire state police department, and is not useful in analyzing the activities of one of its components.

Description of Activities   The description of program activities answers the questions, What will you do? and How will you do it? As Figure 7–3 indicates, this section indicates the approaches, activities and kinds of employees and equipment recommended to get the job done.

Consequences of Not Performing the Activity   This section is undoubtedly the most painful for a line agency manager to fill out, and she or he is thus likely to forecast the downfall of the republic if the activity should be eliminated. Both line managers and central staff agency ZBB analysts should mull this entry over very carefully, for it is the package item most likely to be deliberately or inadvertently inaccurate.

Performance Measures   Performance measures or evaluative criteria have already been identified as crucially important and discussed in Chapters 2 and 6. Item 10 in Figure 7–3 lists the measures used in the Georgia State Highway Patrol decision package.

Costs   It is difficult to know just how much cost information to provide. Some information is absolutely necessary for managers to make a rational decision, but some is detail which may not be necessary. Monthly cost figures, for example, become quite burdensome, and are not essential to get the job done. They may be useful, but not useful enough to justify the added effort for most activities. Yet in some very expensive new projects, they may be considered essential. No easy rule of thumb can be given.

Benefits   Benefits are usually more difficult to measure than costs. One reason for this is that they often include qualitative judgments (beauty of the environment) as well as countable considerations. The benefits listed in item 8, "Achievements from Action," of Figure 7–3 illustrate the less precise nature of benefit forecasting. At the same time, these projected achievements are concrete enough to be measured and evaluated in the future.

Alternatives   Pyhrr states that "the key to zero-base budgeting lies in the identification and evaluation of alternatives for each activity."[15] He further recommends considering two different types of alternatives for each decision package. The first identifies different ways of getting the job done. One of these is selected for the decision package as the best way, while the others are listed with brief explanations of why they were rejected. Figure 7–3's item 13 illustrates such a listing of alternatives for one governmental activity.

The second kind of alternative involves different levels of effort needed to perform the function. These involve a minimum level and other, more ambitious levels. *Each additional level should be identified as a separate decision package*, as is done in item 12 of Figure 7–3.

Why should managers identify different levels of effort rather than recommend the levels they feel appropriate? The rationale behind this procedure lies in the fact that line managers usually know the results of their programs better than other budgetary decision makers. By breaking programs into specific packages, they may avoid the complete elimination of certain functions which would occur if only one package were identified. Chief executives and legislators usually make across-the-board slashes or increases in agency budgets. For example, if the overall budget is to be cut 5 percent, most agencies will be cut at a level close to this figure. But if the budget decision makers realize fully the consequences of cuts, they may not want to chop across the board. Rather than eliminate entire functions or programs, they can reduce current levels of effort in a selective way.

Establishing Decision Packages   How can managers apply the general principles above in formulating decision packages? They should begin with this year's budget, identify activities, and calculate the cost for each activity. If managers can then relate these activities to the division's or program's goals and to factors such as employee wage increases, number of clientele served, addition or reduction in facilities, and planned changes in operations (e.g., expansion into another area), some careful budget planning can be done.

After this information has been assembled, managers can begin to develop packages. The starting point is the status quo, or business as usual. After this level has been established, other packages that involve different levels of effort or different ways of doing the job or new activities and programs can be developed.

For example, to return to Figure 7–3, the status quo would be the program listed in item 7 *minus* the functions headed "Replace," "Reduce," and "Increase." These new functions would become part of the final decision package.

Where Should Decision Packages Be Prepared?   Pyhrr states that ZBB decision packages may be prepared at different levels, and several factors determine the appropriate choice.

The first factor is the size of the organization. In a smaller operation, the manager may have to decide that the only appropriate decision package that can be developed would apply to the organization or one of its divisions as a whole, rather than to a subdivision. In a larger organization, the subdivisions could more easily make their own decision packages. The reason for this difference is that specific functions in a smaller division (e.g., teaching of French and Spanish in a small school) may be performed by the same person. If this is so, it makes no sense to put together a Spanish decision package, which involves only a fraction of a man-year and thus cannot be eliminated to save a position. A meaningful decision package here would have to include *both* languages. For this reason, Pyhrr concludes that size of the function analyzed is the most important factor determining how and where decision packages are put together.

Another factor is the number of realistically available alternatives. For example, if an agency rents office space and has a five-year contract for same, decision packages weighing the consequences of moving out of that space do not make sense until the lease is up. Federal and state grants usually have strings attached prohibiting consideration of many alternatives by the grant-receiving agency. For example, most states and many federal grants are apportioned on a formula basis (e.g., so much per school pupil) and cannot be moved from one school district to another even if need indicates that such a move would be appropriate. This means that decision packages on an interschool district level would be a waste of time. Decision packages should be formulated, rather, within each district.

Another crucial factor is the constraint of time. Lower levels of the organization, especially during the initial installation of ZBB, may lack the ability to put together decision packages in time to meet budget deadlines. Obviously, the learning process will take a while, and during this period of education, decision packages may have to be prepared solely by higher organizational levels.

Presenting the Package   How detailed should the decision package be? This depends on several factors. One is the size of the organization and the type of communication it uses. In a smaller organization with more face-to-face contact, it may be possible to use brief written decision package statements. Such brevity is possible if the managers have a chance to make verbal presentations at all organizational levels. In larger organizations, the package statement and documents will probably have to be longer, since the number of packages and levels in the organization will not allow superiors to spend so much time discussing packages with subordinates.

Another consideration is special and supporting analyses. The decision package should *not* be designed to handle every possible question which might arise, or it will be impossibly detailed and cumbersome. Instead, such supporting documents can be attached as appendices to the package, or be made available on request.

Finally, additional details required after the budget decision has been made should also be provided *after* the decision. This information includes cost details, program responsibilities, and other fine-tuning adjustments. Because such details are very time consuming, it makes sense to do necessary detail work *after* the budget decision has been made. There seems little point in assembling all the necessary minutiae for decision packages which may be rejected.

Ranking Decision Packages   Ranking forces management to ask how much it should spend on each function and where it should spend it. The ranking process accomplishes these steps by listing all the decision packages in order of decreasing benefits to be derived from them.

Like MBO, the ranking process begins at the bottom of the bureaucracy. Managers at the lowest level rank their packages in order of priority and present them to their immediate superiors, who repeat this process all the way up the line.

Figure 7–4 details the ranking process for decision packages in the New Jersey Department of Health. Level 1 packages have top priority, while level 5 have least priority. Note how the sheet enables decision makers to identify priorities at a glance and then, if desired, to request the detailed package information, so that further analysis can be made of each package. Figure 7–4 also identifies the cumulative funding level, so that total budget impact of each of the packages can quickly be identified. Further comparative data for the present fiscal year allow budget decision makers to examine trends. Thus, if there is a substantial increase or no reduction in effort proposed, as is true for the health economics category in Figure 7–4, the decision packages can be selected out and gone through with a fine-tooth comb.

Not every decision package can be reviewed by the top management of a large organization. Rather, there must be some consolidation of packages. At the same time, management must be careful not to overconsolidate. How can this balance be achieved?

Pyhrr recommends that management focus its review efforts on lower ranked activities. To do this, a cutoff spending total must be established at each organizational level. Then, only the decision packages which did not make the cutoff would be reviewed in detail and ranked. Packages retained will be listed, but not reviewed in this probing fashion. Furthermore, to keep down the number of decision packages which will accumulate, the expenditure cutoff total has to be increased at each successive level. For example, a cutoff point of 60 percent of the present year's budget can be set for the lowest organizational level, while the next level will allow 70 percent, and the final level 80 percent. This phasing prevents too great an accumulation of decision packages for review at each successive level and effectively *decentralizes* much of the decision-making process.

In applying this approach, ZBB managers and analysts must be very careful not to become overly mechanical. A cutoff point of 60 percent can easily panic line agency managers. *The point of the process is to concentrate manage-*

FIGURE 7–4 AGENCY PRIORITY SPENDING ANALYSIS PREPARED BY THE NEW JERSEY DEPARTMENT OF HEALTH

Health
Department

BUDGET REQUEST FY 1978

360-100
Account Number

(Thousands of Dollars)

Activity (1)	Program Code (2)	Expended 19 76 (3)	Appropriated 19 77 (4)	Level 1 (5)	Level 2 (6)	Level 3 (7)	Level 4 (8)	Level 5 (9)	Cumulative Total (10)	Recommended Budget Bureau (11)
Interest on Public Constr. Bds.	22150	297	286	143					143	
Interest on Public Constr. Bds.					72				215	
Interest on Public Constr. Bds.						71			286	
Dept. Mgmt. & Genl. Supp.	various	2430	2236	1118					1404	
Dept. Mgmt. & Genl. Supp.					559				1963	
Dept. Mgmt. & Genl. Supp.						559			2522	
Dept. Mgmt. & Genl. Supp.							559		3081	
Dept. Mgmt. & Genl. Supp.								207	3288	
Diagnostic Services	24110	1441	1468	734					4022	
Diagnostic Services					367				4389	
Diagnostic Services						367			4756	
Diagnostic Services							229		4985	
Diagnostic Services (new)								440	5425	
Health Economics	23120	366	746	373					5798	
Health Economics					187				5985	
TOTAL										

FORM DD104-D REV. 51

ment's time on the low-priority packages, not to cut the budget by an arbitrary fixed figure. Careful communication and reassurance must be carried out in a Theory Y atmosphere if terror and resistance are not to result. The purpose of the cutoff point procedure is simply to make ZBB manageable.

Besides reviewing only the lowest ranked packages, management must be careful to keep the number of budget decision-making levels down. But it should not reduce them so much that all ranking decisions are made only at very low levels, because top managers will find it difficult and time consuming to rank decisions made at those levels. A compromise is necessary and will probably have to be arrived at by trial and error in each organization.

Who should rank packages, and how should it be done? As is also true for MBO, Pyhrr recommends that packages be ranked first at the organizational level where they are originally developed. And where lower level ranking can be done by the manager in charge, higher level ranking should be done by a committee made up of managers whose packages are involved. After all, top managers will not be intimately familiar with all these packages, and will thus need the advice of these subordinates in committee to make sensible decisions.

In a large organization, such as a state government, the chief executives cannot review all the decision packages. For example, Governor Jimmy Carter faced 10,000 decision packages while governor of Georgia. He focused his review on policy questions, major budget increases and decreases, new programs, and some special problem areas. Carter was actually reviewing and making final decisions on packages and rankings put together by line managers and budget division staff. They set the agenda for him to make the final decisions on.[16]

Managing ZBB   Pyhrr, like advocates of MBO, argues that ZBB is dynamic and flexible, able to adapt to changing conditions in little more than the twinkling of a lash. For example, ZBB packages and rankings can be modified or eliminated individually. This means that a change in organizational goals does not necessitate reform of the entire budget. Only packages directly affected by the new plan need be changed, as is also true for their rankings. Such specific adjustments would take place if the budget were decreased or increased.

GOVERNMENTAL USE OF ZBB

The Federal Government

As mentioned earlier, ZBB is currently being implemented in the federal government.[17] The schedule set by President Carter calls for the budget for fiscal year 1979 to be prepared under ZBB guidelines. While across-the-board federal experience with ZBB has just begun, there exist earlier cases of federal use of ZBB. One such ZBB experience took place in the Department of Agriculture, beginning in 1962. Budget scholars Aaron Wildavsky and Arthur

Hamman investigated the results of this experiment in 1963 and concluded that only a few minor changes took place as a result. In the authors' words, "There was widespread agreement that the zero-base budget did not significantly affect outcomes."[18]

However, before we rush to generalize from this example, note that *the ZBB approach used in Agriculture is not the same as that described in this chapter.* In the words of budget authorities Allen Schick and Robert Keith, "Whatever the conceptual affinities of the earlier and present efforts, they share few practical similarities. . . . [In Agriculture] none of the distinctive methods associated with current ZBB activities were present."[19] We cannot, then, draw conclusions from this use of ZBB which will be relevant to future federal experience.

State Government

After Jimmy Carter's initiation of ZBB for Georgia State government in 1971, the technique spread to another 11 states by 1976. In addition, another 6 used some but not all of the techniques associated with ZBB; and another 3 decided not to use ZBB, because they had just introduced PPBS, which they felt would accomplish the same ends.[20]

However, the states that use ZBB apply it differently. For example, in California, Rhode Island, and Tennessee, decision packages are either not used or used alongside the traditional line-item system. Moreover, while some states, including Georgia, require that the first decision package be set at a level just adequate to barely sustain the program, others, such as Illinois (90 percent) or Montana (80 percent), set a given percentage of the current budget as the level for the first decison packages. Third, priority rankings are found in all states but California, which applies ZBB selectively rather than across the board.

Schick and Keith conclude that state ZBB does not really require that the budget be built up from nothing each year, but that it shifts "the bulk of budget preparation from increments above the budget base to decrements below the base."[21] In other words, as used in the states, ZBB seems designed primarily to halt large increases in spending.

One state, New Mexico, has tried and abandoned ZBB. Schick feels that the two principal causes for this relinquishment were the enormous paperwork generated by ZBB and a failure to take ZBB seriously after a huge (and temporary) budget surplus came into being.[22] It should also be noted that New Mexico ZBB was instituted by the legislature, without equal enthusiasm from the executive branch.[23]

Determining the results of ZBB is extremely difficult. As Allen Schick has remarked, no one knows quite how to take before-and-after snapshots of budgets.[24] There are too many factors, such as changing economic trends and political variables, to make easy judgments about what ZBB produces. For example, while the budget of the Office of the Massachusetts Secretary of the

Commonwealth declined by 10 percent in two years of ZBB, this does not mean that it would not have dropped 10 percent without ZBB.[25] We shall see later in our New Jersey ZBB case study that state spending dropped drastically after ZBB was initiated, but we shall also see that it is difficult to attribute that drop to ZBB.

More likely to be true are claims like that made by Texas Budget Director Charles Travis: "ZBB itself doesn't save money. What it does is to provide better information for the decision makers." Similarly, a 1974 study of Georgia budget analysts found that state employees understood the workings of government better as a result of ZBB. The study concluded that ZBB had improved the quality of management information and brought about greater involvement in the budgetary process by lower level personnel. (Only 2 of 13 Georgia government department heads felt that ZBB "may" have reallocated resources, while only 7 of 32 Georgia budget analysts felt ZBB caused "some" shifting of financial resources.)[26] While Schick and Keith report that most states using ZBB are pleased with it, they are *not* pleased with it because it has caused major changes in budget appropriations.[27] Yet we should not minimize the importance of a budgeting system which can provide higher quality program data, a crucial concern for results-oriented managers.

Local Government

ZBB has also been used in a number of local governments, including Wilmington, Delaware; Garland, Texas; and Yonkers, New York. By the time these words appear in print, it is safe to predict that a much larger number of our 80,000 local governments will be trying variations of ZBB. At present, however, we lack a survey of local ZBB practices comparable to the one of state practices. In its place, we have only inflated claims offered without evidence, such as one article's assertion that ZBB in Yonkers lowered tax rates and allowed high-priority budget items to be funded.[28] Readers will no doubt have a chance to observe and evaluate ZBB at work in their own or a nearby local government very soon.

TECHNICAL PROBLEMS AND HOW TO MINIMIZE THEM

As mentioned earlier, ZBB is the latest in a series of budget reforms designed to make government more effective and efficient. Like its predecessors, ZBB is not without problems—as Pyhrr himself admits. Lest our analysis in this section seem too negative, we quote the words that Frederick C. Mosher, a leading scholar of public administration, wrote in 1969 about planning-pro-gramming-budgeting systems (PPBS):

> After I had written a mildly critical review of PPBS, I received a confidential letter from one of the top PPBS leaders in a major federal department. He wrote, in effect, that he agreed with everything I had written, but that I had

no business writing it, since it might hurt the cause. On the other hand, I think a more realistic and a more public view of the cost and effectiveness of PPBS itself would be useful.[29]

Our comments should be taken in the same vein. They are intended to help users of ZBB arrive at a realistic picture of this budgeting system.

Even more than is true for MBO, ZBB could easily drown everyone in a paralysis of paperwork, as reported in our discussion of New Mexico. The time, effort, and paper needed to generate and rank decision packages also involve substantial cost to any organization. Former Deputy Director of the federal Office of Management and Budget Paul O'Neill stated in 1976 that ZBB would produce "mountains of paperwork" with few results.[30] As noted above, Pyhrr feels that being inundated by paper can be avoided *if* steps are taken to focus on low priorities and to minimize the number of organizational levels involved.

Another tactic is to use ZBB intermittently rather than annually. We do not recommend this approach, however, because it throws the baby out with the bathwater. Not only is paperwork dispensed with but so is ZBB. If the agency is serious about it, ZBB should be a regular process. The process will become much easier to follow after the first year, as employees get used to it. And many of the decision packages will doubtless remain the same from one year to the next, which should further reduce the paperwork.

A more fruitful way to cut down on the workload is to follow the tactic of selective installation already advocated in previous chapters. While Pyhrr believes that ZBB can be installed across the board in government organizations with good results, we disagree. It is far better to try ZBB out selectively and then eliminate the bugs encountered.

An analysis of ZBB in Georgia made during its first year of operation concluded that "the quality of the decision packages and analysis is generally poor to mediocre."[31] Who was the author of this statement? None other than Peter Pyhrr, the champion of ZBB! However, we quote his words here not to indicate that ZBB is a fiction, but to note his frank acknowledgment of the difficulties in implementing it. Pyhrr notes that the first year of trying anything new is going to be difficult and that most problems encountered can be traced to management shortcomings within the organization. For example, the lack of a planning process, the absence of incentives for greater effectiveness, problems in obtaining data, and resistance of agency managers to an approach which might threaten their autonomy were the key stumbling blocks. Pyhrr's point in identifying these difficulties is not to discourage tryouts, but to give a realistic picture of what the "debugging" process will be like.

Another reason to be so selective is the existing state of the art in evaluation, discussed in the previous chapter. Since ZBB is at bottom a tool for integrating evaluation of programs into the budgetary process, a strong evaluative capacity must exist. But as William Gorham, President of the Urban Institute, noted in July 1976, "to try to review 20 percent of all federal programs (each year) would undermine . . . credibility . . . even if the act were laced with extra evaluation funds."[32] In other words, the technical resources for such a mammoth task just are not there. While Pyhrr notes this difficulty, he makes the point that "At least the identification of meaningful measures of evaluation usually initiates the development of statistical records for future evaluation, and the lack of work measures on any package should automatically be a red flag to raise the question of whether or not there *are* any meaningful measures."[33]

Another problem area discussed by Pyhrr is ranking decision packages for dissimilar functions. When the packages move up to a higher level of review, how does the manager removed from the scene of direct action review these packages? For example, if one police precinct house puts a ranking on preventive patrol, special anti-mugging squads, and a police neighborhood storefront resource, how is someone at headquarters going to rationally review these rankings? Pyhrr suggests that the reviewer who jumps in with both feet and gets started will probably find that the task is a lot easier than suspected. The reader has a right to be skeptical about this suggestion, for review is much easier said than done. There is no question that the superior will have to take a certain amount of the information and analysis provided by subordinates at face value. The superior's job will be to carefully review these materials and ask hard questions about them. The superior cannot do the same lengthy job of developing and ranking the package that the subordinates did, but must run spot checks or look for suspicious signs instead.

One of the most searching critiques of ZBB has come from Robert N. Anthony, professor of management control at Harvard Business School, who states flatly that ZBB is a fraud.[34] As he notes, the bulk of the decision packages put together are not given a searching review. Instead, only those considered least essential are examined thoroughly. In most cases, Anthony notes, a figure of 70 percent or 80 percent of current budget effort is set as the cutoff point. As Pyhrr notes, packages below the cutoff point will not receive the thorough scrutiny that the less essential ones above it will. In Anthony's words, "80 percent is a long way from zero."

In defense of Pyhrr, we should note that all decision packages are ranked. But no one above the initial level reviews those which fall below the cutoff point, so that Anthony's charge that ZBB is not truly zero-base *review* is correct. And even more crucially, traditional budget methods do not examine the difference between funding levels of 80 percent and 100 percent.

Anthony further argues that the large numbers of decision packages are too much for top management to review. Here, though, he may miss the point. Top management cannot review all MBO goal statements and action plans, either. ZBB vests much of the ranking and review process in the hands of managers below the top level, who are not expected to review all the details of these plans. But Anthony's argument that if the chief executive delegates the ranking job to others, "the whole idea of comparing priorities is compromised"[35] carries a lot of weight. And Anthony also argues that "even if the numbers of decision packages were reduced to a manageable size, it is not possible to make a thorough analysis during the time available in the annual budget process."[36] The time for this analysis is during the planning and action plan implementation phases, which precede the budgetary process, according to Anthony. Time and the demands of other budget duties simply do not allow such analysis. (Note, as reported in the implementation section, that Pyhrr felt that Governor Jimmy Carter *was* able to make a meaningful ZBB review of Georgia State government, even though Carter did not look at most of the 10,000 packages.)

The crucial point is whether ZBB is a useful tool for results-oriented managers, not whether it truly starts from zero or whether the chief executive can look at all packages. We feel that ZBB does have this potential, if it is carried out on a selective basis using a Theory Y orientation. ZBB is no more a panacea than any of the other approaches examined in this book, but it raises questions that are ignored in the usual line-item budgeting process. While it cannot work miracles, ZBB can point to areas in which budget decision makers may want to look long and hard.

POLITICAL PROBLEMS AND HOW TO MINIMIZE THEM

The political problems confronted by a comprehensive output-oriented budgeting system such as ZBB dwarf even the substantial technical difficulties faced. The basic problem here is political support for programs that may be only slightly related to an agency's stated goals. If powerful interest groups and legislators support certain agency programs, the task of the ZBB operative will resemble that of Sisyphus, the figure in ancient Greek myth who kept rolling a huge boulder to the top of a mountain, only to see it plunge to the bottom again when he had finally ascended to the peak. An example is the U.S. Army Corps of Engineers' river-dredging program. Objective studies have shown that many of these projects do not generate sufficient return to justify them, but the projects continue nevertheless.[37] They continue because Congressmen, local politicians and businessmen, and the Corps of Engineers want them to. As Peter Pyhrr has said himself, "I must unfortunately agree that those who will expect large savings will undoubtedly be disappointed. Although program effectiveness may be dramatically increased in some instances, and programs reduced or eliminated in other instances, the political will does not exist to significantly reduce costs for health, education, welfare, defense, etc."[38]

Analysis of federal, state, and local budgetary systems indicates that the chief executive and his budget analysts simply cannot control much of the budget. "Uncontrollable" items include trust and special funds, such as federal and state highway funds, social security, retirement and pension programs, and perhaps even the local library's budget. These trust funds cannot be diverted to other programs; nor, in many cases, can budget officials redirect the flow of money within the trust fund. The laws governing social security, for example, do not allow budget officials to raise or lower benefits to retirees after running a ZBB program. Nor can highway funds be directed to mass transit without amending the legislation governing the highway trust fund.

As noted in the section on implementation, similar restrictions exist for federal and state formula grants-in-aid to local government. If a ZBB analysis concludes that County X really does not need these grants, there is no way to stop the flow of grant money unless the original legislation is amended. This will be a task for Sisyphus, since political decision making in this country is characterized by bargaining and compromise, and few people will want to discriminate against County X, lest they get the ax themselves the next time around.

Another uncontrollable item is payment of debt. Governments finance their large-scale ("capital") expenditures through bonding and then pay interest on the bonds. Whether it is the national debt, the debt incurred for state highway construction, or the debt for the new school building, all governments *must* pay interest on their bonds, or no one will buy future bonds.

These relatively uncontrollable items now account for over half of the annual federal budget and for large, if varying, percentages of state and local government budgets.[39] For this reason, Robert D. Lee, Jr., and Ronald W. Johnson, academic specialists in budgeting, conclude that "the zero-base approach makes the unrealistic assumption that decision makers have the capacity to eliminate programs. In reality, the political forces in any jurisdiction are such that few programs in any given year can be abandoned."[40] This passage, however, may miss the point. Astute users of ZBB may very well realize the presence of mandated and uncontrollable costs. In fact, these costs can constitute the minimum of 50 percent, 70 percent, 80 percent, or a higher funding level of different decision packages. This is one way of differentiating controllable from uncontrollable costs.

And we can also recommend here that ZBB advocates follow the advice of economist and former U.S. Treasury official Murray Weidenbaum.[41] He advocates "selling" the legislature on the desirability of a careful review of uncontrollables. Which trust funds, for instance, are essential to getting a job done if they are dissolved? Social Security funds, certainly; but this is *not* the case for highway funds, which were financed out of operating budgets until the 1950s. Good salesmanship would focus on the relatively high cost and low benefits of these candidates for controllability.

We wish we wielded a wizard's wand that we could offer to the reader, but there is no substitute here for persuasion. And some attempts to persuade will resemble an encyclopedia salesperson's bad days. Only when the correlation between lowering or stabilizing taxes and modifying or eliminating low-priority programs comes home to the legislator will she or he support a ZBB approach. But since legislative constituents are concerned with the tax rate, the potential for legislative change may be greater than anyone now thinks. Certainly some liberal United States senators, like Edmund Muskie of Maine, who demanded increased government spending without analysis just a few years ago, have changed their minds. Muskie is now demanding stringent analysis of programs to see their existence is justified. What could be closer in spirit to ZBB?

A caustic critique of ranking comes from Anthony, who states that "Honest agency heads will admit that program priority is influenced by the amount of funds likely to be available, rather than the other way around."[42] Anthony says that federal government attempts to rank programs, which date from 1960, have been abandoned. After all, administrators can rank priorities in such a way as to downgrade essential or popular programs. These downgraded programs will then be funded by the legislature, while other, higher ranked programs will be safe.

While Anthony is skeptical about this crucial aspect of ZBB, he suggests that ZBB can be used as a means of achieving some very useful budget reforms. In effect, he argues that ZBB should be used about once every five years instead of on an annual basis, and that stress on goals and programs to achieve them become part of the regular budget process. Anthony specifically notes the close intellectual relationship between MBO and ZBB, stating that ZBB could work to strengthen MBO, "particularly to focus more serious attention on the development of better output measures."[43] While we feel that ZBB should become an annual process, some agencies might want to go in Anthony's direction.

Ranking programs will not be easy. In 1977, one federal agency budget chief called ranking "crazy," because ranking different U.S. Department of Agriculture programs like food stamps, meat inspection, or maintenance of national forests serves no purpose except to upset supporters of these programs. All three programs must continue, or disaster would result in each area.[44] Agency resistance to ranking may be strong, but this criticism misses the point. The real value of ZBB is the rankings *within*—not *between* or *among*—programs. This is not to say there are no difficulties. As a review of Georgia state government ZBB by Pyhrr concluded, many managers developed their rankings to protect their employees and were extremely unhappy about changes recommended by the budget bureau.[45] Again, all the ZBB proponent can do here is to sell ZBB to the agencies, pointing out that it is designed to reward the most effective programs. But the task of the salesperson will be long and hard, even when conducted under the aegis of Theory Y. Agencies will be apprehensive for some time.

CASE STUDY:
ZBB IN NEW JERSEY STATE GOVERNMENT

After Brendan Byrne took office as governor of New Jersey in January 1974, he confronted a state budget which had grown at an annual rate of 16.8 percent during the previous decade. Byrne and his staff concluded that this pattern of growth would no longer be possible in New Jersey, which had still not recovered from the 1970 recession. The politically acceptable limits of budget growth had been reached.

Having made this decision, Byrne had to go about the unpleasant task of cutting the budget. He chose ZBB as the method by which to make cuts, rather than reducing appropriations across the board by a fixed percentage. The budget presented in January 1975 was drastically different from its predecessors, since it proposed an increase of only 1.8 percent. This "increase" actually represented a cut, since the rate of inflation and previously agreed-on wage and salary hikes would have increased the budget by much more than this amount, had no other changes been made. The legislature chopped this budget even more, adopting as its final version a budget with a 3 percent *cut.* The following year the budget which was adopted increased by only 2.1 percent over 1975.

New Jersey, then, was able to halt its rapidly growing budget increases. But the question remains, what role did ZBB play in this reduction?

The 1974 adoption of ZBB followed the state's 1960 commitment to planning-programming-budgeting, which emphasized output-oriented evaluation and long-range planning. In this sense, then, the state budget division was already involved with results-oriented budgeting. ZBB was adopted above all to cut down levels of expenditure.[46]

Schick and Keith have noted that "New Jersey's ZBB process calls for an identification of the qualitative and quantitative effects of a zero-funding level, and this may be the closest that any state comes to pure zero-base budgeting."[47] As Figure 7–4 (p. 185) indicates, the New Jersey approach includes the kind of information which Pyhrr says is necessary to operate ZBB. Figure 7–4 lists rankings for some health department programs. Note that five different priority rankings are involved.

In its formal aspects, then, New Jersey ZBB gets high grades. But how does it actually *work?* This question is much harder to answer, but we can provide the reader with the differing perspectives of two state government officials intimately familiar with the state budgetary process. Before we do this, note that many areas (over 59 percent of the 1976 New Jersey budget) cannot be changed by using ZBB. These include debt payments, employee pension and health benefits, federally mandated Medicaid and welfare benefits, and state grants-in-aid mandated by law.[48]

What has ZBB achieved in the other 40 percent of the budget? A state budget official strongly critical of ZBB told me in the spring of 1977 that only about 10 percent of the budget was subject to ZBB analysis. Two of the largest departments, Human Resources and Higher Education, were not evaluated by ZBB, nor were a number of smaller entities. Therefore, even if ZBB were totally effective, it could not affect the total budget picture very much. In addition, the official felt that forms such as those in Figure 7-4 were not meaningful without backup analytical studies. That is, without such analyses, which have not been carried out under ZBB, the numbers listed on the forms would not be substantiated. Finally, he noted the difficulty of attempting ZBB in the political environment of New Jersey. For years, under ZBB, PPBS, and line-item budgeting, cutbacks in funds for agricultural experiment stations have been recommended. Yet the state legislature has always restored them.

A differing viewpoint comes from a high-level New Jersey State budgeter. This official, also interviewed in spring 1977, noted that ZBB was an incremental addition to the already existing PPB system, which stressed planning and evaluation. Thus, ZBB should not have been expected to radically change budget decisions. The fact that there is nothing a budgeter can point to and label as a result of ZBB (e.g., "We kept or cut this item") should not be construed to mean that ZBB is just a paperwork shuffle. In this official's words, "What has improved is that departments now look at programs from a ZBB perspective. There have been substantial shifts in priority, although nothing which would appear that dramatic to the public."

The official claimed that the Department of Higher Education budget was already subjected to a zero type of analysis, so it seemed superfluous to integrate it into ZBB. He noted that several million dollars had been cut from the request in 1975, indicating that a process similar to ZBB already existed. (Yet the chief financial officer of one state college stated that nothing like ZBB analysis was used in making up the college's own budget request to the Department of Higher Education).

The budget official noted that the Department of Human Services, which is the largest state agency, had so many "technical" problems with ZBB that it was initially "let off the hook." However, it was expected to get into ZBB in a serious fashion in the next fiscal year. Departments that had used ZBB most successfully were Agriculture and Health, while priorities had shifted to economic development in the Department of Labor and Industry and to health care in Health as a result of ZBB.

Questions

Two different opinions of ZBB in one state have been given. We regret being unable to give the reader a definitive picture of ZBB's impact in New Jersey. Instead, the following questions are intended to sort out the reader's thoughts on this matter.

1. What was the primary reason for adopting ZBB in New Jersey?

2. Does New Jersey ZBB seem to follow the guidelines laid down by Peter Pyhrr?

3. What are some types of limitation on New Jersey ZBB's usefulness? Specifically, what limitations exist in the areas of grants-in-aid, technical difficulties, and politics?

4. Do you think ZBB in New Jersey is worth the effort put into it? Explain your reasons.

PROSPECTS AND PROBLEMS FOR ZBB

As has been noted in this chapter, ZBB has enjoyed great and growing popularity in the late 1970s. But a look at the historical ebb and flow of budget systems in the United States raises the strong possibility that ZBB may just be the latest of several budgetary fads. Performance budgeting and PPBS had their respective days in the sun in the 1950s and 1960s. Their champions pronounced inexorable and ineluctable growth for them, only to see them abandoned by the local, state, or federal governments that had initially embraced them.

What caused this fickleness? At bottom, oversell of the potential benefits and failure to mention the real costs and likely problems involved killed these budget systems. For example, it is no surprise that PPBS did not last in the federal government. Instead of being gradually refined and introduced in a few agencies at a time, it was implemented across the range of the entire federal bureaucracy in 1965. Promising young boxers are not thrown in the ring with the heavyweight champion at the first opportunity. They are, rather, carefully trained in fights with lesser opponents until the time when it is felt they have a realistic chance to beat the champion. It makes no more sense to throw a new budgeting system against the entire bureaucracy at once, but this has been the rule in the budgetary arena. When the Office of Management and Budget announced in spring 1977 that ZBB would be installed across the board in the federal government in time to produce the fiscal year 1979 budget, old budget hands smiled wryly and wondered why budget innovators never seem to look at the record. A five-year introductory period, in which all agencies have used the new system once by the end of the fifth year, seems more sensible.

A second point, noted by one of our sources in the New Jersey case study, is that ZBB without detailed evaluations or performance audits is a meaningless exercise. That is, ranking packages without examining the reasons given for ranking them means that the system still rests on untested assertions. Without evaluation, myths and assumptions are decked out in fancy new garments but remain just as inscrutably impenetrable as ever.

While writing critiques of PPBS, budget specialists Allen Schick and Aaron Wildavsky noted in 1969 that the budgetary process may be the wrong location for policy planning and evaluation. Schick contended that "If policy analysis is to flourish, it will have to be rescued from budgeting."[49] Schick believes that budgeters' concern with financial control and management lead them to downgrade planning and evaluation. Likewise, if "analytical" budgeters take over, budgetary management and control are likely to be downgraded and/or spun off to some other staff agency. There is no question that a gap separates budgeters, planners, and evaluators, and that Schick has correctly described the predominant orientation of the first group. And while Schick does *not* say that ZBB will not work, we believe that the reasons he has given for wanting to separate planning and evaluation from budgeting could apply as well to ZBB as they do to PPBS.

For reasons which seem to apply just as strongly to ZBB as they do to

PPBS, Wildavsky reached much the same conclusion: "To collect vast amounts of random data is hardly a serious analysis of public policy. The conclusion is obvious. The shotgun marriage between policy analysis and budgeting should be annulled."[50] Wildavsky suggests that planning and evaluation be delegated to department heads, who should run studies lasting 6–24 months. If the department head and central budget agency approve, the studies' findings should be translated into programs and budgetary funds.

We have already stated our concern that planning and evaluation may be sidetracked by the budgetary process. But this concern does not worry Peter Pyhrr, the creator of modern ZBB. Pyhrr's book *Zero-Base Budgeting* is not a naive or foolish work. The author constantly points out problems, never claims that ZBB is a panacea, and generally displays an impressive and thorough knowledge of both government and business. And since Pyhrr draws explicit distinctions between PPBS and ZBB, perhaps the objections we have raised above do not apply to ZBB.

Pyhrr defines PPBS as a "macroeconomic tool for centralized decision making on major policy issues and basic fund allocation," while ZBB "provides the microeconomic tool to transform these objectives into an efficient operating plan and budget and allows managers to evaluate the effect of various funding levels on programs and program elements so that limited resources can be more effectively allocated."[51] This microeconomic tool focuses particularly on efficiency, something that Pyhrr says PPBS neglects. PPBS also fails to provide line managers with tools for program implementation or any mechanism to evaluate the effect of different funding levels on programs. In short, ZBB is an operational tool for line managers, whereas PPBS is a planning tool for staff analysts and top management.

In the words of public administration professor and consultant John Rehfuss: "ZBB is really a bottom-up process, just the opposite of PPBS. It isn't a planning tool—it is a management, cost/efficient process. What ZBB really does is develop the skills and expand the views of lower level management and give them control of their budget process."[52]

Pyhrr believes that ZBB and PPBS are compatible and complementary, rather than contradictory and competing. He feels that ZBB, like MBO, is a Theory Y decentralizing approach which "taps a large reservoir of program knowledge and analytic resources ignored by PPB—the operating managers throughout the agency hierarchy."[53]

This emphasis is a proper one. Harnessed closely to competent and thorough evaluation, ZBB can be a mechanism to bring about badly needed change in government programs.

NOTES

1. Jesse Burkhead, *Government Budgeting* (New York: Wiley, 1956), p. 2.

2. Robert D. Lee, Jr., and Ronald W. Johnson, *Public Budgeting Systems*, 2nd ed. (Baltimore: University Park Press, 1977), p. 11.

3. Cf. Allen Schick, "The Road to PPB: The Stages of Budget Reform," *Public Administration Review* 26 (December 1966): 243–58.

4. Allen Schick, "A Death in the Bureaucracy: The Demise of Federal PPB," *Public Administration Review* 33 (March–April 1973): 146–56.

5. Thomas D. Lynch, *Policy Analysis in Public Policymaking* (Lexington, Mass.: D.C. Heath, 1975), p. 49.

6. Harry P. Hatry, "Status of PPB in Local and State Governments in the United States," *Policy Sciences* 2 (1971): 177–89, at 178.

7. Stephen M. Fletcher, "From PPBS to PAR in the Empire State," *State Government,* Summer 1972, pp. 198–202.

8. Allen Schick, *Budget Innovation in the States* (Washington, D.C.: Brookings Institution, 1971), p. 153.

9. Eli B. Silverman and Francis C. Gatti, Jr., "PPB on the State Level: The Case of Pennsylvania," *The Bureaucrat* 4 (July 1975): 117–46.

10. James E. Skok, "Sustaining PPBS in State Government," *The Bureaucrat* 6 (Fall 1977): 50–63.

11. *Local Government Budgeting, Program Planning, and Evaluation,* Urban Data Service Report (Washington, D.C.: International City Management Association, May 1972).

12. Hatry, op. cit., p. 179.

13. Edwin L. Dale, Jr., "ZBB and Sunset: What's The Difference?" *New York Times,* August 7, 1976, Business sect. p. 1.

14. Peter A. Pyhrr, *Zero-Base Budgeting: A Practical Management Tool for Evaluating Expenses* (New York: Wiley, 1973).

15. Ibid., p. 6.

16. Ibid., p. 97. See also Aaron Wildavsky, *Budgeting* (Boston: Little, Brown, 1976), pp. 295–96.

17. See Donald F. Haider, "Zero Base, Federal Style," *Public Administration Review,* July–August 1977, pp. 400–7.

18. Aaron Wildavsky and Arthur Hamman, "Comprehensive versus Incremental Budgeting in the Department of Agriculture," *Administrative Science Quarterly,* 1965, pp. 321–34. In early 1977, the federal House Appropriations Subcommittee tried a ZBB experiment with the Consumer Product Safety Commission. The commission identified 35 percent of its current program levels as the minimally acceptable level. See Joel Havemann, "Management Report: Zero-Base Budgeting," *National Journal,* April 2, 1977, pp. 514–17.

19. Council of State Governments, *Zero-Base Budgeting in the States* (Lexington, Ky.: Council of State Governments, 1976), p. 2.

200 Budgeting for Results

20. Ibid., pp. 4, 12.

21. Ibid., p. 5.

22. "Carter and ZBB: He Tried It in Georgia," *Congressional Quarterly,* November 27, 1976, p. 3257.

23. John D. LaFaver, "Zero-Base Budgeting in New Mexico," *State Government* 47 (Spring 1974); 109–18.

24. Conversation with Allen Schick, May 13, 1977.

25. "Zero-Base Budgeting: A Way to Cut Spending, or a Gimmick?" *U.S. News and World Report,* September 20, 1976, pp. 79–80.

26. George S. Minmeier, *An Evaluation of the Zero-Base Budgeting System in Governmental Institutions* (Atlanta, Ga.: School of Business Administration, Georgia State University, 1975).

27. "Zero-Base Budgeting . . . ," loc. cit.

28. Karl A. Miller, "Zero-Base Budgeting Works in Yonkers, N.Y.," *Government Executive,* January 1977, pp. 39–40.

29. Frederick C. Mosher, "Limitations and Problems of PPBS in the States," *Public Administration Review* 29 (March–April 1969): 160–67, at 161.

30. Dale, loc. cit.

31. Pyhrr, op. cit., p. 130.

32. Dale, loc. cit.

33. Pyhrr, op. cit., p. 31.

34. Robert N. Anthony, "Zero-Base Budgeting Is a Fraud," *Wall Street Journal,* April 27, 1977, p. 26.

35. Ibid.

36. Ibid.

37. John A. Ferejohn, *Pork Barrel Politics* (Stanford, Calif.: Stanford University Press, 1974).

38. Letter to the Editor, *Public Administration Review* 37 (July–August 1977): 439.

39. Asher Achinstein, "Constraints on Policy Analysis and Policy Implementation in the Federal Agencies," in U.S. Congress, Joint Economic Committee, *The Analysis and Evaluation of Public Expenditures: The PPB System, Vol. I,* 91st Cong., 1st sess., (1969), vol. 3, pp. 369–415; and Murray L. Weidenbaum, "Institutional Obstacles to Reallocating Government Expenditures," in Robert H. Haveman and Julius Margolis, eds., *Public Expenditures and Policy Analysis* (Chicago: Markham Publishing Co., 1970), pp. 232–45.

40. Lee and Johnson, op. cit., p. 120.

41. Weidenbaum, op. cit.

42. Anthony, op. cit.

43. Ibid.

44. Havemann, op. cit., p. 517.

45. Pyhrr, op. cit., pp. 131, 133.

46. Michael J. Scheiring, "Zero-Base Budgeting in New Jersey," *State Government,* Summer 1976, pp. 174–79; and statement of Richard C. Leone, State Treasurer of

New Jersey, before the Subcommittee on Intergovernmental Relations, Committee on Government Operations, U.S. Senate, March 25, 1976.

47. Council of State Governments, op. cit., p. 5.
48. Leone, op. cit.
49. Allen Schick, "Systems for Analysis: PPB and its Alternatives," in U.S. Congress, Joint Economic Committee op. cit., vol. 3, p. 833. See also Schick's "Beyond Analysis," *Public Administration Review* 37 (May–June 1977): 258–63.
50. Aaron Wildavsky, "Rescuing Policy Analysis from PPBS," *Public Administration Review* 29 (March–April 1969), 189–200, at 196.
51. Pyhrr, op. cit., p. 153.
52. Letter to the author, October 26, 1977.
53. Pyhrr, op. cit., p. 158.

8
Productivity

LEARNING OBJECTIVES

TO UNDERSTAND:
> **The meaning of productivity and what productivity
> is not**
> **How to implement a productivity program**
> **The productivity achievements of American gov-
> ernments**
> **Thayer's critique of productivity**

*T*he word *productive* has a positive ring. We talk about how productive Smith was, or, conversely, how a failed effort was unproductive. Yet many
workers have come to be suspicious of the term *productivity*, because they
believe it to be a euphemism or cover-up for forcing them to work harder
without additional compensation. Our concern in this chapter is the explanation
of the positive aspects of productivity. Unfortunately, productivity is often used
as a label for any number of practices which are not consistent with our definition, and the reader should bear this in mind. As we shall see, many of the
things labeled productivity are *not* productivity as we use the word.

DEFINING PRODUCTIVITY

Productivity is defined here as the relationship between inputs used to produce
a service and the output or results of that service. Productivity increases can be
simply defined as either getting a job done with less, or getting more or better
work done with the same resources. If two men and one truck can pick up as
much garbage in the same time, and with the same result in sanitary or cleanliness standards, as four men and two trucks did previously, we would say that
productivity has increased. Likewise, if the four men and two trucks increase
the amount of garbage they haul this year with the same results, compared to
last year, their productivity has also increased.

To put it more technically, productivity is the total of an organization's outputs divided by inputs for a given year. This relationship can be stated as a percentage. For example, if an organization manufactured 10,000 widgets with 700 man-years of labor in 1978, productivity during 1978 would be 10,000 divided by 700, or a ratio of 14.3. If the same firm had produced 11,000 widgets of the same quality with 900 man-years in 1977, its productivity for that year would be 11,000 divided by 900, or a ratio of 12.2. In this case, productivity has increased from 1977 to 1978 by 16.9 percent, a figure we arrive at by dividing $\frac{10000}{700}$ by $\frac{11000}{900}$. In other words, each unit of input (manpower-years) produces more output (widgets) in 1978 than was the case in 1977.[1]

In productivity measurement, one year is usually selected as a base year against which to measure the record of future years. In the example just given, 1977 might become the base year for the next decade.

John W. Kendrick has written that the "broadest and most useful concept of productivity is one in which output is related to *all* associated inputs, in real terms—labor, capital, and purchased materials, supplies and outside services, combined (weighted) in proportion to their relative costs in a basic period."[2]

The most important thing to remember about productivity is that it is concerned with the output or results of activity, not with activity itself.[3] As one professor critized for working only nine hours a week in the classroom responded, he could be likened to a bull. The time that he and the bull spent on the job was much less important than the quality of their output.[4]

We have to remember that productivity is only a technical measure of the relationship between inputs and outputs. It does not tell us whether the goals set for the program or the outputs achieved are wise or appropriate ones. For example, the Nazis devised a diabolical device for occupying the time of some concentration camp prisoners. They forced the prisoners to dig large holes—and then fill them in again. If one were to assemble productivity figures for this activity, they would be as meaningless as the activity itself. Likewise, if the productivity of file clerks involved in Medicare billing increases because the Medicare program itself is encouraging unnecessary use of medical facilities, such an increase is of very limited value. Productivity, then, is only a means to an end and can be no more useful than the end itself. Productivity stresses efficiency in attaining a goal, not the effectiveness of the goal.

PRODUCTIVITY BECOMES POPULAR

Productivity is now enjoying a period of renewed popularity. In 1970, President Nixon set up a National Commission on Productivity, largely because productivity increases in the United States economy slowed down after 1965. Politicians, government officials, and many private citizens have become concerned with government productivity now that government eats up about one-third of the gross national product every year. Now that one-third of the average citizen's income is paid in taxes to federal, state, and local government, "at long last," as former New York Deputy Mayor Edward K. Hamilton puts it, "the public seems to care about productivity."[5]

Since all projections of the growth rate in government employment and budgets indicate that government will continue to grow at a faster rate than the private sector, the public will presumably care increasingly about government productivity in the years ahead. This means that government officials will have to investigate different approaches to increased productivity to see if any benefit is to be gained thereby. In the near future, many of them may be issuing statements similar to that made by Wisconsin Governor Patrick J. Lucey when he ordered a productivity campaign in 1972:

> *As a matter of policy, all state agencies will be required to improve their management efficiency in the 1973–75 budget years, maintaining essential public services but cutting service delivery costs by at least 2.5 percent annually.*

SPECIFIC INSTRUCTIONS

1. Each state agency must submit a preliminary productivity improvement report to the Bureau of Planning and Budget by June 15, 1972. The report should identify the proposed areas of improvements in methods, the timing of those improvements and the estimated savings associated with them.
2. Productivity improvements must be reflected in the budgets for all general fund, program revenue and segregated fund state operations, excluding debt service and those costs which will be identified as aids to individuals and organizations and local assistance. To the extent possible, federally funded programs should be handled in a manner to maximize state fund savings.
3. The continuing level budget request for the 1973–74 fiscal year should be reduced by 2.5 per cent of the 1972–73 base for state operations. In the second fiscal year, 1974–75, the continuing level budget should be reduced by 5.0 per cent of the 1972–73 base, reflecting an additional 2.5 per cent increase in productivity above the first year's level.
4. Agencies with several appropriations or programs may apply different amounts of savings to different programs or appropriations but must meet a grand total equal to 2½ per cent the first year and 5 per cent the second year for all programs or appropriations. Agencies are expected to propose the most significant productivity improvements throughout the department, and that may well not occur uniformly among programs and organizational units.
5. Limited shifting between years within the biennial total may be approved (for example, a first-year reduction of 3 per cent and second-year reduction of 4½ per cent).
6. Agencies may propose limited offsets to the productivity savings for investments in the purchase of equipment, systems studies or other investments that are directly tied to improved productivity.

7. The dollar amount of these productivity improvements should be shown as a net cost reduction in the Methods Improvement columns of the B-2 forms. These cost reductions should be shown as a separate decision item in the continuing level for each affected program. Budget narratives should describe the productivity improvements to be made.

8. Agencies are expected to propose means of controlling costs or increasing productivity in all other categories of appropriations: local assistance, sum sufficients and aids to individuals. Agencies are to accompany their budget request with a separate report on cost controls in these other areas.

9. Agencies are not permitted to propose elimination of programs or make major reductions in services as a part of this productivity improvement policy. This policy is intended to improve the efficiency of governmental services, without reducing essential public services.

To further assist you in this effort, a checklist of improvement criteria is available in a separate pamphlet entitled, "Governor's Productivity Improvement Program." You may wish to contact the Chief of the Management Development Section for assistance in studying and selecting potential productivity improvements.[6]

IMPLEMENTING PRODUCTIVITY[7]

The following steps are recommended for implementing productivity improvement. If the program is to work, the steps should be carried out in a Theory Y atmosphere and approach. Employees should be consulted and their ideas for improving productivity carefully solicited. Further, they should receive bonus awards and credit toward promotion if their ideas are adopted. In this way they will become part of a productivity team, rather than recalcitrant resisters of results-oriented management. An example showing the value of this approach is that of the Georgia Highway Department employee who suggested to Governor Jimmy Carter's budget team that grass on the sides of the highway be mowed only 30 feet from the center line of the road. Previously, tractors had mowed down into drainage ditches, which destroyed the natural vegetation, caused erosion, and caused tractors to turn over. The suggestion was adopted and cut maintenance costs by 15 percent, earning the employee a cash bonus award. No top executive would have been likely to come up with this idea. Productivity was enhanced by involving lower level line employees in the process.[8]

The first step in the productivity planning process is to prepare basic policy statements which will clearly explain the goals of productivity to employees and seek their participation in the program. Productivity should be explained as an approach designed to get more output from inputs. To stave off immediate strong resistance, it should be carefully explained *in writing* that productivity will not lead to layoffs. Otherwise, a job action or strike may ensue; at the very least, the work atmosphere will be poisoned with suspicion and hostility. Any reductions in the work force made possible by productivity measures can usually be made through normal turnover, as employees quit, retire, or are transferred to other divisions. After they leave, their job positions can be eliminated. (There is, for example, a normal turnover of 5 percent annually in federal civilian employment.) Hand in hand with assurances that layoffs will not take place should go the announcement of a plan in which employees will share in savings caused by productivity improvement. It can also be pointed out that improved performance reports are likely to improve the agency's likelihood of getting the budget requests it makes. Just as the most able people are the busiest, because they are given work because they can do it, the most effective agency is likely to be given more and more responsibility and the resources to do the job if it demonstrates a record and capacity for work achievement.

Having clarified the goals of productivity and having sought to involve employees in the process, the next step is to work on priorities for analysis. Productivity managers should be cautious here, because *crash programs are usually crashing failures*. Attempts to apply a new approach across the board just do not work.[9] Time is needed to explain a new system to employees, and manpower and equipment must be devoted to the productivity analysis. A comprehensive approach is likely to cause confusion and chaos as the entire organization wrestles with productivity. It is far better to start in one of several selected areas, examining programs that are relatively easy to measure. For example, a municipal manager would be well advised to start productivity improvement in the public works or sanitation departments. Measures relating to the amount of garbage picked up or the miles of streets washed, plowed, or paved can be developed. These tangible achievements are easier to analyze than the services provided by the schools or the police department. It makes sense to begin with public works and learn by experience, and then to go on to schools and police.

It also makes sense, in all cases, to start first with more routine and uncomplicated operations such as police traffic law enforcement rather than more complex programs such as drug abuse control.

The following criteria can be useful in determining which priority areas to select for productivity improvement. First, operations which use a large share of an agency's budget or employees will yield a far greater return than smaller operations if productivity gains are made. Gains among public works road crews are likely to exceed gains made by garage mechanics in the same department, because the road crews make up the bulk of the work force.

Second, divisions which have large backlogs of work (welfare recipients yet to be visited at home or buildings to be inspected for fire risks) are divisions which may not be working well. Perhaps more resources are needed, but chances are that productivity could be dramatically improved in such a situation.

Third, bureaus with obvious management problems (dissension in the ranks and low morale) or operational problems (snow is not plowed until several hours after the storm is over) are good candidates for productivity studies. Improvements will be visible and known, and will provide positive incentive for further changes.

Fourth, new technologies (a leaf pickup machine) or automated processes (new computer programs) which could boost program output should be carefully considered. Of course, cost is a factor here, and the consideration must be careful for that reason alone. If the equipment costs more than it could possibly return in productivity gains, it is not worth the investment.

Fifth, supervisors should be evaluated on the basis of their receptivity to new ideas and their ability to follow through on productivity improvement. Those who can pick up the ball and run with it should be promoted and given additional responsibility. They are the key to the success of the program, especially for their ability to sell it to their subordinates.

Development of a program with proven results will make productivity more acceptable in other programs which are more difficult to measure. At the same time, open-mindedness and humility on the part of the productivity analyst are needed. Productivity gains and methods used in one area (teaching reading) may not apply in another area (teaching arithmetic). One is reminded of the Louisiana logger who compiled an enviable record and then moved to the Maine woods to try his luck. He was very productive and began to feel superior to his Maine colleagues until the winter came. Then his productivity declined drastically, because he could not cope with the rigors of cutting and hauling wood in ice, snow, and mud.

To implement the productivity approaches discussed in this chapter, employees must be trained.[10] They must be aware not only of the goals of the program in general but also of the detailed nitty-gritty of what is expected of them. This training may include mundane and menial steps which are nonetheless essential. New procedures must be carefully gone over with employees. They cannot just be given a ball and told to run with it. Rather, they need instruction in the rules and methods of the new game—whether it is a different approach to record keeping, recreation, or urban renewal. In addition, supervisors should be instructed in the various productivity study techniques and procedures so they know what is going on and can explain the program adequately to their subordinates. A short briefing or a memo is no substitute for this kind of training, without which a productivity program will flounder.

The process of educating managers to identify their needs and the information necessary for better management is a slow and difficult one. Managers need to know how to take a productivity report and extract from it what is relevant for them to do a better job of management. (Some examples of productivity studies which managers must be trained to interpret are given in the following sections on work measurement.)

A key figure in the productivity program's success is its director. In larger organizations, this should be a position with no other responsibilities. Candidates for the job should include the productivity-oriented supervisors mentioned above. The director will be responsible for selecting productivity analysts, establishing a reporting system, setting reporting criteria, monitoring the program to keep it on the track, and identifying areas for future analysis.

In the initial stages of the project, key staff members will probably have to be brought in from outside the organization. The specialized skills for productivity analysis are unlikely to be found internally. Productivity specialists who can work full time and not get lost in daily routine are needed. At the same time, an internal analytical capability, building on productivity-oriented supervisors, should be developed for the long haul. These in-house people should also become full-time analysts if they are capable of doing the work. Nothing can be more futile and frustrating than to expect them to perform both their old jobs and productivity analysis at once.

A timetable, which specifies target dates for the attainment of each productivity objective, must be established. It should include periodic evaluation sessions with management, supervisors, and productivity analysts to review accomplishments and adjust objectives and target dates accordingly. This procedure and structure will enable management to know what productivity improvement is accomplishing, decide whether a project needs more resources, and determine whether the project should be continued. If a fire department, for example, finds it can handle fires with a crew only three-fourths the size it previously used in one station house, it can continue with this productivity improvement. But if the smaller crew is found unequal to the task, this approach will have to be abandoned.

The final, and perhaps most crucial, element of the productivity program is its reporting and control system. This system should produce monthly reports (some analysts recommend *weekly* reports) on the performance of each unit or division. This commitment to regular monthly reports is absolutely necessary if the program is to work. Regular reports signal that management is truly committed to productivity improvement; they convey that productivity is a *permanent* program, rather than a one-shot or sporadic review. And information must be gathered at regular short intervals if management is to monitor trends, spot problems, and get to work on them as soon as they develop. Without this routine and regularized reporting, productivity programs cannot proceed.

One Approach to Productivity: Work Measurement

One commonly used approach to productivity improvements is called *work measurement*, and we will examine it in some detail here, to give the reader a feeling for one productivity measure.[11] One concept crucial to this approach is the *work standard*, or the time required by a well-trained employee to complete an assignment while doing work of acceptable quality. If the work standard for picking up 100 garbage cans is one hour, the employee who takes

FIGURE 8–1.　PRODUCTIVITY STANDARDS

Following is a list of local government activities illustrating the kinds of work standards that have been developed:

Law enforcement—Fingerprint classification, traffic or parking citation standards.

Probation activities—Caseloads for investigation, review and supervision of probation cases.

Health and welfare—Caseload standards, hospital laundry operations, claims processing.

Solid waste collection—Pickup times, tonnage standards, collection tasks, vehicle maintenance and repairs.

Street maintenance—Pothole repairs, sanding, plowing, sweeping, snow removal.

Building maintenance—Janitorial tasks (sweeping, cleaning, etc.).

Utilities—Water meter repairs (in the shop or in the field), meter reading tasks.

Inspections—Buildings, restaurants, wiring and safety, weights and measures.

Clerical—Transcription, typing (especially for special repetitive forms, e.g. medical, welfare or police records).

Data processing—Entry of data onto cards or tape, verification.

Library services—Cataloging.

Parks and recreation—Park maintenance activities such as pruning, raking, grass cutting.

75 minutes to do the job has a performance that is 80 percent of standard. Figure 8–1 lists areas in which work standards have been developed.

In calculating the work standard, the analyst must be sure to include not only the time necessary to do the work without interruption (*normal time*) but also allowances for unavoidable delays such as fatigue, telephone calls, or employee trips to the bathroom. Such allowances usually average between 10 percent–15 percent of normal time. The total time assigned to the job as a work standard is called *standard time.*

Standard time values are expressed in terms of units of work accomplished. For instance, garbage collection time could be measured by applying the following standard time values to the work unit:

1. Standard hours per route mile (a measure of travel time between stops).
2. Standard hours per site (a measure of pickup time).
3. Standard hours per nonroute mile (a measure of travel time to and from garage and disposal site).

It is often useful to express standard time by a single easily measurable limit of output, such as standard hours per cubic yard collected.

There are many means of work measurement. They include many techniques, some of which are listed below:

1. *Time study*—direct observation of a task and the recording of the time it takes. The analyst must make important judgments here, determining the

amount of delay and interruption that must be estimated and added to normal time to get standard time. Table 8–1 illustrates a time study done for water meter reader routes.

2. *Predetermined time values*—a prescribed time is assigned to each action involved in a task, such as a reach or a typewriter stroke. Unlike the time study, no judgment is involved in rating employee performance, because the method draws from a large previous study to determine very precise values.

3. *Time log*—each employee lists beginning and ending time for an action in a log book. For example, a clerk notes that he spent the 48 minutes between 8:04 and 8:52 filing 130 invoices. If the analyst works closely with employees and supervisors, time logs can be accurate to within 5 percent.

4. *Work Sampling*—work sampling is done at random intervals to determine allocation of employee time to different tasks. Table 8–2 is an example of a work-sampling study.

5. *Standard data*—a storage bank of time data used in previous studies of types of work commonly found throughout government provides standard data.

6. *Historical record*—the agency's past experience in using inputs to produce a given output is reviewed.

What is the manager to make of this myriad of methods? The following guidelines are not infallible, but may be of help in selecting an approach.

1. Time study and predetermined time values can be used in most local

TABLE 8–1.   METER READER ROUTING

	TIME REQUIREMENTS (IN MINUTES)				
	Route 1	Route 2	Route 3	Route 4	Route 5
Nonroute travel	30	40	57	65	15
Time per stop					
Inroute travel	0.35	0.40	0.45	0.35	0.55
Read meter	0.65	0.65	0.65	0.65	0.65
Total per stop	1.00	1.05	1.10	1.00	1.20
Workload Balancing					
Total available time	480	480	480	480	480
—nonroute travel	30	40	57	65	15
Net available time	450	440	423	415	465
Meters Assigned (Net available time ÷ Total time per stop)	450	419	385	415	388

TABLE 8–2. WORK SCHEDULE FOR PARKS MAINTENANCE GROUNDS KEEPER*

Time	Work Task	Measured Work Hours	Standard Hours
8:00 A.M.	Check in, get equipment	0.08	0.08
8:05	Travel to park site	0.25	0.25
8:20	Unload equipment	0.08	0.03
8:25	Police 6 acres grass areas	1.08	1.05
9:30	Rest break	0.25	—
9:45	Mow 4 acres grass areas	2.25	2.08
12:00 P.M.	Lunch	—	—
12:30	Mow 2 acres grass areas	1.00	1.04
1:30	Clean 2 restrooms	0.75	0.68
2:15	Rest break	0.25	—
2:30	Grade and line baseball diamond	1.58	1.60
4:05	Load equipment	0.08	0.03
4:10	Travel to district office	0.25	0.25
4:25	Unload equipment, check out	0.08	0.08
4:30	Off duty		
	Total Hours*	8.00	7.17
	Utilization: 89.6 percent		

*Figures are rounded.

government operations. The former is less time consuming, but the latter is useful for high-volume and repetitive work and does not require measurement of employee performance while on the job.

2. Work sampling does not require as much analytical effort as the first two techniques, but it is also not as precise a measurement. This technique is useful to determine the percentage of time spent on a particular task, such as telephone inquires or time spent by mechanics waiting for parts.

3. Time logs are best used for low- or medium-volume jobs, jobs with a long processing cycle, or varied work fragmented among a number of employees. It is most easily applied to clerical operations.

4. Time data from historical records can be used for work scheduling and input allocation, but should not be used for measuring employee performance. Time study and predetermined time values alone would be accurate here.

Common Applications of Work Measurement   Work standards can be useful in improving productivity in a number of areas. One is the calculation of staffing needs. In a hospital admitting room, for instance, workloads fluctuate greatly from one time period to another. Table 8–3 shows how on Friday and Saturday nights, for example, admissions run much higher than they do Monday through Thursday. Friday night shifts may be understaffed and Monday shifts overstaffed. Adjustments can be made in staff assignments to cover expected workload as a result of such a study.

Another area where work standards can be usefully utilized is in setting up

TABLE 8–3.   DAILY STAFFING REQUIREMENTS, COUNTY HOSPITAL ADMITTING ROOM

	DAYS OF THE WEEK						
TIME PERIOD	M	T	W	T	F	S	S
Shift I (8 A.M.–4 P.M.)							
Number of Admissions	50	42	45	35	35	31	25
Work Hours Required	20.0	16.8	18.0	14.0	14.0	12.4	10.0
Number of Staff Required	2.5	2.1	2.3	1.8	1.8	1.6	1.3
Actual Staff Assigned	2	2	2	2	2	2	2
Over (Under) Requirements	(0.5)	(0.1)	(0.3)	0.2	0.2	0.4	0.7
Shift II (4 P.M.–12 A.M.)							
Number of Admissions	40	36	35	30	45	50	32
Work Hours Required	16.0	14.4	14.0	12.0	18.0	20.0	12.8
Number of Staff Required	2.0	1.8	1.7	1.5	2.3	2.5	1.6
Actual Staff Assigned	2	2	2	2	2	2	2
Over (Under) Requirements	—	0.2	0.3	0.5	(0.3)	(0.5)	0.4
Shift III (12 A.M.–8 A.M.)							
Number of Admissions	10	12	8	8	20	28	12
Work Hours Required	4.0	4.8	3.2	3.2	8.0	11.2	4.8
Number of Staff Required	0.5	0.6	0.4	0.4	1.0	1.4	0.6
Actual Staff Assigned	1	1	1	1	1	1	1
Over (Under) Requirements	0.5	0.4	0.6	0.6	—	(0.4)	0.4
All Shifts							
Number of Admissions	100	90	88	73	100	109	69
Work Hours Required	40.0	36.0	35.2	29.2	40.0	43.6	27.6
Number of Staff Required	5.0	4.5	4.4	3.7	5.0	5.5	3.5
Actual Staff Assigned	5	5	5	5	5	5	5
Over (Under) Requirements	—	0.5	0.6	1.3	—	(0.5)	1.5

balanced routes for functions like meter reading and garbage pickup. Different crews can be assigned different routes which should take about the same time, and more productive readers can be rewarded. Table 8–1 shows how this can be calculated for meter readers.

Daily work scheduling can also be improved through work standards. Since employees who are scheduled for only six hours of work in an eight-hour day are utilizing only 75 percent of the time even if they perform with 100 percent efficiency when they do work, maximum possible utilization should be sought. Table 8–2 shows a planned work schedule for a parks grounds keeper which aims for 90 percent utilization.

Performance reporting is perhaps the most beneficial by-product of work standards. This approach usually involves a manpower utilization report comparing hours worked by the unit to standard hours set for tasks performed. Such reports, as detailed in Table 8–4, include the following:

TABLE 8–4.   MONTHLY MANPOWER UTILIZATION REPORT, CITY POLICE RECORDS SECTION

Standard Description	Unit measure	Number Units Completed	Standard Per Unit	Actual Measured Hours	Standard Hours	Manpower Utilization (70)
1. Type and file master index cards	Each card as filed	9,613	0.05	520	480.7	93
2. Type and file crime reports	Each report as filed	3,261	0.32	1247	1043.5	84
3. Conduct name/location search	Each request as received	10,431	0.08	911	834.5	94
4. Process arrest records	Each record as filed	1,042	0.77	853	802.3	94
5. Update teletype information	Each entry as completed	5,403	0.03	153	162.1	106
6. Maintain warrant files	Each warrant as received	315	0.23	75	72.5	97
7. Miscellaneous/administration	Each day as completed	30	10.2	407	306.0	75
TOTAL				4166	3701.6	89

SUMMARY OF HOURS

Total assigned hours   5440
Net adjustments   (451)
Total available hours   4989
Unmeasured Hours:
  Nonstandard Work   (231)
  Supervision   (520)
  Training   (72)
  TOTAL   (823)
Total Measured Hours   4166

Adjustments

Plus:
  Overtime   72
  Part time   51
  Temporary   —
  Borrowed   —
  TOTAL   123

Minus:
  Sick Leave   158
  Vacation Leave   240
  Other Leave   16
  Vacancy   160
  Loaned
  TOTAL   574

Net Adjustment Hours:
  123
  (524)
  (451)

1. Available hours, including overtime, part-time help, and personnel borrowed from other agencies, as well as hours lost due to vacancies, leave, or loaned personnel. These factors must be included or subtracted to get an accurate reading.

2. Unmeasured hours, such as training, conferences, supervision, or unscheduled work, must be included. These must be subtracted to get accurate work standards.

3. Measured hours spent on each job should be arranged separately, if possible, so that utilization for each task can be calculated.

Manpower performance should fluctuate between 85 percent–100 percent, because of different levels of personal skill and variations in work pace and volume. Performance lower than 85 percent indicates that a productivity analysis would be useful. When a service is provided on a demand basis (hospital admissions or library reference desk), it makes sense to search for other tasks for these employees to do in their slack periods.

Units consistently achieving over 110 percent work standards performance should be carefully analyzed, since they may well be overstaffed, not performing work properly, or working under inaccurate standards.

Quality and Local Condition Factors

Performance reporting is perhaps of greatest value as a safeguard against declining service quality or effectiveness. For example, if employees take shortcuts to maintain production quantity, quality is likely to fall. But the consequences of decline may not be visible for a long time, as is true in the work of a building inspector. A poorly built building may collapse years after the inspector has. Performance reporting can provide an early warning that something is amiss and lead to corrections before the house caves in.

Since our discussion up to this point has stressed quantitative work factors, such as hours worked and number of personnel, we need to emphasize what we said earlier. Productivity gains are meaningful only if the work done is at least of the same quality as that done before the productivity campaign began. Some productivity publicists like to label certain practices as productivity gains when they are nothing of the kind. Take a sanitation department which used to pick up trash from peoples' back porches or garages. If it decides to increase tonnage picked up per shift, it can require residents to leave their garbage by the curbside for pickup. This should result in increased tonnage hauled, since workers will save time by not going to the porch or garage and can apply this time to curbside pickup. But in this situation if more trash is hauled, we cannot say that worker productivity has increased. *Rather, some of the burden has been shifted on to other shoulders,* in this case those of the residents who must now carry their trash from the porch to the curb.[12]

To measure productivity, we have to measure the same activity which occurred before the study began. Otherwise, we cannot compare the two situations and cannot make any conclusions about productivity. Government official and taxpayer alike must beware of public relations panegyrics and be sure that a claimed productivity increase is not really just the result of shifting a burden. This is not to say that shifting a burden might not be desirable or a good way to save money. It could be both, and could be decided on as a wise public policy. But it is not the same as a productivity increase. *Money is saved at the cost of a decline in the quality of the service provided when burdens are shifted.*

A focus on quality must go hand in hand with careful consideration of local characteristics which can affect productivity. When studying and interpreting the work of the public schools, relevant quality or output factors would include student performance on achievement tests in such subjects as reading and math. Suppose two fifth-grade classes in a school differ drastically in student scores. Should the teachers with high-scoring students be given productivity bonuses and those with low-scoring students be given the ax? Not necessarily, because the conditions peculiar to each class may make direct comparisons inappropriate. Suppose that the students in the high-scoring class are from middle-class professional families, while the low-scoring class is made up of poor students. Scores of studies show that the poor are likely to do worse in school than the middle class, probably because of the relative lack of intellectual stimulation and encouragement to succeed academically which they get at home. Thus, productivity studies must consider these and similar factors before blindly rushing in and concluding that School A is doing a better job than School B.[13] Table 8–5 provides a list of workload measures, quality (output) factors, and local conditions for ten local government service functions to give an idea of the range of factors to consider before making a judgment on productivity.

The need for care in drawing conclusions does not mean that productivity analysts must throw up their hands and declare that the job is impossible. For example, productivity measurement in the two classes would be better spent in internal rather than external comparisons. Are students *in the same class* doing better or worse than they did in the past? Even if student composition has changed, there are plenty of ways for skilled productivity statisticians to take this change into account and come up with a valid conclusion that output has risen, stayed the same, or fallen.

A finished productivity measurement presentation might look like Table 8–6, which surveys solid waste pickup productivity. Note that Table 8–6 includes both input costs, workload measures, and output measures. In this case, tons of solid waste is the workload measure, while street cleanliness and population satisfaction with the program are used to calculate output. Cost is expressed both in current cost and in terms of the base year, which controls for inflation. With these data, the analyst can make conclusions about how much input was expended per workload unit and what the true measure of productivity is, by dividing items 1–3 in Table 8–6 by costs and then calculating the change from 1970–1971. Note that while more tonnage was hauled in the latter

TABLE 8–5. ILLUSTRATIVE SET OF WORKLOAD MEASURES, QUALITY FACTORS, AND LOCAL CONDITION FACTORS THAT SHOULD BE CONSIDERED IN PRODUCTIVITY MEASUREMENT[a]

Selected Service Functions[b]	Illustrative "Workload" Measures[c]	Illustrative Quality Factors (i.e. Measures of Citizen Impact That Should Be Considered in Interpreting Productivity	Illustrative Local Condition Factors That Should Be Considered in Interpreting Productivity[d]
1. Solid waste collection	Tons of solid waste collected	Visual appearance of streets "Curb" or "backdoor" collection Fire/health hazard conditions from solid waste accumulation Service delays	Frequency of collection Private vs. public collection Local weather conditions Composition of the solid waste (including the residential-commercial-industrial mix; type of waste, etc.)
2. Liquid waste treatment (sewage)	Gallons of sewage treated	Quality level of effluent, e.g., "BOD" removed and remaining after treatment Water quality level resulting where dumped	Initial quality of waterway into which the sewage effluent is released Community liquid waste generation characteristics
3. Law enforcement (police)	Number of surveillance-hours Number of calls Number of crimes investigated	Reduction in crime and victimization rates Crime clearance rates, preferably including court disposition Response times Citizen feeling of security	Percent of low-income families in population Public attitude toward certain crimes
4. Law enforcement (courts)	Number of cases resolved	No. of convictions/no. of plea-bargain reduced sentences Correctness of disposition Delay time until resolution	Number and types of cases

TABLE 8–5 (cont.)

Selected Service Functions[b]	Illustrative "Workload" Measures[c]	Illustrative Quality Factors (i.e. Measures of Citizen Impact That Should Be Considered in Interpreting Productivity	Illustrative Local Condition Factors That Should Be Considered in Interpreting Productivity[d]
5. Health and hospital	Number of patient-days	Reduced number and severity of illnesses Conditions of patients after treatment Duration of treatment and "pleasantness" of care Accessibility of low-income groups to care	Availability and price of health care Basic community health conditions
6. Water treatment	Gallons of water treated	Water quality indices such as for hardness and taste Amount of impurities removed	Basic quality of water supply source
7. Recreation	Acres of recreational activities Attendance figures	Participation rates Accessibility to recreational opportunities Variety of opportunities available Crowdedness indices Citizens' perceptions of adequacy of recreational opportunities	Amount of recreation provided by the private sector No. of individuals without access to automobiles; and the available public transit system Topographical and climate characteristics Time available to citizens for recreation activities
8. Street maintenance	Square yards of repairs made	Smoothness/ "bumpiness" of streets Safety Travel time Community disruption: amount and duration Dust and noise during repairs	Density of traffic Density of population along roadway Location of residences, homes, shopping areas, recreational opportunities, etc.

217

TABLE 8–5 (cont.)

Selected Service Functions[b]	Illustrative "Workload" Measures[c]	Illustrative Quality Factors (i.e. Measures of Citizen Impact That Should Be Considered in Interpreting Productivity	Illustrative Local Condition Factors That Should Be Considered in Interpreting Productivity[d]
9. Fire control	Fire calls Number of inspections	Fire damage Injuries and lives lost	Local weather conditions Type of construction Density of population
10. Primary and secondary education	Pupil-days Number of pupils	Achievement test scores and grade levels Continuation/drop-out rates	Socioeconomic characteristics of pupils and neighborhood Basic intelligence of pupils Number of pupils

[a]More extensive lists of workload measures and quality factors (often called measures of effectiveness or evaluation criteria) can be found in references #1, 6, 9, 10, 16, 17 and 26 of the Bibliography in "Improving Productivity and Productivity Measurement in Local Governments."

[b]Numerous subfunctions each with its own submeasures could also be identified. However, care should be taken to avoid going into excessive, unuseful detail.

[c]Dividing these by total dollar cost or by total man-days yields workload-based productivity measures.

[d]Such local conditions as population size and local price levels are relevant to all service functions.

SOURCE: *Improving Productivity and Productivity Measurement in Local Governments,* by Harry P. Hatry and Donald M. Fisk, The National Commission on Productivity, 1971, p. xvi-xvii.

year, streets were not as clean, and costs rose. Thus, while workload productivity rose 3 percent, output productivity declined 14 percent in 1970 dollars. In other words, increased productivity quantity occurred along with *decreased* quality. In this case, of course, local conditions, such as more trash, might be the cause. The productivity analyst must carefully consider these conditions before rendering a final verdict on the success of the program.

PRODUCTIVITY ACCOMPLISHMENTS IN GOVERNMENT

Productivity has been studied and used more intensively at the federal level of government than at the state and local levels. For this reason, we examine a major federal productivity effort in the case study in this chapter. And there are plenty of state and local productivity efforts, some of which we examine in this section.

In their 1974 study, John P. Ross and Jesse Burkhead argue that even "studies of federal government productivity have been relatively unsophisticated as compared with the work that has been done in the private sector,"[14] but that "compared to the work done on local government productivity, federal

**TABLE 8—6.   ILLUSTRATIVE PRODUCTIVITY MEASUREMENT
PRESENTATION: SOLID WASTE COLLECTION EXAMPLE**

Data	1970	1971	Change
1. Tons of solid waste collected	90,000	100,000	10,000
2. Average street cleanliness rating[a]	2.9	2.6	−$0.3
3. Percent of survey population expressing satisfaction with collection[b]	85	85	−$5
4. Cost (current)	$1,200,000	$1,500,000	+[a]$300,000
5. Costs (1970 dollars)	$1,200,000	$1,300,000	+[a]$100,000
Productivity Measures			
6. Workload per dollar (unadjusted dollars)	75 tons per thousand $	67 tons per thousand $	$11%
7. Workload productivity (1970 dollars)	75 tons per thousand $	77 tons per thousand $	[a]3%
8. Output index: (unadjusted dollars) $\frac{(1) \times (2) \times (3)}{(4)}$	0.185	0.139	$25%
9. Productivity index: (1970 dollars) $\frac{(1) \times (2) \times (3)}{(5)}$	0.185	0.160	$14%

[a]Such rating procedures are currently in use in the District of Columbia. The rating in line 2 is presumed to be based on a scale of "1" to "4," with "4" being the cleanest.

[b]The figures in line 7 indicate some improvement in efficiency, but line 6 suggests that cost increases such as wages have more than exceeded the efficiency gains. Productivity has gone down even further on the basis of decreases in the street cleanliness ratings and decreased citizen satisfaction. However, such indices have to be studied carefully and interpreted according to local circumstances to be fairly understood.

SOURCE: *Improving Productivity and Productivity Measurement in Local Governments,* by Harry P. Hatry and Donald M. Fisk, The National Commission on Productivity, 1971, p. 19.

efforts appear to be a mature area of endeavor."[15] But since Ross and Burkhead wrote these words, teams of productivity analysts have worked to try to increase sophistication in productivity at all three levels of government.

Federal Productivity Efforts

As mentioned earlier, President Nixon established a National Commission on Productivity in 1970. At the same time, federal agencies were directed by the Office of Management and Budget (OMB) to begin analysis of program productivity possibilities. The seriousness of these efforts is reflected in OMB requirements that every federal agency of over 200 employees must report annually on progress made in productivity.

A study begun in 1971 by OMB, the General Accounting Office (GAO) and the Civil Service Commission produced a measure of productivity covering 64 percent of the civilian work force, or 1.8 million employees in 24 major functional areas with similar tasks (e.g., records management.)[16] This study group later added the General Services Administration and acquired semi-permanent status under the title of Joint Financial Management Improvement Program.

The 1977 *Annual Report* of the National Center for Productivity and Quality of Working Life stated that federal productivity rose at an average annual rate of 1.2 percent from 1967–1976. There were wide variations among functions, ranging from an increase of 8.2 percent in communications to a decline of 2 percent in printing and duplication. Many federal line agencies, as well as the OMB, the GAO, and the National Center for Productivity, continue to press for productivity improvement at the federal level.[17]

Productivity in the States

A 1975 study of state government productivity efforts concluded that the states had a long way to go before they could adequately gauge the efficiency and effectiveness of their programs.[18] Researchers examined state budget documents and other reports, and then surveyed 32 states with questionnaires. Of the 32, 11 had only "barely adequate" effectiveness measures, while 10 had "adequate or quite adequate" efficiency measures.

While much remains to be done, some states are trying hard to make productivity work. Wisconsin Governor Patrick J. Lucey announced in 1972 that he was setting a productivity improvement goal of 2.5 percent annually.[19]

A 1977 report claimed that $47 million in productivity gains was "targeted" by agencies in this program between 1973–1976. Yet the report documented only $2.1 million in savings.[20] Examples included $25,000 in the Department of Motor Vehicles, a saving made possible by replacing 2.5 clerks with a letter-sorting machine. Apparently the machine cost nothing, since the clerks' salary and fringe benefits must have come to $10,000 a year. Likewise, an investment of $247,000 for a new air heating and cooling system in one building which saved $131,000 per year in fuel was counted as a $131,000 gain. The reader has to raise questions about such claims. While the figure of $47 million is close to Governor Lucey's 2.5 percent productivity target, the $2.1 million achievement is far below. Our point here is not to heap abuse on the Wisconsin program, but to note that this example indicates that it is not easy to wave a wand and get productivity gains.

In 1971, California Governor Ronald Reagan called for productivity analysis and reform of state welfare spending. At that time, over 10 percent of the population was receiving welfare, at a cost of over $2.5 billion per year, while gigantic future increases were forecast. But in the first year of the productivity program, the state spent $400 million less than forecast, while increasing by 30 percent grants to those who had no other income. For example, consider the techniques used in Los Angeles County, which has 40 percent of the welfare recipients in the state. Previously, welfare applicants were given a "service assessment," an in-depth analysis of their needs by a social worker. A "service plan," an elaborate document without measurable activities or events, was then concocted. The process took many hours, but did not generate data which productivity analysts could examine to check agency performance.

This system was changed to a "contract" method, in which an applicant coming into the office is given a list of available services. If the applicant feels that any service is needed, an interview with a service worker follows. They discuss the situation and then sign a "contract" detailing the service and the length of time it is to be provided. Paperwork is minimal, and the interviews usually run 10–15 minutes. Proponents of the system claim that it not only saves money but is also less paternalistic, giving the applicant more of a say in which services to be given. Supporters of the program point to a survey which found that 75 percent of welfare recipients were satisfied with the new contract approach. However, proponents say nothing about the obvious morale problems which must have resulted from employee layoffs. But, as the authors of an article on the program state, "California's reform of social services deserves close scrutiny and assessment."[21] We agree.

Local Government Productivity

Hundreds of local governments are experimenting with productivity. Let us examine the record of several cities, studied in depth by administrative scholar and former New York City Budget Director Frederick O'R. Hayes.[22]

Dallas, Texas, has made gains by concentrating on areas with high potential for payoff and low likelihood of employee resistance. Examples include the following:

1. Lowering the cost of cleaning public buildings from $2.00 per square foot in 1971 to $0.96 in 1975, while improving building cleanliness at the same time. Savings were accomplished by a new training program, standardization of equipment and supplies, and continued reexamination of policies. As an example of this last practice, it was found cheaper to replace flooring more frequently than to wax it.

2. Massive reductions in use of energy for cooling, heating, and lighting. Many offices were found to have more lighting than needed, so lighting could be reduced. Likewise, by putting building cleaning crews on a day schedule, air conditioning could be turned off at night. One large city building cut energy costs 55 percent through these and related measures.

3. A study of Dallas Fire Department deployment enabled four new fire stations to be manned by the transfer of existing fire companies, saving over $600,000 a year.[23]

Milwaukee, Wisconsin, has been using productivity improvement methods since the early 1950s, longer than any other big city in the country. Accomplishments include the following:

1. Reorganization of garbage collection in 1971, saving $3.8 million annually in 1974 prices. These savings resulted from a combination of pickups of combustible and noncombustible trash, more efficient scheduling, two-way

radios (enabling trucks to eliminate checking in and out of headquarters) and a host of other innovations.

2. A $500,000 annual saving in the repair and maintenance of water pipelines. Overly large crew sizes and overly specialized position classifications were changed to make response and repair faster and far more efficient.

3. Building inspection functions of the Health, Building, Fire, Water, and Public Works departments were consolidated into one Building Department, at an annual savings of $270,000 a year.[24]

Phoenix, Arizona, estimates that it saves over $7 million annually through work measurement and related studies which have been implemented. In addition, reorganization of such functions as garbage collection, park maintenance, and street repair has saved millions. Hayes concludes that "few cities in the country have done as much to improve productivity and have been as successful in doing so as Phoenix."[25]

Before the reader succumbs to euphoria, however, note that productivity has failed in such places as Detroit, Michigan, and Nassau County, New York. And the Hayes study finds that productivity improvement tends to be most successful in areas where public employee unions are relatively weak or passive, as is the case in Phoenix and Dallas. But since these unions are definitely *not* weak in Milwaukee, we can conclude that productivity improvement is indeed possible at the local level.

TECHNICAL PROBLEMS AND HOW TO MINIMIZE THEM

Productivity analysis, like all the approaches discussed in this book, is not something a beginner is likely to be able to implement without a hitch. As stressed above, it takes careful planning, consultation, and continued adjustment. In many cases, persons with advanced technical skill are needed to conduct a valid productivity analysis.

Because of these technical requirements, line managers and employees may view productivity as a mass of mysterious measures. The federal government study group mentioned above in our discussion of state productivity concluded that many federal managers were baffled and bewildered by productivity indexes which had been constructed. The remedy for this problem is simple: plan enough time to explain the meaning of these measures to all affected employees. This solution should be a part of any Theory Y approach to management, which does not just announce productivity measures, but plans to see them emerge from constant consultation.

The federal study group also found that many managers who understood the productivity indexes could not see their value. At the same time, "field managers . . . perceive a great need for the means of educating their employees—and themselves—in the ways of measuring and enhancing productivity."[26] The solution to this problem is the same as that just offered above:

educate employees through mutual consultation. Failure to do so will result in the pattern Wisconsin Governor Lucey uncovered. Agencies responded to his directive to raise productivity 2.5 percent by cutting their budgets 2.5 percent. *While expenses were cut, nothing was done to raise productivity.* And it was certainly possible, under these circumstances, that productivity might have declined.[27]

There are some technical limitations to productivity data. The federal study group concluded that they are not well suited to external comparisons. That is, comparisons of Public Health Service and Veterans Administration hospitals may not be as useful as they first seem, since each type of hospital has a different task and a different kind of patient. Productivity data are more useful for charting an organization's present record against its past history.[28] Analysts should beware of trying to use the data for purposes for which they are not suited.

An additional limitation on the work of the productivity analyst is dependence on line agency employees for information. The analyst cannot directly inspect all claimed gains in quantity and quality unless he or she has a huge staff. This fundamental fact means that figures can be fudged by line officials who want to make themselves look good. While the vastness of the areas to be examined poses a problem, the analyst can deal effectively with it by making spot checks. That is, the analyst can sample the work of employees in the office or the field, rather than examine every single arrest record, voucher filed, or pothole filled. This is the technique used by auditors, and the errors found by using it can alert the analyst to serious difficulties in a program, if these exist.

Another problem is the comparative difficulty in measuring government work, which is labor intensive. Government does not manufacture many items; rather, it provides services ranging from mail delivery to fire protection to sanitation. Productivity experts have known for a long time that productivity is more difficult to measure in service industries than in manufacturing.[29]

Service productivity is more difficult to measure because there is no tangible item, like a manufactured product, which describes a unit of service. This problem is complicated and compounded for *government* services, for which there is no set market price. Welfare, health, and educational services are not priced and sold to the public in the same way that private goods and services are.

Government productivity analysts substitute the cost of government service *inputs* for market price when computing productivity measures. That is, they calculate the total cost of wages, salaries, fringe benefits, equipment, and supplies used in delivering the service. This measure is a reasonable one. The problem comes when the attempt is made to measure *output*. How do we measure a police officer's or teacher's output? The city of Orange, California, rewards policemen with a bonus if the crime rate declines.[30] But since the police are universally acknowledged to *not* always be the key factor in determining the rate of crime, they could be doing a better job while the crime rate is simultaneously rising, and police personnel would receive no recognition for their increased productivity. There is no easy way out of this technical thicket, no matter what measure of police productivity is used,[31] because it is not as easy, and never will be as easy, to measure the output of governmental services as it is to measure private goods or even private services. The only solution is to keep working at the task of creating better measures of productivity, while being aware of the inherent problem involved. Such awareness will prevent one from making too much of a 5 percent productivity increase in an area notoriously difficult to measure. At the same time, if productivity in this area increases dramatically, say, by 20 percent, the chances are that there has been a significant productivity gain, assuming that the measures were well constructed and data were gathered and analyzed equally well.

A related problem inherent in government productivity stems from the monopoly position of government. It has no competitors, so comparative assessment of program costs is more difficult than in the private sector. Attention to and interest in this problem has led a number of governments to contract out services—whether management of the school cafeteria, garbage pickup, or other operations—to private firms, to see if they can provide the service at a cheaper price. One high school cafeteria recently turned over its operation to McDonald's and reported that at least now students were eating their meals, instead of leaving them on the trays as they had done before.

Productivity studies will cost additional money, lost employee time, and other resources while they are being run. This problem must not be ducked, but confronted. By selling productivity as an investment which will yield returns in greater program efficiency and effectiveness, the analyst is on safest ground. Pooh-poohing or minimizing costs will not get one very far in today's tax-conscious government environment. Here, as in other areas, honesty, coupled with good selling techniques, is the best policy.

Another inevitable problem in productivity is assigning work not included in an employee's position description to that employee. Almost all government agencies have such job descriptions, spelling out the responsibilities of workers who hold a given position, whether that position be secretary II, sergeant, or psychiatric social worker. If a productivity program is to have any impact, employees will eventually be assigned to certain duties they never performed before. Road crew pothole fillers, for example, may be assigned to drive the truck.[32]

When such a new assignment is made, the employee response is often one of resistance: "I can't do that, because it's not in my job title statement." Threats to file a union grievance are also to be expected. The best way to handle this situation is to stress the positive. In the short run, make clear to employees that if the job they are newly assigned gets a higher wage than their usual duties, they will get the higher wage. On the other hand, if it pays less, they will get no decrease in pay. At the same time, a position analyst should come in and look to see whether the job should be reclassified with a new title. A manager can motivate employees out of title to higher performance by noting that the position analysis may result in an upgrading of the job in title and salary.

Additional problems relate to the information generated by productivity reporting systems.[33] While highly accurate reports on workload and output are needed, often only incomplete and inaccurate data are available. Poor and careless reports, or reports which come in late, may also be a problem. These difficulties provide ammunition for critics of productivity in the organization, who conclude that the entire effort is useless.

To get valid and thus useful data, managers must make clear that these reports are highly valued. Since actions speak louder than words, managers should also reward employees who do a good job in this area with added responsibilities, pay, and promotions. Then other employees will get the message and produce better reports. Symbolic gestures of approval such as letters from, visits with, and photographs with the boss can be very successful means of motivating employees. No one who has done a job well and knows it resents a pat on the back and sincere thanks from the boss—quite the opposite. In other words, technical problems and their solution often depend in part on knowing how to bring employees around to a productivity outlook. Here we enter the world of organizational politics, discussed in the next section.

POLITICAL OBSTACLES AND HOW TO MINIMIZE THEM

The sanitation director of an eastern city was told that Inglewood, California, had used one-man garbage crews for over 10 years, with greatly reduced cost, fewer injuries, and increased personnel satisfaction. His first reaction was disbelief, an unsurprising response given the four-man crews he used per truck. When he was convinced that Inglewood used one-man crews, he stated that Inglewood's streets and geography were probably very different from his city's. When he found out that conditions were roughly the same, he lamented that local residents would never accept a lower level of service. When he discovered that service levels were the same, he argued that his men would not accept a faster pace and harder work conditions. When he learned that Inglewood's workers prefer their system because they can set their own pace and suffer fewer injuries caused by co-worker carelessness, he asserted that the city council would never agree to such a large manpower reduction. Told that Inglewood moved surplus sanitation men into other departments, he noted that he was responsible for only the sanitation department.[34]

The reaction of this department head is not an absurdly extreme example of resistance to productivity. Rather, it is all too common. The sanitation director had come to identify himself with the system his department used, so that any proposal for change meant that he would have to change his outlook and behavior in a way that he would find most painful. For change can be traumatic for those who are used to a given system and have succeeded in it. They are likely to feel that change, or "rocking the boat," as they might say, may turn over the boat and throw all those in it into the water. If they stay with their existing mode of operation, life is likely to be a good deal more tranquil. Why?

Perhaps the most important reason is what Anthony Downs has called "the law of counter-control."[35] Downs argues that any time top management tries to change procedures and tighten control over lower levels in the organization, these lower levels will resist. Thus, our manager was not acting irrationally when he said that his men would not accept new work conditions. In fact, their initial reaction to such a proposal would almost certainly be an outraged and angry one. If they had a union, union leaders might threaten a strike and initiate job slowdowns to protest the proposal.

Workers are not necessarily responding irrationally by acting this way. Their natural apprehension is that their livelihood will be threatened. And it is indeed threatened by certain budget cuts made in the name of productivity. Such cuts, in reality, may have no relation to productivity, but just be part of a budget reduction campaign. Under such an approach, a given percentage of every division is cut, regardless of its record of achievement. Workers who have been through such an experience are unlikely to trust anything called *productivity* for a long time thereafter. For this reason, it is crucial to assure workers that their jobs are not threatened by productivity, that at worst—unless they fail to meet minimum standards jointly set by management and labor—they will be transferred, not fired. Few managers relish this kind of hassle.

Anyone claiming to be able to introduce productivity improvement without political hassles would not be able to deliver on this promise. But there are better and worse ways to go about this task. If productivity planning and implementation take place in a Theory Y atmosphere, where employees are consulted at every step, political problems will be minimized. But if employees are suddenly told that productivity plan X is to be started tomorrow, the law of countercontrol will immediately come into play.

Unfortunately for results-oriented managers, the law of countercontrol is not the only cause of resistance to productivity improvement. Our sanitation manager may have had other understandable reasons for his chariness about the Inglewood example. If productivity analysts come on the scene, the manager will have to share power with them.[36] In other words, the manager will have less control of the operation and less leeway to bargain in the political process. This is so even if the manager and the productivity analysts are pretty much in agreement. A marriage can be a happy one, but each partner still has less individual discretion than when she or he was single. Thus, productivity data is often ignored by managers. One federal study found that

> most civilian agencies did not make use of unit costs in the management process even when such data seemed to be readily available sources of valuable insight. In fact, middle managers made relatively little use of measurement data of any kind in planning and evaluating results of their operations.[37]

Also, managers, just like low-level employees, may fear that productivity data will be used to set arbitrary productivity increases, or be misinterpreted to make forced comparisons with uncomparable activities (e.g., drug versus alcohol rehabilitation programs) in other agencies. Since public management takes place in a political climate, the potential for misuse and public relations shenanigans is always present.[38] Such abuses have frequently happened, and workers may know of, and be nervous about, them.[39] As a Wisconsin State University official remarked when informed of the governor's productivity program, "We have a quality system. I for one am unwilling to preside over its decline."[40]

A study of federal productivity found cases where productivity increases had been mandated without any serious study of whether they were attainable.[41] Small wonder, then, that managers who have been through or heard of such hair-raising experiences may prefer to conceal rather than measure productivity.

While there is no panacea for these problems, they can be reduced to the minimum possible by constant and continuous consultation with employees. Perfunctory and pro forma consultation is not enough. The manager who wants to implement productivity must be completely honest and candid with employees about top management's motives. The manager must also vigorously denounce any improper use of productivity data for political purposes. Any deviation from these high standards will bring the law of countercontrol into effect.

An example of the successful application of this Theory Y approach is that of the City Manager of Tacoma, Washington, in the 1960s, Bill Donaldson. Donaldson did not push productivity as a crusade, nor did he emphasize monetary savings or work force reductions to be made. Instead, to induce his agencies to think over their problems, he kept a low profile. By not coming on strong and frightening subordinates, this manager was able through this consultative approach to make significant productivity gains in a number of departments.[42]

Another and more difficult hurdle in the quest for greater productivity are statutes and collective bargaining agreements which restrict the authority of management to initiate change. As Edward K. Hamilton, former Deputy Mayor of New York City, has noted: "Work rule agreements and traditions—which the New York courts often invest with the force of contractual obligation—are replete with restrictions upon flexible use of manpower. Parts of state civil service laws sometimes appear to have been written precisely to frustrate a productivity effort."[43]

Examples of these rules would include a requirement for a minimum of 2 officers to ride in a police patrol car, or a maximum of 20 students to a class, regardless of what productivity studies may show are needed to get the job done efficiently and effectively.

These kinds of barriers are more difficult to surmount because they are embedded in the law or contracts. A recent approach to dealing with them has already been mentioned—productivity bargaining. When labor and management sit down to negotiate contracts, management insists that it will pay more only if labor productivity is increased. In so doing, labor may have to agree to a change in work regulations which restrict management.

A related legal rigidity is the ceiling on individual worker cash bonus awards for productivity. In Georgia State government during Governor Jimmy Carter's administration (1971–1975), there was a $2,000 limit on the amount of bonus money paid to a worker whose suggestion saved the state money. Such a restriction seems counterproductive: if a worker saves the state a cool million, why not award 5 percent or 10 percent, instead of a measly thousand or two? Such a policy might turn many good minds from the lottery to thoughts on productivity. Unfortunately, there is no substitute for working in the legislative and rule-making process to amend these legal restrictions.

Another statutory rigidity arises from the controls placed on funds by legislatures. No matter what productivity analyses show, less than 1 percent of the Pennsylvania State Department of Education budget is subject to the discretion of the department head.[44] This situation—in which the vast majority of funds is earmarked no matter what—is typical of most government programs. And the only way out of this impasse is for productivity professionals to become adept diplomats and salespersons, persuading legislators to follow their suggestions even though the agency affected and its interest group clientele will probably fight the recommendations tooth and nail.

Another rigidity is governmental fragmentation. Wisconsin's Governor Lucey has bemoaned the fact that he cannot appoint or remove the heads of many of the agencies technically under him.[45] (*No* governors, and very few mayors and managers, have complete appointment and removal power over line agency heads in their government.) Governmental reorganization to increase the authority of the chief executive, discussed in Chapter 3, is necessary to change this situation, and such reorganization can only take place after a long and bitter struggle.

Another political reality, if productivity is to succeed, is the need for strong and persistent support of top management. Lack of such support explains why Detroit's productivity program never got off the ground. Without such support, productivity efforts cannot be adequately staffed, nor given the authority and responsibility that will make line agency heads sit up and pay attention to them. Small or poorly trained staffs are often regarded as a technical limitation to productivity, but the real problem here is a political one. If the decision were made to commit the government or agency to a sustained productivity effort, funds would be appropriated and staff recruitment would begin overnight.

CASE STUDY:
PRODUCTIVITY IN THE UNITED STATES POSTAL SERVICE[46]

Largely because of criticism of its productivity record and mounting deficits, the U.S. Post Office Department was reorganized into the U.S. Postal Service in 1970. The reorganization involved more than a change in title, because the Postal Service is a government corporation, with more management authority vested in its director than had been the case when it was a regular line department of the federal government. The law that created the Postal Service really mandated increased productivity, since it charged the Postal Service with providing uniform quality service while charging fair rates, paying adequate employee wages and benefits, and becoming financially self-suffcient by 1982.[47] Fulfilling all these stipulations would be no mean achievement, since the Post Office had been running up billions of dollars of debt even while postage rates were increasing. (If fees from postage charges do not meet costs, Congress appropriates an amount equal to the deficit.)

The Post Office Department was also embarrassed by the record of the United Parcel Service (UPS) and other private parcel carriers, which were able to move parcels faster and more cheaply than the Post Office. Part of the problem of the Post Office Department and Postal Service is its obligation to deliver mail anywhere in the United States, whereas UPS emphasizes highly populated high-parcel-density areas. The Postal Service operates 40,000 post offices, and the number of delivery points in the country increases 2 percent per year.[48]

To run this system the Postal Service had 700,000 employees, 200,000 vehicles, and a budget of $14 billion in 1976. In spite of these resources, 5 percent of the 51.4 billion pieces of first-class mail delivered in 1975 were late. The Postal Service received 5,000 complaints per day about its service in 1976.[49]

Confronted with these various problems, Postal Service managers embarked on a wide-ranging productivity improvement campaign. Since 86 percent of the 1970 budget went to labor costs and 90 percent of postal operations were manual, productivity analysts concentrated on these areas. The actions which resulted from these studies included hiring freezes, reassignments, mechanization, and work simplification. Some specific policies include

1. A reduction in the number of mail collection boxes.
2. The reduction in the number of times mail is picked up from these boxes.

FIGURE 8–2.   EXCERPT FROM POSTAL SERVICE GUIDELINES, 1976

IV. STREET MANAGEMENT PROCEDURES

In the past, too little emphasis has been placed upon street management. Yet most of the carrier's workday is spent on the street. The detailed management planning procedures which follow will assist delivery unit managers in improving the efficiency of street service. First, existing street service will be documented on maps to visually enhance the manager's comprehension of what is presently happening. The maps will then be analyzed to discover potential opportunities for improvements. Next, the manager will travel each route to examine first hand whether his preliminary ideas can be applied successfully. At the same time he will look for other conditions which may require attention. Finally, he consolidates all his ideas and implements the service improvements he has determined to be appropriate:

A. Planning Efficient Street Service

The delivery unit manager must conduct a detailed preliminary review of all street service. This review will include observing carrier work methods and examining vehicle lines of travel, foot-travel patterns, collection and relay points, park and loop locations, dismount deliveries, etc. Throughout this review the delivery unit manager will analyze existing street service to determine the best delivery procedures and carrier work methods for his unit:

1. Obtain Local Maps

Obtain two or more maps of the local delivery area with a scale anywhere from one inch equals two hundred feet, to one inch equals twelve hundred feet. Useful sources of such maps include the courthouse, the tax assessor's office, the city engineer's office, or the chamber of commerce. Check the maps to be certain all streets and blocks in your delivery area are shown. Any streets which are not shown must be added as accurately as possible. When the maps are up to date and ready for use they may be covered with thin transparent material, such as 0.005 inch acetate, which will keep them clean and serviceable. Such a clear covering also permits making revisions without preparing a new map.

2. Plot Present Service

On one map indicate the boundaries of each carrier route with narrow colored lines and identify each route by its number. The delivery unit manager, while working with the carrier, should accurately record the exact lines of vehicle and foot travel presently being used to serve the entire route, and immediately implement any obvious improvements noted. Denote vehicle travel on the route with a dotted line. Then using a solid line, denote the foot-travel path the carrier takes through every block. (NOTE: Colored lines are easier to follow since they provide distinctive identification.) The location of each relay box should be marked "R," the location of each collection box marked with a "C" and use "X1," "X2," "X3," etc., to sequentially designate each parking location from which the carrier normally

FIGURE 8–2 (cont.)

serves each loop. Use a "D" to indicate each place the carrier is authorized to dismount for delivery. Be sure to indicate the delivery pattern where more than one delivery is served from a dismount stop.

3. Identify Potential Improvements

   When the map is complete and it shows all the routes in the delivery unit, the delivery unit manager will use the map to analyze each route in detail, to plan the most efficient street service. The following items must be included in his analysis:

   a. Travel to and from the Route: Establish the most efficient line of travel to and from the route. Designate this as the authorized line of travel and record the daily authorized mileage for each route. Distance, time of day, traffic conditions, and travel times must be considered.

   b. Travel to and from Refueling Location: Schedule refueling of USPS-owned or leased carrier vehicles on known light days. The frequency of this servicing will depend on actual need. Normally, a vehicle used on a park and loop route will not need gas more than once a week. Vehicles used for curbline delivery, parcel delivery, special delivery, or collections may require more frequent servicing. The delivery unit manager will also establish the line of travel to and from the refueling location and record that mileage for later confirmation that authorized lines of travel are being followed.

   c. Vehicle Travel on the Route: Determine the most efficient vehicle lines of travel on motorized and drive-out routes. Avoid retracing. Proceed through route in an orderly manner.

   d. Parking Locations: Select the best parking locations on park and loop routes. These locations should be selected so that the maximum area is covered by each loop or swing and the need for replenishment is minimized. More than ten parking locations indicate probable inefficient delivery patterns and the need for re-examination. Designating a parking location at a delivery point which receives several parcels each day can reduce the number of stops and dismounts.

   e. Relay Points: Select the best relay points on foot routes. Determine the number of relays necessary for each foot route. Minimize the trips to relay points by utilizing the full 35-pound mail carrying capacity of the satchel. The carry out relay should be of adequate size so that the carrier does not have to wait at the first relay box for the relay truck. To help assure relays are properly planned they must be weighed.

   f. Delivery Patterns: Optimize the delivery pattern for each delivery segment; e.g., block or group of blocks on the route. The three patterns used in city delivery are:

FIGURE 8–2 (cont.)

(1) The "U" Shape Pattern: A carrier travels up one side of a block or group of blocks and returns to his starting point via the opposite side of the street.

(2) The Criss Cross Pattern: The carrier travels through a block or group of blocks serving several deliveries on one side of the block; he then crosses over to serve several deliveries on the opposite side. This pattern is repeated until the entire block is delivered.

(3) One Side Only Delivery: The carrier only delivers to one side of the block and will avoid deadheading back through the block whenever possible.

NOTE: When selecting a delivery pattern or combination of patterns, the most important criterion is to minimize foot and vehicle travel.

g. Collections: While carriers are returning to the delivery unit from their route, they should be scheduled to collect mail from boxes along their authorized line of travel. Doing so may improve service to customers and eliminate the need for a later collection.

h. Travel to and from Lunch: Determine the most efficient lines of travel to and from authorized lunch locations following the same procedures described for travel to and from the route.

4. Travel the Routes

After the delivery map is complete and an analysis of each route has been made to find ways to improve street operations, the delivery unit manager must go on the street and travel each route. There is no substitute for familiarization of delivery territory. A personal review of delivery territory on each route will confirm or revise earlier conclusions regarding the benefit of the potential changes which were contemplated when the delivery map was examined. Local conditions which could not be determined from the map alone will become apparent:

a. Dismount Deliveries: Dismount deliveries must be kept to a minimum. They can only be approved by the delivery unit manager. Areas to be served by dismount delivery must be carefully analyzed to assure maximum cost effectiveness.

(1) Criteria for Approving: Consideration should only be given to using a dismount delivery if the following conditions exist:

(a) One-side of the street delivery over a rather lengthy distance with no possible means for connecting this with other delivery territory, or

FIGURE 8–2 (cont.)

           (b) <u>Boxes Not Accessible from Vehicle</u>: If many curbline boxes are located where they cannot be served by the carrier without dismounting, the delivery unit manager should change these deliveries to park and loop delivery when delivery cost can be reduced.

    b. <u>Authorizing Service to Out-of-Bounds Boxes</u>: Delivery managers should encourage customers to use post office boxes rather than out-of-bounds boxes. However, customers who reside outside of a delivery area may receive mail in boxes erected along a carrier's line of travel if approval is granted by the delivery unit manager after he has considered the operational impact. When out-of-bounds service will be approved, the customer is to be instructed to display his address on the box along with the names of all persons who will receive mail through the box.

    c. <u>Parcel Post Delivery</u>: Separate parcel post routes are not to be established or allowed to continue in territories covered by motorized letter routes. This does not preclude the use of auxiliary assistance or the delivery of directs by other carriers where volumes warrant.

5. <u>Prepare Map Showing Results of Analysis</u>

Complete another master map showing the entire revised street service picture including all the improvements decided upon. In addition, an individual route map showing the revised street service must be placed in each carrier's route book. This may necessitate obtaining and completing an additional map of the delivery area, or reproducing the new map showing the complete service picture after all revisions. The additional map or the copy of the new map will then be cut into individual route maps which must always reflect the current delivery patterns, etc. Delivery managers and route examiners will use these maps during on-the-street management activities.

3. Mechanization of mail sorting.
4. Replacement of door or curb delivery with large cluster boxes in one location in a neighborhood.
5. Carrier verification of mail while walking the route (see Figure 8–2).
6. Carrier use of shortcuts (e.g., across lawns; see Figure 8–2).
7. Reduction in number of post offices.
8. Reduction of post office hours of service.

What have been the results of this campaign? From 1971–1976, the Postal Service trimmed 65,000 employees from its payroll, a saving of about $1 billion annually, and reduced overtime pay 14 percent, for a $75 million saving. The closing of 250 rural post offices saved $2 million a year, while reduced mail delivery in nine eastern cities saved $4 million. From July 1–September 30, 1976, the Postal Service had a $15 million surplus, its first ever. (Skeptics point out that this occurred during a United Parcel Service strike, which greatly increased Postal Service business, and that the deficit ballooned to $652 million at the end of fiscal year 1977).[50] Furthermore, average delivery time for all letters decreased from 1.65 days in 1971 to 1.49 in 1976.[51] The primary productivity criterion used by the Postal Service is pieces of mail moved per man-year. There was an increase in this measure of 14 percent for carriers and 8.9 percent for clerks between 1971–1976.

While positive achievements have been made, skeptics point to other facts. The mechanical sorters often damaged or misdirected mail. Several new machines developed for sorting at a cost of $43 million were evaluated by the U.S. General Accounting Office and found to be inappropriate for large-scale use.[52] Some work measurement studies of carrier routes did not take into account such variables as snow, dogs, and vehicle breakdowns. The Letter Carrier Route Evaluation System plan implemented in a Portland, Oregon, post office caused higher, not lower, unit costs. Union officials have often complained about lack of consultation by management in the development of productivity improvements. The National Center for Productivity concluded that postal productivity rose only slightly in fiscal year 1976, after dropping in 1974 and 1975.[53]

Political pressures by voters and Congress have called into question the continued viability of the Postal Service. Proposals were made in 1977 to raise first-class mail rates and eliminate Saturday deliveries, in order to meet the estimated $2.4 *billion* deficit of fiscal year 1978.[54] Congressional committees reacted to these proposals with proposals of their own for returning the Postal Service to cabinet department status, ending its existence as a government corporation, and downgrading the productivity campaign. Congressional pressure has kept open 12,000 rural post offices which the G.A.O. estimates could be eliminated without impairing service.[55] Stressing that the key function of the Postal Service is service to their constituents, these congressional critics oppose efforts which they feel would interfere with this service.

Questions

The productivity record of the Postal Service, then, is a mixed one which has met with a mixed reception. The following questions are designed to let the reader apply the principles of productivity analysis to this specific case.

1. Review the list of eight measures taken to improve Postal Service productivity. Do all these steps further productivity as you understand the concept? If not, explain which ones do not and why they do not.

2. Do you feel that there is any tension or contradiction among the goals spelled out in the law creating the Postal Service? Explain the reasons for your opinion.

3. Do the achievements of the productivity campaign indicate that it has been successful?

4. How serious is the criticism of the productivity campaign? Do you feel the points raised by the critics make the productivity effort questionable? Explain.

PRODUCTIVITY: PROBLEMS AND PROSPECTS
FOR THE CONCEPT

Problems

This chapter has recommended productivity studies as a means of improving program efficiency and effectiveness. But the reader must be made aware that some cogent critiques of productivity conclude that it is only of marginal value, or even counterproductive. Frederick C. Thayer has written what is probably the most trenchant criticism of today's productivity efforts.[56]

Thayer argues first that tying wage and salary increases to productivity gains is a self-defeating effort, since industries will lose whatever competitive advantage they might have gained, and inflation will continue. This argument does not apply to the public sector as it does to the private sector, however, so we can question Thayer's logic here. Governments do not compete against each other in offering services, since they act as monopolies within their own boundaries. The question of inflation is an important one that goes beyond the boundaries of this book. Suffice it to say that inflation with productivity gains would seem to be preferable to inflation without such gains.

Thayer is on firmer ground when he contends that suitable productivity standards cannot be devised for service employment. We have already examined this subject and noted some of the difficulties. Thayer unnerves us with a discussion of the National Bureau of Economic Research report which said that the work performed by surgeons can be measured through the device of the "hernia equivalent," or HE. While a group of surgeons estimated that 10 HEs a week was a reasonable workload, the specter of requiring it and getting physicians to think in quantitative rather than qualitative terms is a frightening one. And Thayer says that such a shift is inevitable when productivity is emphasized. As we have acknowledged earlier, this is a problem to be aware of—yet not an insuperable one, as Thayer thinks.

Thayer next discusses the social costs of productivity. While productivity improvement may work well for one organization, he argues, one cost will be an increase in the number of unemployed workers in the society as a whole. As David B. Walker has said, there is real social utility in big sanitation crews in cities with large low-income and low-skill populations, because otherwise these workers would be unemployed. On the other hand, an affluent suburb can be tougher about cost effectiveness without putting its own residents out of work.[57] Thayer is saying that there are more important human values than efficiency, and that the ability to support oneself is one of them. This criticism cannot be easily sloughed off, yet job training to increase skills seems to be a better approach to this difficulty than does continuing the practice of featherbedding. At the same time, it must be admitted that job training programs for the unskilled have not netted impressive results in gaining better jobs for trainees. On the other hand, unemployment might diminish or disappear in an economy geared to greater productivity.

Thayer's strongest criticism of productivity is that it tends to turn administrators into heartless beasts who treat their employees like machines. Here he invokes the ghost of Frederick C. Taylor, the founder of "scientific management," which developed at the turn of the century the techniques for work measurement described earlier. Taylor felt that there was always "one best way" to do a job, and that the job of the analyst was to discover this way. Some of his followers even developed a measurement called the "therblig," a fundamental hand motion for manual work, and compiled a list of seventeen of these. Thayer feels that the inevitable result of this approach would be a "speed-up" by management in work done to the point where workers become alienated from their work instead of enjoying it and being proud of their accomplishments. He cites the example of the automobile plant in Lordstown, Ohio, where workers often quaff a quart of wine during the lunch break so that they become numb enough to finish their shift. These workers are surrounded by productivity experts determined to push one more car per hour through the assembly line. One result is that cars produced in Lordstown have had to be returned at a staggering rate for repairs.

Anyone who has seen the Charlie Chaplin film *Modern Times* can understand the nature and effects of the speedup, even if he has been lucky enough never to have directly experienced it. And Thayer is absolutely correct in stating that the speedup is the inevitable result of productivity—in a Theory X atmosphere. It is the argument of this book that the only way any results-oriented management approach can succeed—increasing quantity, maintaining quality, and increasing worker enjoyment in the job—is through the cooperative Theory Y approach outlined throughout this book. Not that developing such an approach is easy. But without it, productivity efforts will either fail or not be worth the candle because of the social costs they generate.

Prospects

Conditions encouraging productivity programs in government have never been more favorable. Both leaders and average citizens are increasingly coming to realize that we live in a world of limited resources. We can no longer squander energy and food sources as we once did, without running out of them in the near future. Rising taxes reflect increased demand for governmental services, and the only way to keep the services without going broke to pay for them is to increase productivity. Paradoxically, the advent of an age of unparalleled public affluence has caused a need for greater efficiency and effectiveness. We are now used to, and dependent upon, high levels of service provided by government. Since few are unwilling to dispense with these services—whether they be for education, public transportation, or public health—the only way to avoid being inundated with greater taxes is through results-oriented public management systems which stress greater productivity.

Contemporary conditions favor increased productivity, but will not cause it by themselves. Leadership from elected officials and Theory Y–oriented managers and analysts is necessary if productivity is to become more than a slogan. It is a safe bet to predict that productivity will be no more than an empty phrase in many jurisdictions, where this leadership is lacking. But it is also safe to predict that productivity will be tried for the first time between 1979 and the end of the century in more governments than have used it up to 1979.

NOTES

1. Thomas D. Morris et al., "Productivity Measures in the Federal Government," *Public Administration Review* 32 (November–December 1972): 754.

2. John W. Kendrick, "Public Capital Expenditures and Budgeting for Productivity Advance," *Public Administration Review* 32 (November–December 1972): 804.

3. Morris et al., loc. cit.

4. Lyle C. Fitch, "Remarks," *Public Administration Review* 32 (November–December 1972): 843.

5. Edward K. Hamilton, "Productivity: The New York City Approach," *Public Administration Review* 32 (November–December 1972): 786.

6. See Patrick J. Lucey, "Wisconsin's Productivity Policy," *Public Administration Review* 32 (November–December 1972): 795–99.

7. This section is based primarily on Daron K. Butler and Jay G. Stanford's fine *Checklist for Planning and Implementing a Productivity Improvement Program in Governmental Units,* Intergovernmental Brief (Austin, Tex.: Texas Advisory Commission on Intergovernmental Relations, June 1976).

8. Jimmy Carter, "Making Government Work Better," *National Journal,* October 9, 1976, pp. 1448–49.

9. A very relevant example is that of planning-programming-budgeting (PPB), implemented across the board in the federal government, several states, and several large cities in the 1960s, but pretty much abandoned today. PPB is gone largely because it was comprehensively mandated instead of tried out on a pilot basis.

10. These remarks on training are based on Herb Simon, "Policy Implications and Implementation Issues in Creating a Productivity Program," in *Public Productivity: State of the Art,* Papers from the Tenth Annual Conference on Management Analysis in State and Local Government (Windsor Locks, Conn., October 1973), pp. 28–39.

11. This section is based primarily on Patrick Manion, *Improving Municipal Productivity: Work Measurement for Better Management* (Washington, D.C.: Government Printing Office, November 1975).

12. See Harry P. Hatry, "Issues in Productivity Measurement for Local Governments," *Public Administration Review* 32 (November–December 1972): 777.

13. Ibid., pp. 774–78.

14. John P. Ross and Jesse Burkhead, *Productivity in the Local Government Sector* (Lexington, Mass.: Lexington Books, 1974), p. 78.

15. Ibid., p. 83.

16. Peter G. Peterson, "Productivity in Government and the American Economy," *Public Administration Review* 32, (November–December 1972): 741; and Neal R. Peirce, "Productivity Is Slogan for Taming Spiraling Expenses," *National Journal*, April 12, 1975, p. 538.

17. National Center for Productivity and Quality of Working Life, *Annual Report* (Washington, D.C.: Government Printing Office, 1977), pp. 72–76.

18. National Center for Productivity and Quality of Working Life, *The Status of Productivity Measurement in State Government. An Initial Examination* (Washington, D.C.: Government Printing Office, 1975).

19. Lucey, op. cit., p. 797.

20. Wisconsin Department of Administration, "Survey of State Agencies' Management Improvements," January 1977, p. 1.

21. Ralph C. Bledsoe et al., "Productivity Management in the California Social Services Program," *Public Administration Review* 32 (November–December 1972): 799–804.

22. Frederick O'R. Hayes, *Productivity in Local Government*, (Lexington, Mass.: D. C. Heath, 1977).

23. Ibid., pp. 20–37.

24. Ibid., pp. 57–69.

25. Ibid., p. 167.

26. Morris et al., op. cit., p. 757. Cf. Simon, op. cit.

27. Lucey, op. cit., p. 797.

28. Morris et al., op. cit., p. 762.

29. Jerome A. Mark, "Meanings and Measures of Productivity," *Public Administration Review* 32 (November–December 1972): 751–52.

30. Paul D. Staudohar, "An Experiment in Increasing Productivity of Police Service Employees," *Public Administration Review* 35 (September–October 1975): 518–22.

31. For some valiant attempts, see Joan L. Wolfle and John F. Heaphy, eds., *Readings on Productivity in Policing* (Lexington, Mass.: Lexington Books, 1975).

32. Simon, op. cit., p. 37.

33. Ibid., pp. 37–38.

34. *Improving Productivity in State and Local Government* (New York: Committee for Economic Development, 1976), p. 46.

35. Anthony Downs, *Inside Bureaucracy* (Boston: Little, Brown, 1967), p. 147.

36. Eli B. Silverman, "Productivity in Government: A Note of Caution," *Midwest Review of Public Administration*, June 1973, pp. 150–53.

37. Morris et al., op. cit., p. 755. Cf. Simon, op. cit.

38. Morris et al., op. cit., p. 757.

39. Silverman, op. cit., p. 151.

40. Lucey, op. cit., p. 797.

41. Morris et al., op. cit., pp. 755–57.

42. Hayes, op. cit., pp. 210–11.

43. Hamilton, op. cit., p. 785.

44. Silverman, op. cit., p. 149.

45. Lucey, op. cit., p. 798.

46. This case study is based primarily on an unpublished paper by Gregory D'Alessio, "Productivity in the U.S. Postal Service," December 1976.

47. See Ernest Holsendorph, "Postal System, Beset by Problems, Faces Challenges to Independence," *New York Times*, March 14, 1977, p. E–3, and "Are We Meeting Our Goals?" *Postal Life*, July–August 1976, pp. 3–10.

48. "Save Our Service," *The Postal Record*, May 1976; Maury Delman, "What's Wrong? Our Sad Mail Sack," *American Legion Magazine*, October 1976, pp. 14–21; and U.S. General Accounting Office, *A Summary of Observation on Postal Service Operations from July 1971 to January 1976* (Washington, D.C.: Government Printing Office, 1976).

49. See note 48.

50. "Are We Meeting Our Goals?" op. cit., and Associated Press, "Mail Cutbacks Advised," *News-Times* (Danbury, Conn.), December 7, 1977, p. 13.

51. See note 50.

52. Holsendorph, op. cit., and "Save Our Service," op. cit.

53. "Save Our Service," op. cit., and National Center for Productivity . . . , *Annual Report,* op. cit., p. 77.

54. Ernest Holsendorph, "Will the Public Pay More for Less Service?", *New York Times*, June 12, 1977, News of the Week in Review sect., p. 3.

55. C. W. Borklund, "The Postal Service," *Government Executive*, September 1976, pp. 12–19.

56. Frederick C. Thayer, "Productivity: Taylorism Revisited (Round Three)," *Public Administration Review* 32 (November–December 1972): 833–39.

57. Peirce, op. cit., p. 539.

9

Personnel Performance Appraisal

LEARNING OBJECTIVES

TO UNDERSTAND:
The usual methods of evaluating personnel performance
The concept of validity and its relationship to results-oriented personnel appraisal
Types of results-oriented performance appraisal
Minimizing problems of performance appraisal
Linking training to appraisal

Anyone who has consulted a text on personnel administration can attest that the topic is a huge and heavy one. It is not our purpose here to provide a summary of the field, but to focus on results-oriented performance appraisal of employees. The success of government programs rests on the quality of the employees carrying them out; in this sense, personnel evaluation can be considered the most important management approach we examine in this book. For this reason it is especially unfortunate that, in political scientist N. Joseph Cayer's words, "most performance rating systems in the public service fall far short of their aim. More often than not, they are haphazard and lead to deterioration in employee-supervisor relationships."[1]

241

DEFINING PERFORMANCE APPRAISAL

This chapter focuses solely on evaluating the work done by public employees, and does not include such closely related topics as the selection of applicants from outside the agency for certain jobs. Our concern is to determine how well employees are doing, to help them do a better job, and to determine whether or not they should be promoted or disciplined. *Performance appraisal* means just that: it is an evaluation of the employee's work based on observation and experience of how well the individual carries out the duties entailed in the job.

Results-oriented management requires performance appraisal. If employees are not rated and rewarded on the basis of results, all the processes of program planning, organization, supervision, management by objectives (MBO), program evaluation, budgeting for results, and productivity examined earlier will be empty exercises. There can be no incentives for achieving better results without performance appraisal.

CURRENT PERSONNEL APPRAISAL METHODS

Why is public personnel appraisal a "haphazard" endeavor? Primarily because public employees are often evaluated according to arbitrary criteria which have nothing to do with the quality of their work. These criteria include political patronage, personal favoritism, seniority, required background characteristics, and high performance on unvalidated examinations. Let us look briefly at each of these factors.

Political Patronage

Many governmental jobs and promotions are obtained by loyalty to the political party in power. An applicant for a position in the Indiana State Highway Department is asked if she or he is a registered member of the party which controls that department. If so, the applicant must be endorsed by local party leaders and is expected to contribute 2 percent of total salary to the party.[2] Teachers of the North Bergen, New Jersey, public schools who wish to be promoted to administrative positions have to be prepared to carry out tasks like trimming trees in neighborhoods which have requested such help from city hall. Over half of the jobs in state and local government are exempt from civil service merit system coverage, which usually means that the political party in power is the personnel department. There is a great range in the extent of merit system coverage. Two New England cities of 150,000 illustrate different cases. Hartford, Connecticut, has extensive coverage, while Providence, Rhode Island, has none. Almost 90 percent of federal employees are covered by merit systems, but attempts to get around the spirit and the letter of the Civil Service Act can be found in any administration. Such abuses reached their high watermark in recent history during the Nixon administration, in which procedures similar to those of the Indiana Highway Department were used.[3]

Personal Favoritism and Animosity

Personal favoritism for a protégé or friend has existed since the beginning of recorded history and will presumably exist to the end of the world. Nepotism, or the bestowing of rewards on employees who just happen to be relatives of the boss, is common in both the public and private sectors. And just as some unworthy individuals are undeservedly promoted, some outstanding workers are fired or kept in place.

Witness the case of a Connecticut state employee admonished to wear a hard hat by his foreman while at work in a powerhouse. The employee noticed that the foreman frequently went without a hard hat himself. The employee began to note the occasions when the foreman appeared hatless by writing them in the powerhouse log, even though the foreman warned him not to do so. Finally, after recording the latest hatless appearance of the foreman, the employee was told to remove the entry from the log at once. The employee did so with the paintbrush he was using at the time, and was then charged by the foreman with defacing state property.[4]

While political patronage may be eliminated some day, personal favoritism or prejudice will never be. It may, however, be possible to reduce favoritism, as we shall see in the section on implementing performance appraisal.

Seniority

Many state and local civil service systems tend to promote employees by seniority, or the length of time served in the organization. This policy is also often supported by unions, which believe it minimizes arbitrary actions of management and rewards long and faithful service. Unfortunately, there is little relationship between seniority and performance in the job. The best performers are often the most junior members of the organization. Nothing can be more demoralizing for capable employees than to have to wait many years for promotion while they watch less competent colleagues with more time in the job being promoted. It is difficult to view seniority as anything but an obstruction to results-oriented management.

Required Background

Some agencies stipulate that a person have a certain background, most typically an educational degree, to be hired or promoted. It is assumed that the degree, whether an A.A. for a police officer, an M.A. for a social worker, or a Ph.D. for a school superintendent, is a predictor or prerequisite of performance. Almost never, however, is this assertion proved by those who require the degree. Indeed, many cases exist to disprove such a contention. At worst, requirement of the degree becomes a way for an agency to continue to staff positions with the same type of people rather than undesirable newcomers. State of Connecticut welfare social workers bitterly protested a 1972 experiment which showed that welfare recipients trained to do social work were as effective at the job as those with the M.S.W. Any governmental employee can give examples to illustrate that earning a degree in itself does not turn a sow's ear into a silk purse. As the saying goes, we all know what B.S. means, and M.S. means "more of the same," while Ph.D. means "piled higher and deeper." Requirement of a degree reaches ridiculous heights when public managers with impressive career records, extensive publications, and ample experience in public speaking find it hard to become teachers of public administration after they retire because they lack a Ph.D. Background requirements intended to improve public management can have exactly the opposite effect.

Testing

Written tests are given for performance appraisal in many state and local agencies, though rarely in the federal government. If these tests had been validated, or proven to test for job capabilities, there would be no problem. Unfortunately, most tests are not validated. Indeed, aptitude tests do not show a positive correlation with job achievement of more than 0.5 out of 1.0, and are of least use in appraising applicants for managerial positions.[5]

Some persons are good test takers but lack the competence to do a job well. When such an individual is promoted and then shows lack of decisiveness or wisdom, of what value is the test which led to the promotion? It is not only worthless but also counterproductive. In Wallace Sayre's words, the situation has "become characterized more by procedure, rule, and technique than by purpose or results."[6]

New Jersey municipal employees who work in civil service systems must take tests administered by the state civil service agency to be promoted. Civil service draws its questions from a repository of some 10,000 items. Study groups of employees pool the questions they remember from previous tests, giving their members a huge advantage over nonstudy group test takers. In one case, a test taker was wired for sound and whispered all the questions to his study group, which received the message on a radio in a car parked outside the examination center. In another case, a test taker managed to throw the examination questions to study group members waiting outside a window. While these examples may be more titillating than typical, unvalidated examinations—whether written or based on physical or other requirements—are no laughing matter. They sabotage attempts to improve agency management.

Oral examinations can be just as useless as bad written tests, even though they are designed to size up personal qualities first hand. In 1974, a New Jersey county employee taking the state civil service oral exam was told to keep his answers short, for only 20 minutes would be allowed for the oral exam. Following this advice, he was amazed to receive the following comments back from the examining officer:

1. Inability to stimulate and motivate subordinates.
2. Insufficient knowledge of overall function of Prosecutor's Office.
3. Demonstrated lack of self-confidence; was ill at ease and did not demonstrate ability to express ideas: shallow in presentation of ideas and would find difficulty in accepting ideas of others.
4. Unable to articulate ideas forcefully. Did not project ideas with force in such a manner that others would follow his direction. Generally ill at ease under pressure. Lacks leadership qualities necessary for this position.
5. Demonstrated very little originality or imagination.
6. Candidate didn't seem to grasp situation presented in order to draw proper conclusion. Explanation of polygraph matter and plea bargaining was shallow and insufficient.
7. Presentation appeared brief, uncertain, and disorganized. Hesitant in speech. Grammar and vocabulary limited.

The thought that a 20-minute discussion could justify such far-reaching conclusions seems laughable, but both written and oral exams draw such unvalidated conclusions everyday.

IMPLEMENTING PERFORMANCE APPRAISAL

There is an abundance of alternative approaches to performance appraisal. In this section, we will survey some of them.

Performance Standards

Standards similar to those used in measuring productivity can be used to evaluate employee performance. Such *quantitative* standards are best used in jobs (garbage collection, typing and filing, voucher processing, etc.) where production can be easily measured. The employee can be assigned a certain point score for each standard, and his or her record can be summed up on a sheet and compared to average performance or an established minimum score.

Personnel appraisal would be much simpler work if this approach were sufficient for all jobs. *Qualitative* factors, however, are also important in determining the work done. For instance, is the employee tactful to clients and effective in interactions with fellow employees? It is extremely difficult, if not impossible, to derive quantitative measures for jobs such as teaching and police work, so that the appraisal may have to depend primarily on assessing the qualitative. Figure 9–1 lists the appraisal standards used by one government, most of which are qualitative in nature. Figure 9–3, in the case study section, shows a rating scale; note that items 1, 2, and 4 are quantitative measures, while the other items are qualitative measures. While qualitative factors can also be assigned a point score, we are now on more shaky ground, and different evaluators may differ in their assessment of the same employee.

FIGURE 9–1.   EVALUATING A COG DIRECTOR

Executive Director Performance Evaluation Guidelines

Administration (Factor I):

1. *Manpower Development:* Does he/she appoint and train effective subordinates? Has he retained excellent people who were tempted to go elsewhere?

2. *Supervision:* Does he direct his group and control their efforts? Does he encourage their initiative? Does he know what is going on with all CVAG projects? Is he available to his employees for guidance and counselling? Does he evaluate his key personnel and suggest ways for them to improve?

3. *Execution of Policy:* Does he understand and comply with the overall policy, laws, and philosophy of the organization? Do his efforts lead toward successful accomplishment of goals? Does he measure results against goals and take corrective action?

4. *Budget:* Is his budget realistic? Is it prepared in a good format? Is it reasonable? Does he control expenses within the set levels of the budget?

5. *Reporting:* Does he submit accurate and complete staff reports on schedule? Are they readable? Are staff reports concise, to the point, and submitted with appropriate recommendations when necessary?

6. *Planning:* Is he familiar with the Association's policies, objectives, and practices? Does he translate these policies, objectives, and practices into specific programs?

7. *Leadership:* Does he motivate others to maximum performance? Is he respected as demanding but fair? Does he get enthusiastic response to new ideas and needed reorganizations?

8. *Job Organization:* Does he delegate responsibility but handle job details efficiently? Does he use time productively? Does he program activities in an orderly and systematic way?

9. *Communication:* Does he keep appropriate people informed? Does he present his thoughts in an orderly, understandable manner? Is he able to convince people to adopt his viewpoint? Is his written correspondence clear and concise and an accurate representation of Association policy?

Other Approaches

One variation of the qualitative approach is a focus on *critical incidents.* This method asks evaluators to list actual important occurrences, both favorable and unfavorable, relating to the job. For instance, a nursing floor supervisor might receive praise and credit for effective leadership in organizing the floor to care for the victims of an earthquake, or be criticized for losing control, shouting at, and publicly berating a subordinate who committed a minor error. This approach has the advantage of compiling evidence to support ratings, but care must be taken that the rater does not become obsessed with recording every incident. If this happens, a decentralized participative approach to management will become impossible.[7]

Another variation on the qualitative approach is the use of a *narrative report.* Here the supervisor or evaluator writes a summary of the employee's work. Some narratives are highly structured, while others allow the rater more discretion. Personnel specialists believe that narratives are most useful when they are confined to factual statements, instead of summing up the employee's performance worth. They can be used to supplement overall ratings like those in Figures 9–1 and 9–3, but are less likely to threaten the employee. Superior and subordinate may be able to understand each other better when the narrative is restricted to this kind of description.[8]

A perennial problem with appraising qualitative factors is a tendency to focus on traits rather than performance. Figure 9–3, in the case study section, lists the traits of leadership and effectiveness under stress. Even if there is an adequate definition of these traits—which is not the case in a large proportion of public personnel ratings—it is unlikely that all raters will concur in their judgment of an employee. One social worker may perceive a subordinate as taking

External Relationships (Factor II):

10. *Community Reputation:* What is the general attitude of the community to this man? Is he regarded as a man of high integrity, ability, and devotion to the Coachella Valley Association of Governments?

11. *Professional Reputation:* How does he stand among others in the public administration profession? Does he deal effectively with other city and county managers? Is he respected by other professional and staff representatives of the cities and county? Does he enthusiastically and constructively attend seminars and conferences?

12. *Intergovernmental Relations:* Does the executive director work closely with other federal, state, and local government representatives? Is his relationship with others friendly? Does he provide requested assistance to other cities and the county?

13. *Community Relations:* Does he skillfully represent the Coachella Valley Association of Governments to the press, radio, and television? Does he properly avoid politics and partisanship? Does he show an honest interest in the community? Does he properly defend CVAG and its reputation?

Personal Characteristics (Factor III):

14. *Imagination:* Does he show originality in approaching problems? Does he create effective solutions? Is he able to visualize the implications of various approaches?

15. *Objectivity:* Is he unemotional and unbiased? Does he take a rational, impersonal viewpoint based on facts and qualified opinions?

16. *Drive:* Is he energetic, willing to spend whatever time is necessary to do a good job? Does he have good mental and physical stamina?

17. *Decisiveness:* Is he able to reach timely decisions and initiate action, but not be compulsive?

18. *Attitude:* Is he enthusiastic? Cooperative? Willing to adapt?

19. *Firmness:* Does he have the courage of his convictions? Is he firm when convinced, but not stubborn?

COACHELLA VALLEY ASSOCIATION OF GOVERNMENTS

EXECUTIVE DIRECTOR PERFORMANCE EVALUATION FORM

Date: _____

Name: _____

Title: _____

Period Covered by This
 Rating: _____

Factor I—ADMINISTRATION:

Factor II—EXTERNAL RELATIONSHIPS:

Factor III—PERSONAL CHARACTERISTICS:

OVERALL EVALUATION

Less Than Satisfactory	Satisfactory	Excellent	Outstanding

substantial initiative, while another may perceive the same subordinate as taking only moderate initiative. Many supervisors tend to be subverted by the "halo effect" and to evaluate their subordinates' personalities rather than concentrating on subordinates' performance when they rate traits.[9] Ernest Dale and Alice Smith note that someone like Abraham Lincoln would probably not have scored very high on a trait checkoff list.[10] For this reason, complementary use of critical incident or narrative reports can serve as a helpful corrective to trait ratings.

Two additional variations on qualitative rating are *forced distribution* and *forced choice*. The former, which is in much more frequent use in business than in government, was designed to cope with the common problem of superiors giving their subordinates undeservedly high ratings. For example, of 88,000 state employee evaluations in New Jersey between 1972–1974, only 419 (less than 0.5 percent) were unsatisfactory.[11] Such an absurd aberration takes place because supervisors are trying to protect their subordinates from what they consider to be arbitrary personnel ratings, and because supervisors may have given up trying to fight a system which makes it almost impossible to fire unsatisfactory employees.

The forced distribution approach asks managers to list their top 10 percent of employees, next 20 percent, and so on, down to the bottom 10 percent. In this way, lenient ratings are eliminated. But while this method is easy to administer, it has an almost fatal flaw. It assumes all work groups have the same proportion of good, average, and poor employees. The contrary is more likely to be true, especially in small groups.[12]

Forced choice was developed by the U.S. Army near the end of World War II to rate officers. The rater is given statements such as those listed in Table 9–1.

The rater is asked to check two items. One of these should be most characteristic of the subordinate; the other, least characteristic. But only one of the favorable items gives credit, while only one of the negative items detracts from the overall rating. The rater does not know which items count and which do not, and is deliberately kept in the dark to minimize bias. Forced choice is not used much outside the military. It is expensive to install, because it must be individually tailored to each organization. Even worse, it is often resented by

TABLE 9–1.   FORCED CHOICE RATINGS

	Most	Least
1. Doesn't try to pull rank	——	——
2. Knows limitations and capabilities of subordinates	——	——
3. Low efficiency	——	——
4. Speaks in steady monotone	——	——

superiors, because its implicit operating assumption is that they cannot be trusted. Nor can it be used to help employees do a better job.[13]

Yet another approach is the behavioral or skills method of Robert N. McMurry.[14] McMurry's system supposes that the past foretells the future. An employee who feels past supervisors have been incompetent will probably feel the same way about future supervisors. An interview is conducted with the employee to probe such traits as creativity ("Have you ever created anything?"), leadership ("Led anything?"), and loyalty ("What do you think of past employers, schools, parents, etc.?"). This "patterned" interview assumes that people do not change their behavior without plenty of personal pain or pressure. George Odiorne, a leading authority on MBO, argues that McMurry's approach is better than many others. At the same time, it is deterministic and not primarily results-oriented. It asks not what the employee has done, but what the employee's attitudes about certain key traits are.[15]

Smoothing the Way to Performance Appraisal[16]

Installing performance appraisal in an agency which has never used it before is no easy task. The following considerations should be kept in mind while doing the job.

Ample time must be allotted to gain full agreement from line management. Performance appraisal cannot be implemented overnight, because managers must be instructed in how to use the new system. Further, frank discussion sessions about the purposes and usefulness of the new approach should be held. Managers should be encouraged to express any feelings they may have about shortcomings in the plan.

The best way to "sell" performance appraisal is to note that it is likely to improve employee morale if properly done, because it is not an arbitrary approach. While this will not convince subordinates who expect a promotion soon on the basis of other criteria such as seniority, it should improve overall morale.

Supervisors should be asked to help in drawing up the appraisal form to be used. Otherwise, they will view it as a dumb and dictatorial demand by top management and only go through the motions of using it.

Subordinates and the union should be fully briefed on the purpose, nature, and format of the performance appraisal. Time should be allotted for discussing the plan and distributing copies of appraisal forms.

Coordination among divisions of the agency to achieve uniform appraisal procedures is a must. For example, if employees of one section consistently get much higher ratings than those in another section, a very careful study of rating practices should be made to see if the same criteria are in use in both cases. Morale will suffer if employees in one division are rated in a way that is unfair to other departments.

Perhaps the most crucial step is the interview between subordinate and superior held to discuss the superior's evaluation. Superiors must realize that this is a tense and trying time for the subordinate. No one likes to be criticized, even if one recognizes that the criticism is correct. And criticism from the boss is especially threatening. Attention to the following procedures should help to reduce employee anxiety levels considerably.

First, the superior should indicate that the purpose of the interview is to help the subordinate to do a better job. The subordinate is not being called on the carpet, but is participating in a regularly scheduled periodic conference.

Next, the superior should go over the evaluation, *starting with positive points*. This reduces the subordinate's anxiety and makes it easier to listen to criticism later on. Supervisors should stress that the evaluation is performance and not personality oriented. The employee is not being criticized as a person.

Third, the superior should ask for the subordinate's response. The subordinate must be allowed to show hostility about negative comments and thus release tension. The superior should not contradict or argue with the subordinate, for this would only be likely to get the subordinate so tense and angry that he or she would not listen to anything else the superior had to say.

Fourth, the subordinate should be asked to state where he or she stands and how to improve his or her own performance. The superior must be a sincere listener, or this step will be a waste of time. The subordinate can quickly ascertain whether the superior is genuinely interested in what the subordinate is saying.

Finally, the subordinate and superior should discuss what the former can do to overcome weaknesses and what the latter can do to help the subordinate. The subordinate is then given several days to submit any comments on the evaluation.

If the evaluation is part of an ongoing process, it will not contain any great surprises for the subordinate, because the supervisor will have already mentioned key achievements or problems in the course of work. The interview session is part of a process, not an end in itself.

Toward Maximum Achievement: Personnel Appraisal by Objectives

If the title of our preferred approach—personnel appraisal by objectives—sounds familiar, it is because MBO began primarily as a way to manage and evaluate personnel. By the very act of setting goals and reviewing them, the employee is appraising his or her own performance record.

Remember that MBO entails conferences between superior and subordinate for both goal setting and periodic performance review. During the performance review, superior and subordinate discuss the record of goal attainment, possible improvements, and goals to be set for the next period. Rather than having the superior write a lengthy performance appraisal, the subordinate writes a self-report of accomplishments. This suggestion will doubtless raise a lot of eyebrows. After all, why would one downgrade oneself? Interestingly enough, however, the record shows that "most subordinates normally have an understandable wish to please their bosses and quite willingly adjust their targets or appraisals if the superior thinks they are unrealistic."[17] This is to be expected if a Theory Y ambience prevails. The subordinate will not feel threatened and pressured to lie or act defensively in such an environment. Instead, the employee can act as a member of a goal-oriented team. In writing up the self-report, the subordinate will probably gain a good deal of insight on how to improve attitude and behavior.[18]

Of course, the superior's behavior is crucial in determining whether there will be real personnel appraisal by objectives. The subordinate should be asked to tell the superior how to help or stop hindering the subordinate from performing better. In this way, the fact that the subordinate's job performance is affected by the superior is explicitly recognized. The subordinate can now feel freer to bring up any problems that he or she might have been reluctant to air before.

Table 9–2 lists sample objectives for one job, as well as more specific measures which can be used to determine how well objectives were met. Remember that in MBO the attempt to quantify should be made whenever possible.[19]

In no system is a subordinate going to be completely on his or her own in drawing up the performance appraisal. Even in an MBO appraisal system, the superior will have great indirect influence on the subordinate. And there is no reason why the MBO approach cannot be used jointly with the ratings of superiors. For most governments, MBO appraisal by subordinates might be viewed as too radical a step if it were the only appraisal method. For this reason, it makes sense to introduce MBO as one of several criteria to use in evaluating work done.

TABLE 9–2.　SAMPLE JOB OBJECTIVES FOR HOSPITAL FLOOR GENERAL NURSING SUPERVISOR

Objectives	Indicative Past Achievements
1. To select nurses to be head of different floor shifts	Has supervisor picked a shift head before? Does she or he have definite notions about shift head's duties?
2. To train nurses in the work of the floor	How many nurses has the supervisor trained? How many have been promoted, disciplined, and dismissed?
3. Quality of care	How many supervisors, clients, and outside experts rated quality of care in this supervisor's terms? What techniques for improvement has the supervisor used?
4. Employee relations	What are the turnover rates, grievance rates, and absenteeism? How do they compare to previous rates and average hospital floor rates?

Any performance appraisal is meaningful only if it is done on an ongoing basis. All too many superiors make a last-minute scramble to fill out evaluation forms, which naturally results in a superficial and impressionistic write-up. Performance appraisal should be seen as a continuing responsibility which involves setting objectives, training and coaching subordinates, and setting and revising job standards throughout the year. After all, appraisal should be based on a subordinate's total performance, rather than the superior's memory of how that individual seemed to perform during the year. For these reasons, the MBO approach, with its periodic conferences and active role for the subordinate, should be part of any ideal system of performance appraisal.

USE OF PERFORMANCE APPRAISAL IN AMERICAN GOVERNMENT

The Federal Government

Under the requirements of the 1950 Performance Rating Act, federal agencies must set up their own performance rating systems. Evaluation may not be made on nonperformance-related criteria. Written tests are only allowed if approved in advance by the U.S. Civil Service Commission. The federal government is far ahead of most state and local governments in stressing performance criteria. Relatively little patronage exists at the federal level, seniority is a factor in positive evaluation only if directly related to job performance, and written tests are not used. But these conditions alone do not guarantee a perfect performance appraisal process.

A 1978 Government Accounting Office report stated that current federal ratings did not provide management with information on which to base personnel decisions necessary to improve agency effectiveness. The GAO found that the ten performance-rating systems it examined were not meeting the objectives of the 1950 act. Performance appraisals have taken a Theory X approach, leaving the job entirely up to supervisors. As a result, subordinates received inadequate information on their work and the improvement of it. Finally, and crucially, there was little linkage between accomplishment on the job and rewards such as salary increases and promotions.

Additional efforts have to be made at the federal level before a truly results-oriented performance appraisal system is installed in all agencies. President Carter acknowledged this fact in 1977 when he appointed public administration professor Alan Campbell head of the Civil Service Commission and gave him a mandate to eliminate the bottlenecks to good management in the federal personnel system.[20]

State Government

While state governments are not so deeply committed to performance appraisal as the federal government, they seem to be moving in that direction. A 1975 survey found that 8 of the 39 states surveyed measured employee goal achievement in their appraisals. These results-oriented systems were quite new, averaging less than two years in age.[21] Presumably, then, performance criteria are increasing in popularity and may continue to advance. Examples of performance-oriented state personnel systems are found in Wisconsin and California, for positions covered by civil service. California state civil service rules read as follows:

> Performance appraisal shall be governed by the following:
> a. The appraisal of work performance provides recognition for effective performance and identifies aspects of performance which could be improved.
> b. Performance appraisal is a continuing responsibility of all supervisors, and supervisors shall discuss performance informally with each employee as often as necessary to insure effective performance throughout the year.
> c. Each supervisor . . . shall make an appraisal in writing and shall discuss with the employee his over-all work performance at least once in each twelve calendar months . . . for the purpose of informing the employee of the caliber of his work, helping the employee recognize areas where performance could be improved, and developing with the employee a plan for accomplishing such improvement.
> d. Performance appraisals shall be prepared and recorded in the manner prescribed by the executive officer or board and may be appealed to the board only on the basis that they have been used to abuse, harass, or discriminate against an employee.
> e. Each employee shall be given a copy of the written appraisal covering his own performance. . . .

Local Government

While we know that local governments have the longest distance to move toward performance appraisal, we lack a detailed survey of appraisal techniques in our 80,000 local governments. One example of a city using performance appraisal is Amarillo, Texas, which requires its Civil Service Commission to "make rules and regulations providing for a system of efficiency ratings for all employees in the classified service and shall require that such ratings be used for purposes of promotions, demotions, reductions in force, and reinstatements."

An interesting experiment taking place in Dayton, Ohio, is *performance contracting*. This approach ties managerial pay increments to achievement of results. Managers who achieve the most get the largest rewards. In this way, managerial ratings go beyond the judgments of superiors to a clear-cut focus on what the manager's subordinates are producing. Such a results-oriented approach in performance appraisal is needed if employee effectiveness is to increase.

The U.S. Civil Service Commission, through the Intergovernmental Personnel Act of 1970, assists localities and states in developing performance appraisal systems. A community receiving such help is the town of Holden,

Massachusetts, which uses performance appraisal for deciding whether to grant periodic increment salary increases and special merit increases. It would not be surprising for the federal government to eventually insist that state and local governments move toward performance appraisal of personnel as a precondition for receiving grants in aid. There is a clear precedent for this step in increasing federal requirements of evaluation and performance auditing, so that the most performance-oriented level of the United States government may spur the other levels in its own direction.

TECHNICAL PROBLEMS AND HOW TO MINIMIZE THEM

Substantial technical problems beset, besiege, and beleaguer backers of performance appraisal. As is true for all the methods described in this book, performance appraisal entails substantial investment of money, time, and effort. The situation can easily get out of hand, as a 1974 survey of New Jersey State civil service found: "The amount of time and effort necessary to carry out the assignment of formulating performance descriptions and performance standards for each and every employee was felt to constitute an almost impossible task for the supervisor. . . ."[22] But the situation is not a hopeless one. In this case, the way out lies in having standards set for groups and classes of employees rather than for individual employees. And like all the results-oriented approaches in this book, costs involved should be viewed as an investment. The question is not whether the cost is too high, but whether the approach yields benefits sufficient to justify the cost.

One limitation of performance appraisal is that it can only measure how well an employee has done in past assignments. The employee may have the potential to do far better in the future in a different kind of position. Certainly, few expert observers would have concluded that Senator Harry S. Truman would do a good job as President, yet he received high grades from these same experts after completing eight years in the oval office. There are two principal ways to get around this limitation. One is to use aptitude tests, which are explicitly designed to measure potential. As we have mentioned before, however, aptitude tests have only limited validity, especially for managerial positions. The other approach is to ask raters to appraise potential as a factor separate from performance. Several federal agencies, according to public personnel specialist O. Glenn Stahl, have used this approach, with fair to middling success.[23] While we are clearly on treacherous ground in advocating it, such a subjective guesstimate seems the most useful tool in an ambiguous situation *if* the following safeguards are employed. First, ratings for potential should be made by several different supervisors who know the employee well. Second, a decision based on this collective rating should be made only if there is definite agreement and consensus on the employee's potential by most of the raters. In this way, individual prejudices and misjudgments can be minimized.

One reason why written tests came into vogue is that these objective mechanisms replaced arbitrary ratings based on political party and personal contacts. Unfortunately, as we have mentioned, objective tests are not necessarily valid tests. And performance appraisal inevitably has a strong subjective element. One rater's poised and mature employee may be another rater's arrogant and stodgy subordinate. How do we combine objectivity and validity?

One intriguing proposal has been put forth by personnel specialist Lawrence R. O'Leary, who advocates what he calls *job assessment centers*.[24] These centers employ multiple raters and multiple exercises, examine only behavior, and require that raters justify their rankings among themselves. If all these steps are followed, subjectivity in ratings will be reduced. O'Leary has used this approach in the Kansas City, Missouri, Police Department. It does not replace written tests and oral examinations, but is a substantially different supplementary approach.

During a two-year period, over 250 candidates for the positions of sergeant, detective, and captain were evaluated in the Kansas City assessment center. Basically, the center put candidates through a one-day series of exercises to make them display behavior which could be observed and measured by raters. Interviews with employees who had actually held the kind of posts the candidates were applying for were used to derive rating criteria. This information was used to fashion a number of exercises simulating the duties and responsibilities of the position. Applicants performing these exercises were rated by 20 observers who had once reported to superiors holding the rank which applicants were being evaluated for, who then held the rank themselves, and who presently were supervising officers at that rank. These observers spent two days of intensive training learning how to rank for observed behavior before actually beginning the task.

Raters who had supervised a specific candidate within the last year were asked to disqualify themselves. All raters had to justify their reasons for rating candidates as they did to their fellow raters. Both raters and employees rated felt that the assessment center was an appropriate means of performance appraisal. Specifically, 99 of 117 applicants for sergeant felt that the assessment center was job related to a great or very great extent, while 15 of the 20 raters felt that a supervisor should put a very great or great deal of reliance on assessment center results. O'Leary notes that the 6 minority group members and 1 woman evaluated for sergeant scored higher than average, and concludes that the assessment was job related, culturally fair, and highly objective.

Even our optimal approach, personnel evaluation by objectives, has some substantial snags. It will not work without a Theory Y atmosphere. That is, if the boss is decisively dictatorial, the subordinate is simply going to set the kinds of goals he or she thinks the boss wants. Indeed, all the political and technical problems discussed in Chapter 5, on MBO, can come to haunt personnel appraisal by objectives.

POLITICAL PROBLEMS AND HOW TO MINIMIZE THEM

Certain political obstacles to performance appraisal, such as political patronage, are difficult or impossible to modify or minimize. The only way to get rid of the problems of patronage would be to abolish the entire system and replace it with a functioning merit system—no easy task.

Unfortunately, civil service, designed to stop the arbitrary and inefficient practices of patronage personnel, has spawned a host of problems of its own. To understand these, a brief sketch of the historical evolution of civil service in the United States is necessary. Advocates of civil service reform decried the lack of performance criteria in selecting government employees. Their criticism gained more and more momentum in the last quarter of the nineteenth century, as government work became more complex. The rapid growth of industrial technology had repercussions for government as well as business. The typically unskilled, unindustrious party hack proved increasingly unequal to the new work of government.

The initial civil service laws, such as the federal Pendleton Act of 1883, were designed to keep the "bad guys," or party politicians, off the government payroll. Written examinations and a probationary period were required for new employees. The heritage of civil service reform has retained the predominantly negative "keep out the bad guys" orientation for a long time. That is, in many state and local governments, there is no stress on performance appraisal or performance-related job training. Instead, the system protects its own by making it very difficult to remove any civil servant, no matter how inefficient or ineffective. Many civil servants, including those at the department head level, earn tenure in their position. This means they can be removed only for "cause," an arduous and exhausting achievement. For example, Connecticut State Statute Section 7-278 states that "No active head of any town commission . . . shall be dismissed unless he has been given notice in writing of the specific grounds of such dismissal and an opportunity to be heard in his own defense, personally or by counsel, at a public hearing before the authority having the power of dismissal." These requirements discourage chief executives who wish to replace department heads with new appointees oriented to their own way of thinking. While this regulation restricts patronage, it also acts against chief executives who wish to improve performance.

Civil service may become even more rigid at lower levels of the organization. The head of the New Jersey state prison system told the state legislature in 1976 that civil service procedures made it almost impossible for him to dismiss incompetent guards. And the New Jersey Department of Youth and Family Services uses private agencies to provide residential care for disturbed children because civil service rules make it impractical for the department to give such care. In addition, the so-called rule of three in promotion, under which management gets to pick among the three top-scoring candidates for a post, does not apply to New Jersey military veterans. A top-scoring veteran must be promoted, regardless of other considerations. These rigidities are not peculiar to New Jersey; similar restrictions are to be found in most state and local "merit" systems. While we can sympathize with the reasons for their original creation, these rules interfere with agency effectiveness. For instance, if we wish to reward veterans for their service, why not give them pensions or other benefits? If they are not the most qualified applicants, they should not serve in government.

While a persistent manager may be able to weed out some incompetent civil service employees, major change is going to be impossible without a thorough overhaul of restrictive civil service regulations. While this is no small task, it must become a top priority for advocates of increased governmental effectiveness.

Government employee unions also cause decreased effectiveness, as we have noted in the preceding chapter, on productivity. As far as personnel policy is concerned, unions typically push for seniority as the top criterion for promotion or protection against layoffs. Since there is no correlation between performance and longevity in the job, one must agree with Stahl's contention that seniority "is one of the most insidious sappers of incentive for superior performance and the most vicious denials of the merit idea that exists."[25]

Managers who wish to get unions to de-emphasize seniority must realize that union adherence to the concept is a result of arbitrary actions by management in the past. Unions were formed as a response to management dismissal of, or refusal to promote, qualified individuals for personal reasons. Sometimes a worker with an enviable career record would be fired when she or he began to slow down in late middle age. The natural union response was to settle on the "objective" criterion of seniority in the job as a qualification for promotion.

Realizing this, the manager must act according to Theory Y to convince the union to let up on its demands for seniority in promotion. In business executive Robert Townsend's words, "If you already have unions, then deal with them openly and honestly. Abide by their rules."[26] While not easy, it is also not impossible to get unions to give ground on seniority. One private firm, for example, gave in during one bargaining session to union demands that seniority be applied to all promotions. But three years later, during the next contract negotiations, the union agreed to go back to a merit promotion system in return for higher wages and fringe benefits. This turnaround was caused by a series of reforms in supervisory practices made in the period between the two bargaining sessions. The union became convinced that supervision had become much fairer and could be counted on to promote truly qualified workers, rather than playing favorites.[27] Theory Y and fair play may induce unions to be less adamant about the seniority principle. Certainly, blustering and bullying will get management nowhere on this matter.

Another source of substantial dissatisfaction for supporters of merit evaluation is a series of new federal government regulations. The federal government gave over $70 billion in aid to state and local governments during 1977 and attached various strings to many of the grants. The string that concerns us here is the insistence that a certain type of person be hired with grant funds, regardless of qualifications. For example, grants under the Comprehensive Employment and Training Act (CETA) require that hiring preference be given to women, minority groups, the handicapped, and those under 18 and over 45 years of age. As a result, many CETA employees are working in departments where they could not have entered if they had been required to pass performance requirements, and where they often perform far below par.

Federal "affirmative action" programs push for the hiring of women, minorities, and the handicapped in federal, state, and local governments. Although a quota system with fixed percentages is not supposed to operate under affirmative action, agencies are given "guidelines" which amount to a quota and told that they will lose federal aid or be subject to other pressures if they balk at following the "guidelines." There is no question that there has been a substantial history of discrimination toward women and minorities, but one should not be called either a bigot or a male chauvinist pig for wondering whether quotas are the best way to attack the problem. It would seem more reasonable to begin to apply stringent measures to agencies which consistently refuse to promote minority, handicapped, or female employees with strong performance records. The blanket approach taken by affirmative action may elevate personnel with dubious credentials and discourage those with proven performance capacity. It is difficult to give advice to the practitioner in this area. Skilled managers and personnel directors may be able to protect their top performers by delaying tactics, strong counterattacks, or outright refusal to go along. But the penalties, especially for state and local government agencies who lose grants, may be severe. The best overall strategy seems a long-range one, emphasizing legal attacks in the courts, demands to legislators to change the law, and the protective tactics outlined above.

CASE STUDY:
PERFORMANCE APPRAISAL IN A POLICE DEPARTMENT[28]

This study deals with the installation of performance appraisal in Caldwell, a northern New Jersey suburban police department of less than 50 officers. Previous to the adoption of performance appraisal, all promotions, including that to the rank of chief, had been on a strict seniority basis. No performance appraisal was used for purposes of discipline or monitoring, either.

In 1962, patrol officer James Brown circulated a petition advocating the substitution of a merit appraisal system for the seniority system. Although every patrol officer signed the petition, and the Police Commission endorsed the idea in principle, it never got any further. None of the commissioners was willing to work to translate the idea into operating policy.

Ten years passed. The patrol officer who had circulated the petition for performance appraisal was now a sergeant, and he tried again to interest the chief and the Police Commission. After his pleas fell on deaf ears, he began an in-depth study of performance appraisal after being assigned to the FBI Academy in Quantico, Virginia. (The FBI has extensive training programs for state and local police officers, and the sergeant spent three months there.) He soon found that no performance appraisal system was without problems. His two preferences—forced choice ratings and assessment centers—were just too costly for a small department. But he felt that most of the other systems lacked adequate safeguards against bias. Furthermore, a really drastic break with the past might prove unpalatable to departmental employees.

With these factors in mind, the sergeant chose the so-called Windsor system of appraisal, which the police department in Windsor, Ontario, Canada, had used for some 20 years. The Windsor plan uses three factors in determining promotion: scores on a written aptitude examination, specific to police work; performance appraisal by trait; and seniority. The applicant can earn up to 15 out of 100 points on the written test; up to 40 points on performance appraisal; and up to 45 (3 points per year, up to a 15-year maximum) for seniority.

Note that this is not a total performance appraisal system, since it also considers test scores and seniority. But it was a giant step forward for a department whose sole criterion for advancement had been seniority.

By 1975, the sergeant had become a lieutenant. As the operations officer of the department, he pressed for a trial run of the Windsor system. As Figure 9–2 indicates, the system is designed for

Department of Police BOROUGH OF CALDWELL

P.O. Box 191, Caldwell, New Jersey 07006 / Essex County / (201) 226-2600

James B. Brown, Jr
Chief of Police

SUPERVISOR'S DAILY REPORT

SUPERVISOR:_____ DATE:_____ SHIFT:_____

DURING MY TOUR OF DUTY I SUPERVISED THE FOLLOWING OFFICERS AND OBSERVED THEM ACTIVELY ENGAGED IN POLICE DUTIES:

OFFICER:_____ OFFICER:_____

OFFICER:_____ OFFICER:_____

PRIOR TO ASSUMING PATROL DUTY I CONDUCTED AN INFORMAL INSPECTION OF THE OFFICERS AND THEY WERE PROPERLY DRESSED, CLEAN, AND PREPARED FOR DUTY UNLESS OTHERWISE NOTED.

NOTATIONS

ADDITIONAL NOTATIONS REGARDING EXCELLENT AND/OR DEFICIENT PERFORMANCE OF DUTIES BY OFFICERS:

SIGNATURE OF SUPERVISOR:_____

OFFICER EVALUATED: I CERTIFY THAT THIS REPORT HAS BEEN VIEWED BY ME. MY
SIGNATURE DOES NOT NECESSARILY INDICATE AGREEMENT.

SIGNATURE: _____ DATE: _____

IF THE EVALUATED OFFICER DESIRES A CONFERENCE WITH THE REVIEW OFFICER, INDICATE
UNDER COMMENTS SO APPROPRIATE ARRANGEMENTS CAN BE MADE.

COMMENTS:

𝔇epartment of 𝔓olice BOROUGH OF CALDWELL

P.O. Box 191, Caldwell, New Jersey 07006 / Essex County / (201) 226-2600

James B. Brown, Jr
Chief of Police

PERFORMANCE EVALUATION REPORT

EVALUATOR:_____ DATE:_____

OFFICER EVALUATED:_____

STANDARDS

	1	2	3	4
1. OBSERVANCE OF WORK HOURS.............				
2. ATTENDANCE...........................				
3. APPEARANCE...........................				
4. COMPLIANCE WITH RULES AND DIRECTIVES.				
5. PUBLIC RELATIONS.....................				
6. HUMAN RELATIONS SKILL................				
7. CONCEPTUAL SKILL.....................				
8. TECHNICAL SKILL......................				
9. QUALITY OF WORK......................				
10. ACCEPTS RESPONSIBILITY..............				
11. ACCEPTS DIRECTION...................				
12. ACCEPTS CHANGE......................				
13. EFFECTIVENESS UNDER STRESS..........				
14. INITIATIVE.........................				
15. LEADERSHIP.........................				

1=UNSATISFACTORY.

2=SOME IMPROVEMENT
IS NEEDED.

3=MEETS STANDARDS.

4=EXCEEDS STANDARDS.

CHECKS IN COLUMNS 1, 2 OR 4 MUST BE EXPLAINED ACCORDING TO INSTRUCTIONS.

THE EVALUATOR CERTIFIES THIS REPORT REPRESENTS HIS BEST JUDGMENT:

SIGNATURE OF EVALUATOR:_____

more than promotion alone. Daily reports by supervisors enable superiors to judge whether an officer has problems or is excelling in performance. Figure 9-3 is the periodic evaluation sheet which is used for promotion and to give a detailed picture of officer performance.

The lieutenant was able to nullify potential opposition by senior officers to the trial run for two reasons. First was the inclusion of the seniority criterion in the Windsor system. Second, there were just three patrol officers with 15 years of seniority, all of whom the lieutenant had personally broken in as rookies. They were willing to go along with him out of a combination of loyalty and respect, based on the fact that Brown was known as a person who always kept his word. Thus, when he explained to them how the system worked, they could be sure that there were no ulterior motives involved.

After the trial run was over, the Windsor system became official departmental policy on January 1, 1976. The lieutenant credits this achievement to one member of the Board of Police Commissioners, who became a supporter of the plan. This was the difference between 1975 and earlier attempts to get performance appraisal. This commissioner ran interference and convinced both peers and the chief that the Windsor system should become departmental policy. He argued that "this is no longer a sleepy little hamlet. We have homicides, rapes and other serious crimes against people and property. To deal with the situation, we need a department of professionals, not a collection of cronies." The Patrolmen's Benevolent Association (PBA), bargaining agent for the rank and file, endorsed the plan and even insisted that it be included in the contract signed at the beginning of 1977.

The crucial test for the implementation of the Windsor system's performance appraisal began in January 1976. The lieutenant felt that the key to success lay in persuading the three departmental road sergeants, who were the first-line supervisors, to take the new approach seriously. He explained to them that they would be expected to fill out the supervisor's daily report (Figure 9-2) and to justify, with evidence, any comments they made. The system was not designed to praise protégés or stab disliked subordinates in the back.

After the first six weeks, the lieutenant called the road sergeants in for a conference. He noted that they were not filling out the daily reports. When one of them argued, "Aw, that's not necessary —we're all cops, you know what it's like out there. You can trust us to do our job," the lieutenant indicated that such a defense would get the sergeants nowhere. He expected them to cooperate fully; and if they did not, he would come down on them hard for the first minor infraction on duty in any area. Since the lieutenant usually overlooked minor breaches of the departmental code, the supervisors knew that he meant business, and they began filling out the daily reports.

After this conference, some officers and sergeants began to criticize the lieutenant and the Windsor system to their patrol officers. The lieutenant's response was to get both the chief and the Police Commission to read the riot act in personal conference and by official memorandum to the entire department. Once this was done, everyone was put on notice that the Windsor system was to be taken seriously. It was official departmental policy with strong support at the top, not just the pet project of the lieutenant.

At the next conference with the road sergeants, the lieutenant went over the daily reports they had filed. He picked up one which indicated that one patrol officer assigned to school crossing guard duty spent too much time chatting with adults who were passing by and did not pay enough attention to crossing the children. What had the sergeant done about this situation? the lieutenant inquired. When the sergeant replied that he had done nothing, the lieutenant stated that he considered the evaluation to be a worthless one. It is the responsibility of supervisors to begin corrective action when they spot flaws in subordinate performance. The sergeant should have talked to the patrol officer involved, and then noted in future reports the subsequent actions of this subordinate. The lieutenant told the sergeants that if they failed to do so and could not justify their reasons for rating the subordinates as they did, he would point this out in his annual rating of *their* performance to the chief.

The formal performance evaluation rating (Figure 9–3) must be endorsed not only by the road sergeant with primary responsibility for the subordinate but also by the other two sergeants as well. (The three sergeants are each in charge of one of the three daily shifts, so each has some knowledge of every patrol officer in this small department.) If the sergeant cannot persuade his peers that his appraisal is justified, he will have to keep revising the report until he can persuade them. And after the three sergeants concur, they have to justify their recommendations to the lieutenant. In this way, the lieutenant feels he can minimize the problem of personal bias which has concerned him ever since he made a thorough review of performance appraisal.

Once the performance evaluation report is accepted by all four officers who have to approve it, the road sergeant shares it with the subordinate. A subordinate who feels that he has been given a raw deal, that the report is unacceptable, is sent to talk to the lieutenant. The lieutenant informs him that the report has been approved by four different superiors, and that the subordinate had better respond constructively in his weak areas if he wants to do well in the department. He is also told he can talk to the chief or file a grievance if he still disagrees. So far, no disgruntled subordinates have done either.

What has the Windsor system actually accomplished in the Caldwell, New Jersey, Police Department? At the time of this writing, no superior slots had opened up, so it could not be used for promotion. However, it had been used to evaluate performance in terms of standards developed by the department. The standards involve the number of motor vehicles cited for moving violations (speeding, reckless driving, etc.) by each officer. They were derived by figuring the average number of such citations issued per year for each officer over the three years from 1973–1975. The average number was 20, so it was felt that it was reasonable to expect each officer to issue 10 such citations per year. The number 10 was felt to be reasonable enough (only half of 20) so that it would not act as a quota, forcing patrol officers to issue inappropriate citations. And since the officers who issued the most citations also made more arrests for other offenses than average, the number of citations seemed to be correlated with productivity in general.

When it was announced that issuing less than 10 citations a year would count against patrol officers in the performance appraisal, all officers who had previously performed below par issued at least 10 per year in 1976. And the lieutenant also noticed a change for the better in personal appearance, one item on the checklist in Figure 9–4. Scruffy looking officers tidied up, and one 5-foot 10-inch 265-pounder shed 25 pounds and continued to diet.

The lieutenant felt that the new performance appraisal, despite all the headaches involved in installing and implementing it, was well worth the trouble. While he noted that the Windsor system would not "win any popularity contests for me," he felt confident it had already improved performance and would continue to do so in the future.

Questions

1. Do you think the Windsor system is a good method for initiating performance appraisal? Explain your reasons.

2. Is the Windsor system an output-oriented personnel evaluation system? Explain your reasons.

3. Do you think another type of personnel appraisal system would have been a better choice for this department? Explain your reasons.

4. Detail the constraints limiting the choice of personnel appraisal systems open to this department.

5. Would you have implemented the Windsor system in the same manner that the lieutenant did? Explain your reasons.

6. Would you say that the Windsor system is more of a Theory Y approach than a Theory X approach? Explain your reasons.

PROSPECTS AND PROBLEMS FOR PERFORMANCE APPRAISAL

Like the other results-oriented techniques examined in this book, performance appraisal is likely to enjoy increased popularity in the last fifth of the twentieth century. To be fully effective, however, it must be carried out in a Theory Y ambience, and must be closely linked to other crucial considerations of any personnel system. Let us examine each of these points in turn.

Theory Y and Performance Appraisal

We have already indicated that personnel evaluation by objectives is our preferred approach. We return to the topic again to explain a severe disadvantage of other performance appraisal techniques. This presentation is based on the writing of Douglas McGregor, the originator of the terms "Theory X" and "Theory Y."[29]

McGregor notes that both superiors and subordinates are often uncomfortable with performance appraisal procedures. Even managers most sympathetic to performance appraisal find it difficult to give ratings, because subordinates react defensively and angrily to low ratings. This painful situation is exacerbated when the manager uses an evaluation plan which discusses employee personality traits. At this point, McGregor says, we are "close to a violation of the integrity of the personality. Managers are uncomfortable when placed in the position of 'playing God.' "[30]

McGregor argues that traditional performance appraisal fails to achieve desired administrative, informational, and motivational purposes. While the best appraisal systems can discriminate among outstanding, satisfactory, and unsatisfactory performance, in attempting to make fine distinctions, "we are quite probably deluding ourselves."[31] This means that performance appraisal leaves a lot to be desired as a means for administering discipline, promotions, and transfers.

As an informational tool, designed to improve superior-subordinate communication, traditional performance appraisal fails because of the immense anxiety generated by the appraisal interview, a fact we have already mentioned. There is no easy way out of the dilemma. For instance, if the superior tries to present unpleasant news in generalities, the subordinate will probably ask the boss to be more specific. Once given specific examples, the subordinate will usually try to point out extenuating circumstances for the concrete occurrences cited. Most of us find criticism hard to hear and accept, because it is painful to our egos and feelings of self-worth. Accordingly, the greater the criticism, the less likely we are to accept it. In McGregor's words, "If our managerial strategy emphasizes this childlike dependence, this schoolboy reliance on teacher's grade, we should not be surprised if the reactions to an objective appraisal are sometimes immature."[32] A superior who comes on strong may be able to communicate the details and reasons for low ratings to the subordinate, but only at the price of a decline or rupture in their relationship.

In a situation so fraught with tension, small wonder that the appraisal interview can often become a meaningless ritual in which managers avoid unpleasant truths. These managers have found that the two assumptions behind the appraisal interview—first, that employees want to know just where they stand; and, second, that when they are told, they can change—are not necessarily true. Strauss and Sayles argue that there is no point in a manager's pointing out faults which are very difficult or impossible for a subordinate to correct. If told about these faults, the subordinate's anxiety will increase and his or her performance may decline.

For instance, what is the point of telling an intensely shy or anxious person that he or she is shy or anxious? Nothing short of extensive psychotherapy is likely to help.[33] Thus, in McGregor's judgment, traditional performance appraisal also fails the test of motivating employees to change their behavior. Moreover, the semi-annual or annual evaluation typical of performance appraisal is inferior to more frequent and informal consultations held right after an employee's achievement or failure.

For all these weighty reasons, an MBO approach to appraisal, which makes superior and subordinate a real team, is to be preferred to the typical appraisal, which is a disservice to superior and subordinate alike. While hardly a flawless approach, as we have already noted, MBO is the only way for an organization to tap its full potential.

Linking Appraisal to Training

Results-oriented personnel systems cannot stop with performance appraisal. Further *training* of employees—whether done in house, at colleges, special institutes, workshops, or elsewhere—is an inescapable necessity today. We live in an age of scientific revolution, where innovation constantly outdates past methods.[34] More scientists are alive today than in the entire previous history of the world. Every five years, the quantity of published scientific research is doubled. Some engineers find that half of what they learned in school is outmoded five years after they have graduated. Specialists in even the most specialized areas of human behavior, such as results-oriented public management, simply find it impossible to keep up with all the new developments in their area of expertise.

In such a turbulent environment, the need for continued training is apparent. And there is more training for government employees than there has ever been before. Yet many agencies, including many which use performance appraisal, neglect training. Training is usually seen as a luxury and is the last thing added to the budget and the first thing cut.

No doubt, part of the reason for this sad state of affairs is the poor record of some training programs. More important factors include resistance from senior department members, who fear what will happen to themselves if younger subordinates become more proficient through training. The reaction of senior police department employees to the federal Law Enforcement Educational

Program (LEEP) has often been to ridicule the "college boys," a reaction based on fear. Another reason is the tendency of lay budget decision makers— whether a city council, county commission, or board of finance—to view training as a "frill" which the department must sacrifice in a time of tight budgets.

Yet training is an indispensable means of ensuring greater efficiency and effectiveness in our rapidly changing world. If performance appraisal recommendations are not supported by training, many of them will be worthless. That is, if employees have good overall performance scores and are highly motivated but are deficient in some areas, it makes sense to train them to overcome these deficiencies. Perhaps a formal training session will be needed. If so, it should be regarded as an *investment*, and a calculation made to determine whether the likely benefits will exceed the costs. The civilian public service lags greatly behind both the corporate sector and the professional military in training employees. In particular, state and local governments could do much more to train their workers. This is an area where the federal government has again taken the lead, through such programs as the Intergovernmental Personnel Act and LEEP. Further investment in this area by all three levels of American government will both improve performance and enhance the efficacy of performance appraisal systems.

NOTES

1. N. Joseph Cayer, *Public Personnel Administration in the United States* (New York: St. Martin's Press, 1975), p. 81.
2. Douglas M. Fox, *The Politics of City and State Bureaucracy* (Pacific Palisades, Calif.: Goodyear Publishers, 1974), p. 51.
3. See U.S. Congress, House Committee on Post Office and Civil Service, *Final Report on Violations and Abuses of Merit Principles in Federal Employment Together with Minority Views*, 94th Cong., 2nd sess., 1976.
4. "Hard-nosed Foreman Gets the Brush from Hard Hat in Dispute," *Government News* (Hartford, Conn.), April 1977, p. 5.
5. George S. Odiorne, *Personnel Administration by Objectives* (Homewood, Ill.: Richard D. Irwin, 1971), p. 265.
6. Wallace S. Sayre, "The Triumphs of Techniques over Purpose," *Public Administration Review* 8 (Spring 1948): 134–37, at 135.
7. See O. Glenn Stahl, *Public Personnel Administration*, 6th ed. (New York: Harper & Row, 1971), p. 198; and George Strauss and Leonard R. Sayles, Jr., *Personnel: The Human Problems of Management*, 3rd ed. (Englewood Cliffs, N.J.: Prentice-Hall, 1972), p. 515.
8. Stahl, loc. cit.
9. See Felix A. Nigro and Lloyd G. Nigro, *The New Public Personnel Administration* (Itasca, Ill.: F. E. Peacock, 1976), p. 202.

10. Ernest Dale and Alice Smith, "Now Report Cards for Bosses," *New York Times Magazine*, March 31, 1958, p. 56.

11. *Administration of the New Jersey State Civil Service System* (Trenton, N.J.: New Jersey State Legislature Office of Fiscal Affairs, January 1975), p. 163.

12. Strauss and Sayles, op. cit., p. 514.

13. Ibid., pp. 514–15.

14. Robert N. McMurry, "Validating the Patterned Interview," *Personnel* 23 (January 1947): 263–72.

15. Odiorne, op. cit., p. 268.

16. This subsection is based primarily on Paul Pigors and Charles A. Myers, *Personnel Administration: A Point of View and a Method*, 7th ed. (New York: McGraw-Hill, 1973), pp. 300–1; Town of Newington, Conn., *Performance Evaluation Instructions*, 1976; and Strauss and Sayles, op. cit., p. 517.

17. Douglas McGregor, "An Uneasy Look at Performance Appraisal," *Harvard Business Review* 35 (May 1957): 91.

18. O. A. Ohmann, "Executive Appraisal and Counselling," *Michigan Business Review* 9 (November 1957): 24.

19. Table 9–2 is based on the approach described in Odiorne, op. cit., pp. 271–72.

20. United States General Accounting Offiice, *Federal Employee Performance Rating Systems Need Fundamental Changes* (Washington, D.C.: Government Printing Offiice, 1978).

21. Hubert S. Field and William H. Holley, "Performance Appraisal: An Analysis of State-Wide Practices," *Public Personnel Management* (May–June 1975): 145–50.

22. *Administration of the New Jersey State Civil Service System*, op. cit., p. 164.

23. Stahl, op. cit., p. 188.

24. Lawrence R. O'Leary, "Objectivity and Job Relatedness: Can We Have Our Cake and Eat It Too?" *Public Personnel Management*, November–December 1976, pp. 423–33.

25. O. Glenn Stahl, *The Personnel Job of Government Managers* (Chicago: Public Personnel Association, 1971), p. 74.

26. Robert Townsend, *Up the Organization* (Greenwich, Conn.: Fawcett Crest Books, 1970), p. 77.

27. Douglas McGregor, *The Human Side of Enterprise* (New York: McGraw-Hill, 1960), pp. 136–37.

28. The author is indebted to Chief James Brown of the Caldwell, N.J., Police Department for the information contained in this section.

29. Douglas McGregor, "An Uneasy Look at Performance Appraisal," *Harvard Business Review* 35 (May–June 1957): 89–94.

30. Ibid., p. 90.

31. McGregor, *The Human Side of Enterprise*, op. cit., p. 82.

32. Ibid., p. 86.

33. Strauss and Sayles, op. cit., p. 519.

34. See George E. Berkley, *The Administrative Revolution* (Englewood Cliffs, N.J.: Prentice-Hall, 1971).

10
Putting Results-Oriented Approaches Together

LEARNING OBJECTIVES

TO UNDERSTAND:

The interrelationship of different approaches to results-oriented management

The place of Theory X in results-oriented management

Why results-oriented approaches should be tried even though they have often failed

---

A RECAPITULATION AND COMPARISON OF RESULTS-ORIENTED APPROACHES

By now the special attributes of each major approach to results-oriented management should be evident. The questions to be considered here are their similarities and differences, and the special utility of each. We begin this analysis by reviewing each of the approaches in turn.

Program Planning

Planning was the first approach examined, and appropriately so. Without the identification of problems and setting of goals and objectives that plan-

271

ning involves, there can be no results-oriented management. Results are only meaningful in terms of the goals set by the agency. Goals are the guideposts by which the agency charts its way. Planning, then, is a necessity for any kind of results-oriented management.

The planning process can be a part of approaches such as management by objectives (MBO), planning-programming-budgeting (PPB), and zero-base budgeting (ZBB). It need not exist separately if these approaches are used in a comprehensive manner by the agency, because MBO, PPB, and ZBB all entail goal statements. A reexamination of Figure 1–1 illustrates this point, since the figure relates each of the principal approaches to the functions of planning, organizing, supervising, and controlling. Where comprehensive MBO, PPB, and ZBB exist, then, it probably would be needless duplication to set up a separate planning process for the agency.

Reorganizing for Results

Agencies vary greatly in size, task, and function, and these variables determine which principles of reorganization will be useful to an agency. For example, a building inspection department, where inspectors do almost all of their work individually, would not benefit nearly as much from instituting joint accountability as would a fire department, where teamwork is essential in almost all aspects of the job. Another example, already mentioned, is irrelevance of project management for routine or repetitive tasks such as mail delivery. Likewise, the need for decentralization may be much less in small agencies with few employees than in giant organizations with thousands of workers. Reorganizers should always be guided by Harvey Sherman's flexible pragmatism, that is, by asking whether the organizational tailoring works toward the desired result, or not. Nice neat organizational charts may look impressive, but they are meaningless if they bear no relationship to the structure of work.

Output-Oriented Supervision

Supervision which always focuses on organizational goals and the work to be done is an absolute requirement for results-oriented management. If employees are not motivated to achieve goals by their managers, programs will never live up to their potential. Here is an area where an enormous amount of work needs to be done in the public sector, for managers are rarely adequately trained and rewarded to work toward results. This situation explains many of the failures of government agencies. Output-oriented supervision is a must in any organization concerned with accomplishing goals.

Management by Objectives

As noted in chapter 5, MBO involves far more than planning alone. It is also concerned both with implementing the plan and monitoring the results of the implementation. These two tasks are vital ones for any goal-oriented agency, because the most impressive and incisive plan is meaningless unless carried out and carefully scrutinized for achievements. If some managers shy away from the abbreviation *MBO* as yet another management gimmick, let them do so. The important thing is to carry out the implementation of the plan in a careful and methodical manner, regardless of the label.

Program Evaluation

Where MBO-type implementation and review is useful in just about any agency, the greater cost and technical difficulties of evaluation make the latter approach less meaningful for smaller agencies with small budgets. The need for evaluators to determine *why* something occurred—going beyond the monitor's concern with *whether* it occurred—will always make evaluation more expensive and difficult than monitoring. Some of the best known authorities on evaluation have taken pains to point out that not all programs can or should be evaluated. Evaluation should be applied selectively, with larger programs or those which are in trouble receiving special attention.

Results-Oriented Budgeting

Results-oriented budgeting systems entail substantial implementation costs. The additional paper they generate is testimony to the effort put into these approaches. If an organization already has thorough-going planning and MBO systems at work, the need for planning-programming-budgeting may be minimal. Planning and MBO would also reduce the need for zero-base budgeting, with one important difference. ZBB is a bottoms-up process, where budget analyses develop in the depths of the organization. If managers feel that putting their subordinates to work on ZBB would develop these employees' analytical skills and develop more of an awareness of the relationship between organizational goals and budgets, they may well want to launch ZBB.

Note that there is a real kinship between MBO and ZBB, although MBO is not a budgetary system. Both stress the involvement of the bottom of the bureaucracy in results-oriented management. In so doing, they are both consistent with Theory Y decentralized organization and delegation of authority. Since ZBB and MBO are so closely related, it may not be necessary to use them both simultaneously for maximum results. One or the other may get the job done perfectly well at less cost, especially in smaller organizations. Larger organizations may find it beneficial to use both approaches simultaneously in an integrated manner.

Productivity

Since productivity improvement stresses increased efficiency, it can be used in disparate, specialized, and narrowly focused areas. This means it can perhaps be used more universally than any of the other approaches examined in this book. But, as we noted in Chapter 8, productivity will go off the track if it is not implemented with a focus on organizational goals. To be most meaningful, productivity should stress program results rather than increased efficiency in and of itself, as Table 8–6 indicates. With these warnings in mind, almost any agency may be able to increase efficiency by carrying out productivity studies, which should be carefully considered by all managers.

Personnel Performance Appraisal

We advocate that results-oriented employee appraisal be used in all agencies. Just as supervisors should focus on results in directing the work, employees should be rated and rewarded on how well they achieve the stated objectives of the organization. While it is often difficult to determine the results achieved by an employee, the effort should be made. A variety of methods to do so is mentioned in Chapter 9, and there should be an approach tailored to the size and budget of any agency.

Recapitulation

We have stated above that we believe planning, output-oriented supervision, MBO, productivity improvement, and personnel performance appraisal to be indispensable to real results-oriented management. Results-oriented budgeting approaches are extremely useful and could perhaps be used in place of MBO, just as MBO could substitute for them. Program evaluation, while very helpful, seems less suitable for smaller agencies with good monitoring systems. Finally, while we believe that the principles of results-oriented reorganization listed in Chapter 3 are usually useful, they should be applied with an emphasis on results, not for their own sake.

Management professor and consultant Myron Weiner has stressed how related results-oriented approaches should be combined into a complementary "repertoire."[1] Weiner notes, as we have done in this chapter, how the approaches work best in tandem with others. For example, as we stated, program planning without MBO-type implementation and monitoring is useless. Likewise, output-oriented supervision will not get very far without personnel performance appraisal. While the examples Weiner gives are far more elaborate and complex than anything discussed in this book, the principle is the same. None of the approaches discussed in this book should be used in isolation. Rather, a reinforcing repertoire of approaches should be established.

What about the other results-oriented approaches such as program evaluation and review technique (PERT), critical path method (CPM), and operations research (OR), discussed (in less detail) in Chapter 2? These approaches are of maximum utility in analyzing regularly recurring situations which involve a great number of objects or variables, such as highway traffic flow or construction of a large physical facility. In other words, when the problem deals with physical objects that can easily be subjected to quantitative analysis, the techniques are very useful. When the emphasis is on qualitative factors like the nature of nursing care or educational instruction, the techniques will be much less useful, or not useful at all.

We have tried to stress throughout this book that none of these approaches is a panacea, and that some of them are not worth the effort to install under certain conditions. While none of these approaches can make the sun stand still in its path, all of them can gather more meaningful information for agency employees to analyze. The improvement in the quality of data and analysis can well lead to more effective programs. We say *can* rather than *will*, because, in the last analysis, the use to which these approaches will be put depends upon the desire and the competence of agency managers to implement them.

THEORY X AND THEORY Y: SOME FINAL WORDS

Most government agencies follow a variant of Theory X management, and trying to change that approach may be difficult, if not impossible. Such is especially likely to be true if top management is not fully behind the change, leaving middle managers who want to move to Theory Y on their own. And while these managers can make certain changes, they are unlikely to be able to transform the organizational atmosphere from that of Theory X to Theory Y.

In these circumstances, managers may well want to institute results-oriented approaches in a Theory X atmosphere. While our preference for participatory management is obvious, results-oriented Theory X management is superior to activity- or input-oriented Theory X. Indeed, by its rational stress on accomplishments, it may set the stage for a transition to Theory Y.

Some of the case studies in this book illustrate this point. These studies sketch modest beginnings, indicating that most agencies are unlikely to try a comprehensive approach at first. This is probably just as well, since we have noted the fate of such comprehensive crash programs. And these modest beginnings, as the case studies point out, are hardly pure Theory Y. They are, instead, bridges from Theory X to Theory Y. Managers who wish to go to results-oriented approaches may have to have some confrontations at first, if no other way of getting employees to respond works. Orders and confrontations should be avoided at all cost, but may have to be used if nothing else succeeds. For instance, subordinates who refuse to fill out ZBB or MBO forms will have to be reminded that the agency is serious about these approaches, and that those who do not cooperate are unlikely to get along very well with their superiors in the future. Most of the resistance is likely to be concentrated among more senior personnel, who balk at changing their ways after a career of doing things differently. Here the managerial skills of supervisors, who may implicitly present past IOUs to their subordinates for payment, are crucial. Note how the police lieutenant in the personnel appraisal case study in Chapter 9 was able to do just this, getting his senior patrol officer to accept the new approach without cracking any heads. Once the new approach is installed, it can gradually be converted further and further in the direction of Theory Y.

Here the MBO case study in Chapter 5, dealing with the Passaic County Prosecutor's Office business manager, is relevant. The business manager began by setting objectives for employees and planned to eventually involve employees in setting objectives themselves. In agencies with less disastrous histories of Theory X management of more junior employees, more rapid movement to Theory Y is possible. But in both cases, managers should keep their eyes firmly fixed on Theory Y. If they are sidetracked from that goal by the inevitable difficulties they will confront, all the work involved may come to nothing. To be sure, a Theory X results-oriented approach will yield some benefits, but these will be small compared to those of Theory Y.

DO RESULTS-ORIENTED APPROACHES ACHIEVE WORTHWHILE RESULTS?

As the reader has noted, we have listed many examples of failed efforts to increase agency effectiveness. Why should the manager want to try approaches which have often failed? The manager should try, we argue, because they are the *only* way to improve agency performance.

We grant that some jurisdictions would not be fertile ground for results-oriented management. Many Hudson County, New Jersey, municipalities, for example, are so ridden with patronage politics that a department head wanting to introduce MBO or ZBB would not get very far. But changes *can* be made if political support from high places can be gained. Jersey City, the largest city in Hudson County and the one with the most spectacular history of government corruption, commissioned a police department productivity study in 1974. To the amazement of many, its recommendation that several precinct houses be closed down and consolidated with others was accepted and implemented. A reform mayor, Dr. Paul Jordan, supported the measure and proved that it is not impossible to change even governments like Jersey City's.

Of course, without the mayor or key party leaders supporting department managers, changes to results-oriented management will be impossible in jurisdictions like Jersey City. But most governments in the United States do not have the extreme case of patronage politics pathology that Hudson County does, and so allow for more possibilities for change.

What *kind* of changes will results-oriented management introduce? Those who expect dramatic dollar savings will often be disappointed because of the difficulties in phasing out government programs. Yet cumulative savings can be substantial, as the examples from productivity programs in Dallas, Texas, and Milwaukee, Wisconsin, indicate. Even more important, though, are increases in *effectiveness*.

Government programs cannot be effective if basic information about how they work and what they are accomplishing is absent. This information enables managers to form better policies, and is the most important contribution of the various approaches examined in this book. From planning through MBO to evaluation; from results-oriented budgeting through reorganization to productivity; and from output-oriented supervision to personnel performance appraisal; all the approaches help the manager decide where to go and how things are working out once the journey begins.

Note that while this book lists plenty of failures, it also lists many accomplishments, with many managers stressing the importance of the improvement of the quality of information to them. This means that results-oriented approaches will work if conditions are right. One of the key focuses of this book is methods to minimize obstacles to achieving these right conditions. While we promise no miracles, management can and has been improved by the approaches described in this volume. Results-oriented managers will want to ponder and peruse these approaches, which may well lead to better results in their own jurisdictions.

NOTE

1. Myron E. Weiner, "Management Repertoires," *Connecticut Government*, Winter 1977, pp. 8–12.

Books, Articles, Magazines, and Organizations Relevant to Results-Oriented Public Management

This listing makes no claim to be comprehensive and inclusive, but is a compilation of some of the information the author has found most useful.

1. INTRODUCTION

Books and Articles

Chris Argyris, *Management and Organizational Development* (New York: McGraw-Hill, 1971). Argues that the cumulative weight of past studies of business organizations supports the assumptions of Theory Y. Discusses problems and strategies involved in implementing Theory Y in business corporations. One of this noted author's many books on this theme.

Robert Dubin et al., *Leadership and Productivity: Some Facts of Industrial Life* (San Francisco: Chandler, 1965). This review of past research concludes that there is an ambiguous relationship between supervisory style and productivity. Some of the assertions championing Theory X (e.g., p. 42) are not supported.

Willis D. Hawley and David Rogers, eds., *Improving Urban Management* (Beverly Hills, Calif.: Sage, 1976). A variety of approaches to measuring, organizing, and delivering urban public services in several different policy areas.

Hugh Heclo, *A Government of Strangers* (Washington, D.C.: Brookings Institution, 1977). Pages 191–234 argue that neither Theory X nor Theory Y will suffice in federal government management, and that a combined approach is necessary.

International City Management Association, *Developing the Municipal Organization* (Washington, D.C.: International City Management Association, 1974). Good introduction to results-oriented management, although the chapters need expansion and more examples.

Rensis Likert and Jane Gibson Likert, *New Ways of Managing Conflict* (New York: McGraw-Hill, 1976). Likert's "System 4," roughly the same as Theory Y, is the desired goal in this expansion of the argument made in Likert's earlier *New Patterns of Manage-*

ment. Stresses converting destructive conflict into constructive conflict. Based on extensive studies.

Michael Maccoby, *The Gamesman* (New York: Simon & Schuster, 1976). Pages 217–44 are a very cogent argument against the usefulness of Theory Y in the business world.

Douglas McGregor, *The Human Side of Enterprise* (New York: McGraw-Hill, 1960). The classic statement of Theories X and Y. This is not an empirical study, but an argument based on experience and examples.

Robert N. McMurry, *The Maverick Executive* (New York: AMACOM, 1974). Disputes Theory Y, arguing that a "benevolent autocrat" is the most effective executive. No more empirical than the McGregor book in the preceding entry.

James L. Mercer and Edwin H. Koester, *Public Management Systems—An Administrator's Guide* (New York: AMACOM, 1978). This valuable volume has chapters on capital budgeting, management information systems, incentive contracting, hardware and software, and a host of other management topics. While it is expensive, and perhaps optimistic about obstacles to implementation, it is a welcome addition to the literature.

John S. Morse and Jay W. Lorsch, "Beyond Theory Y," *Harvard Business Review,* May–June 1970, pp. 61–68. Authors present data indicating that Theory Y is best applied selectively, not universally.

Elinor Ostrom, ed., *The Delivery of Urban Services: Outcomes of Change* (Beverly Hills, Calif.: Sage, 1976). Analyzes the impact of institutional managements on service delivery in several different local policy areas.

Brian W. Rapp and Frank M. Patitucci, *Managing Local Government for Improved Performance: A Practical Approach* (Boulder, Col.: Westview Press, 1977). This treatise by two seasoned government officials would be much more useful if they told the reader *how* to work to overcome technical and political obstacles to the approaches they recommend.

Alice M. Rivlin, *Systematic Thinking for Social Action* (Washington, D.C.: Brookings Institution, 1971). Superb provocative treatment of many of the key issues involved in results-oriented management.

Robert Townsend, *Up the Organization* (Greenwich, Conn.: Fawcett Crest Books, 1970). An unusually well-written book by a business executive who tried Theory Y in the Avis Rent-a-Car Corporation and who credits it with taking the company out of the red. Difficult to put down.

Magazines

Brookings Bulletin, Brookings Institutution, 1775 Massachusetts Ave., N.W., Washington, D.C. 20036. The Brookings Institution is a research organization which publishes several excellent management studies every year. Its bulletin, published quarterly, gives a brief description of each and has several lengthy articles as well. Can be obtained at no charge by writing and asking to be put on the mailing list.

The Bureaucrat, Sage Publications, Beverly Hills, Calif. 90212. Focuses on items of current, concern in federal administration, and cannot be ignored by those interested in the topic. Quarterly.

Congressional Quarterly Weekly Report, 1735 K St., N.W., Washington, D.C. 20006. This report on the activities of Congress contains excellent summaries of both executive and legislative interest in federal management innovations. Weekly.

Government Executive, 1725 K St., N.W., Washington, D.C. 20006. Covers the waterfront of federal, state, and local government with short reports by and on practitioners. Tends toward superficiality, with an occasional trenchant article. Monthly.

Harvard Business Review, Harvard Business School, Cambridge, Mass. 02138. The leading journal in business management, *HBR* publishes many articles relevant to the government manager. Six issues a year.

Midwest Review of Public Administration, Park College, Parkville, Mo. 64152. Most articles focus on the Midwest. This small journal has been steadily increasing in quality. Two issues a year.

National Civic Review, Pforzheimer Building, 47, E. 68 St., New York, N.Y. 10021. Published by the National Municipal League. Short articles rarely surpass the superficial, but news and notes of ongoing developments are often of substantial interest. Monthly.

National Journal, 1730 M St., N.W., Washington, D.C. 20036. Though fabulously expensive ($300 a year in 1977), this magazine has many fine articles on federal management. If your organization's library subscribes, you can get your own subscription for $52 a year. Weekly.

Policy Studies Journal, 361 Lincoln Hall, Urbana, Ill. 61801. Tends more to the academic than the practical, but a healthy minority of articles are practitioner oriented. Quarterly.

Public Administration Review, 1225 Connecticut Ave., N.W., Washington, D.C. 20036. *PAR* is the journal of the American Society for Public Administration, discussed in the following section on organizations, and can only be obtained by ASPA members. It is the leading journal of public administration in the United States, with articles on a wide variety of topics. Six issues a year.

Public Interest, 10 E. 53 St., New York, N.Y. 10022. While the predominant editorial viewpoint is skeptical about broad new initiatives in government, a variety of viewpoints can be found. Format is general exposition of new ideas or criticism, rather than detailed blueprints of how to do it. Quarterly.

Public Management, International City Management Association, 1140 Connecticut Avenue, N.W., Washington, D.C. 20036. Magazine of the city management profession. Though not usually profound, these articles deal with important management issues of current concern. Monthly.

Public Policy, Littauer 118, Harvard University, Cambridge, Mass. 02138. An excellent journal, focusing on a wide range of problems, often in more depth than the *Public Interest.* Quarterly.

Search, Urban Institute, 2100 M St., N.W., Washington, D.C. 20037. Similar to the *Brookings Bulletin,* summarizing Urban Institute publications. Those who request it will be put on the mailing list at no charge.

Southern Review of Public Administration, Department of Government, Auburn University, Montgomery, Ala. 36117. *SRPA* began publication in June 1977 with an emphasis on concerns of the South. Quarterly.

State and Local Government Review, Institute of Government, University of Georgia, Athens, Ga. 30602. Practitioner-oriented journal. Quarterly.

State Government, Council of State Governments, P.O. Box 1190, Iron Works Pike, Lexington, Ky. 40511. Focus on state government, with an increasing emphasis on management issues. Quarterly.

Organizations

American Management Association, 135 W. 50 St., New York, N.Y. 10020. This business management association has some public sector members, and publishes many fine books on management which are relevant to government.

American Society for Public Administration, 1225 Connecticut Ave., N.W., Washington, D.C. 20036. This generalist organization, which had 18,000 members in 1977, draws from federal, state, and local government, as well as from academia and the nonprofit sector. This most important general purpose group for public administration has active state and regional chapters. We strongly urge the practitioner to join ASPA.

International City Management Association, 1140 Connecticut Ave., N.W., Washington, D.C. 20036. The professional organization of America's city managers, ICMA publishes a variety of books on many public management topics. Though some of these need updating and a more lively style, they are solid treatments of their topics. To date, ICMA has cooperated on results-oriented research and guides for the practitioner with such groups as the Urban Institute. Individuals who are not city managers can join as associate members.

Public Administration Service, 1313 E. 60 St., Chicago, Ill. 60637. This venerable organization provides consulting services and issues research reports on a variety of topics.

Urban Institute, 2100 M St., N.W., Washington, D.C. 20037. This federally funded research organization has published many excellent results-oriented guides for the practitioner, several of which are cited in this text.

2 . PROGRAM PLANNING

Books and Articles

Jack Byrd, *Operations Research Models for Public Administration* (Lexington, Mass.: Lexington Books, 1975). Good description of OR as applied to public management.

Robert Lee Chartrand, *Systems Technology Applied to Social and Community Problems* (New York. Spartan Books, 1971). Originally prepared as a study for Congress, the book ranges over a broad variety of topics and contains a good deal of useful material.

John Dearden and F. Warren McFarlan, *Management Information Systems* (Homewood, Ill.: Richard D. Irwin, 1966). Ch. 4 is a good summary of PERT and CPM.

John M. Fitzgerald and Ardra F. Fitzgerald, *Fundamentals of Systems Analysis* (New York: Wiley, 1973). A good introduction to systems analysis.

Harry Hatry, Louis Blair, Donald Fisk, and Wayne Kimmel, *Program Analysis for State and Local Governments* (Washington, D.C.: Urban Institute, 1976). Excellent guide for the practitioner, full of both technical and political advice.

Ida R. Hoos, *Systems Analysis in Public Policy: A Critique* (Berkeley, Calif.: University of California Press, 1972). A brilliant and devastating critique of those who argue that systems analysis techniques can be translated wholesale from the private to the public sector. Must reading.

Kenneth L. Kraemer, *A Systems Approach to Decision-Making Policy Analysis in Local Government* (Washington, D.C.: International City Management Association, 1973). Planning principles for city managers and other local government managers. Would be more useful were its tone less academic.

George L. Morrisey, *Management by Objectives and Results in the Public Sector* (Reading, Mass.: Addison-Wesley, 1976). This discussion of MBO contains an excellent treatment of the planning process.

Magazines

Policy Analysis, University of California Press, Berkeley, Cal. 94720. Not limited to planning, this excellent journal is also concerned with evaluation. Quarterly.

In addition, most of the magazines listed for Chapter 1 frequently carry articles on program planning.

Organizations

American Institute of Planners, 1776 Massachusetts Ave., N.W., Washington, D.C. 20036.

American Society of Planning Officials, 1313 E. 60 St., Chicago, Ill. 60637.

The membership of these two organizations is made up primarily of professionals who call themselves planners and who are concerned principally with making changes in the physical environment. Of late, more and more planners have become concerned about the social aspects of change as well. While these associations hardly have a monopoly on planning—which we have defined in a broader sense than the practice of most of their members—their activities and publications may be of interest to some readers.

National Planning Association, 1606 Connecticut Ave., N.W., Washington, D.C. 20009.

See also the organizations listed for Chapter 1.

3. REORGANIZATION FOR RESULTS

Books and Articles

George A. Bell, "States Make Progress with Reorganization Plans," *National Civic Review*, March 1972, pp. 115–19, 127. A good survey of general trends and prospects, whose major theses have not been outdated since it was written.

Robert C. Casselman, "Massachusetts·Revisited: Chronicle of a Failure," *Public Administration Review* 33 (March–April 1973): 129–35. Excellent discussion of the reasons why this reorganization stopped short. This study has general implications, since almost all government reorganizations are not adequately followed through.

Marshall E. Dimock, *The Executive in Action* (New York: Harper & Row, 1945). A fascinating and unique account of the application of organizational principles to the creation of a wartime agency which the author headed. Well worth the trouble to search out.

Herbert Emmerich, *Federal Organization and Administrative Management* (University, Ala.: University of Alabama Press, 1971). A good survey and summary of developments in federal reorganization.

Douglas M. Fox, "The President's Proposals for Executive Reorganization: A Critique," *Public Administration Review* 33 (September–October 1973): 401–6. Argues that Nixon's reorganization proposals would not only not have led to better management but also were not primarily designed for that goal. Nixon was instead more concerned with subduing career bureaucrats and reducing the power of clientele groups who did not vote Republican.

Luther Gulick and Lyndall Urwick, eds., *Papers on the Science of Administration* (New York: Institute of Public Administration, 1973). Classic statement of the "principles" which reorganizers espouse to this day.

Harvey C. Mansfield, "Federal Executive Reorganization: Thirty Years of Experience," *Public Administration Review* 29 (July–August 1969): 332–45. An incisive review of federal reorganization, which concludes that we have to move far beyond the classic "principles."

Edward C. Schleh, *The Management Tactician* (New York: McGraw-Hill, 1974). A brilliantly iconoclastic dissection of classical management "principles," with suggestions for implementing new approaches.

Harold Seidman, *Politics, Position, and Power: The Dynamics of Federal Organization*, 2nd ed. (New York: Oxford University Press, 1975). A superb survey of the political realities of federal organization. To replace the classic principles, which he claims are irrelevant, Seidman offers a new set of "principles."

Harvey Sherman, *It all Depends: A Pragmatic Approach to Organization* (University, Ala.: University of Alabama Press, 1966). Arguing that there are no immutable principles of organization that can be applied in all cases, Sherman argues for a science of organization which will guide administrators by advising them which type of approach to use in particular cases. Powerfully provocative, the book is full of examples from the experience of this scholar-practitioner.

Herbert A. Simon, "The Proverbs of Administration," *Public Administration Review* 6 (Winter 1946): 53–67. A devastating attack on the Gulick-Urwick "principles."

Schuyler C. Wallace, *Federal Departmentalization: A Critique of Theories of Organization* (New York: Columbia University Press, 1941). An outstanding critique of the classical theories of organization which shows few signs of age. Worth searching for.

Magazines

While no journal specializes in administrative organization and reorganization, many of the magazines listed for Chapter 1 publish articles on reorganization.

Organizations

There is no association that specializes in reorganization as such. The Council of State Governments, P.O. Box 1190, Iron Works Pike, Lexington, Ky. 40511, publishes research on state reorganization on a regular basis.

4. OUTPUT-ORIENTED SUPERVISION

Rather than repeat the books, magazines, and organizations mentioned under Chapter 1, we list here only some additional books.

Louis A. Allen, *The Management Profession* (New York: McGraw-Hill, 1964). Well-argued multidisciplinary approach which could use more examples.

William F. Dowling, Jr., and Leonard R. Sayles, *How Managers Motivate: The Imperatives of Supervision* (New York: McGraw-Hill, 1978). This is the best single book on supervision this writer has seen. Written in a lively manner and replete with engaging examples, it covers all the important issues.

Effective Supervisory Practices (Washington, D.C.: International City Management Association, 1965). A valuable series of bulletins, which could use more examples.

Vincent W. Kafka and John W. Schaefer, *Open Management* (New York: Peter H. Wyden, 1975). Stresses the importance of motivating different employees differently. Excellently done, with many fine examples.

Henry C. Metcalf and Lyndall Urwick, eds., *Dynamic Administration: The Collected Papers of Mary Follett* (New York: Harper & Row, 1942). The work of a major student of administrative behavior, who stressed depersonalization.

James K. Van Fleet, *The 22 Biggest Mistakes Managers Make and How to Correct Them* (West Nyack, N.Y.: Parker Publishing, 1973). This popular treatment is well argued, with many relevant examples.

5. MANAGEMENT BY OBJECTIVES (MBO)

Books and Articles

Peter F. Drucker, *The Practice of Management* (New York: Harper & Row, 1954). Drucker, one of the world's most respected authorities on management, is generally acknowledged as the originator of the MBO concept. This does not mean that no one managed by objectives before this book, but that Drucker was the first to write systematically on the topic. Drucker has also written many other books dealing in part with MBO since 1954.

John W. Humble, *MBO in Action* (Maidenhead, Berkshire, Eng.: McGraw-Hill, 1970). Humble is an outstanding British authority on MBO who writes well. This book contains a checklist of questions to guide the manager toward MBO.

Harry Levinson, "Management by Whose Objectives?" *Harvard Business Review,* July–August 1970, pp. 125–34. Argues forcefully that MBO without Theory Y is counterproductive.

Dale D. McConkey, *MBO for Nonprofit Organizations* (New York: American Management Association, 1975). Series of provocative case studies supplements the author's basic argument. Based on this writer's experience with one of these organizations, however, some of the assessments may be a little too glowing.

George L. Morrisey, *Management by Objectives and Results in the Public Sector*

(Reading, Mass.: Addison-Wesley, 1976). Perhaps the best introduction to the topic, because it provides a wealth of detail. But while logically organized and argued, with excellent chapter summaries, it could use more examples to cut down on a series of dull "laundry lists." Contains four case studies and a fine bibliography as well.

George S. Odiorne, *Management Decisions by Objectives* (Englewood Cliffs, N.J.: Prentice-Hall, 1969). Odiorne has written several fine books abut MBO, but this is my favorite. It is written superbly, with lively examples and a command of the language which keep the reader going. Odiorne is the dean of writers on MBO, and deservedly so.

Richard Rose, *Managing Presidential Objectives* (New York: Free Press, 1976). One of the few attempts to look seriously at the impact of MBO on government. Not an exhaustive empirical study, but a good start

Magazines

Management by Objectives. This British journal is available through MBO, Inc., 157 Pontoosic Road, Westfield, Mass. 01085. Quarterly.

MBO Newsletter. A six-page bulletin written by George Odiorne, surveying current literature and organizational achievements. Also available through MBO, Inc. Monthly

Organizations

MOB, Inc., 157 Pontoosic Road, Westfield, Mass. 01085. George Odiorne's consulting service, through which the above magazines are available.

Annual International Conference on MBO: State of the Art. Sponsored every summer by the Management Center, Bowling Green State University, Bowling Green, Ohio 43402.

6. PROGRAM EVALUATION

Books and Articles

James S. Coleman, "Problems of Conceptualization and Measurement in Studying Policy Impacts," in Kenneth M. Dolbeare, ed., *Public Policy Evaluation* (Beverly Hills, Calif.: Sage, 1975). Superb exposition of the basic problems encountered in evaluation and suggestions about how to deal with them.

Harry P. Hatry et al., *Practical Program Evaluation for State and Local Government Officials* (Washington, D.C.: Urban Institute, 1973). In spite of some murkiness in distinguishing inputs, activities, and outputs in ch. 1, this book is easily the most valuable introduction to evaluation. Every results-oriented practitioner should have a copy.

Pamela Horst et al., "Program Evaluation and the Federal Evaluator," *Public Administration Review* 34 (July–August 1974): 300–38. A superb treatment of the obstacles confronting the evaluator and what to do about them.

Peter H. Rossi and Sonia R. Wright, "Evaluation Research: An Assessment of Theory, Practice, and Politics," *Evaluation Quarterly* 1 (February 1977): 5–52. An impressive survey of the field, with suggestions about the usefulness of different approaches in different situation.

Edward A. Suchman, *Evaluative Research* (New York: Russell Sage Foundation, 1967). A basic, if not the leading, work in the field.

Carol A. Weiss, ed., *Evaluating Action Programs* (Boston: Allyn and Bacon, 1972). An exceptional collection of crucial articles in the field.

Carol A. Weiss, *Evaluation Research* (Englewood Cliffs, N.J.: Prentice-Hall, 1972). An incisive treatment of the major technical and political issues involved in evaluation. Hopefully, a revision with more examples will soon appear.

Magazines

Evaluation Quarterly, Sage Publications, P.O. Box 776, Beverly Hills, Calif. 90213. This new (born 1977) journal is off to an excellent start and promises to be a very valuable one.

In addition, most of the journals listed under Chapter 1 carry articles on evaluation, as does *Policy Analysis*, listed under Chapter 2.

Addresses of Organizations

The Annual Summer Institute in Evaluation Research was held from 1975–1977 at the University of Massachusetts, directed by Professors Rossi and Wright, Social and Demographic Research Institute, University of Massachusetts, Amherst, Mass. 01003. Presumably, similar programs will continue there or elsewhere in the future.

The Urban Institute and the International City Management Association, listed under Chapter 1 have devoted substantial attention to program evaluation.

7. BUDGETING FOR RESULTS

Books and Articles

Robert N. Anthony, "Zero-Based Budgeting Is a Fraud," *Wall Street Journal*, April 27, 1977, p. 26. A frontal attack on ZBB, backed up by relevant data. An expanded version has been scheduled for *Government Accountant* magazine.

Logan M. Cheek, *Zero Based Budgeting Comes of Age* (New York: American Management Association, 1977). A how-to-do-it volume, stressing the steps necessary to motivate employees to accept ZBB.

Judy Gardner, "ZBB Undergoes Limited Test," *Congressional Quarterly*, March 12, 1977, pp. 441–43. A fall 1976 experiment in two federal agencies showed that ZBB generated much more paperwork, but not necessarily enough information for decision makers. The study indicates that it would be difficult if not impossible to implement ZBB across the board in the federal government in less than two-to-four years.

David L. Leininger, "Start Budgeting from Scratch," *The American City and County*, April 1976, pp. 69–70. This brief account by the Fiscal Services Director of Garland, Texas (pop. 110,000) claims savings in the millions of dollars with no decline in services as a result of ZBB.

Peter A. Pyhrr, *Zero Base Budgeting* (New York: Wiley, 1973). The how-to-do-it book by the man who started ZBB as we currently know it.

Allen Schick and Robert Keith, *Zero-Base Budgeting in the States* (Lexington, Ky.: Council of State Governments, 1976). Survey of ZBB procedures and practices in the states.

Charles L. Schultze, *The Politics and Economics of Public Spending* (Washington, D.C.: Brookings Institution, 1969). The best introduction to PPBS. Frankly discusses difficulties the approach is likely to encounter and realistically assesses its likely achievements.

David W. Singleton, "Zero-Based Budgeting in Wilmington, Delaware," *Governmental Finance*, August 1976, pp. 20–29. This article by two Wilmington (population 80,000) budget officials and a consultant sketches the process used in detail. Interestingly enough, the mayor and city council prefer ZBB to the former budget process. Yet insufficient time had passed to allow definitive conclusions about what ZBB had accomplished in results.

Aaron Wildavsky, *Budgeting* (Boston: Little, Brown, 1975). Chapter 14 deals with ZBB and concludes that some butterflies were caught, but no elephants stopped. Schick and Keith's book cited above disputes Wildavsky's reasoning.

Magazines

Governmental Finance, 1313 E. 60 St., Chicago, Ill. 60637. The publication of the Municipal Finance Officers Association, this magazine covers practices and innovation in local budgetry. Monthly.

See also *National Civic Review*, cited under Chapter 1; this publication has a section in each issue on taxation and finance.

Addresses of Organizations

Municipal Finance Officers Association, 1313 E. 60 St., Chicago, Ill. 60637. The national professional association of local budget officials.

National Association of State Budget Officials, Iron Works Pike, Lexington, Ky. 40511. The national professional association of state budget officials.

8 . PRODUCTIVITY

Books and Articles

Daron K. Butler and Jay G. Stanford, *Checklist for Planning a Productivity Improvement Program in Governmental Units,* Intergovernmental Brief (June 1976), Texas Advisory Commission on Intergovernmental Relations, Austin, Texas. A Model of precision and concision, this checklist is an excellent outline of the steps to be taken in starting a productivity program.

Committee for Economic Development, *Improving Productivity in State and Local Government* (New York, Committee for Economic Development, 1976). A useful introduction, with some good examples, this book makes no mention of Theory Y participatory management.

Frederick O'R. Hayes, *Productivity in Local Government* (Lexington, Mass.: Lexington Books, 1977). The first thorough review of productivity accomplishments in eight cities and a county finds a mixed record of achievement. Key factors related to high achievement are the political cultures and tradition of the jurisdiction, strong support from the chief executive, and weak labor unions. A model of practical research that will hopefully be emulated in all the areas of results-oriented management covered in this book.

Marc Holzer, *Productivity in Public Organizations* (New York: Dunellen, 1975). A useful collection of key articles in the field.

Patrick Manion, *Improving Municipal Productivity: Work Measurement for Better Management* (Washington, D.C.: National Center on Productivity and Work Quality). A fine technical guide to use in implementing work measurement, a valuable technique for improving productivity.

Chester A. Newland, ed. "Symposium on Productivity in Government," *Public Administration Review* 32 (November–December 1972): 739–850. The best collection of articles on the subject yet to appear in one place. Available from ASPA (see address under Chapter 1 listings).

John P. Ross and Jesse Burkhead, *Productivity in the Local Government Sector* (Lexington, Mass.: Lexington Books, 1974). An excellent review of the concept and the state of the art, with case study illustrations. Indicates that local productivity studies had a long way to go to match those in the private sector at the beginning of 1972.

Eli B. Silverman, "Productivity in Government: A Note of Caution," *Midwest Review of Public Administration*, June 1973, pp. 143–53. Some well-phrased words to the wise not to expect that productivity will be a panacea.

Frederick C. Thayer, "Productivity: Taylorism Revisited (Round Three)," *Public Administration Review* 32 (November–December 1972): 833–39. Part of the excellent symposium cited under Newland, above, this article warns that productivity contains a number of extreme dangers if not applied in a Theory Y ambience.

Magazines

Public Productivity Review, Center for Productive Public Management, John Jay College, 445 W. 59th St., New York, N.Y. 10019. This new journal contains some excellent pieces, though to date it is much stronger on prescription than description of what productivity programs actually accomplish. Quarterly.

Organizations

Center for Productive Public Management, John Jay College, 445 W. 59th St., New York, N.Y. 10019. Publisher of *Public Productivity Review* and numerous other materials and sponsor of symposia and workshops, CPPM acts as a clearinghouse of information on productivity.

National Center for Productivity and Quality of Working Life, Washington, D.C. 20036. Formerly the National Commission on Productivity and Work Quality, NCPQWL is concerned with both public and private productivity. In spite of very limited funds, which rule out having its own research staff, the center has aided productivity efforts through its publications, conferences, and joint work on productivity improvement with selected federal agencies.

Public Technology, Incorporated, International City Management Association, 1140 Connecticut Ave., N.W., Washington, D.C. 20036. Set up by a Ford Foundation grant and run by a board with representatives from the national associations of city managers, mayors, governors, counties, and states, PTI advises governments about technological innovations which may help them increase productivity.

The Urban Institute (see address in listings for Chapter 1) publishes more how-to-do-it guides to productivity than any other organization except NCPQWL itself. Its excellent books should be perused by the productivity practitioner.

In addition, Frederick O'R. Hayes lists several other organizations doing important work in productivity studies in *Productivity in Local Government* (Lexington, Mass.: Lexington Books, 1977), pp. 264–84.

9. PERSONNEL PERFORMANCE APPRAISAL

Books and Articles

Herbert S. Feild and William H. Holley, "Performance Appraisal: An Analysis of Statewide Practices," *Public Personnel Management,* May–June 1975, pp. 145–50. Comprehensive survey which finds goal-oriented appraisal on the rise, though it is found in only a small minority of the states.

Douglas McGregor, "An Uneasy Look at Performance Appraisal," *Harvard Business Review* 35 (May–June 1957): 89–94. Argues that conventional appraisal is a failure and should be supplanted by joint supervisor-subordinate goal setting.

George S. Odiorne, *Personnel Administration by Objectives* (Homewood, Ill.: Richard D. Irwin, 1971). Probably the best text written from an MBO-participatory management perspective, but it could contain much more material on performance appraisal.

O. Glenn Stahl, *Public Personnel Administration,* 7th ed. (New York: Harper & Row, 1977). This leading text contains all the basic information needed on performance appraisal, except examples which would both illustrate points and enliven reading.

George Strauss and Leonard R. Sayles, Jr., *Personnel: The Human Problems of Management,* 3rd ed. (Englewood Cliffs, N.J.: Prentice-Hall, 1972). Perhaps the best personnel text, outstanding in both style and content in its treatment of performance appraisal.

Most specialized books on performance appraisal either apply exclusively to the private sector or are frankly disappointing, compared to the treatments of the major general textbooks.

Magazines

Personnel, American Management Association, 135 W. 50 St., New York, N.Y. 10020. Short articles about personnel developments, almost entirely in the private sector. Monthly.

Personnel Journal, 1131 Olympic Blvd., Santa Monica, Calif. 90404. Articles tend to be written in more depth than those in *Personnel,* and are more likely to be based on empirical research. Somewhat greater coverage of nonprofit and public organizations than *Personnel.* Monthly.

Public Personnel Management, 1313 E. 60th St., Chicago, Ill. 60637. Journal of the International Personnel Management Association, and indispensable to those seriously interested in public personnel matters, including performance appraisal. 6 issues a year.

Organizations

International Personnel Management Association, 1313 E. 60th St., Chicago, Ill. 60637. The national association of professional public personnel managers. State and regional chapters hold regular meetings.

Index

decision packages *(cont.)*
  alternatives in, 181–182
  benefits, 181
  and consequences of not performing activities, 181
  costs, 181
  definition of, 177
  description of activities, 181
  establishing, 182
  goal statement of, 181
  level of preparation of, 182–183
  performance measures, 181
  presenting, 183–184
  ranking, 184–186, 187, 190–191, 193, 197
  in state government, 187, 189
Defense, U.S. Department of
  planning in, 32, 44
  PPB in, 174
delegation
  of authority, 86
  of tasks, 86
depersonalization
  in consensus building, 95–96
  and conveying bad news, 89, 90
  definition of, 81, 83
  practicing, 98
  and punishment, 92
Detroit, Mich., 222
diagramming, 20, 21
director, in productivity program, 207–208
Dodge Commission on Urban Problems, 164
Donaldson, Bill, 227
Donohue, Leo V., 66
double-loop learning, 102, 103
Dougan, William R., 106
Dowling, William F. Jr., 87, 89
Downs, Anthony, 226
Drucker, Peter F., 3, 117
Dye, Thomas, 63

education, as requirement for employment, 243–244
  see also training
education boards, 65
educational programs, evaluation of, 155
Eisenhower, Dwight D., 62, 80–81
effectiveness
  definition of, 3–4, 102
  estimating, 16, 26, 27, 29–30
    case study of, 34, 35
  in MBO, 125

effectiveness *(cont.)*
  and productivity, 276
  of program, 224, 237
  in reorganization, 55, 57, 76
  and training, 269
  in ZBB, 191
efficiency
  definition of, 3–4, 102
  and functional integration, 50–51
  of program, 224, 237
  in reorganization, 55, 57, 76
  and training, 269
Ehrlichman, John, 48
emotions, communicating, 87
employee participation, *see* Theory Y
Energy, U.S. Department of, 49
Energy Reorganization Act (1974), 152
ethics, 164, 167–168
evaluation, program, 141–169, 273, 274, 277
  and budgetary process, 197, 198
  case study of, 165–166
  defining, 141–142
  differentiating from planning, 16
  implementing, 142–151
    the controlled experiment, 142–144
    data collection, 147–151
    ethics of, 164, 167–168
    nonexperimental approaches to, 144–146
    the quasi-experiment, 144
    supporting, 151
    when to use, 151
  in PPB, 174, 175
  political problems of, 160–164
    experimental design, 160–164, 167–168, 169
    nonexperimental approaches, 161–164
  problems and prospects of, 167–169
  pseudo-, 162–163
  technical problems of, 156–160
    controlled experiments, 156–160
    nonexperimental approaches, 158–160
  use of, in American government, 151–155
  in ZBB, 189–190
evaluation criteria
  in case study, 33
  in program evaluation, 143, 158, 159, 160
  specifying, 16, 24–26
  in ZBB, 181
evaluative manager, 7

Pennsylvania
  Department of Environmental Resources, 122
  PPB in, 122
performance appraisal, *see* personnel performance appraisal
performance audits, 152, 154–155, 175, 197
performance budget, 173–174, 175, 197
performance contracting, 253
Performance Rating Act (1950), 252
performance reporting, 212–214
performance standards, 245
personal favoritism, 6, 243, 255
personnel appraisal methods, 242–245
personnel performance appraisal, 241–269, 274, 277
  case study of, 259–266
  defining, 242
  implementing, 245–252
  political problems of, 254–255
  prospects and problems of, 267–269
  technical problems of, 254–255
  use of in American government, 252–254
Peter, Laurence, J., 6
Peter Principle, 6
Phoenix, Ariz., 173–174, 175, 222
pilot study, 30
planning, program, 15–45, 271–272, 274, 276
  and budgeting process, 173, 198
  case study of, 33–36
  comprehensive, 44–45
  defining, 12, 15–16
  differentiated from evaluation, 16
  evaluation in, 157, 158
  implementing, 18–30
  lack of, 189
  in MBO, 106, 272
  political problems of, 30–31, 37, 40–43
  in PPB, 173, 174, 272
  prospects and problems of, 43–45
  small scale, 44
  and systems analysis, 16–18
  technical problems of, 37–40
  use of in American government, 30–32
  in ZBB, 272
planning-programming-budgeting (PPB), 16, 173, 174, 175–176, 198, 272, 273
  in government, 30–31, 44–45, 174, 175–176, 188–189, 194, 195, 197

policy
  definition of, 16
  differentiating from program, 16
  in productivity planning process, 205–206
political patronage, 6, 10, 242, 252, 255, 256, 276
political problems
  in MBO 121, 127–130
  in planning, 30–31, 37, 40–43
  in productivity, 225–228
  in program evaluation, 160–164, 167–168, 169
  in reorganization, 58, 68–69
Port Authority of New York and New Jersey, 3
postponement in program evaluation, 162–163
posturing, 162
President's Committee on Administrative Management, 62
price change projections, 37–38
problem identification, 15–16, 18–21
productivity, 202–238, 273–274, 277
  defining, 202–203
  in government, 203–205, 218–222, 223–224, 237, 276
  implementing, 205–218, 225
  political problems of, 225–228
  popularity of, 203–205
  problems of, 236–237
  prospects for, 237–238
  service, 223–224, 236
  social costs of, 236
  technical problems of, 222–225
productivity bargaining, 228
productivity indexes, 222
professional ratings, 147, 151
program
  definition of, 2, 16
  differentiated from policy, 16
  see also planning, program
program budgets, 173
program evaluation and review technique (PERT) 16, 17, 274–275
programming, 109, 114
  project management, 60–62, 65–66
  definition of, 52
  problems with, 70–71
Providence, R.I., 242
pseudo–evaluations, 162–163
punishment, 90, 91–93
Purdy, Lawson, 93–94